Oxford Socio-Legal Studies

Law's Community

LAW'S COMMUNITY

Legal Theory in
Sociological Perspective

ROGER COTTERRELL

CLARENDON PRESS • OXFORD

Oxford University Press, Great Clarendon Street, Oxford OX2 6DP

Oxford New York
Athens Auckland Bangkok Bogota Bombay
Buenos Aires Calcutta Cape Town Dar es Salaam
Delhi Florence Hong Kong Istanbul Karachi
Kuala Lumpur Madras Madrid Melbourne
Mexico City Nairobi Paris Singapore
Taipei Tokyo Toronto

and associated companies in
Berlin Ibadan

Oxford is a trade mark of Oxford University Press

Published in the United States
by Oxford University Press Inc., New York

© Roger Cotterrell 1995

First published 1995
First issued in paperback 1996

British Library Cataloguing in Publication Data
Data available

Library of Congress Cataloging in Publication Data
Cotterrell, Roger (Roger B. M.)
Law's community : legal theory in sociological perspective / Roger
Cotterrell.
p. cm. — (Oxford socio-legal studies)
Includes bibliographical references and index.
1. Sociological jurisprudence. I. Title. II. Series.
K376.C68 1995
340'.115—dc20 94-49560
ISBN 0-19-825890-9
ISBN 0-19-826490-9 (Pbk)

Printed in Great Britain
on acid-free paper by
Bookcraft Ltd., Midsomer Norton, Somerset

*For Ann, David
and Linda, once more.*

General Editor's Introduction

It is now sixteen years since the first books appeared in the original series of Oxford Socio-Legal Studies. The first eight were published by Macmillan, but since 1983 the series has carried the Oxford University Press imprint. In the last twelve years, a further twenty-two volumes have appeared. While the series is now well-established, the appearance of three more works—Roger Cotterrell's *Law's Community*, *Rules and Government*, by Robert Baldwin and *Wills, Inheritance, and the Family* by Finch, Masson, Mason, Haynes, and Wallis—marks a new beginning. Oxford Socio-Legal Studies will now have a wider institutional basis and a broader sweep in its intellectual interests. The series will continue to be comprised of original works which examine the nature of law in its social setting from a variety of disciplinary perspectives, but it is intended that it will also be one which publishes theoretical, as well as empirically-informed works of high quality, and one which is international in scope. Professor John Baldwin, Director of the Institute for Judicial Administration at the University of Birmingham, Professor William Felstiner of the University of California at Santa Barbara, and Professor Simon Roberts of the London School of Economics are joining the existing Editorial Board, and an International Advisory Board has also been appointed.

Roger Cotterrell's *Law's Community* reflects one important aspect of the extension of the new series' intellectual scope. Professor Cotterrell is highly respected in Britain and abroad as a distinguished analyst of legal theory and the sociology of law. *Law's Community* consists of a series of original essays by the author, some of which have previously been published, some of which are appearing for the first time. The previously published essays have been edited by the author and integrated into the course of the book's argument, giving it coherence, while maintaining the integrity of the earlier work. What now appears represents a consistent approach to the theoretical analysis of law, reflecting the author's position that law has to be analyzed as a social phenomenon.

Professor Cotterrell has a number of objectives: to explore legal theory as an aspect of social theory; to identify aspects of law that would be regarded as problematic in a sociologically informed legal theory; and to develop an agenda for legal theory in relation to some of the important practical and political issues which it now confronts. The author wants to raise questions about the nature of the relationship between law and community; and about the moral foundations that may be possible for law, and how they relate to the present forms of state regulation. Professor Cotterrell's concern is to stress the importance of understanding the nature of contemporary legal regulation in its social context and of ensuring the development of legal theory that always recognises the social roots of law.

This book engages with many of the big questions in the sociology of law. What follows is for social theorists, sociologists of law, and political scientists, but it is also for socio-legal researchers. It is the first such work to have appeared in Oxford Socio-Legal Studies, and it is good to be able to publish a book that will surely come to be regarded as a major contribution to the field.

Keith Hawkins

Preface

The studies in this book are products of my work in legal theory since the early 1980s. They are presented here in the belief that, taken together, they suggest a consistent theoretical outlook on law and a systematic approach to legal inquiry, applied in various closely interrelated contexts. This approach assumes that legal ideas cannot be adequately analysed without study of their social origins, social conditions of existence, and social consequences. It treats legal theory as a particular aspect or area of social theory —that is, theory seeking to explain systematically and generally the structure of societies and social relationships and the conditions of social stability and change.

My aim here is to explore the potential of legal theory viewed in such a way. One aspect of this project is to clarify a conception of law that will serve as the focus for a sociologically oriented legal theory. Thus, the book develops a conception of law as institutionalized doctrine within a wider view of the nature of legal experience. It builds on this, especially in the chapters in Part I, to analyse distinctive general characteristics of professionalized legal thought. It considers how professional understandings of law are socially constituted and assesses the ways in which sociological research has been able to clarify the nature of these understandings.

A further important concern is to identify general aspects of law that, from the standpoint of a sociologically oriented legal theory, are fundamental or particularly problematic today. The chapters in Part II use resources from classic social theory to do this. The themes emerging from these chapters—especially about legality and political legitimacy, the Rule of Law, law and ideology, law and power, law and morality, and the nature of critique in legal and social theory—underpin discussion throughout the remainder of the book.

Part III is concerned to develop an agenda for legal theory that combines a sociological sensitivity to the changing character of contemporary regulation with a focus on pressing practical and political issues confronting legal theory today. What are these issues? Law now appears as a technically complex, policy-driven instrument of state control of social life. Sometimes, perhaps often, in individual citizens' lives it seems practically inaccessible, largely uncontrollable, and morally remote. The question is whether law might become something more, or something different: regulation that embodies the moral aspirations of individuals and diverse groups in the context of a non-repressive, cohesive, and co-operative, but also diverse and vital, community life. This question reflects enduring themes in the literature of social theory and sociology of law, as well as in contemporary political theory and moral philosophy. I seek to give a positive answer to the question posed. But the primary aim is to suggest directions and ideas that a sociologically informed legal theory might pursue, and to provide a theoretical context that demonstrates their significance.

Three chapters (Chapters 1, 14, and 15) consist entirely of previously unpublished material. Others are based on papers produced on diverse occasions and published in diverse places. Each chapter, apart from the introductory and concluding ones, is prefaced by a new linking summary clearly separated from the main text. All of the material has been revised to take account of the context of presentation in which it now appears. In some instances, paragraphing has been altered, phrasing that was highly specific to the original context of publication has been altered or removed, and wording has been changed or supplemented where removal from the original context made statements in the text unnecessarily obscure. Where appropriate, I have replaced references to superseded editions of books with references to corresponding current editions. Case citations have also been amended in a few instances to refer to more recent and more authoritative reports and one footnote has been altered to note a change in the law. Apart from this, references to source materials have not been updated or supplemented in any way. For reasons of consistency of presentation, a new section heading has been added in each of Chapters 7 and 10, some other section headings have been moved, and in Chapter 9 the original section numbers have been replaced with headings.

Beyond these presentational matters, the substance of previously published papers has not been changed. The ideas set out in them remain in all respects as they were when put into print elsewhere. There is a real danger in what has been called the 'retrospective fallacy': the temptation to explain or represent ideas from one's past so as to impose on them an order, coherence, or sequence of development that was not present in the actual processes of their production over a period of time. Emphases in my work on legal theory have certainly changed over time, a matter that is addressed directly in Chapter 1.

Nevertheless, all of the chapters present research that has been produced with the aim of elaborating a constant theoretical outlook, albeit with a number of different aspects. Most of the previously published studies explicitly relate to each other (all of the present cross-references in them to other chapters correspond to references in the original publications). When the papers on which these chapters are based were originally written it seemed important to me to establish their exact relation to work I had done before in legal theory. Each of these studies was produced in a conscious attempt to advance a continuous, long-term project of developing and applying a unified, internally consistent, sociologically based legal theory.

The contents of the book as a whole are intended as a contribution towards reclaiming legal theory from what might seem to be a degree of philosophical isolation; an isolation that arises because of an inadequate recognition in some legal philosophical literature of the need to examine, systematically and empirically, change and diversity not only in the character of contemporary regulation but also in the social contexts in which law is applied and invoked. The aim here is to to suggest positions from which legal theory might further engage with certain fundamental moral and political questions: what is law's relation to the idea of community (and, indeed, what meaning can usefully be attached to the idea of community in contemporary industrialized Western societies)? What moral foundations can be identified or constructed for contemporary law? What is the relationship between contemporary forms of state regulation and these foundations?

Many people have helped to create conditions in which it has been possible to develop the ideas set out in these pages. I am grateful to David Nelken and Tim Murphy for the stimulus derived from numerous discussions in and around the postgraduate University of London law and social theory course which we taught together for many years. In first systematically exploring social theory I gained immeasurably from Paul Hirst's teaching. More recently Gunther Teubner's generosity in debate has helped to focus certain issues. William Twining and Neil MacCormick, viewing legal theory from different perspectives from my own, have provided much appreciated encouragement in many ways over a long period. More generally, I have been privileged to work, throughout more than a decade during which the contents of this book were researched, in a supportive and congenial faculty at Queen Mary (later Queen Mary and Westfield) College. That colleagueship has been important. Thanks are also due to John Whelan of Oxford University Press for encouraging this publication and for the care and enthusiasm he has brought to it. Finally, and most importantly, Ann Cotterrell has read at various times all of the writing that has gone into this book and improved much of it through careful criticism. The opportunity I have had to develop these ideas derives in considerable measure from the support she has provided.

Roger Cotterrell

Queen Mary and Westfield College
University of London
April 1994

Acknowledgements

. For permission to reproduce previously published material in revised form I am grateful to: Philip A. Thomas and Basil Blackwell Publishers for Chapters 2, 3, 12, and 13; Dott. A. Giuffré Editore SpA for Chapter 4; Edinburgh University Press for Chapter 5; Routledge for Chapter 6; David Sugarman and Academic Press Ltd. for Chapter 7; the *Modern Law Review* for Chapter 8; The Law and Society Association for Chapter 9; Antoinette Hetzler and *Tidskrift för Rättssociologi* (Sweden) for Chapter 10; JAI Press Inc. for Chapter 11.

The following previously published papers form the basis of particular chapters: 'The Sociological Concept of Law' (1983) 10 *Journal of Law and Society* 241–55 [Chapter 2]; 'Law and Sociology: Notes on the Constitution and Confrontations of Disciplines' (1986) 13 *Journal of Law and Society* 9–34 [Chapter 3]—the text is from a 1992 update prepared for P. A. Thomas (ed.), *Law and the Social Sciences* (Aldershot: Dartmouth Press, forthcoming); 'Sociology of Law in Britain: Its Development and Present Prospects' in V. Ferrari (ed.), *Developing Sociology of Law: A World-Wide Documentary Enquiry* (Milan: Giuffré, 1990) [Chapter 4]; 'Sociological Perspectives on Legal Closure' in A. Norrie (ed.), *Closure or Critique: New Developments in Legal Theory* (Edinburgh: Edinburgh University Press, 1993) [Chapter 5]; 'Conceptualizing Law: Problems and Prospects of Contemporary Legal Theory' (1981) 10 *Economy and Society* 348–66 [Chapter 6]; 'Legality and Political Legitimacy in the Sociology of Max Weber' in D. Sugarman (ed.), *Legality, Ideology and the State* (London: Academic Press, 1983) [Chapter 7]; 'The Rule of Law in Corporate Society: Neumann, Kirchheimer and the Lessons of Weimar' (1988) 51 *Modern Law Review* 126–40 [Chapter 8]; 'The Durkheimian Tradition in the Sociology of Law' (1991) 25 *Law and Society Review* 923–45 [Chapter 9]; 'Critique and Law: The Problematic Legacy of the Frankfurt School' (1986) 3 *Tidskrift för Rättssociologi* 99–112 [Chapter 10]; 'Law's Images of Community and Imperium' in A. Sarat amd S. S. Silbey (eds.), *Studies in Law, Politics and Society* (Greenwich, Connecticutt: JAI Press, 1990) [Chapter 11]; 'Feasible Regulation for Democracy and Social Justice' (1988) 15 *Journal of Law and Society* 5–24 [Chapter 12]; 'Law's Community: Legal Theory and the Image of Legality' (1992) 19 *Journal of Law and Society* 405–22 [Chapter 13]. Chapter 14 is adapted from the previously unpublished text of a plenary address to the Socio-Legal Studies Association, delivered at the University of Exeter in March 1993.

Contents

Part II: Law in Social Theory

Part III: Law, Power, and Community

PART I

Law and Sociology

1 Introduction—Explaining Law's Power

This book is intended to illustrate a particular approach to theoretical analysis of the nature of contemporary law. Central to this approach is the claim that general patterns of development in law, as lawyers understand it, cannot be adequately explained unless legal study is grounded in sociological analysis. In other words, the study of law needs to be rooted in empirical analyses of the social conditions in which legal ideas are formed and used, and which underpin their moral significance, determine their authority or legitimacy, inform the regulatory demands made of them, and provide the sources of their power to regulate and control.

Legal theory with this orientation does not dissolve into general sociological inquiries. Its task is to develop systematic explanations of the general nature of legal phenomena. Its focus remains clearly on law as a special field. But the identification of this field is a matter of analytical convenience and practical appropriateness—a way of drawing together and focusing on what can be thought of as legal aspects of social life, including especially lawyers' professional practice and the specialized knowledge that informs it. The studies in this book seek to specify theoretically the nature of this special field of law. At the same time they recognize that law's significance as a social phenomenon is determined by its character as one aspect of social life; a certain focus of governmental problems and practices, as well as interpretations of (and sometimes attempts to influence) social relationships and social change.

Law in its broadest sociological sense is a *field of experience* shaped and structured by problems of government, social control, and social order.[1] Lawyers and others whose work is directly concerned with the operation of the state legal system are much concerned with a specific *professional* experience of law. This is an experience of interpreting, reformulating, systematizing, supplementing, and applying an accumulation of officially recognized practices,

---

[1] See especially Ch. 13, below.

precedents, and prescriptions, which relate to problems of government and of maintaining social order and control. In other words, lawyers and legal officials experience law, professionally, as *doctrine*: established rules, regulations, procedures, guiding principles, and normative concepts, together with specialized modes of reasoning with these various legal ideas.

Legal doctrine, as lawyers recognize it, is *institutionalized* doctrine. That is to say, this doctrine is focused on, developed in, and given its distinctive characteristics by particular kinds of agencies regularly concerned with its creation, interpretation, application, or enforcement. Among the most visible, but not necessarily always the most socially important, of these agencies are courts of law. Legal doctrine is, thus, shaped by the practical contexts of its use in the business of governing and ordering social life, and also by the institutional characteristics of the agencies that monitor and control that use.[2]

Law and Power

From the standpoint of the lawyer's clients, however, and from that of lawyers thinking in terms of their clients' interests, the experience of the state legal system necessarily appears broader and more diffuse than the professional experience of interpreting legal doctrine. It appears more generally as an experience of *social power*. Sometimes it is an experience of power available for the citizen's use; an experience of having the ability to coerce, influence, make things happen, and get things done; of being able to invoke the aid of the state or, at least, to make use of certain procedures, practices, or circumstances of state agencies to further or protect one's interests. When law gives power, aiding citizens, agencies, or collectivities (for example, business corporations) with enforceable rights, it strengthens and emboldens the legally supported person, as though the agents of interpretation, application, and enforcement of legal doctrine were an army of retainers available to be brought into play to ensure full respect for the just demands or interests of the person invoking law.

Conversely, legal experience is often an experience of power being exercised over the citizen; it involves feelings of vulnerability

[2] The idea of law as institutionalized doctrine is developed in Ch. 2.

and insecurity, of being subject to official control or interference. It is often an experience of being threatened in precise, calculated, and complex ways by other individuals, agencies, or collectivities, which are able to invoke law against the person or to neutralize means of defence that that person might otherwise have against moral demands, as well as against exploitations, victimisations, nuisances, or inconveniences. It may also be an experience of being made helpless by the technicality and obscurity of regulations and practices, which one does not understand but which nevertheless envelop and trap the individual as in— to use Max Weber's famous term—an 'iron cage' (Weber 1930: 181) of bureaucracy and routinized procedures. The power of law in these senses is felt not only by people who formally have the full legal rights and capacities of citizens but also, and often, by others who are, according to legal doctrine, marginal in some way to the society of fully participating legal actors (for example, aliens, children, mental patients, or prisoners).

Legal experience may also be, very importantly, a relatively unfocused experience of *general security*; of power neither exerted nor suffered but kept in balance. This experience is one of social peace, or of dangers held at bay; the sense, for example, of safe streets and secure homes, reliable transactions with others, and of plans and investments in which reasonable expectations will not be frustrated. The experience of legal security is based on the belief that power is being used in unseen ways to protect the citizen from unknown others (individuals, corporations, groups of various kinds) who might pose threats through unpredictable or irresponsible action, and from political or military authorities that might otherwise seem uncontrolled or unaccountable. Unlike the power that citizens seek from law by specifically calling upon lawyers, courts, police, or administrative agencies to protect their rights or to pursue their claims, this general legal security is effective in so far as it is unobtrusively pervasive. It is diffused, like air, throughout all the environments of everyday life. It seems available, and reliably permanent and continuous without specific invocation; in other words, without the need to seek aid from such as police or lawyers. Legal security in this sense is a public resource, a shared benefit, not a matter of individualized claims or demands.

The range of terms used above—coerce, influence, 'make things happen', 'get things done', 'hold at bay', control, interfere, threaten—indicates something of the immense variety of ways in which power is experienced. These in turn suggest the ambiguity of the concept of power itself. The theoretical analysis of law reveals many forms of power at work through law, or related to it in intricate ways. Indeed, one of the most important tasks of legal theory is to reveal and explain the characteristics and limitations of law's power as a means of defining and guaranteeing justice and order.

While power can be conceptualized in a variety of ways as a social phenomenon (see e.g. Cotterrell, 1992: 112–13) it can be most simply and conveniently treated here as the capacity to control, protect against, or affect the conduct of some person or persons. Law's power is easy to recognize in state coercion (the use of police and other enforcement power) that may be brought to bear on those who defy legal doctrine. It is obvious also that, for a host of reasons, some individuals and collectivities have more control or influence over the coercive power of the state than others, and more opportunity or possibility to invoke the aid of law to achieve their objectives; while others are more likely to be subject to legal coercion, more likely to be the recipients of unwanted attention from legal officials and agencies (Galanter 1974; Black 1976; Hagan 1982; Black 1989: 41–6).

The formal allocation of authority by legal doctrine (through the fixing, in terms of legal rules, of official governmental powers and responsibilities, and private rights and duties) does not give reliable information as to how power actually operates in social life. It does not, for example, reveal patterned disparities in the ability of different categories of individuals or social groups to invoke the aid of legal agencies, such as lawyers or courts. For this reason, among others, sociological study of the operation of legal agencies and of citizens' access to them is fundamental as a basis for rigorous theoretical analysis of law. This is a centrally important part of the field of empirical sociology of law (Cotterrell 1992: chs. 6, 7, and 8). It follows that if legal theory is to be able to examine law's power rigorously the nature of the general relationship between sociology of law and legal professional understandings of law must be clarified. Chapters 3, 4, and 5 of this volume explore confrontations between sociology and legal studies, especially so as to consider how far sociology of law is able to bring to legal inquiry perspectives that challenge the views of social reality that lawyers' professional legal reasoning typically presents or assumes.

Questions about the relationships between the activities of legal officials and agencies and the needs and demands of lay citizens are far from exhausting the foci of theoretical concerns with the ways in which power is expressed legally. It is important that a sociologically oriented legal theory should examine law's power as a *system of ideas*, developed and applied in practical contexts, to influence the way that citizens think and act. Indeed, law's particular power in these respects might even affect the way that citizens tend to think about power itself; the way they understand its place in their lives. I argue in this book that legal ideas help to define the kinds of power that individuals identify as available to be invoked and relied on as well as the kinds that are most readily perceived as threats. Legal theory is centrally concerned with the nature of law as doctrine. And one important aspect of this concern must be with the fact that legal doctrine gives rise to systems of cognition and evaluation that help to define the way people understand the general character of the social world in which they live.

These matters have been discussed in legal and social theory in a variety of ways. Sometimes they have been addressed in terms of law's symbolic (e.g. Arnold 1935; Corwin 1936; Edelman 1964; Aubert 1966; Hay 1975) or rhetorical (e.g. Goodrich 1987; 1990) power; its capacity to focus the consciousness of a legal community (Conklin 1989); or to 'constitute social reality' (e.g. Gordon 1982) by shaping the very concepts (for example, property, contract, ownership, fiduciary relationship, responsibility, liability, rights, and duties) which citizens use in describing and explaining (to themselves and to others) social reality and the nature and significance of social relationships. The power of legal ideas has also been widely and productively discussed in terms of the concept of ideology.

Law and Ideology

Analysis of legal ideology is one way of trying to examine extremely diffuse and hard-to-define forms of power which law as institutionalized doctrine may exert. It is a way of emphasizing that law regulates not only by coercing those who create disorder and by empowering those who sustain and reproduce order, but also by helping to fix and maintain 'common sense' understandings of the nature of society and social relationships in general. These understandings, if widely diffused and firmly established, may contribute importantly to regulation: they may help to define acceptable behaviour; to influence individuals' choices of projects; to colour, promote, or constrain individuals' ambitions; to specify the limits of possible or desirable social change; and to measure the relative value of particular social institutions and social practices.

Clearly law alone cannot create such understandings, shaping the entire regulatory climate of thought in which people live their lives. Law may be less important than other more direct influences on the ideological climate in which individuals live. Neither does legal doctrine act as an independent force shaping society. Law as institutionalized doctrine is shaped by pre-existing patterns of power which, in legal doctrine's particular institutional settings, it may formalize, systematize, divert, and influence but which in various ways it reflects. If legal ideas have the power to influence, they are themselves produced, in these institutional settings, in response to wider social pressures. Law is an aspect of society, not an autonomous force acting on it. Thus, the claims made in this book about law's ideological power are not mainly about the extent or sources of this power but about its nature. The argument here is that if law's capabilities (its limits and potential) as an agency of regulation in contemporary society are to be understood it is important to recognize that these may lie as much in providing a structure of social understandings as in ordering a system of state coercion. Indeed, the claim is that *both* elements of law—the structures of reason to which legal doctrine contributes and the coercive power that it channels—are inseparable and vital foci for legal theory's attention.

In recent decades, in the effort to shift the agenda of legal theory to a broader terrain than that of liberal legal philosophy and the traditional questions of English analytical jurisprudence, the concept of ideology has served an important purpose. Initially, it enabled critical scholars in legal studies, no less than in other fields of inquiry, to distance themselves from currents of ideas and modes of thought generally treated by other scholars as the self-evidently correct frame of reference for interpretation, analysis, and reflection. It enabled these critics to treat taken-for-granted, 'obviously correct', or 'common sense' currents of ideas and established modes of thought as *objects for study in themselves.* By labelling ways of thinking that were to be subjected to examination as 'ideology' or 'ideologies' critical scholars could radically separate the ideas under examination from the modes of analysis and interpretation used to examine them. Marxist critics, for example, tended to use for this purpose distinctions between 'ideology' (the ideas under analysis) and 'science' (the ideas, usually provided by Marxist theory, employed by the analyst); or between 'false consciousness' (the mystifications, delusions, and contradictory or blinkered understandings characteristic of ideological thought) and 'true consciousness' which somehow freed itself, in the analyst's mind, from these defects.

When these critical approaches were being introduced in Britain and elsewhere into the theoretical analysis of law during the late 1970s serious problems of Marxist theory and especially of Marxist approaches to the study of ideology were already apparent. The problem of distinguishing in some analytically rigorous manner between true and false consciousness or between ideology and science remained an unsolved problem for Marxist thought. The problem of the science–ideology distinction inspired genuinely rigorous and sophisticated theoretical work by the French philosopher Louis Althusser, but Althusser seemed to solve the problem ultimately only by erecting Marxism into a mechanistic and dogmatic explanation of the structure of societies[3] and by discarding the humanistic elements in Marx's thought that had seemed especially liberating and morally relevant to many of his followers.

Despite these difficulties, the general approach of trying to look at currents of thought and belief as specific matters for analysis in a distanced, sceptical way has great relevance for legal theory. Legal doctrine, after all, typically appears as an intricate and powerful system of ideas. Lawyers, as noted earlier, experience law especially as a matter of interpreting and applying this doctrine, of thinking 'within' it, and of using it to make legal sense, in their clients' interests, of social relationships and situations. The task

[3] See Ch. 6, below.

10   *Law and Sociology*

of a sociological study of law is not just to observe behaviour in legal contexts but to understand the social significance of lay and professional legal thinking. Sociological study of law should contribute to legal theory by helping to show the nature of legal thought as a social phenomenon, treating law as institutionalized doctrine.

It should help, therefore, to reveal the diversity of legal thinking and interpretation in its social contexts—recognizing, for example, the variety of lay and professional understandings of law, changes in these understandings, and variations in modes of interpretation and application of legal doctrine in different institutional settings. A sociology of legal doctrine will recognize that this doctrine is typically presented, by those whose professional task is to interpret and apply it, in ways that emphasize and enhance its moral and intellectual consistency and continuity.[4] Yet it will also observe that legal doctrine is adaptable, malleable, and subject to continuous internal conflicts and tensions produced in the political, cultural, and social confrontations that lawyers think of as processes of legal interpretation.

Legal ideology is not to be equated with legal doctrine in all the latter's complexity, technicality, particularity, inconsistency, and changeability. Legal ideology consists of currents of 'common sense', taken-for-granted understanding, and belief that are informed and sustained by legal doctrine and which, in turn, reinforce it and are to some extent expressed in it. It comprises the more general structures of values and cognitive ideas that legal doctrine presupposes or invokes. Legal ideology includes, for example, currents of understanding and belief about property and contract, punishment and compensation, obligation and responsibility, authority and personality, individual freedom and social bonds, justice and order,[5] among many other matters. It also includes beliefs and assumptions about the nature of law itself[6] and about its inevitable and appropriate functions.[7]

Although the concept of ideology has its greatest prominence in Marxist literature, the view of legal ideology developed

---

[4] See especially Chs. 3 and 5, below.   [5] See pp. 154–7, below.
[6] Among the most important of these is the belief that legal doctrine, taken as a whole, is an autonomous, and ultimately consistent and comprehensive, system of knowledge and evaluation. This aspect of legal ideology is considered in Ch. 5.
[7] See Ch. 12, below.

throughout this book is not Marxist. Chapter 6, based on a paper published in 1981 (the earliest study presented here), suggests reasons why, although much of value remains in Marx's writings on capitalism and law, Marxist legal theory seems inadequate. One main reason for rejecting it, indeed, is a consequence of applying the particular conception of ideology used in this book.

I argue that ideological thought is to be distinguished from scientific thought not by its content but by its self-perception. Ideological thought assumes its own completeness and its unassailable integrity; it purports to offer a total picture, a *full* and *true* understanding within its sphere of concern. Ideology presents itself as a comprehensive perspective, a self-evidently correct understanding, not subject to doubts, caveats, and revision. Its evaluations are absolutely and obviously justified. Ideological thought closes off inquiry because within its sphere answers are already known, specified in advance of any observation of the complexity and contradictions of experience. As such, ideological thought is highly resistant to modification through experience; indeed, it mediates experience, reinterpreting this continually in ways that preserve ideological structures of understanding. Only when intellectual and emotional resources for this process of reinterpretation run out does ideology collapse.

Viewing ideological thought in this way it is possible to distinguish it from scientific thought.[8] The distinction is not, as Marxist theory has often claimed, that one kind of thought is 'true' (science) and and the other 'false' (ideology), but that one kind (ideology) views itself as truth while the other (science) recognizes explicitly its provisional character, always fated for revision, reinterpretation, or rejection in the light of better data or reasoning. Because of this recognition, scientific thought demands continually improved means of observation and interpretation of

---

[8] The term 'science' is used here in relation to the study of social phenomena despite its avoidance in much contemporary social and legal theory. Many adverse connotations of the term can be removed once it is clear that what is being considered is far from positivist conceptions of science, with their limited view of means of deriving scientific knowledge and their inflated valuation of the particular forms of knowledge they approve. Scientific knowledge is not an accumulation of 'truths' or 'data' but the provisional interpretations of experience produced in an endlessly self-critical process of systematic empirical inquiry. It follows that science is an aspiration and an ideal; not the specific disciplinary practices and 'intellectual capital' of scientific professionals.

experience. It remains permanently critical of its own procedures and protocols. It worries incessantly over questions about the rigour of its inquiries and the means of improving their systematic character. And it searches less for convincing verification of its claims than for indications of their inconsistencies and inadequacies. It seeks better knowledge and modes of establishing knowledge, and it treats the criteria of 'better' as, themselves, matters of permanent controversy. It welcomes new evidence and new challenges to its existing understandings. It lives willingly with uncertainty, basing today's judgements on what it treats as best current understandings while assuming that tomorrow's understandings will be different.

Ideological and scientific thought are implacably hostile to each other. From the perspective of ideological thought, scientific inquiry relating to matters within the sphere of ideological thought is often offensive, pointless, mischief-making, subversive, heretical, or misguided. From the perspective of science, ideological thought is itself an object of inquiry. But ideology's complacent certainties are a denial of all that the ideal of science stands for, and frequently a powerful threat or deterrent to scientific efforts to make sense of experience. Indeed, the practice of scientific inquiry is itself easily subverted by ideology when scientific knowledge is treated as truth by those who ally it with their established beliefs or who have substantial emotional, intellectual, or other investment in it.

These ideas about ideology and science are applied in many ways in this book. In the light of the conception of ideology just outlined, Marxism itself is revealed as ideological thought in so far as it proclaims the 'truth' of historical materialism. Viewed scientifically, Marx's work, like the other literature of social theory discussed in the following chapters, remains a storehouse of valuable insights in so far as these insights can be treated as provisional knowledge, a partial perspective on experience, and an imperfect way of making sense of certain aspects of history. Marxism as ideology—as a set of 'inevitable truths' about historical change and its interpretation—has collapsed with the regimes that tried to make history conform to that ideology. But I include in this book a critique of Marxist legal theory, written long before the collapse, to suggest that the unmasking of Marxism's ideological pretensions does not remove the need to appreciate the

contribution that Marxist thought has made to the development
of social theory of law. The task of unmasking ideology goes along
with that of recognizing the partial perspective on experience that
even ideological thought may offer.

Marxist views of ideology are flawed by Marxism's own character as ideological thought. Ideology is typically viewed in Marxist
theory as a unity, as in the claim that there may be an overarching
'dominant ideology'[9] in a society. It is more promising, however,
to envisage ideology not as unified but as a complex interweaving
of ideological currents of thought in any given social context,
often with incompatibilities and tensions between them. A useful
analytical approach recognizes the indeterminate outcomes of this
interweaving, noting that diverse structures of ideological thought,
all of them arrogating claims of truth within their sphere, may co-
exist in a society. There is also no reason to accept that ideology
is necessarily connected in some relatively direct way with patterns
of economic interests (although there is no reason either to deny
important connections between particular ideological ways of
thought and economic considerations). Neither is it appropriate
to see ideology as having some permanent, theoretically definable
function to fulfil in society as Marxists have usually claimed,[10] nor
to see it as necessarily connected with the interests of some particular social class. Indeed, Marxist concepts of social class are
difficult to apply to the variety of social and economic groups in
contemporary Western societies (Cotterrell 1992: 111–12).

Ideology is a valuable concept when it is used to identify structures of taken-for-granted, 'common sense', self-evidently 'true' or
unquestioned modes of reasoning and interpretation which may
influence the way people in particular spheres of activity make
choices and decisions, interpret possibilities and constraints, and
evaluate their own and other people's attitudes, beliefs, and actions. Important battles are fought around ideology. Many major
conflicts in contemporary society are fought, not with violence,
but with the weapons of ideas, and especially by encouraging people
to accept as 'common sense', inevitable, and natural that which is
in fact contingent, calculated, and controvertible. It follows that
the analysis of ideology should be concerned not only with the

[9] See the critique of this conception in Abercrombie, Hill, and Turner 1980.
[10] See especially the critique of Louis Althusser's theory of ideology in Ch. 6,
below.

beliefs that people hold but equally with the ways in which they are discouraged by particular intellectual and moral climates from independent thinking and questioning.

Law and Critique

Sociological analysis of legal ideas is much influenced by the German social theorist Max Weber's writings on rationality. Weber is important in this context because he highlights particular ideological aspects of legal doctrine and legal reasoning and suggests important connections between rationalization in legal thought and other aspects of social organization. In Chapter 7, Weber's ideas on the relationships between legal ideas and political legitimacy are a special focus of attention. Weber does not develop a conception of legal ideology as such but he suggests in striking ways how the dominance of certain modes of legal reasoning can contribute to the structure and stability of political systems. Elsewhere in his writings he locates legal developments within a vast theoretical picture of the changing culture of modern Western societies.

Chapter 8 takes up themes that Weber's work establishes, addressing one of the most important components of legal ideology—the doctrine of the Rule of Law. Although the concern is to emphasize here (and also in Chapter 12) the ideological character of the doctrine as it is widely interpreted, this is not to denigrate it nor to belittle its fundamental importance. It is to suggest— as with all discussions of ideology in this book—that the partial perspectives on experience provided by ideological thought are important in presenting elements of that experience in striking, readily understood ways. To progress further in understanding, however, it is important to analyse what remains unpresented and unseen in these partial perspectives. Ideological thought is not 'untruth' or false consciousness; it is limited knowledge and partial understanding masquerading as something more. The need is to recognize and transcend these limits and this partiality, even though scientific thought accepts that knowledge will never achieve completeness.

It might be asked why we should want or need continually to transcend these limits. And the question is reasonable. It seems impossible to live in a state of continuous uncertainty and perpetual questioning of all received knowledge. Individuals necessarily accept much of their understanding of the social and moral environment as amounting for all practical purposes to 'truth'. For many people, a prerequisite for orienting themselves to the circumstances of their existence is a faith in certain fundamental truths—religious or otherwise. Even the professional scepticism of the scientist often goes along with a strong religious faith. The possibility of continuous questioning, of permanent commitment to the advancement of scientific thought, may well be dependent on an unshakeable faith in certain absolutes that provide security for this questioning. This may, for example, be a faith, at least, in the value of scientific inquiry itself, or in the human progress that it can produce; or a belief that one of the purposes of human existence (perhaps *the* purpose) is to seek restlessly for deeper understanding of the conditions of that existence.

Consequently, the subjection of ideological thought to scientific analysis is often motivated by a faith that something better can be built (for example, a better understanding of the conditions of social existence and hence a better response to those conditions) as a result of the questioning and contextualizing of ideology's assumptions of its own truth. Such a motivation underlies the studies of legal ideology contained in this volume.

As in the case of many other legal analysts attracted to sociology of law, my original aim (in the mid-1970s) was to discover new, more 'objective' and 'realistic', ways of observing and interpreting law. These new approaches would produce less time-bound and transient analyses than what appeared at the time as the value-laden, policy-oriented, even casuistic arguments and analyses in much orthodox legal literature. It seemed important to find a more intellectually convincing, more securely grounded approach to legal study; one that would bear comparison with the efforts evident in the best work in the social sciences to develop rigorous theoretical understandings of social experience. This approach would allow the development of knowledge of law to be cumulative and guided by strong theoretical frameworks. Like other researchers with similar aims and dissatisfactions I nailed my flag to the mast of social science and assumed, initially without explicit analysis, that such an approach would be liberating and progressive in so far as it revealed facets of law that traditional forms of legal study missed.

The studies in this book record, however, a process of trying to develop a critical, analytical view of the scientific quest itself and a reflexive attitude to the faith in science on which it is founded. Chapter 3, for example, attempts to set out reasons why sociology—treated not as a distinct academic discipline but as a set of methodological and theoretical orientations, and as a repository of insights reflecting human beings' self-consciousness about the conditions of their social existence—is an appropriate resource for this scientific endeavour. The claim in essence is that the sociological tradition happens to fit, for complex historical and intellectual reasons, the protocols of sceptical, self-questioning, endlessly provisional scientific thought that have been described earlier. It provides an analytical setting in which these protocols can be applied to the study of social (including legal) experience. 'Sociology', like 'science', is thus to be understood in an ideal way that frees it from the rigidities, distortions, and sheer crassness now often thought to be linked with the very idea of trying to develop a science of social life. As an ideal of research practice it is to be freed even from the constraining outlooks of some 'professionalized' academic sociology itself! Sociology is to be understood as a process and an aspiration: a process of working towards, and an aspiration to achieve, knowledge that transcends partial perspectives on social experience. Sociology's self-critical outlook as regards its observations and interpretations of experience, and as regards the methods by which they are accomplished, reflects the fact that the effort to achieve this transcendence is never-ending.

Gradually, however, the need to go beyond attempts to justify a particular vision of science has seemed pressing. Like other sociologically oriented legal observers, I have moved towards a more explicit concern with the nature and purposes of critique. Chapter 10 provides a very brief sketch of some ideas on this theme. The need is not only for a scientific means of revealing facets of law often hidden from sight but also for a coherent 'moral vision'; a means of articulating and defending values that lie at the base of scientific curiosity and that provide the ultimate motivation for it.

In the most recent studies presented here the values and ambitions that underpin a faith in the need for sociological inquiry about law are made explicit. It is no accident that the work collected in this volume has been produced for the most part during a particular period of a decade and a half and in a particular country in which the conditions of social cohesion and solidarity (and eventually of public security and order) have seemed increasingly precarious. The conviction (made explicit in the chapters in the final section of the book) that underpins the effort to develop a reflexive social science of law in these studies is a conviction that law can and must be made to serve purposes beyond those to which it is presently directed. Those new purposes centre on the need to redefine radically the nature of community, to recreate conditions of community as a strengthening of the moral bonds that unite citizens in a pluralistic political society, and to develop regulatory structures that will allow the conditions of community in this sense to flourish.

Law and Community

How should we begin to think of these possibilities for law? It has been argued above that law is experienced as a matter of power. So power can be said to be, in this sense, its social essence. But law has, also, another face—its utopian, aspirational face. Law would not have been the focus of so many hopes of emancipation and progress throughout modern history—aspirations invoking the name of justice, the ideal of the Rule of Law, the symbolic security and progressivism of bills of rights, the moral appeals of natural law and human rights discourses—had it been seen as no more than the allocation of power.

Certainly, part of law's aspiration can be understood in terms of this allocation. In so far as law allocates power it may channel it in relatively predictable ways, requiring that it be exercised in certain forms rather than others, through particular procedures whose operation can be formalized and known in advance by those likely to be affected by them. Law's power may require that informal modes of coercion or influence be restricted or surrendered in return for access to the power of law itself. One must, for example, give up or limit many possibilities of self-help (the use of direct violence, feud, or vendetta, military coercion, and perhaps certain forms of economic compulsion) if processes of enforcement and order-maintenance through legal processes are to be effective and respected. Thus, as suggested earlier, law's modes of expressing, channelling, and formalizing power can create a sense of general security; security for *all* who live subject to law.

The promise of this general security is the appeal of the Rule of Law. The doctrine of the Rule of Law offers some security even to the least powerful among citizens. It does so by requiring that when power (for example, physical, economic, administrative, or political power) is exercised over them this is done in predictable, formalized ways. Hence rational general law is often praised as a restraint on power. But, most importantly, it is a regularization of power. It does not usually take away the prerogatives of the economically, politically, militarily, or cultural powerful. It may, however, require that their power be exercised through relatively predictable procedures. This, in itself, may make the exercise of that power somewhat more bearable to those subject to it.

I argue, especially in Chapters 8 and 12, relying on the German jurist Franz Neumann's work, that the ideal of the Rule of Law, as a means by which formalized, predictable, regularized power is substituted for (and outlaws) arbitrary—that is, unpredictable and informal—power is not enough as a basis for law's aspirations to contribute to the ordering of a cohesive society. Law's aspiration is towards something more than this, and something more than the society of morally unconnected, rights-possessing individuals that liberal philosophy tends to presuppose.

Thus, in Parts II and III of the book the theoretical emphasis gradually shifts from a focus on aspects of law's discursive or ideological power towards an exploration of what law's aspiration might be. The ultimate aim is to try to clarify the almost terminally vague idea of community. The notion of community needs to be translated into a concept that can be used to analyse in relatively concrete ways the contemporary situation of law in advanced Western societies. For this purpose, many older ideas of community in the literature of social theory are relatively unhelpful, but some important keys are provided in the writings on law of the French sociologist Émile Durkheim, which are discussed in Chapter 9.

In Part III of the book the question of the meaning of community is approached from several contrasting starting points. The approach is essentially that of deriving elements of a legal concept of community from the conclusions of a range of separate studies of legal ideology. I argue that much of the power of contemporary

law is ideological in the sense that law helps in important ways
to sustain taken-for-granted, 'common sense' understandings of
the nature of society and of life within it. If this is so, it may be
important to see how the notion of community appears in legal
ideology. This matter is addressed directly in Chapter 11, where
comparisons are made between, on the one hand, notions about
community evoked in judicial opinions of the United States Supreme Court and in some American legal writings and, on the
other, significantly different ideas expressed in some English legal
literature and in judgments from English courts. The idea of
community that legal ideology presents seems, however, as might
be predicted, a 'commonsense' and traditional one, characterized
essentially by shared values and beliefs. The major difficulties with
this conception are in locating the source of shared values in
contemporary conditions, and in determining how these shared
elements of community are created and how they are reliably and
authoritatively to be expressed.

Legal ideology, in conformity with its nature as ideological
thought, tends to proclaim or assume broad consistencies of
values and social understandings when, in fact, the detail of
legal doctrine reveals complexity, fragmentation, and diversity.
Contemporary legal doctrine in advanced Western societies does
not constitute legal systems as unified, stable systems of reason or
principle but as loosely interrelated, overlapping, and sometimes
conflicting patterns and structures of piecemeal regulation.

Further, the proliferation of law's technical intricacies seems to
mirror the fragmentation and diversity of contemporary advanced,
industrialized societies. In so far as some overarching unity in
regulation and social organisation is discernible much of this seems
to derive from economic imperatives—from the increasing size
and sophistication of capitalistic economic and social structures of
trade, commerce, employment, investment, production, and product distribution in consumer markets and from the extension of
these aspects of capitalist organization to more and more spheres
of life in advanced Western societies. Beyond this network of
economic life there lies considerable moral, social, and cultural
diversity and division, reflected often in misunderstandings, confrontations, and tensions between different populations within the
same political society, or in passive tolerance and general avoidance. In other respects the lack of strong moral bonds within

particular localities encourages largely privatized or isolationist life-
styles (Baumgartner 1988). In these circumstances the question of
what 'community' means in contemporary conditions is a difficult
one. To some people it might seem an unreal question to ask.

Chapter 12 attempts to combine further explorations of legal
ideology with tentative steps towards clarification of what a legally
relevant conception of a community and its regulation might entail.
The aim is to take certain prevailing assumptions about law's
appropriate functions and, through a critical examination of these
assumptions, show how they can be transformed into a different
view of legal activities which implies some ideas about a different
kind of society that law might help to shape. The elements of democracy and active participation by ordinary citizens in decision-
making, noticeably absent from most invocations of the idea of
community in legal ideology, receive some discussion here.

The matter is taken further in Chapter 13 by elaborating the
idea of a plurality of communities and thus, as a necessary corre-
late, a plurality of interlinked legal orders, or realms of regulation. If we are to recognize the fragmentation and diversity of
contemporary societies—the plurality of values, aspirations, life-
styles, and cultural preferences and beliefs of different sections of
the population of contemporary societies such as Britain—it is
important also to recognize that concern for 'community' means
concern for a plurality of communities each with much regulatory
autonomy, yet integrated and co-ordinated under the protective
umbrella of state regulation. Chapter 13 attempts to look at these
matters in terms of the tasks of legal theory. It links them with
claims about the apparently dramatically diversifying, fragmenting, and highly pragmatic character of the regulation which the
centralized state now produces.

Chapter 14 considers similar matters from a different standpoint, that of empirical social scientific study of regulation and its
contexts. The message expressed here is that some shift of emphasis not only among legal theorists but also among social scientists
concerned with law might be beneficial. Their concern might
appropriately be less sharply focused on the orthodox image of
modern law as centralized state regulation—now increasingly driven
by transnational policy imperatives. Instead it might shift further
towards the consideration of appropriate forms and structures of
regulation emerging out of more local conditions of life. I call

these conditions 'local moral milieux'; that is, local cultures and patterns of social interaction that vary with the great diversity of spheres of social life. These local cultures and social patterns can spontaneously generate elements of mutual trust within a population which sow the seeds of community.

Ideas, expressed in general terms, about the moral necessity for devolution of regulation are not new. Durkheim wrote passionately at the beginning of the twentieth century (Durkheim 1984: xxxi–lix) of the need for a vast delegation of legislative and regulatory power from the centralized modern state to what he termed (seeking analogies in the medieval guild systems) corporations— organizations representative of particular sections of the population defined by common interest, professional or occupational experience, and shared moral outlook. In England, Harold Laski, G. D. H. Cole and others developed pluralist theories of the state (Hirst, ed., 1989) which stressed the necessity and even inevitability of decentralization, not only geographically but also in terms of the delegation of specialized functions and the creation of local autonomy. The inadequacy of most of these theories is often in their insufficient attention to specific principles of regulation and accountability, their failure to conceptualize clearly in general terms the character and basis of cohesion of the collectivities, corporations, or communities in which regulatory responsibilities and powers might reside, and their general failure to theorize adequately the functions of the state in co-ordinating a diversity of communities and policing their relations with each other effectively.

In the concluding chapter I try to confront some of these large issues, at least in a tentative, exploratory fashion. The main challenge that faces the legal imagination at the present time is to envisage what 'law's community' might be; to draw on the vast accumulated experience of modern legal regulation to imagine and to work towards regulatory structures that are responsive to local moral milieux and that clearly reflect the diversity of social experience of citizens. This is a task of making law morally meaningful as an aspect of everyday existence, rather than an alien intrusion, an inaccessible resource, or a special component only of particular professional or commercial settings.

As Chapter 15 seeks to make clear, the idea of a plurality of systems of legal regulation mirroring the moral diversity of contemporary society does not imply an unimportant, non-interventionist role for the centralized state. Law's community should not be seen as in some way contrasted with law's power. Regulatory power is a necessary guarantee of community stability and centralized state power is necessary to the protection and co-ordination of whatever structures may be envisaged as regulated communities. The essential questions are about what law's power can effectively be used to achieve. The following chapters explore facets of this power, especially the power of legal ideas, and try to offer perspectives on the character of contemporary law that may show some of its familiar aspects in an unfamiliar light while indicating possibilities for rethinking and reshaping law in new, perhaps liberating, ways.

2 The Sociological Concept of Law

What should sociology of law take as its central subject-matter? What should it treat as 'law'? The answers are not self-evident but must be the basis of any attempt to develop a sociological theory of law. A wide variety of approaches is advocated in the literature. In studying systematically organized regulatory practices, however, a concept of law as institutionalized doctrine seems particularly useful. This does not restrict law to state law or 'lawyers' law', but it treats the regulation produced and applied by agencies of the centralized state as the dominant form of contemporary law. Arguments around the concept of law serve as an essential starting point for trying to reinterpret legal theory and the field of law in sociological terms.

This chapter is concerned with a familiar problem of jurisprudence but transplanted to the context of the sociology of law. The central problem of much of jurisprudence has been that of the definition of law or the specification of the appropriate meaning of the word 'law'. For a great deal of modern jurisprudence this problem has been virtually identical with that of achieving a scientific understanding of law. For John Austin, the English nineteenth century jurist, to define law was to designate the field of a science and to characterize the essential elements of its subject matter. Among more modern writers the search for a definition has been abandoned in favour of the attempt to formulate a concept of law—a model of law in something of the manner of the models that natural or social scientists use as guides for the construction of theories and for the formulation of hypotheses to be tested by empirical research. Yet the problem of the concept of law remains central to jurisprudence; something more than a starting point for inquiry.

For sociology of law the objectives of specifying a concept of law are often different from—although not indifferent to—the concerns of many jurists. My purpose in this chapter is to outline in general terms some approaches to specification of a concept of law that have characterized modern sociological study of law, to consider some of their implications, and to suggest reasons why some conceptualizations of law may be more useful to sociology of law than others.

Differing Uses of a Concept of Law

The terms jurisprudence and sociology of law are too vague and refer to too many diverse objectives and methods of legal analysis to allow generalization. For that reason I propose to use a distinction between normative legal theory—a centrally important part of the territory of contemporary jurisprudence, in a sense its heart—and empirical legal theory, which is central to the concerns of sociology of law. By normative legal theory I mean theory that seeks to explain the character of law solely in terms of the conceptual structure of legal doctrine and the relationships between rules, principles, concepts, and values held to be presupposed or incorporated explicitly or implicitly within it. By empirical legal theory I mean theory that seeks to explain the character of law in terms of historical and social conditions and treats the doctrinal and institutional characteristics of law emphasized in normative legal theory as explicable in terms of their social origins and effects.

The Concept of Law in Normative Legal Theory

Contemporary jurisprudential writings, like earlier ones, reflect in their normative legal theory the lawyer's professional approach to knowledge of law. To fix the meaning of legal ideas is to explain the reality of law; to make explicit a concept of law compatible with lawyers' assumptions about legal doctrine is to know law since law is understood by normative legal theory to exist only in concepts, rules, and other elements of doctrine developed in or implicit in legal practice. So, in jurisprudence, the enterprise of fixing the meaning of law is often merely the most general and abstract form of the lawyer's natural professional concern with definition. Specifying what is law is the same as specifying what is valid as law, what can be relied on in arguments before a court, or how to determine what the legal result should be when rules are interpreted and applied by courts or other legal authorities. In contemporary normative legal theory the object of specifying a concept of law is that of explaining the possibility of logical system and coherence in legal doctrine; showing how the professional doctrine of the lawyer constitutes an integrated totality. The construction of a professionally plausible and logically coherent concept of law as doctrine is both the starting point for and the final expression of knowledge of the nature of law from the standpoint of normative legal theory. This is notwithstanding the fact that the techniques of normative legal theory can be and are applied to analysis of normative systems other than that suggested by lawyers' professional doctrine.

The Concept of Law in Empirical Legal Theory

The numerous approaches to legal analysis that can be categorized as sociological in the broadest sense are unified only by their deliberate self-distancing from the professional viewpoint of the lawyer. It is implicit in the aim of empirical legal theory that law is always viewed 'from the outside', from the perspective of an observer of legal institutions, doctrine, and behaviour, rather than that of a participant, although participants' perceptions may be taken into account as data for the observer. Indeed, from a phenomenological standpoint the interpretation of participants' perceptions may be of primary importance. Yet that interpretation becomes possible only through a scientific distancing as determined and thoroughgoing as the empathy which the observer may seek with the observed. Sociological analysis of law has as its sole unifying objective the attempt to remedy the assumed inadequacy of lawyers' doctrinal analyses of law.

Beyond this, sociological analysis may have a variety of aims. It may be a supplement to professional doctrinal analysis, revealing the social consequences, environment, or causes of legal policy and doctrinal or institutional development[1] so as to aid the lawyer's legal policy debates. Alternatively, with other social

---

[1] Gurvitch 1947: 7. Such objectives may offer the greatest prospect of sympathetic support from lawyers at 'the level of mutual service' (cf. Willock 1974: 5–6) and help to disarm 'powerful antagonists' (cf. Gurvitch: 1947: 1). See also Carbonnier 1978: 369 ff.

scientific approaches, it may claim to provide a substitute for doctrinal analysis revealing the 'unreality' of legal concepts[2] or the need for legal policies that bypass doctrinal disputes (for example, through use of statistics or 'Brandeis briefs', importations of psychology, and positivist 'treatment' approaches in criminal justice and elsewhere). Finally, it may seek to explain in sociological terms law as doctrine, practices, or institutions, treating these as the subject matter of scientific analysis and hence distancing itself from the manifest functions or purposes of the law which, in themselves, are treated as part of the subject matter of inquiry. Behind such an objective usually stands the motive of adopting an epistemological standpoint from which a radical critique of and challenge to lawyers' professional conceptions of law becomes possible. For some critics this is a step towards the fundamental reshaping of legal institutions; for others it may be part of the means of demonstrating the need for and exploring the possibility of a social order dispensing with law—at least in its accepted forms.

Although such a classification of objectives certainly cannot imply any useful corresponding classification of the research to which they give rise (cf. Nelken 1981a; Nelken 1981b), it can highlight differences of emphasis in the literature. The third objective of sociological study of law specified above is in the fullest sense the basis of a sociology of law (as opposed to a sociology in aid of law or a sociology in place of law) treating the nature of law as its centre of attention rather than being primarily concerned with the effects of laws or legal practices. At the same time it is the objective that is most directly related to the development of empirical legal theory and that most clearly demands the development of a rigorous concept of law, while much other sociological inquiry related to law can and does merely employ common sense views of the meaning of law informed by lawyers' assumptions.

[2] See e.g. Podgorecki 1974: 47, suggesting sociology of law as an empirical replacement for jurisprudence. Eugen Ehrlich (1936: 339–40), following the tenets of the *Freirechtslehre* jurists, argues for sociology of law partly as a substitute for conceptual analysis and partly as its scientific basis. Typical of much writing from a psychological perspective is Meehl 1977. For an early polemic emphasizing the roots of this approach within 'realist' jurisprudence see Cohen 1935; 'Legal concepts are supernatural entities which do not have a verifiable existence except to the eyes of faith' (Cohen 1935: 821).

In fact sociological concepts of law are extremely varied; much more so than those presented by the modern Anglo-American literature of normative legal theory. Oppositions in basic conceptualizations of law tend to be easy to categorize in normative legal theory (for example, positivist/natural law, rules versus principles) and the minority positions tend to display (as with Ronald Dworkin) or are interpreted as displaying (as with Lon Fuller) not so much a coherent and adequate alternative conception of law as a set of criticisms of the prevailing orthodoxy presupposing the fundamental concepts within it. Thus Fuller's central ideas of the functional character of law tend to be under-emphasized in favour of stress on the positivistic elements in his theories and his answers to questions of importance to positivists—particularly the question of legal validity and the normative criteria of the existence of legal systems.[3] It is, thus, easy to identify powerful orthodoxies which are, no doubt, to be explained to a considerable extent in terms of the underlying common professional aims and outlook of lawyers in these societies, which also inform or influence the outlook of jurists. The variety of aims with which sociological study of law may be pursued and its lack of commitment to legal professional concerns have, however, already been suggested above. We should therefore expect less uniformity in basic conceptualizations of law in sociologically oriented literature.

Sociological concepts of law are also, in general, formulated in a less sophisticated and elaborate manner than in normative legal theory. In part this is because, as suggested above, for normative legal theory definition or conceptualization of law is an end in itself. It constitutes knowledge of law rather than, as with sociological study of law, a preliminary stage in organizing empirical study beyond legal doctrine as well as within it. Yet it can be suggested that sociological studies have been in some measure intimidated by the massive bulk of existing conceptual analysis of law within the literature of normative legal theory. The problem here is that a concept of law must take account of, though not necessarily treat as central, the nature of law as doctrine—unless, as for example in Donald Black's (1976) work, doctrine is almost entirely

---

[3] See e.g. Lloyd 1985: 60–1, 131–3; Summers 1971; Villanova Law Review Symposium 1965. Cf. Summers 1978, where, in the course of a sympathetic discussion, the changing attitude to Fuller's work in recent commentaries is noted.

excluded from a concept of law framed in strictly behavioural terms. Thus a sociology of law which seeks, *inter alia*, to analyse the social significance of legal doctrine must confront jurists' conceptions of the nature of legal doctrine. The legal sociologist must become a lawyer in order to challenge or go beyond lawyers' conceptions of law.

Sociological Concepts of Law: A Sketch of a Typology

Juridical Monism

Sociological concepts of law fall into three broad categories, the last of which needs to be further subdivided. In the first category, law is understood in terms of lawyers' conventional definitions of law. In contemporary Western societies, therefore, as in many others, law is understood to be, in essence, the law of the state as recognized by lawyers and state courts and enforced by state agencies. Whatever the position in stateless societies, in politically organized societies the effect of this conceptualization of law is to remove by definition many problems of the relationship between law and state. If for Kelsen the state is merely the legal order seen from a particular point of view (Kelsen 1945: 190–1), for many Marxist analysts law has been the state seen from a particular viewpoint, or a technical apparatus of state power. As such, while the state has long constituted an important focus of Marxist concern, law has, until relatively recently, been of little interest; an empirical theory of law has seemed unnecessary when knowledge of law is seen to depend solely on a proper understanding of the nature of the state.[4] Even contemporary Marxist analyses—whether based in commodity form, state derivation, or relative autonomy theories—of law in advanced capitalist societies do not consider the possibility or utility of conceptualizing law as potentially or actually wider in scope than lawyer's law or the law created,

---

[4] Pashukanis' work provides the most interesting exception to this, where an attempt is made to combine a Leninist conception of the state with a theory of law derived from Marx's analysis of the fetishism of commodities. But the result is a vague and ambiguous analysis of the legal functions of the state inappropriate to the political project of Soviet Marxism at the time in which he wrote, and which provides a major reason for the rejection of the theory in Marxist politics. See Pashukanis 1978: ch. 5; Cotterrell 1979.

interpreted, and enforced by what can be understood in common sense terms as state agencies.[5] Conventional definitions generally appear adequate in a tradition of inquiry that does not include law as such among its primary theoretically specified objects of analysis.

Many non-Marxist sociological approaches to legal study adopt a similar conception of law. Donald Black, who in other respects offers a radical behaviouralist critique of lawyers' conceptions of law as doctrine, characterizes law as governmental social control, the normative life of a state and its citizens.[6] Adam Podgorecki (1974: 46) preserves a practical definition of law as 'lawyers' law' alongside a theoretical definition in wider terms. Roberto Unger (1976) offers three concepts of law arranged in a historical matrix of modernization. Modern law in this view is the official and autonomous legal order of the modern state. In Talcott Parsons' major writings on law (e.g. Parsons 1962; 1966; 1971), law is assumed to be the lawyers' law of politically organized societies, a distinct species of social norms. In these lawyers' law conceptions other normative systems in a society may be seen as derived directly or indirectly from law, or as created or maintained by 'delegation' from it (Carbonnier 1978: 208), or as sources influencing the content of law. They are, however, distinct from and ultimately subordinate to it.

Juridical Pluralism

It might be thought that these standpoints on the concept of law are in many respects obvious and realistic. Yet even in contemporary

---

[5] This despite the fact that several sophisticated recent Marxist analyses of the state have deliberately rejected its common sense connotation of government agencies in preference for a conception that stresses the pervasiveness of state controls in the 'private' sphere. Most important in this respect is the work of Nicos Poulantzas and Louis Althusser, and modern interpretations of Antonio Gramsci's insights. Law, however, tends to remain conceptualized in these writings as lawyers' law applied by and to government agencies, although, notably in Althusser's concept of ideological state apparatuses, its pervasiveness as ideology through many levels of social relations is accepted.

[6] Black 1976: 2. See also Black 1972: 1096, where the concept is held to be 'more inclusive than an American lawyer might deem proper' but to exclude such forms of social control as 'bureaucratic rules in private organisations'. While the concept undoubtedly lacks precision and in Black's view can encompass 'any act by a political body that concerns the definition of social order or its defence' it is clear that in research practice it functions as a strictly behavioural version of the state law conception.

conventional Western usage law refers not only to state law but also to the law created and applied by international agencies and to transnational religious law (for example, canon law), and historically it has included numerous forms of law (for example, customary, territorial, mercantile, personal, ecclesiastical) whose creation, interpretation, and enforcement have not in any way depended on state agencies. Such usage has undoubtedly influenced a second kind of sociological conceptualization of law which emphasizes 'juridical pluralism' (Carbonnier 1978: 208–18; 1988: 16–20).

The essence of these concepts of law is that state or lawyers' law is only one form of law and is not necessarily to be seen in sociological terms as dominant. Law exists in various layers or levels (Gurvitch 1947); it may exist in associations (Gierke 1900; 1934; 1977; Ehrlich 1936), institutions (Romano 1975; Broderick 1970), or social systems of various size and nature. Social groups of whatever size may be seen as having the same fundamental legal needs (Llewellyn 1940).[7] Law may be seen as including unofficial as well as official and intuitive as well as positive forms (Petrazycki 1955).

What is the significance of such conceptualizations? Invariably it is to claim through the very definition of law that legal ideas and the fundamental problems of legal thought with which lawyers are familiar pervade, in some sense, social life. Thus, in Georges Gurvitch's work a phenomenological approach to the analysis of law is suggested by the very definition of the juridical sphere. If the state law conception emphasizes the political importance of law and the relationship between law and the power of the state, the juridical pluralism conception tends to stress the pervasive social importance of legal ideas as responses to fundamental problems of social interaction quite independent of the state yet developed at one particular level in the political life of the state. The fundamental problem of most such pluralist approaches is that of explaining the relationship between levels of law (Fitzpatrick 1983a). Hence these concepts seem to many writers to be wholly inadequate to confront the political dimensions of law, while for others they imaginatively open up the possibilities of interpreting its complex social dimensions.

---

[7] And cf. Llewellyn's remarks on 'folk-law' in Llewellyn 1930: 462–3.

State Law as the Dominant but not Exclusive Form of Law

The third type of sociological conceptualization of law offers a kind of compromise between the two previous ones. Its essence is that law is defined to extend beyond lawyers' law or state law, and lawyers' practical definitions of the legal are considered sociologically inadequate; yet the sociological definition entails that a particular and clear analytical primacy attaches to state law in contemporary societies, so that, for many but not all purposes, law in these societies can be largely equated with law as the lawyer understands it. These approaches treat a particular institutional characteristic of contemporary state law as essential to the definition of law. Law exists to the extent that this institutional characteristic is present.

Three variants of this approach are represented in the literature, focusing on three institutional characteristics: enforcement, dispute processing, and doctrinal development. Thus Max Weber's (1978: 34) major definition of law relies on the existence of particular *sanctioning processes*: 'an order will be called ... law if it is externally guaranteed by the probability that physical or psychological coercion will be applied by a staff of people in order to bring about conformity or avenge violation'. The essence of law is the existence of recognizable police power (see also e.g. Hoebel 1954: 26; Radcliffe-Brown 1933, 1934) which may exist in many social groups or systems but reaches a particularly significant level of development in the state, so much so that state law dominates in social reality and in sociological analysis of law.

Similarly, the fashionable recent emphasis on *dispute processing* has provided a means of avoiding limitation of study to formal 'lawyers' law' processes and has made possible not only important advances in anthropological analysis of social control mechanisms but also theoretical study of the relationship between formal and informal dispute institutions in Western societies (Abel 1973). Yet there is no doubt that in much of the recent discussion of informal, community-based dispute institutions in Western societies, the ultimate dominance of the state system of courts is assumed and informality appears as its support and extension (see e.g. Abel 1981; Bankowski and Mungham 1981; cf. Cain and Kulcsar 1982).

Finally, a third approach focuses on the concept of law as *doctrine or discourse*, as a particular way of reasoning and problem-solving. In this view law typically appears as a variety of social rules, distinguished from others by relatively developed institutional mechanisms for their creation/revelation/discovery, interpretation, or application. Unlike the first and second institutional approaches, this one specifies neither enforcement processes nor adjudicative processes as central, but emphasizes the integrity of doctrine whatever the nature of the institutional processes in which doctrine is developed. 'Legality', in some such approaches, becomes a centrally important concept—indeed, the essence of the legal—implying procedural prerequisites and consequences of the coherent development of doctrine (see e.g. Selznick 1969; Skolnick 1975) and important moral overtones (Fuller 1969; Selznick 1961). Its *alter ego*, 'legalism', with implications of the adverse or pathological consequences of rule-bound reasoning in social organization, forms a focus for other, often more critical, analysts (Shklar 1964).

The danger of this doctrinal focus is that of assuming that contingent doctrinal characteristics of particular legal orders constitute an 'essence' of law; a failing that has been mercilessly exposed by critics of certain early sociological conceptions of law as doctrine that entail excessively rigid characterizations of the sociological implications of the existence of legal rules (e.g. Black 1970; 1972).

Discussion

The Significance of a Concept of Law not Restricted to State Law

Important work has been done on the basis of concepts of law within each of the categories outlined above. Is it necessary, then, or indeed possible to make any general remarks about the relative utility of these approaches? It is hardly necessary to say that a definition of law does not prevent the researcher from studying other social phenomena outside the definition but seen, for certain purposes, to be relevant to legal analysis. Yet the usage of the term 'law' in studies of regulation or social order is important since, like any such designation, it suggests an integrity in the object of study which separates it from other phenomena that may appear similar in certain respects.

To tie law to state law or lawyers' law imposes definite limits on the extent to which law can be envisaged in radically differing forms while yet retaining important continuities with what is presently familiar to the lawyer. To see law as wider than state law— as compassing so-called private legal systems (Evan 1962) or forms of social order or social interaction in diverse groups, institutions, or associations, is to raise seriously the hypothesis that the problems of legal regulation with which lawyers and legislators concern themselves may arise in some form in many different kinds of normative system. These problems include those of the justifications of legal decision-making and of the authority-bases of adjudicative processes; of the conditions of legitimacy of legal orders; of the relationships between sources of legal authority; of the conditions of effectiveness of enforcement of law; of the interpretation, development, generalization, and systematization of rules; of the translation of goals and policies into regulatory form; of the relationship between rule and discretion as administrative devices, and between certainty and justice as legal ideals.

To assume that these and other problems within or about law are peculiar to lawyers' law is to make an unnecessarily restrictive assumption. The issues involved may undoubtedly be developed most fully and with most sophistication in relation to lawyers' law. Some of these problems may indeed be absent in some other normative systems. And the specification of which of these foci of analysis are central and which peripheral to legal study extending to normative orders other than state law will depend in part on the choice of a particular concept of law. Yet to widen the concept of law beyond the lawyer's view of it is to assert the sociological necessity of considering the possibility that legal thought or legal processes in various empirically analysable forms may be a relatively pervasive feature of social life rather than isolated phenomena of a narrow professional sphere.

Sociology of law may well be best served at the present stage of its development by a plurality of approaches to the problem of the concept of law. Indeed, it is implicit in what was said earlier about the variety of aims of writers in this field that this plurality is probably inevitable, quite apart from any question of its desirability. Yet increasing interest in both phenomenological and anarchist approaches to legal analysis suggests a reorientation towards a serious concern with non-state law systems of regulation in contemporary Western societies and with the processes of social rule formation quite apart from formal law-creating processes.[8] If, however, the dominant concept of law in contemporary sociology of law remains the state law concept the danger is that the problems of lawyers' law may be seen as analytically distinct from those of other actual and potential regulatory systems. Thus the withering away of law can be foretold, by some writers, without serious consideration of the possibility that, like hydra heads, law and its problems and consequences may be chopped off in their most visible forms (as state law) only to remain or reappear in other regions of social life which they in fact pervade.

The problems of an uncompromising juridical pluralism that accords no theoretical primacy to state law have been clearly stated in the literature (see e.g. Carbonnier 1978: 213 ff.), and touched on above. The crucially important relationship between law and state is often treated only peripherally given such a conceptual approach, and the relationship between state law and other forms of normative order remains an unsolved problem. A useful concept of law today must surely treat lawyers' law as central, a primary focus of analysis. Yet if analysis is to be developed to explore fully the reach into society of law as both an instrument and formalization of power and as an ideological phenomenon, there seem good grounds for making central the hypothesis that legal thinking is not merely lawyers' thinking, and that the characteristics which sociology of law identifies in state legal institutions may not be unique to them.

One consequence of this might be to avoid utopian thinking that suggests without empirical demonstration that the features of state law and its institutions which sociology of law identifies will not be replicated in various ways in informal regulatory or adjudicatory processes, or in social systems (for example, regions, collectives, autonomous or semi-autonomous social organizations, or groups) smaller than those of the nation state which forms the

[8] There is also evidence of a growing concern with the conditions of both legal and political pluralism in Western societies among some Marxist writers. See Fitzpatrick 1983a; 1983b; Geras 1981. But whether Marxist theory with its central concern with a 'social totality' conceived in terms of integrated modes of production can accommodate such a pluralistic conception of law is an open question at present. Certainly any such developments would necessitate a radical reshaping of established Marxist concepts.

typical unit of modern legal jurisdiction (Cf. Dahl and Tufte 1974; Newton 1982; Black 1974; Taylor 1982). Another consequence might be to raise seriously the possibility that the experience of forms of social organization quite separate from the official state legal system may yield insights into problems of normative order that are typically considered only in relation to state or lawyers' law.[9] The experience of 'simpler' legal orders of simpler social systems than that of the nation state may offer legal insights in a manner somewhat parallel to the insights into complex societies that anthropologists have often claimed as one special justification for the study of relatively simple societies.

These kinds of considerations suggest links between aspects of the concerns of sociology of law and of sociology of organizations. Indeed, at one stage in the recent development of sociology of law influences from this other field of social research were manifest.[10] Interestingly a recent survey of problems of the field of sociology of organizations (Manning 1982) has called for a re-orientation of emphases to take account of the increasing importance of phenomenological perspectives and other recent developments in theory. Thus Peter Manning notes the failure of sociological studies to find a way of specifying in objective terms the nature of organizations and calls for a recognition of the importance of the conceptions of the organization held by those participating in it. Occupational culture is thus of great importance. It provides the image of the organization for those involved in it; 'the framework around which organizational work is legitimated' (Manning 1982: 125). It acts as a 'grid or screen by which events are defined and also makes relevant internal rules' (Manning 1982: 130).

Using empirical data on police organization as a foundation for analysis, Manning identifies three elements which constitute occupational culture: principles (the most abstract statement of culture),

---

[9] This is, of course, the methodological assumption underlying Karl Llewellyn's 'law jobs' theory (Llewellyn 1940) which boldly encompasses the 'law' of 'a newly wedded couple, a newly formed partnership, a two child casual playgroup'. Cf. the fictional illustration of the 'legalistic child' in Twining and Miers 1991.

[10] Particularly through the influence of writers such as Selznick and Evan. For modern analyses see e.g. Evan 1977; Baum 1976. But present concerns seem to be with organizational problems of the state legal system rather than with the regulatory problems of organizations, analysed as problems relevant to legal theory.

working rules ('by which the principles are translated into the everyday negotiated bases for work') (1982: 125) and actual work practices. He goes so far as to set out a detailed code of such principles and rules for the occupational culture of the police he studied in London and in the United States. It is important to stress that an analysis in terms of the relation of rules and principles offers only one possible and partial approach to the problem of analysis of a structure of normative regulation. Yet the parallel with more familiar issues of legal theory seems obvious.

From an entirely different point of view it might be asked whether a sociology of law tied to lawyers' conventional definitions of law ties itself to a form of regulation that may be gradually decreasing in importance. Numerous forms of bureaucratic regulation and control seem to be developing or to have developed in close alliance with orthodox legal forms yet in substantial independence of the reach of analysis of the lawyer. Much of the analysis of rule and discretion in welfare provision, in prison regimes, and in regulation of the national economy and of particular public and private enterprises is concerned in various ways with this matter. Much social theory now foresees the gradual superseding of lawyers' law in its familiar forms by a variety of technological mechanisms of administration and control.

Whether such analyses have merit is not relevant here (see e.g. Nelken 1982). Neither can it be claimed that sociology of law can usefully consider all aspects of any such transformation and all the varied forms of control that have been discussed in recent critical literature.[11] Yet it can be argued that sociology of law must take sufficient account, as central to its project, of forms of regulation going far beyond the boundaries of state or lawyers' law: sufficient, that is, so as to be able to make assessments of the nature of changes in patterns of regulation fundamentally important to any judgement of the changing social significance of the lawyers' law of the state.

The conclusion to which these arguments lead is that, in general terms, a concept of law that treats state law as central to the concept of law in modern industrialized societies, but treats certain other normative systems in these societies as directly

---

[11] See especially Michel Foucault's various writings, Mathiesen 1980, and Donzelot 1980.

comparable and closely related theoretically within a kind of regulatory continuum, is of particular utility for confronting contemporary problems posed by theory and empirical research in sociology of law. My view, then, is that the kinds of institutional concepts of law discussed earlier which avoid both exclusive concern with state law and also pure juridical pluralism, and treat state law as central to but not the exclusive concern of analysis of law in contemporary Western societies, are potentially fruitful.

Some Arguments for a Doctrinal Focus in the Sociological Concept of Law

It may be appropriate to conclude with some brief remarks on the three foci (enforcement, disputing, doctrine) mentioned above as according limited analytical primacy to state law. Approaches taking *enforcement* mechanisms as of central importance make it possible to stress the importance of coercive social institutions in the frameworks of social order and the varied agencies of organized force in societies. Law may appear in such conceptions as essentially a system of order supported by an organized sanctioning apparatus but not necessarily based in rules or doctrine. One important advantage of such a concept of law is that it offers a relatively simple means of expressing theoretically the position of state law in relation to other forms of law. State law dominates to the extent that it holds a monopoly of organized force; to the extent that its sanctioning agencies can prevail in conflict with those of other normative orders.

On the other hand, however, most socially significant normative structures can be seen as sanctioned even without formal enforcement machinery, and much of state law itself (for example, areas of constitutional law) is not dependent for its recognition by lawyers on the existence of related institutionalized sanctions, as the analytical jurists themselves demonstrated. More seriously, to treat coercion as the key defining element of law raises the problem, familiar from criticisms of early Soviet legal theory such as Stuchka's, of distinguishing legal coercion from other forms of coercion. Thus, as Pashukanis (1978: 83) argued, if law is an expression of class power it is a particular kind of expression of power and it is necessary to explain why class power takes legal form and what the term 'legal form' involves.

The *dispute processing* focus in its modern versions typically recognizes that law may less often resolve disputes than 'cool them out'. Dispute processing thus provides a concept of a system of order which, as with the enforcement focus, does not necessarily entail the existence of rules or doctrine as essential to the existence of law. Yet it can be asked how central dispute processing is to state law, given the relatively small number of disputes processed by courts and other legal tribunals in comparison with those dealt with by other means. For example, while the London Commercial Court has dealt with over 100 cases a year, London commercial arbitration bodies have been handling an estimated 10,000 (cf. Ferguson 1980: 146).

Thus while dispute processing has been an important modern focus of work in sociology of law, it is significant that influential theoretical writing developing this focus has often sought to replace the concept of law with that of dispute processing rather than to take dispute processing as the basis of a concept of law. This suggests a recognition that while dispute institutions are of great social significance, a focus on them is not properly seen as an adequate or appropriate focus for analysis of 'law' as such. What may be much more central to law, understood primarily but not exclusively as state law, is the production of ideologically and technically important doctrine by courts and other state-controlled dispute institutions on the occasion of dispute processing, rather than the processing itself, which concerns only a small minority of disputes arising in society.

These considerations may suggest the special utility of a concept of law that focuses on *doctrine* and distinguishes law from other social rules in terms of the existence of specific institutions and processes for the creation, interpretation, and application of doctrine. Law thus consists, like many other normative systems, of rules, concepts, and principles and is distinguished from them in degree rather than in kind by the existence of an institutional structure for the development and organization of doctrine. This institutional structure can presumably take many forms and may not provide for all three functions of creation of doctrine, adjudication or application, and enforcement. But its centrality in a concept of law would ensure that law is not considered merely as disembodied doctrine. Law appears as doctrine produced in, embodied in, and legitimating institutional practices.

Despite the problems of Louis Althusser's theory of ideology,[12] its cardinal virtue was to affirm the materiality and specificity of ideology as expressed and embodied in social relations (see especially Hirst 1979a: 22–39). In somewhat analogous manner legal doctrine (which can be seen in one aspect as a fundamental basis, support, and elaboration of a more diffuse legal ideology embodied in social relations) can be thought of as embodied in particular institutional practices. These practices vary considerably in the different social systems in which law can be held to exist. In this regard legal professionalization—in the sense of professional monopolization and guardianship of doctrine—appears as a central feature of the emergence of the most developed forms of law.

Such a view of law as doctrine makes it possible to see the ideological aspects of law as of particular importance and also, in a sense, incorporates much that is of major significance in the enforcement and dispute processing foci. As many writers have stressed, ideology cloaks power and class relations at the same time as it protects and guarantees them. Pashukanis (1978: 39) suggested that 'defence of the so-called abstract foundations of the legal system is the most general form of defence of bourgeois class interests'. Also, from another viewpoint, it has been stressed in modern discussions of power that one of its vital forms is the power to set the agenda of debate or decision (Bachrach and Baratz 1970), a matter that depends significantly on ideological conditions (Lukes 1974: 23).

Similarly it can be argued that legal dispute processing is by and large effective to 'cool out' conflicts because of the acceptance of court procedures which depend for their authority on the ideological foundations and effects of legal doctrine. The court is seen to act impersonally in applying the law. To compare various kinds of informal dispute processing mechanisms without analysing as centrally significant the ideological conditions under which legal dispute processing takes place may lead to unrealistic expectations of the effects of informal processes.

Yet it would be as misleading to reduce all questions of power to analyses of ideology as it would be to explain the character of ideology in all its many forms and effects as the direct expression of coercive relations. At the same time as the elaboration of

---

[12] For a discussion of these problems see Ch. 6, below, pp. 126–30.

law as doctrine appears as a means of developing and sustaining ideology it can be seen also as a technical means by which the exercise of power is formalized and so co-ordinated as a precision instrument of control at many 'levels' or in many aspects of social life. The choice of a concept of law is, thus, in social science merely a starting point for analysis. Yet in important respects it may influence the agenda of research and the forms that the sociological imagination takes in legal study.

3 Law and Sociology: The Constitution and Confrontations of Disciplines

> How should law as a discipline or intellectual field be viewed sociologically? Indeed, what does it mean to speak of intellectual disciplines, and how can disciplines confront each other? Law and sociology show similarities but also important contrasts in the way they are constituted as intellectual fields and in their strengths and weaknesses as such. Law's particular weaknesses have allowed sociological ideas to invade legal thought in certain contexts and conditions. But, perhaps ironically, the continuing importance of the sociological tradition as a source of enlightenment about law derives in very large measure from the intellectual consequences of sociology's own permanently insecure and ambiguous disciplinary status.

Some caveats have to be entered before trying to generalize about relationships between law (that is, in this context legal studies or legal scholarship) and sociology. To survey the relationships between two such complex and multi-faceted intellectual fields in a single chapter would be impossible. No more than a subjective choice of what is centrally important and most properly to be compared and contrasted could be made. Consequently what follows in this chapter is limited and perhaps idiosyncratic in its choice of issues.[1]

It takes the form of notes on various matters that seem particularly significant in considering the interaction between two intellectual traditions of great importance. It considers general problems involved in understanding the nature and effects of confrontations between such different fields of knowledge and practice as those of law and sociology; some aspects of law as a field of study (and as a 'discipline') that bear centrally on its relations with sociology; and aspects of sociology's nature and

---

[1] A book-length survey of some important results of the confrontations between law and sociology as knowledge fields is attempted in Cotterrell 1992, which contains extensive references to relevant literature.

history that seem particularly important in explaining the history of its involvement with legal studies. In the light of these considerations comments are offered on aspects of the development of sociology of law and its future.

All of these matters are discussed in the particular context of legal studies and sociology in Britain, though much that is written here should have a more general application. But the ideas in this chapter are intended to have a general application in another sense. It will be contended here that in understanding the problems and possibilities of interaction between legal scholarship and sociological inquiry we are involved in considering fundamental questions about the epistemology of legal studies in general and about the possibility of rigorous understanding of law as both a form of intellectual practice and a social phenomenon.

Intellectual Disciplines and their Relationships

Both law and sociology are commonly referred to as academic or intellectual *disciplines*. When their relations are discussed it is usually in terms of a meeting or confrontation of disciplines. It is, however, not necessary to probe far into the concept of 'discipline' in this context to realize the difficulties of making general comments on the relations of law and sociology, even with regard to particular aspects of each. This is because we are attempting to compare, and generalize about, social constructs—commonly thought of as 'knowledge fields'—that have quite different historical origins or patterns of development, social and institutional contexts of existence, and social and political consequences or effects.

By referring to the disciplines with which this chapter is concerned as social constructs I mean to indicate that they are to be understood primarily as social phenomena rather than as intellectual phenomena; that their character can be understood only in relation to the particular historical circumstances in which they exist and is determined not by pure intellectual necessity but by particular social, political, and economic conditions, patterns of institutional organization, and structures of power of many kinds. All of this is, from one viewpoint, obvious. But much discussion (at least by legal scholars) of the relations between law and 'other disciplines' largely ignores these complicating factors in determining what interaction between disciplines actually can mean. Even when the social foundations of disciplines are recognized, these foundations are rarely given the kind of rigorous theoretical analysis that might indicate how disciplinary boundaries function and in what circumstances, if any, they can be effectively overcome.

From Thomas Kuhn and Michel Foucault we have examples of two highly influential ways of thinking of academic disciplines as social constructs; examples which indicate in particularly instructive ways major problems involved in comparing and relating aspects of legal studies and sociology, and which will serve as a useful basis for further discussion in this chapter. The conception of Foucault which reaches its most explicit and uncompromising level of development in his 1969 work, *The Archaeology of Knowledge*, is of fields of knowledge and practice—such as the disciplines of medicine or economics—as 'discursive formations' (Foucault 1972: 31 ff.).

Relations of *discourse*—common modes of thought and expression—are seen as unifying the social, technical, institutional, and economic factors involved in the practice of a particular discipline. Foucault's characterization of disciplinary fields in terms of unifying discourse is particularly interesting in so far as it stresses the *autonomy* of discourse and hence the appearance of autonomy in the disciplinary practices it unifies; secondly, that discursive practices are rule-governed (Foucault 1972: 46); and, finally, that discursive practices are not organized around but, on the contrary, *produce* the objects of which they speak (Foucault 1972: 48).

We arrive at a position in which the comparison of fields of intellectual practice seems all but impossible since each exists according to its own canons of independent validity and each constructs its own field of knowledge and experience. The discourse that underlies each can be thought of as more or less unified and autonomous; and since discourse determines the way the objects of a discipline are conceived within it there can be no obvious means of comparing fields of intellectual practice in relation to objects that are 'common' to two or more disciplinary fields.

Foucault's introduction of the Nietzschian notion of genealogy in his later works, to make possible more concrete analyses of the interrelation of power and knowledge in the development of specific fields of practice, seems to emphasize still more strongly the incomparability of knowledge fields in any terms except those of their specific historical patterns of formation. Thus, 'truth' and 'objectivity' have meaning only from a particular disciplinary standpoint; in a certain historical situation and in relation to the exigencies of specific practical concerns. From a different standpoint, in a different practical situation, 'truth' appears quite differently.

Analysis, by Foucault and like-minded writers, of discourse tends therefore to lead to a position in which it is impossible to compare intellectual disciplines in any terms other than those of, on the one hand, the history of the power relations forming them and embodied in them and, on the other, what might be called the internal mechanisms of discourse—the modes of thought, expression, analysis, and argument which happen at a given time to underlie and facilitate communication between those engaged in the discourse, and which 'police' the elaboration of knowledge within a disciplinary field. A 'distinct' intellectual discipline is only recognizable in terms of its unique circumstances with regard to each of these two kinds of conditions of existence. It seems that the so-called autonomy of disciplines (cf. Giddens 1984: 286) is not an autonomy of unique methods of analysis, practice, or research; nor an autonomy of a distinct 'field of knowledge', but only an effect produced by discursive conventions and the institutions in which they are expressed, both of which are formed in specific historical conditions.

It is important to note that this view of disciplines as themselves producing the *only* available validations of their own knowledge claims (including their claims to possess an autonomous field, unique methods of analysis, or a distinctive subject-matter) is largely confirmed by other analyses proceeding on rather different bases. Foucauldian ideas on this matter have been developed largely in relation to the human (and especially social) sciences.[2] However, Thomas Kuhn's analysis of disciplinary formations in natural (physical) science equally stresses collective self-validation of scientific work, although for Kuhn the essence of this validation is not

---

[2] The term human sciences, though somewhat vague, is appropriate to include knowledge fields such as medicine and psychiatry with which Foucault's writings have been concerned but which would not normally be termed social sciences.

common adherence to rules of discourse by members of the disciplinary community, as with the Foucault of *The Archaeology of Knowledge*.

Kuhn writes of the 'disciplinary matrix' of a scientific field as made up of at least four elements: symbolic generalizations, models, values, and exemplars.[3] It is clear that, for Kuhn, exemplars— shared examples of good research practice and problem-solving within the discipline—are the central elements cementing together the unity of a scientific community as the sustainers of a specific discipline. Thus, whereas for Foucault in *The Archaeology of Knowledge* it is discourse which unifies a field of practice, for Kuhn it is practices themselves—universally accepted by a scientific community as legitimate and appropriate—which perform this function. Scientific revolutions occur when the exemplars cease to be credible to most members of the scientific community; when the research practice they exemplify no longer seems acceptable; when the results obtained by such practice seem fundamentally wrong. Further, it is an important part of Kuhn's argument that many knowledge fields (for example, the social sciences) seem permanently to lack such generally accepted exemplars. Thus they never attain the condition of normal science with its unity and cohesion.

One major strength of Kuhn's work is that an emphasis on the social processes of validation of knowledge makes clear what more traditional accounts of scientific practice, such as positivist accounts, fail to explain: how it is that inconsistent research findings, perceived illogicalities or confusion in disciplinary practice, or incoherences in theory or methodology, are often suppressed for a long time to maintain the existing intellectual order of the discipline. The actual decision to reject the established disciplinary order—the occurrence of what Kuhn terms a scientific revolution—seems to be very much a matter of personalities, power, and environment; a matter of who innovates, how, and at what time and place the innovation occurs. As Kuhn (1970a: ch. 10) makes

---

[3] Kuhn 1970a (postscript), 174 ff.; and see also Kuhn 1970b and 1974. Kuhn eventually adopted the term 'exemplar' in preference to his famous term 'paradigm' which, as he came to recognize, was used ambiguously in his major work, *The Structure of Scientific Revolutions*, sometimes referring narrowly to what he later called an exemplar, and sometimes much more widely to what he subsequently termed a disciplinary matrix.

clear, scientific revolutions involve a 'change of world view' in the scientific field; not just an accumulation of anomalies but a readiness in the scientific community to accept that the attempt to explain these anomalies in the old terms is fruitless; a 'conversion' to a 'new vision' of the scientific field and of the nature of its problems. It is one of the most valuable aspects of Kuhn's analysis that he shows clearly that changes of scientific world view occur only as a result of intense conflict within scientific communities.[4]

There seem to be two particular problems with a Kuhnian approach that are relevant to this chapter's concerns. First, Kuhn offers no guidance as to where we might find any unifying or integrating elements in disciplines other than those of the natural sciences,[5] since probably only the latter have, in his view, the characteristics of the disciplinary matrix that make normal science possible. The answer may be that for knowledge fields such as law and sociology there is only what we might call a *discipline-effect*—a mirage of disciplinary integrity—not the actual conditions of practice for an integrated intellectual discipline. Foucault's approach, at least in his *Archaeology of Knowledge* phase,[6] seems to suggest that such a discipline-effect is the consequence of rules crystalized by, and at the same time implicit in and governing, discursive practice. In other words, there are no objective tests of what counts as a discipline since each disciplinary field has its own unique discursive character; in effect it quite arbitrarily defines itself as a discipline. Later Foucault is explicit in his writings that the character of the social sciences, and of law as a knowledge field, is shaped by the intimate relationship between knowledge and power;[7] these knowledge fields are structured by their direct relevance to particular configurations of power in society.

[4] On dogmatic conformity and resistance to challenges to basic ideas in scientific fields see also Feyerabend 1975: 298.

[5] This has not prevented numerous attempts to apply his ideas to the social sciences. See e.g. Harvey 1982 and many references therein; Harvey properly notes that Kuhn's ideas have been seriously distorted in much of this literature.

[6] For a most valuable discussion of the evolution of Foucault's thought see Dreyfus and Rabinow 1982.

[7] He insists, however, that the discourse of law is formed in relation to a quite different basis of power—expressed in terms of sovereignty—from those of the human sciences founded in a variety of 'new mechanisms of power', which Foucault thinks of as particularized technologies of social control: see especially Foucault 1980.

Secondly, Kuhn plainly rejects a relativistic conception of knowledge; that is, one which assumes that there can be no ultimate criteria of truth or no possibility of objective knowledge which could adjudicate between the conflicting knowledge claims of, for example, different intellectual disciplines or scientific communities. This is because it is clear that he thinks that when a scientific revolution occurs there is an *advance* of knowledge. Indeed the revolution occurs eventually because the 'old guard' of the scientific community can no longer resist the *better* explanation of scientific findings that the scientific 'revolutionaries' are offering. But the explanations of why the new approaches are considered better, and of how the decision to accept them is eventually made, are the weakest parts of Kuhn's analysis.[8] Although relativism is rejected it is not entirely clear why we are entitled to reject it (cf. Giddens 1977: 76–7; Lakatos 1970). Foucault has no such problems since, as we have already seen, a thoroughgoing relativism is necessarily accepted by him, at least as regards knowledge in the human sciences with which his writings have been primarily concerned.

However, there seems importance both in Foucault's implication in some of his writings that certain knowledge fields (especially, or perhaps solely, the natural sciences) may escape the relativism which his discourse and power-knowledge analyses of the human sciences suggest (Dreyfus and Rabinow 1982: 115–7), and in Kuhn's need to reject relativism despite the insistence of his theory that validation by scientific communities is the only significant measure of scientific 'truth'.

These theoretical positions or problems provide some encouragement for suggesting that we can provisionally hold both to a view of disciplines as social constructs and also to the possibility that forms of knowledge can in some circumstances transcend the particular social conditions of their production. However, it may be that the only way in which knowledge in the human sciences generally (including the study of law) can escape being limited by the particular configurations of power in the human activities that

---

[8] Cf. Kuhn 1977a where a mixture of 'subjective' and 'objective' factors is said to be involved. But Kuhn himself shows in this paper, as elsewhere, that the so-called objective factors (accuracy, consistency, scope, simplicity, fruitfulness) often lose their objectivity in subjective interpretation.

make possible each of these specific disciplines (cf. Dreyfus and
Rabinow 1982: 163) is by confrontation *between* disciplines, or—to
put it another way—the effective challenging of the mechanisms
sustaining the discipline-effect of these fields. Intellectual confrontations of disciplinary knowledge fields may be possible to
advance knowledge beyond that encompassed by each of them. It
should follow, however, that any such effective confrontation will
not merely add to knowledge but ultimately *transform the terms in
which knowledge is sought and conveyed* by disrupting the taken-for-
granted foundations of the disciplines involved.

It should also follow, if disciplines are understood as social
constructs in the ways outlined above, that a confrontation of disciplines will never be a confrontation of 'pure' knowledges or meth-
odologies with its outcome determined by intellectual criteria such
as methodological rigour, sophistication of theoretical analysis, or
depth of empirical reference. Such a confrontation will always ultimately be a *social* conflict (in certain aspects, a political conflict in
the sense of a competition for power or an attempt to exercise
power).

It is thus not possible to bring about any such confrontation
merely by intellectual argument, unless the social conditions for
such a confrontation arise. Thus, critical writing in jurisprudence
importing perspectives from philosophy or various social sciences
has, despite some extremely cogent demonstrations of the inadequacies of prevailing modes of legal thought, often failed to
achieve any lasting reorientation of legal thinking. On the other
hand, if such conditions do exist, an 'intellectual space' may be
opened through the disciplinary uncertainties and self-doubt that
may ensue. And these kinds of uncertainties and doubts are never
far from the surface of serious and imaginative scholarly activity
in disciplinary fields such as those of law and the social sciences if
we accept the implications of Kuhn's and Foucault's analyses that
what exists in them is at best no more than a discipline-effect, a
chimera of scientific unity and autonomy.

The opening of an intellectual space for analysis relatively un-
constrained by existing disciplinary limits holds out the possibility
of intellectual advance; that is, towards the development of wider-
ranging, more powerful theoretical frameworks of explanation, a broadened perspective on experience, a recognition of and
capacity to interpret convincingly a wider range of available data.

This would not, however, be intellectual advance in the sense of a Kuhnian scientific revolution in a particular discipline. On Kuhn's analysis, at least, it would seem that no such scientific revolution can occur in the social sciences since such fields lack universal agreement on appropriate exemplars; hence they have no single orthodoxy to be overthrown.[9] The possibility of intellectual advance in this context probably has to be viewed much more modestly. It may mean (putting the matter in Kuhnian terms) a reduction in the range of seriously competing exemplars, or clarification of their appropriateness, power, or scope; or (in Foucault's terms) a making explicit of the 'hidden' rules or structures of discourse in a particular disciplinary field so as to reveal the contingent character of taken-for-granted disciplinary practices.

The advancement of knowledge is thus a possible by-product of the effective confrontation of disciplines, and not an aspiration that brings about such confrontations. But I see no reason why, just because such advance occurs in unpredictable and very indirect ways and probably cannot be assessed by methods that are free of historical contingency, it need be treated as chimeral in the social sciences and in the study of law in society. The confrontation of knowledge fields formed, as Foucault suggests, by the technological necessities of power in historical conditions may help to reveal the particular social foundations of these knowledge fields more clearly (as Foucault's own work has done) and pave the way for developing broader perspectives on experience, which are freer of the constraints imposed by these historical origins of specific knowledges. It is against this background that we need to consider the respective positions of law and sociology as 'disciplines', the conditions under which confrontations between these knowledge fields have occurred, and some existing intellectual 'by-products' of their confrontation.

[9] Kuhn originally described such knowledge fields as the social sciences as 'pre-paradigmatic' but later rejected this term, recognizing that their problem is not a lack of exemplars but lack of agreement on the status of exemplars. Hence they are immune to the normal processes of development of science. It would seem that they are likely to be stagnant with unchanging dogma, or else subject to unending crisis since the conditions for establishment of normal science are never achieved. It would be a considerable over-simplification (with nevertheless a certain amount of plausibility in it) to see sociology as generally suffering from the latter condition and legal studies from the former.

Legal Science and its Discontents

How should we think of the field of legal studies in the light of the above discussion of the nature of intellectual disciplines? The typical kinds of enquiries about law pursued by academic and practising lawyers and often thought to be encompassed within law-as-discipline are very varied in character and aims. For convenience we will term the whole range of these inquiries *legal science* (cf. Cotterrell 1983: 683), deliberately leaving open all questions whether a single epistemology underlies them, what audiences they are addressed to, and what purposes they are thought to serve.

Is it possible to understand the disciplinary character of this knowledge field by using Kuhnian or Foucauldian perspectives? A Foucauldian concern with unifying discourses would seem potentially helpful if only because of the obviously close, if ill-defined, connection between legal doctrine (the rules, principles, and concepts set out in law books and authoritatively stated in legislation or deduced from judicial decisions) and legal science itself. It is clear that unity is sought in legal doctrine both as a discourse—a mode of organizing and understanding 'legal experience' and going about 'legal tasks'—and as a general integrated system of social regulation. Much of legal science is clearly directed to facilitating or revealing this doctrinal unity. To this extent, however, legal science's own integrity and unity as a knowledge field is usually considered unproblematic, being assumed to be merely a reflection of the unity it postulates for legal doctrine. Thus legal science is thought of as that discipline which professes knowledge of law (as doctrine).

As we would expect, however, from the discussion in the previous section, this postulated unity of legal science turns out on examination to be merely a presupposition or discipline-effect. Legal science views itself, so to speak, in the mirror of the legal doctrine which it has itself organized and 'unified' in particular forms. It cannot derive its disciplinary integrity from 'the law' as a supposedly already unified, integrated object since law only attains this integrity and unity (or the appearance of it) through the activity of legal science. To some extent, then, legal doctrine and legal science appear in a kind of symbiosis in which each seemingly justifies the autonomy and integrity of the other, but is only able to do so by postulating its own autonomy and integrity.[10]

This seems a clear example of the kind of essentially self-validating discourse with which Foucault has been much concerned. As such, if legal discourse is understood in Foucault's terms as having its own historical basis for existence in structures of power and as an intersection and interpenetration of power and knowledge, we should expect it to be largely impervious to serious challenge from other knowledge-fields.

Some years ago, Vilhelm Aubert, trying to describe the typical character of legal thinking, remarked on its intellectual isolation and distinctiveness (Aubert 1963). It is interesting, however, that when the components of legal reasoning and legal analysis are isolated there appears to be little that is truly distinctive about them. The techniques of practical reasoning, modes of interpretation, organization of problem solving, and so on, that are involved appear not fundamentally different from those frequently encountered in what are considered non-legal contexts. This suggests that when law as a knowledge field continually asserts its distinctiveness and autonomy it does so in much the way that Foucault's analyses would lead us to expect: unilaterally and without consideration of other knowledge fields; by seeing the world from within a self-contained framework of discourse which constructs its own objects of analysis and declares irrelevant, because it cannot even recognize (let alone comprehend), other discourses and their objects.

[10] Neil MacCormick offers an interesting and, in some respects, comparable description of the 'circular phenomenon' of legal knowledge, in which the ceaseless interaction of legal science and legal doctrine makes legal knowledge 'an endless belt which is continuously moving through time. Endless but not gapless, the gaps being filled in from what is already there. If the phenomenon we describe is circular, a circular explanation of it is not vicious, but required by veracity': MacCormick 1978: 246. For me, the crucial point is that the gaps are thought to be filled in from 'what is already there'; i.e. already existing components of doctrine. The filling of gaps (legal science activity) is thus seen as an activity controlled by existing doctrine. At the same time, what that doctrine 'really is'—where its limits lie, what its components are, and how they are to be organized, evaluated, related—is determined by legal science. The scope of and nature of legal science and legal doctrine are thus determined by each other in an endless circularity of thought.

Niklas Luhmann describes the legal system as a 'normatively closed system'. Thus it 'produces its own elements as legally relevant units' (Luhmann 1985: 283). Birth, death, human actions, and so on enter legal discourse only in so far as the normative qualities of these occurrences are given to them by this discourse. They are thus accorded 'a special status that is solely relevant for the legal system'. However, Luhmann also suggests that the legal system is 'cognitively open' in the sense that it is oriented to its environment and takes account of facts occurring in that environment. The extent to which it does so can be a basis for evaluation of legal doctrine (Luhmann 1985: 283; see also Luhmann 1986: 113–14). Thus, medical advances may raise the question of the appropriateness of the law's conception of life or death.

This view of cognitive openness can, however, be misleading. Law may find its own good reasons within its own framework of discourse for ignoring even obvious facts of its environment. A good illustration would be the biologically absurd English common law stance on 'precocious toddlers' and 'fertile octogenarians' in the law of perpetuities,[11] or the stubborn adherence to the M'Naghten Rules on insanity despite the weight of psychiatric knowledge.[12] The alteration of doctrine by legislation in both of these areas in no way affects the basic characteristics of legal discourse which give rise to such 'anomalies' and which continue to inspire new ones as quickly as old ones are removed by legislative surgery (cf. Aubert 1963).

It is, of course, one of the great strengths of positivist thought in legal science that it makes it possible to accept simultaneously, on the one hand, that the substantive content of legal doctrine can be changed from 'outside' (from political input into the legal system) and, on the other, that such inputs in no way prejudice the integrity of the discursive formation of law; a formation that can be understood as a 'regularity (an order, correlations, positions and functionings, transformations)' existing 'between objects, types of statement, concepts, or thematic choices' (Foucault 1972: 38). Legal discourse protects itself from (is perhaps immune to) interference from external knowledge fields. Because of its quality

[11] See e.g. *Jee* v. *Audley* (1787) 1 Cox Eq. Cas. 324; *Re Dawson* (1888) 39 Ch.D 155; *Re Gaite's Will Trusts* [1949] I All ER 459. Cf. Perpetuities and Accumulations Act 1964, s. 2.   [12] For general discussion see e.g. Finkel 1988.

of being 'normatively closed' it does indeed construct its own objects of discourse. In this sense it is self-contained.[13]

This kind of analysis helps in understanding some very important reasons why legal science typically maintains its intellectual isolation despite the apparent lack of distinctiveness of its methods and the fact that its object 'law' might be thought to be ambiguously defined or even elusive, multi-faceted in nature, and shared in various ways with several other disciplines. Why does the knowledge field of law apparently maintain its isolation so much more fiercely than do numerous other disciplines? The answer may be that the relationship of legal knowledge with configurations of power in society is so firm, direct, and fundamental that the power-knowledge interpenetration provides an especially strong demand for and guarantee of the maintenance of the autonomy of the legal field and its discipline-effect. In some areas of social science this demand and guarantee may not be so strong. In natural sciences (where the forming, reforming, and cross-cutting of disciplinary boundaries often seems a continuous and flexible process) it may be even more restricted (cf. Dreyfus and Rabinow 1982: 162–3).

Nevertheless, there are limitations on this kind of explanation of the disciplinary character of legal science given that legal science, as defined above, cannot be understood in its entirety as the disciplinary mirror-image of legal doctrine. A diversity of types of study is involved and it seems clear that a variety of different audiences is addressed by legal scholarship. The application of Foucault's discourse analysis to the legal knowledge field postulates a disciplinary unity that should not be assumed without more detailed discussion.

Can a Kuhnian approach help? Kuhn refers to law, in terms that seem compatible with Foucault's approach, as a disciplinary field unified by 'external social need', not by agreement on exemplars (Kuhn 1970a: 19). We should, perhaps, expect to find a range of conflicting exemplars which are the focus of different kinds of analysis of law in legal science. Colin Campbell (1974:

---

[13] It is precisely this aspect of legal discourse which is reflected in Kelsen's claim that norms of law and morality cannot conflict. See Kelsen 1945: 374–5, and cf. Hart 1983: 301 ff. That Kelsen adopts this uncompromising position is a measure of his rigour as one of the very few modern jurists who, while committed to orthodox legal science, seriously address the question of its epistemology.

22) has suggested that agreement on exemplars in legal science *does* exist, with 'a particular "world view", an orientation to practical and pragmatic problem-solving, and set methods for tackling these problems', so as to create the conditions for 'normal science' in Kuhn's sense. Campbell's analysis of what he calls juristic thought finds the basis of these unifying elements in the process of judicial decision-making, which provides a set of exemplars of appropriate reasoning and problem solving. Accordingly, Campbell not only identifies a Kuhnian unity of legal science but also the possibilities of a 'scientific revolution' in this knowledge field as an increasing number of legal scholars have become dissatisfied with the dominant exemplars of juristic thought and legal analysis and research.

It does, indeed, seem appropriate to locate the model of judicial decision-making at the centre of legal science, but only in so far as this decision-making is inseparably connected with the production or refinement of legal doctrine. Legal science has not generally been directed to the study of lower court decision-making but almost exclusively concerned with the activities of those higher, especially appellate, courts whose decision-making adds to legal doctrine. Attention centres on judicial decision-making in these courts to the extent that it clarifies or creates doctrine, indicates doctrinal problems for legal science to solve, or demonstrates methods of reasoning by which such problems can be solved. Hence attention again returns to the link between legal science and legal doctrine. If there are dominant Kuhnian exemplars they are centred on ways of identifying doctrine, filling gaps in it, and manipulating its uncertainties into certainties. Ultimately, therefore, Campbell's identification of Kuhnian exemplars takes us back to the mirror-of-doctrine conception of the unity of legal science which we derived from Foucauldian premises.

Nearly two decades after Campbell's discussion no scientific revolution has occurred in legal studies. The dominant form of legal scholarship remains one that fits the idea of legal science as a mirror of legal doctrine. Now, as then, alternative modes of legal science exist and, indeed, seem to have increased significantly in strength and appeal. But to talk of a possibility of the breakdown of the dominant paradigm of law as a discipline—of a scientific revolution in the discipline of law—misses the point. The thrust of the analysis in the above paragraphs has been to suggest that as long as law exists as an intersection of knowledge and power in Foucault's sense, as long as there is a need for a knowledge field founded in and serving the power relations that law embodies, legal science will necessarily seek *primarily* to act as the mirror of doctrine; as the unifier, rationalizer, second-guesser, and apologist of legal doctrine. In so far as law portrays itself as a discipline it will necessarily do so through these activities. For, as Foucault's acute analysis of the interdependence of power and knowledge suggests, this provides its reason for disciplinary existence. Only in so far as legal studies escape this discipline-effect—through a conscious breaking-down or rejection of disciplinary boundaries or prerogatives—can they assume forms that escape the endless casuistry entailed in the 'mirror-effect' by which legal science and legal doctrine mutually and endlessly guarantee each other.

How far is this breaking-down possible? From the relationship postulated above between conceptions of law-as-discipline and conceptions of legal doctrine we should expect unorthodox exemplars in legal science (especially those drawing from social science) to gain ground and achieve their greatest influence within legal scholarship usually at times when crises of various kinds are perceived in legal doctrine; at times when legal science finds it extremely difficult to portray the unity of legal doctrine convincingly because of particular developments in the legal systems concerned. It may well be that the partial success of American legal realism, as well as the earlier European 'free law' movement, and numerous other apparently radical legal movements in legal scholarship can be understood in such terms.[14]

The adoption of unorthodox exemplars of research by particular scholars can be attributable to numerous diverse reasons, and legal science, today as in the past, certainly appears to contain a variety of conflicting exemplars. However, it can be hypothesized

[14] William Twining emphasizes the roots of American legal realism in the problems of rapid legal and social change in the late nineteenth and early twentieth century USA; and the related and acute problems of 'unification, systematization and modernization' of doctrine (and legal science) as legislation and judge-made law proliferated in the various state and federal jurisdictions. See Twining 1973: 5–9. Interestingly Twining seems to portray the realist movement as an attempt to grapple constructively with the problems of orthodox legal science. By contrast some other writers have seen it as a denial of the whole doctrine-unifying project of orthodox legal science. See e.g. Stevens 1983: 156; cf. Cotterrell 1989: 202–6.

that technical, social, or political factors reflected in the character of legal systems at particular times determine the amount of 'intellectual space' within which alternative modes of legal science can exert *widespread* influence on legal scholarship and legal practice as a whole. Only when, for various reasons, legal science is incapable of satisfactorily demonstrating the unity and integrity of legal doctrine through its normal analytical methods will effective confrontations of other disciplines with law be possible, for only in these conditions is the self-sufficiency of legal discourse seriously put in question.

Accordingly, the often-discussed discontents of legal science—its casuistry and circularities of argument; its ephemeral concern with minute problems of doctrine which have little significance once the law has changed; its isolation from other knowledge fields—cannot be remedied merely by appealing to another discipline such as sociology, for these are part of the very essence of legal science. On the other hand, as the discussion so far in this chapter has sought to demonstrate, both the nature and limitations of an existing 'discipline' such as law can be clarified in important ways by showing the social foundations of the disciplinary claims made in relation to such a knowledge field.

A paradoxical conclusion can be suggested. On the one hand, law as a discipline in modern times is, thanks to the positivist modes of argument developed within it and the basically orderly processes of construction of legal doctrine, remarkably self-sufficient. On the other hand, this self-sufficiency is ultimately a mere discipline-effect, not founded in the relative certainties and security of Kuhnian science but in the social–political imperatives of law as an intersection of knowledge and power, and maintained by what we might think of as a kind of necessary self-deception in the mirror-image mutual reinforcement of legal science and legal doctrine. It does seem that at various times legal science loses confidence in itself, and the fragility of its discipline-effect becomes apparent. Fairly clear evidence of this in the case of the 'scientific method' controversies of the 1920s in American legal education seems to exist (Twining 1973: Chs. 3 and 4). The growth of socio-legal studies generally from the late 1960s[15] and the

---

[15] For general surveys of this development in many countries see Ferrari, ed., 1990.

impact of sociology and other social sciences on legal study in the late nineteenth and early twentieth centuries in several European countries (see e.g. Nussbaum 1940; Cappelletti, Merryman and Perillo 1967: 184–6; Carbonnier 1978: 126–32) may also reflect such situations.

It is not possible to do more than mention here the question whether legal doctrine is losing the characteristics that made possible its portrayal by modern legal science as a unified and autonomous field. Undoubtedly much recent literature, written from many diverse standpoints, raises or implies reasons for uncertainty on this issue. It does so in relation to such matters as the following, which can only be listed here without further discussion: the relationship between rule and discretion as mechanisms of contemporary government (e.g. Adler and Asquith, eds., 1981; Galligan 1986); the proliferation of bureaucratic-administrative regulation and its relationship with other forms of law (Kamenka and Tay 1975); the significance of particularistic and mechanical regulatory forms as well as those involving wide discretion;[16] the attempt to distinguish, as a central task of legal philosophy, legal principles (as elements of legal doctrine) from policies informing law (Dworkin 1977: chs. 2–4; 1986: 221–4, 243–4); a postulated replacement of principle by pragmatism in much legal decision-making (Atiyah 1978; and see Atiyah 1987: ch. 1); discussion of the appropriateness of the use by courts of social scientific and statistical evidence and arguments as the basis of judicial decision-making (e.g. Chesler *et al.* 1988; Monahan and Walker 1986; Sanders *et al.* 1982); doubts about the continued utility of fundamental conceptual categories of legal doctrine (Gilmore 1974; Grey 1980; cf. Gray 1991; Cotterrell 1986); the emergence of technologies of social control both more penetrating and less definable than those of law, yet closely allied with them (see especially Foucault 1977; 1980); and claims about the increasingly subtle interpenetration of state and civil society (Santos 1982; Mathiesen 1980) which may cast doubt on the intelligibility of a clear separation of 'lawyers' law'—the legal doctrine of orthodox legal science—from numerous other normative orders.

All of this literature points directly or indirectly to important perceived changes in the character of legal doctrine, to the

---

[16] For a discussion see Cotterrell 1992: 161–6.

increasing social significance of regulatory forms that seem to blur the distinction between law and non-law, or to the problem of clearly distinguishing legal doctrine, legal knowledge, and legal discourse from 'non-legal' technologies, knowledges, or discourses. It can only be suggested that these doctrinal questions and the wider social and political issues that they parallel or reflect (Cotterrell 1992: ch. 9) may indicate the existence of conditions of crisis or, at least, serious uncertainty in orthodox legal science which have allowed the recent burgeoning influence of social scientific and other disciplines in legal analysis.[17]

Sociology and its Confrontations with Law

The appeal made by legal scholars who seriously seek to escape the disciplinary constraints of legal science is almost always ultimately an appeal to sociology in *some* form. This is because an escape from these constraints requires the explicit recognition of law-as-discipline as a social construct to be understood in terms of its social origins and social effects. Not only must the behaviour of lawyers, judges, legislators, and law enforcers be understood sociologically but so must legal ideas and the processes of their production and reproduction. Only by understanding the way a discipline-effect is achieved can one escape from it. The promise of sociology here is in the prospect of a theoretical understanding of law as social institution, professional practice, and intellectual discipline.

Unfortunately these hopes of enlightenment from sociological inquiry have often been frustrated. There is no reason why, in so far as sociology is itself organized as a discipline in the sense discussed in earlier sections of this chapter, it should be free from the kinds of limitation and distortion of intellectual vision that, according to the argument here, are associated generally with rigid disciplinary commitments. We should expect that the more sociology becomes professionalized, in the sense of becoming organized into a discipline explicitly professed by a self-consciously distinct scientific community of sociologists, the less likely it is that it can offer the kind of resources that legal scholars seeking to

[17] See Ch. 4, below.

escape the constraints of law-as-discipline require. This is because, as has been suggested earlier, the establishment of a self-contained sociological disciplinary discourse is likely to have the effect of making other discourses (such as legal discourse) and their objects (such as 'law' specifically as constructed and portrayed in legal discourse) seem largely irrelevant and even 'unreal' within it.

On the other hand, as will appear, there is something distinctive about the nature of sociological inquiry which tends to put severe limits on the possibilities of treating sociology as an autonomous discipline; that is, developing it as a knowledge field in relation to which a strong discipline-effect exists. The history of sociological inquiries shows that there have been and still are important constraints on the possibility of professionalizing the field of sociology, of portraying it as an autonomous, specialized field of knowledge and practice. To understand sociology's confrontations with law, both in the past and in possible future forms, it is necessary to examine both the tendencies towards professionalization of sociology and also the limits of these tendencies.

The ambiguous character of sociology as a knowledge field is expressed in many ways in commentaries on its scope, methods, and history. Reflecting on the history of British sociology, Philip Abrams (1985) identifies five conceptions of sociology's use as a research enterprise and knowledge field which have been influential.

The *policy-science conception* 'envisages the possibility of authoritative social knowledge' which can be directly applied in rational social planning in an 'increasingly purposive and concerted movement towards a better society' (Abrams 1985: 183). Secondly, and less ambitiously, the *socio-technics conception* still sees the sociologist as providing solutions to social problems but recognizes that he must negotiate with policy-makers or serve as technical assistant to them rather than do their job for them: 'useful work is defined in terms of the reliable, proficient servicing of policy-makers—whether in the form of basic information, analytic data, advice on data-gathering, technical problem-solving, identification of technically best courses of action or evaluation of the effectiveness of policy after the event' (Abrams 1985: 184).

Against these conceptions which see sociology as directly 'useful'—a technological resource in social engineering—can be set others in which sociology's uses are seen as more diffuse. Its knowledge is not considered necessarily directly applicable in social problem-solving but is seen to serve as 'enlightenment'—offering a broader or, at least, a different perspective on the nature of social life or social problems. Thus, Abrams's third conception is that of *clarification* which involves 'demystification, dispelling illusions and unmasking myths . . . reformulating issues or problems by elucidating assumptions or revealing hitherto unperceived realities of social structure or meaning, or . . . changing the possibilities of social action by changing the language of public dIscourse' (1985: 184). As he notes, there is an optimistic view implicit in this conception that the world is 'a reasonable place' in which careful argument and rational analysis will be seriously listened to by non-sociologists. Fourthly, the *advocacy conception* is less grounded in optimism about the triumph of reason and, by contrast, sees sociological argument as a matter of linking good evidence to good causes as a means of political persuasion; as argument for a particular reading of sociological evidence to achieve political results. Finally, in the *education conception*, which Abrams sees as widely advocated by contemporary British sociologists, sociology eschews both politics and government and, recognizing governmental disinterest in or hostility towards many of the truths or scepticisms it proclaims, aims patiently at achieving the gradual dissemination and acceptance of its ideas among citizens. 'It is a matter of changing the world through the next, or the next twenty, generations. Education is seen as a conduit for understandings which for whatever reasons cannot flow through society more directly' (1985: 185).

Abrams' perceptive categorization identifies central dilemmas that have always existed in attempts to organize sociology as a discipline. There is a clear tension between conceptions of sociology as essentially a useful science for solving immediate practical problems and conceptions of it as essentially an enterprise of enlightenment seeking deeper understanding of the nature of social life. The latter often makes sociology appear highly impractical in terms of the concerns of government, or even hostile or subversive of governmental aims, since problems as governments formulate them may appear quite differently in sociology's gaze; perhaps as irrelevant or insoluble in the form presented by government because fundamentally misunderstood in governmental perceptions, or distorted in the way governments present them by ideological considerations, or misrepresented to serve the interests of powerful groups.

A Foucauldian perspective would suggest that sociology's status as an independent discursive formation or discipline is grounded in its utility as a technology of power or control; that the key to its history will be found in the power–knowledge nexus. This utility is not necessarily in providing direct technical aid to government but may be a matter of providing a general understanding of or insight into conditions of malaise or change in societies. Thus, as histories of sociology often affirm, the discipline of sociology is perhaps best understood historically as having gradually formed itself around general problems of order and control posed by the industrialization and urbanization of Western societies in the eighteenth and nineteenth centuries. As such it provided a largely conservative response[18] to these developments by offering knowledge of, warnings about, and guidance in responding to, the processes of social change involved in them.

All this is compatible with an interpretation of the formation of the discipline in terms of the power–knowledge nexus. Yet, in the subsequent history of sociological inquiry, the 'clarification', 'advocacy', and 'education' outlooks which Abrams describes have often encouraged sociology away from being the intellectual support of established structures of social order and towards the possibility of genuinely critical analysis of structures of power, present social conditions, and existing forms of knowledge—including those of sociology-as-discipline itself. In aiming at 'enlightenment', sociology seems to have been able, at least sometimes, to make itself genuinely self-critical, so that it has, at least to some extent, escaped the limitations of its own discipline-effect. It is this remarkable character of sociological inquiry which justifies the appeal made to it by legal scholars seeking to advance knowledge of law beyond the constraints of law-as-discipline.

There is no mystery about the conditions that have allowed and indeed necessitated such disciplinary openness. For a variety of reasons, sociology has been quite unable to maintain even a consistent discipline-effect, let alone the conditions for Kuhnian normal science. In this respect it differs, for example, from

---

[18] See e.g. Bramson 1961; Nisbet 1967: ch. 2. But for an appropriate warning against over-generalization see Hawthorn 1987: 255 ff.

modern economics in which dominant (if not universally accepted) exemplars and theoretical frameworks of inquiry exist, and legal science in which, as has been seen earlier, the mirror-of-doctrine conception has provided a clearly dominant (though again not universally accepted) model of appropriate methods and concerns. The policy-science pretensions of sociology have been criticized since the time of its first serious assertions of disciplinary status in the nineteenth century, on the ground that too much disagreement existed between experts (Abrams 1985: 192). This criticism reflects both the sheer empirical complexity of sociology's subject-matter and the necessarily permanently exploratory and unfinished character of serious inquiry about it.

A specific problem for sociology is that its subject-matter, if taken to be social life or 'society' (cf. Bottomore and Nisbet 1978: viii), necessarily encompasses numerous fields of social experience (for example, law) that are already the concern of other disciplines. Hence not only does it necessarily seek a synthesizing conception of social reality but in doing so it must eventually confront the conceptions of particular aspects of social reality (for example, legal, economic, political, or æsthetic) created by those other disciplines and not necessarily compatible with sociology's vision of social relations and social structures generally. Sociology, seeking a systematic understanding of social reality, thus almost inevitably finds itself in conflict, not only with 'common sense'— the everyday unsystematic social knowledge necessary to individuals living in society, but also with the established knowledge claims of other disciplines.

It has been suggested earlier that disciplines can, in general, often ignore the knowledge-claims and objects set up by other disciplines; but ultimately this is not possible for sociology as a general science of social life since those knowledge-claims must— if sociology is to pursue its inquiries about social phenomena with rigour—become part of its subject-matter.[19] In so far as intellectual disciplines and structures of power in society are closely interconnected, sociology is necessarily eventually drawn by its concern in understanding social structure to make the knowledge-claims of

---

[19] On the problems of integrating sociological inquiries of special fields of social experience within an overall conception of sociology as a discipline see Eldridge 1980: ch. 4; and for a view of sociology as parasitic on other disciplines see Urry 1981.

other disciplines part of its subject-matter (and so merely social data rather than 'truths') so as to examine the contribution of these disciplinary knowledges to the maintenance, organization, and transformation of patterns of power relationships and social structure generally. Thus in seeking to become a rigorous discipline of inquiry into the general character of social phenomena, sociology builds into itself a necessarily subversive or revisionist attitude to the knowledge-claims of other disciplines. In its own search for disciplinary status is an implicit denial of *all* disciplinary boundaries and prerogatives.

Numerous attempts have, of course, been made to avoid this conclusion. Sociology has frequently been portrayed as the unifier (not subverter) of existing social science disciplines (e.g. Durkheim and Fauconnet 1982; Hobhouse 1966: 27; Ginsberg 1956: ch. 16), although when conflicts between sociological and other disciplinary conceptions have arisen this has often metamorphosed into a claim of sociology as the dominant controlling science; as the provider of fundamental theoretical perspectives for all the others.[20] This claim may have some merit if sociology is thought of as a *resource* to be drawn on in the study of special fields and as an *aspiration* towards unified knowledge of the nature of social life. However, such a view has rarely been treated as an acceptable justification of a distinct disciplinary status of sociology since it offers no basis for defining the discipline in terms of distinctive subject-matter (as compared with the aggregated subject-matter of other disciplines) (Urry 1981; Bottomore and Nisbet 1978), or universally accepted methodology or controlling theory governing the field of sociological inquiry.[21]

Perhaps partly in recognition of these problems some micro-sociological approaches have adopted what might be called an 'underworker' rather than 'controlling science' conception of

[20] Thus Durkheim and Fauconnet (1982: 195) conclude that 'the different social sciences must become special branches of sociology'.

[21] For a time, particularly in the USA in the 1950s, it seemed that functional analysis as a 'fully sociological' method of inquiry might provide a distinctive unifying methodology of sociology: see especially Davis 1959. Its failure to achieve this position was largely due to the fact that, quite apart from the method being shared with other disciplines, its dominance was seen as having unacceptable restrictive implications for the scope of sociology's concerns. Sociology as an enterprise seems always ultimately to have rejected intellectual orthodoxies that would enhance its disciplinary unity at the expense of its free development.

sociology. They have emphasized sociology's role in clarifying irreducible *general* mechanisms of social interaction,[22] which could be considered the building blocks of all of the social behaviour and institutions analysed in the specialized disciplines. Most sociologists have, however, found such an abstract focus far too constraining unless conclusions can be drawn from it that bear on the analysis of particular fields of social experience (thus raising again the prospect of confrontation with other disciplines' perspectives on these fields).

What should be clear even from such a brief discussion of sociology's relationships with other disciplines is its inherent critical and subversive tendencies in relation to those disciplines. Thus Abrams (1981: 538) asserts the need to recognize 'the contradictory, unsatisfactory, and uncertain nature of sociology as a venture which is simultaneously criticism and science'. Its pretensions as a policy-science have been demolished above all, first, by the multifaceted nature and complexity of social problems and the impossibility of studying them rigorously without putting them into a context of inquiry far wider than that which is generally useful to or manageable by policy-makers; and, secondly, by sociology's inability to define a discrete realm of inquiry compatible with the prerogatives of other disciplines and avoiding the need for continual conflict with the knowledge-claims of these disciplines and the power structures underpinning them or dependent on them.

The contrasts with the disciplinary character of legal science are very clear. While legal science in its dominant form has typically been supremely self-confident in its undisputed 'usefulness' as a technology of power and control, sociology appears vulnerable. Its claim to provide enlightenment on the most general and fundamental issues of social experience is often seen as merely an indication of its lack of practical utility. Further, while legal science with its apparently secure dominant exemplars sets up clear criteria of success in legal analysis, sociology, with its continually exploratory character, numerous competing exemplars,

---

[22] The approach of the German sociologist Georg Simmel centres on his claim that sociology 'must seek its problems not in the matter of social life, but in its form ... It is upon this abstract consideration of social forms that rests the right of sociology to exist, just as geometry owes its existence to the possibility of abstracting from material things their spatial shapes' (quoted in Durkheim and Fauconnet 1982: 190, where a powerful critique of this approach is offered). Cf. Ginsberg 1956: 259–60. See generally Wolff, ed., 1950.

and provisional, continually revised theoretical frameworks, often appears racked by self-doubt.

As Edward Shils puts the matter: 'Sociology is not at present, and is not likely to become in the near future, a subject which can stand up under the fire of intellectual sharpshooters. Too many points can be scored off sociology by those who regard intellectual activity not as the extension of understanding but a game in which the prizes go for rigour and elegance of formulation and proof, and for proving the other fellow wrong' (Shils 1985: 168). This is hardly a justification for sociological work that does not seek the highest standards of rigorous analysis. Nevertheless, as Shils suggests, 'intellectual sharpshooting' is not always the best way to understanding in considering the most complex and fundamental questions about human experience. 'Discoveries are not made in this way, least of all self-discoveries and the discoveries of the self in one's fellow-man' (Shils 1985: 168). They are sometimes made, however, through the kind of iconoclastic imaginativeness and determinedly exploratory outlook that has frequently characterized sociology's unruly scientific progress.

It is perhaps inevitable that when lawyers have called on sociology for aid they have often seen it or claimed to see it in its 'policy-science' or 'sociotechnics' guises. This is apparent, for example, in the use of sociological material in judicial decision-making in American courts and in the proliferation of studies of the 'impact' or effectiveness of particular laws.[23] In numerous socio-legal inquiries sociology has been required to be useful in the immediate and obvious senses in which legal doctrine or legal decisions are seen to be useful. And since sociological knowledge can certainly sometimes offer insights that are immediately applicable in policy and practice such inquiries have not been fruitless.

Nevertheless, a number of opportunities have been largely missed by the biasing of research towards short-term policy ends. First, sociological inquiry has been devalued since, judged in terms of immediate policy relevance, it has been judged by its weakest characteristics. Secondly, like other social scientific material, sociological material has been used typically not to challenge the perspectives of orthodox legal science but to reinforce them. Frequently what

---

[23] For perceptive comment on 'impact' studies see Rabin 1979. On the use of social scientific material by courts see Chesler *et al.* 1988; Monahan and Walker 1986; Sanders *et al.* 1982.

is involved is thus not a productive confrontation of law-as-discipline with another knowledge field but the selection of social scientific language and data as rhetorical ammunition for argument before courts, tribunals, or legislative bodies. Any appeal to 'outside' knowledge sources such as sociology (or more often, at present, economics) has the potential for weakening legal science's discipline-effect and, according to the arguments of this chapter, only occurs on a significant scale when conditions of uncertainty or crisis in legal doctrine (and so also in orthodox legal science) exist. Naturally, therefore, when it *does* seem necessary to lawyers to call on such knowledge sources attempts are made to use them in ways that minimize any disruption of the image of law as an independent discipline.

The disciplinary character of legal science and attempts to professionalize sociological inquiry, especially in the United States, have combined to shape strongly the dominant character of sociological inquiries on law. British sociologists have long been ambivalent about the idea that they belong to a 'profession' (Barnes 1981; Banks 1967). Their collective outlook has been formed in a tradition shaped by Leonard Hobhouse's and Morris Ginsberg's fusion of social philosophy and empirical research, by ethical stances originally grounded in nineteenth century conceptions of evolutionary progress, by a long history of pragmatic and piecemeal empirical policy-relevant research,[24] and by influences from classic and recent continental European social theory of many kinds.[25] In this context perhaps it is unsurprising that enlightenment rather than engineering conceptions of sociology have dominated. Thus, John Barnes (1981: 22) writes, perhaps optimistically: 'Sociological insights and counter-intuitive discoveries, within a generation, become commonplace truisms. If they do not, there must be something wrong with the insights'. From this standpoint sociology is necessarily evangelical (and also necessarily subject to appropriation by and criticism from an 'informed laity'); the idea of sociological 'professionals' protecting their esoteric knowledge is seen as wholly inappropriate.

It seems to me that this kind of openness expressed by some leading British sociologists is an indication not of the weakness of

[24] See e.g. Perry Anderson's scathing condemnation of this tradition of social research in Britain in Anderson 1968.
[25] See generally e.g. Collini 1979; Abrams 1968; Halsey 1985.

academic sociology in Britain but of its present intellectual maturity, in so far as it is committed to the creation of knowledge not bounded and distorted by disciplinary jealousies and the power relationships that they reflect. It might be thought, therefore, that the traditions of British sociology have favoured the development of broad sociological inquiries in relation to law. That this is not so is due to a complex of reasons. Prominent among them are the lack, until quite recently, of a strong tradition of major theoretical work in British sociology;[26] and the perennially embattled and often relatively insecure position of sociology in British higher education which may have limited its range of concerns.

In Britain as elsewhere, the growth of sociological studies of law has been strongly influenced by the extensive American literature, itself influenced by the much more highly professionalized character of American sociology. The search for secure disciplinary status for sociology in the United States has been pursued primarily through the development of sophisticated research methods, emphasizing quantitative procedures; through a general positivist emphasis on behavioural study; and by a primary and strong commitment to empirical research and a frequent (though far from total[27]) avoidance of theoretical speculation of the kind that trenches on social philosophy.

Shils wrote in 1948 that American sociology's 'hitherto predominant indifference to the formation of a general theory is closely connected with its eagerness for precision in first-hand observation' (Shils 1948: 56). Because of its behavioural orientation American sociology was initially able to approach the consideration of law in a way that largely avoided jurisprudential issues and hence also avoided direct conflict with the disciplinary prerogatives of legal science. Its empirical traditions made it in some respects hospitable to demands for 'neutral' policy-science information

[26] Cf. Shils 1985: 178, bemoaning (in a text originally written in 1960) the lack of 'some resonant works' on theory or methodology. Significantly Hobhouse, who did attempt to develop original theoretical perspectives, also devoted considerable attention to law, especially in his *Morals in Evolution* (1906).

[27] Thus, the strong tradition of empirical sociological research associated with the University of Chicago in the first half of the 20th century, and often seen as having set many of the dominant styles of sociology in the USA, went along with a selective attitude to European social theory ('They drew upon it liberally, but did not swallow it as a whole') and a desire to develop theory 'out of the research process': see Kurtz 1984: 17.

about law and regulatory problems. Finally, its quantitative bias, which has remained a feature sharply distinguishing it from dominant trends in British sociology (Husbands 1981), encouraged the belief that sociological studies of law could indeed provide policy-relevant, useful data to guide lawmaking and law-implementation.

It would be wrong to suggest that, in American sociology and in the fields of research in other countries strongly influenced by it, enlightenment as an aspiration has been wholly discarded in favour of the pursuit of efficient social engineering. It has, indeed, been suggested in this chapter that the character of sociological inquiry is such that the policy-science or socio-technics conceptions of sociology's dominant role cannot consistently and convincingly be maintained. The particular characteristics, mentioned above, of much American sociological work co-exist with claims that sociology's aim is, indeed, enlightenment or the pursuit of scientific knowledge not bounded by policy needs. Also, it should be stressed that many of the most important American sociological writings do not show these characteristics.

But the relatively highly developed discipline-effect of American sociology has tended to produce the kind of limitations and distortions of vision that accompany the establishment of clear disciplinary boundaries and distinct discursive formations. Sometimes, at least in the view of many British sociologists viewing contemporary American sociology, the sociological imagination (cf. Mills 1959) tends to disappear in the effort to appear fully respectable in the arena of intellectual sharpshooting. 'In a host of ways the verve and drive—but noticeably not the technical sophistication—of American sociology seem to have got lost'.[28]

The Past and Future of Sociology of Law

The term sociology of law is in many respects unsatisfactory to refer to the enterprise of inquiry involved in systematically adopting a sociological perspective on law. From the standpoint of sociology-as-discipline, sociology of law is portrayed as a minor

---

[28] Abrams 1981: 534. On the history of American sociology see e.g. Odum 1951; Hinkle 1980; Bulmer 1984; Gouldner 1971; Vidich and Lyman 1985.

subdivision within the discipline of sociology. Yet the classic founders of modern sociology, who refused to confine their vision within narrow disciplinary boundaries, did not usually see law in such a limited way.

Max Weber saw his studies of law as the most complete part of his work (Lachmann 1970: 63). Yet only recently have they received the kind of careful attention that has long been lavished on the rest of his sociology in Britain and the United States. In part this is because Weber treats law primarily as doctrine. Hence much of what he writes has seemed peripheral to sociology-as-discipline in so far as the latter has tended to focus on behaviour and avoid entanglement with the mysteries of jurisprudence. Partly also, the reason undoubtedly lies in the relatively undeveloped state of theory in an Anglo-American sociology of law strongly influenced, on the one hand, by the policy concerns of lawyers and legislators and, on the other, by the tendency in dominant forms of American professionalized sociology to isolate empirical research from broad theoretical perspectives.

Yet Weber also saw, as sociology-as-discipline cannot, that the sociological study of law involves, in its confrontation with legal discourse and its consideration of the social foundations and effects of legal ideas, the most fundamental questions of social theory;[29] that it is not a 'sociological specialism' but central to the task of sociological understanding of contemporary life;[30] that in confronting legal discourse sociology confronts another enterprise of interpretation of the world whose power (social and political) must be recognized. The sociological study of law is thus, above all, a study of (legal) forms and mechanisms of power and of the power of (legal) ideas in controlling and shaping social life.

Similar points can be made in relation to the reception in the Anglo-American world of Emile Durkheim's classic writings which have exerted a major influence on the development of modern sociology. The sociological study of law and legal institutions was

[29] Cf. Unger 1976: 43 ff. Obviously the point can be carried too far. The French writer Jean Carbonnier (1988: 23) properly warns against the dangers of 'panjurism': 'It would be a pity if juridical sociology felt obliged, because it is juridical, to read the universe as if it were a law book'.

[30] In one of his last papers Talcott Parsons forcefully affirmed, from a position of lonely eminence as the doyen of American sociological theory, his minority view, expressed in print a decade and a half before, 'that the core of Weber's substantive view of societies lay in his sociology of law'. See Parsons 1981: 188.

a central concern for Durkheim and for several of his closest
followers who established the Durkheimian tradition in French
sociology (see e.g. Vogt 1983). Yet the works that most strongly
reflect this concern are neglected in Anglo-American sociology
and in many cases have remained untranslated into English.[31] The
sociological study of law has been marginalized in the image of
sociology-as-discipline at the same time as empirical social theory
has been marginalized in the dominant forms of jurisprudence
constrained by the demands of law-as-discipline.

It is, therefore, unsurprising that the nearest we get to a 'crashing classic' in American sociology of law is the uncompromisingly
behaviourist work of Donald Black,[32] which, because it concerns
itself only with what it takes to be observable behaviour, necessarily offers no real engagement with law as lawyers learn it; that
is, with legal doctrine. More generally, in sociology-as-discipline,
issues about law in the lawyer's sense have often been converted
into something more amenable to observational methods of research or, at least, not requiring engagement with the object 'law'
constructed in legal discourse. Thus, sociologies of deviance, of
administration and organisations, of professions and occupations,
of politics and government have shared out such matters amongst
themselves.

Talcott Parsons' monumental sociological writings—arguably the
most important work in sociological theory yet produced in the
United States—do not seriously engage with lawyers' conceptions
of law or with significant issues about the nature of legal doctrine.
Though Parsons frequently discusses law and clearly regards it
as an important matter for sociological analysis, no confrontation with legal discourse takes place. Parsons betrays no recognition of questions that have been raised in so much legal literature,
and mentioned earlier in this chapter, about the nature of transformations occurring in Western legal doctrine in recent decades.[33]
Yet these matters demand sociological analysis.

[31] Georges Davy's *La foi jurée* (1922) and Paul Fauconnet's *La responsabilité* (1928)
spring to mind as important examples of such neglected works. There are numerous others.

[32] Especially Black 1976 and 1989; and see also Black 1984. Black's 1976 book
was termed a 'crashing classic' in comments by the distinguished anthropologist,
Laura Nader, quoted on its cover. For less enthusiastic assessments see Hunt 1983;
Greenberg 1983.

[33] See Parsons 1977: 148, commenting on 'fashionable' worries about the future
of the Rule of Law.

Again, in some of the writings of the so-called Berkeley school of legal sociologists, centred on the work of Philip Selznick, Philippe Nonet, and Jerome Skolnick, an alternative to behaviourism has been sought in theoretical adherence to the central idea of 'legality' as the organizing focus of sociological research on law. In this way sociology of law is held to be able to integrate jurisprudence and policy analysis through the clarification of legal values in relation to the consequences of their invocation (Nonet 1976). Thus, while other approaches to sociology of law ignore legal discourse, this approach seeks to take it over and do its job better. The policy-science and socio-technics conceptions of sociology thus remain strongly present in the arena of American sociology of law.

It must be stressed that the point of this discussion is not to deny the worth of numerous thoughtful and genuinely illuminating empirical inquiries and middle-range theoretical insights, which have emerged from a sociology of law strongly shaped by practical policy concerns of lawyers and legislators and by the disciplinary perspectives of (mainly American) sociology. The rich literature of empirical research on the genesis of legislation, on the social impact of laws and legal institutions, on citizens' access to law and legal agencies, on judiciaries, legal professions, police, and law enforcement, on courtroom interaction, and on administrative and regulatory agencies is testimony to the fruitfulness of this enterprise of inquiry. Such empirical research is the indispensable foundation of all else that may be accomplished in the sociological study of law. But much of it is at its most stimulating when it frees itself from the disciplinary preconceptions of both law and sociology; when it confronts legal discourse with sociological perspectives; when it treats the sociological study of legal behaviour as inseparable from an understanding of the nature of legal doctrine and discourse as social constructs.

A wider set of responsibilities attaches to the sociological study of law than is typically recognized by a view of sociology of law as a sub-field of sociology-as-discipline, or as a peripheral and exotic help-mate of orthodox legal science. Those responsibilities include the advancement of social theory and the application of this theory to reinterpret legal knowledge in a continually broadening perspective. It should follow from the arguments in this chapter that the advancement of knowledge of law in society depends ultimately on the breaking down of disciplinary limits, whether these are constructed by legal science or by professionalized sociology. As has been argued earlier, resistance to this from the legal side is normally necessarily very strong indeed, although at certain times substantial intellectual space for the development and wide influence of sociological perspectives on law has been created, probably by changes in the nature or environment of legal doctrine itself.

That such changes, with their attendant crises for orthodox legal science, may be presently occurring is suggested by the increasing popularity of economic analysis of law as a policy-science substitute for, or supplement to, orthodox legal science analysis of doctrine, and by the emergence of a strong and popular 'internal critique' of legal science and legal doctrine in the form of critical legal studies movements in the United States, Britain, and elsewhere. If so, it is likely to be 'enlightenment' (rather than 'engineering') sociology which will, by its very nature as an enterprise of inquiry transcending disciplinary limitations, provide necessary guides to understanding the processes of transformation going on in legal doctrine. More importantly, it is this kind of sociological inquiry—with powerful and disciplinarily heterogeneous theoretical resources from, for example, Foucault, Habermas, Luhmann, many varieties of Marxist thought, and numerous other classic and contemporary works of European social theory—which holds out the best prospect of overcoming the prisons of our limited disciplinary modes of thought about legal phenomena and about the societies in which they exist.

4 Sociology of Law in Britain: A Case Study

> The general character and evolution of sociology of law was analysed in Chapter 3 in terms of confrontations between law and sociology as fields of knowledge and practice. A more detailed consideration of the particular history of sociology of law in Britain extends this inquiry by providing a concrete case study of interactions between legal studies and the social sciences. It highlights conditions that have promoted and hampered the development of research on law in society, as well as the gradual emergence of a sophisticated sociological perspective on the legal field.

The object of this chapter is to survey the present position and prospects of sociology of law as a field of study in Great Britain in the light of factors that have shaped the development of this field. I shall try to specify what 'sociology of law' can be taken to refer to in the British context, and to what extent a shared outlook is reflected in work within this area. An attempt will also be made to sketch stages of development of sociology of law in Britain, and some major ways in which this kind of legal study has been institutionalized. A particular aim is to highlight the significant growth of interest in sociology of law in Britain over the past two decades.

No attempt, however, will be made to describe particular theoretical developments or empirical work. Only general trends are discussed[1] and references to particular examples of published research are intended to illustrate these trends. It would be unrealistic even to attempt to provide a full survey of the voluminous literature. Consequently, although many monographic publications are referred to for illustrative purposes, it must be borne in mind that a comprehensive bibliographical survey—if such a survey were possible in a field whose boundaries inevitably remain inexact and

[1] For a fuller guide to the literature see Cotterrell 1992.

controversial—would include many items as significant, or possibly more significant, than those to be mentioned here.

Conceptions of Sociology of Law in Britain

Views of the nature and scope of sociology of law are not necessarily uniform in different countries so as to allow direct comparisons of its progress. Further, in Britain, as elsewhere, a variety of views about its scope and objectives exists. Most of these views define sociology of law in terms of one or both of the established intellectual disciplines—law and sociology—to which it is seen primarily to be related. Thus, one writer notes: 'the sociology of law is but a sub-discipline of sociology and, as such, aims at the understanding of that discipline's particular subject-matter' (Wilkinson 1981: 67). Yet it is clear that, in Britain, sociology of law has not developed as a recognized sub-discipline of sociology, although many contemporary writers label it as such. It tends to occupy a very marginal position in relation to academic sociology. In so far as aspects of its subject-matter are widely recognized as fundamentally important to sociology as a discipline in higher education, they tend to be scattered among several branches of this discipline, such as sociology of deviance, sociology of organizations and administration, political sociology, and sociology of knowledge. Thus, to the extent that sociology of law has been drawn into the disciplinary orbit of sociology, 'law' as a distinct object of inquiry has tended to disappear.

Many of those who have been most active in shaping sociology of law in Britain and in contributing to empirical research on legal institutions have not regarded themselves as professional sociologists with a distinct primary allegiance to sociology as a discipline. Major contributions have come also from legal scholars, as well as political scientists and anthropologists. Perhaps because of the immense technicality and complexity of law, many of those social scientists who have not been repelled from research on law by these characteristics of legal doctrine have felt the need eventually for close links with the world of legal scholarship and for immersion in the voluminous literature of law and legal theory. The investment of effort in entering the powerfully integrated, highly developed, and long established intellectual milieu of law has often tended to separate them from colleagues in their parent social scientific disciplines who have adopted other special fields of research outside law. Thus, to the extent that 'law' has been treated as the central unifying focus of sociology of law, explicit disciplinary links with academic sociology have often been loosened. Instead, an explicitly interdisciplinary conception of 'socio-legal studies', calling upon all or any of the social sciences for aid in legal research, has been promoted (see Campbell and Wiles 1976).

It should also be recognized that sociology in Britain has been much less self-consciously professionalized than in the United States (Barnes 1981; Banks 1967).[2] It has been strongly influenced over the past two decades not only by American sociological theory and empirical research, but also by the diverse intellectual concerns represented in contemporary continental European social theory. Because of the more open character of British sociology, as compared with American professionalization, it has been relatively easy in the United Kingdom for scholars from a variety of intellectual backgrounds to adopt the term 'sociology of law' for interdisciplinary or multi-disciplinary approaches to legal studies concerned with the social sources or consequences of law, or with behavioural studies of legal institutions. Sociology of law has, thus, often been taken to refer to much of what, in America, would be termed law and society studies.

The result of this situation in Britain has been partly beneficial and partly disadvantageous. Beneficially, scholars working in many different fields of research have been able to treat social theory not as the monopoly of academic sociology but as a resource available to guide studies in the particular social fields in which these scholars happen to specialize. Thus, academic lawyers increasingly draw on social theory (especially writings of Jürgen Habermas, Michel Foucault, many contemporary and classic Marxist writers and, of course, the classic texts of Weber, Durkheim, and Marx), in their writing and teaching. Less beneficially, because of the limited professionalization of British sociology and the tendency in public opinion to view the gathering of social statistics as sociology, there has been a tendency among non-specialists to use the term sociology of law to cover any kind of

[2] See Ch. 3, pp. 66–8, above.

'fact research' on law and a failure among many lawyers and legal scholars to recognize the theoretical objectives of sociological study of law and the central importance of social theory in defining the aims of this kind of legal study.

Just as sociology of law cannot realistically be taken as a recognized sub-discipline of contemporary academic sociology, so it cannot be taken either as a distinct compartment of legal studies: that is, merely as a particular subject within legal education. It does tend to be taught in Britain primarily in law schools rather than social science faculties, and it is typically taught as a particular subject within the curriculum (Fielding and Fielding 1983). But this is largely a matter of convenience dictated by the vocational setting of legal education. Sociology of law, judged by the scope of its research concerns and theories, takes all law as its province and should intrude into all areas of the legal curriculum. Its researches range over all subjects taught in the law school. In this situation its compartmentalization is a matter of educational convenience within a vocationally oriented environment.

Whether it will eventually escape this compartmentalization is uncertain since it challenges the perspective of self-sufficient legal knowledge unrelated to other intellectual fields which is presupposed by the still-widespread traditional methods of teaching and learning legal doctrine. A recent survey indicated that, while sociology of law tends to be taught in a vocationally oriented way on, for example, social work courses, those teaching it also to law students tend to see the subject as 'theoretically oriented and not purely instrumental' (Fielding and Fielding 1983: 189). Put bluntly, the legal sociologist's elementary commitment 'is not to law departments, the law or reform of the law, but to furthering knowledge and understanding of the law in terms of the wider social order' (Campbell and Wiles 1976: 555).

At the same time, sociology of law presupposes much more than 'contextualism': that is, the study of law in social context. Contextualism, which established itself as an alternative to traditional approaches to legal education in Britain from the late 1960s, has been accommodated within the existing organization of legal education. It requires only that particular legal subjects—as defined by lawyers—be studied with a broad awareness of social consequences and social origins of the law. A sociological perspective on law presupposes, however, that lawyers' definitions and interpretations of the field of law are insufficient; that law itself needs to be understood not merely in terms of lawyers' categories, but in the light of a theoretical understanding of the nature of the societies within which legal systems exist. In other words, law is to be understood in terms of social theory. Legal theory is to be seen as a particular branch or application of social theory.

To the extent that this outlook is shared by many teachers of and writers on sociology of law in Britain, it makes it difficult to see an easy route to accommodation with more traditional perspectives informing legal scholarship, except in so far as sociology of law must treat lawyers' participant perspectives on law as part of its subject-matter, to be explained, incorporated, extended, and accounted for within the broader perspective on law which the sociology of law seeks to offer. Thus, sociology of law appears not as a sociological or legal specialism but a perspective or set of perspectives on law and legal study.

What unites sociology of law as a coherent intellectual enterprise in this conception is, first, a concern to understand legal doctrine and legal institutions in terms of their social origins and effects and in relation to systematic empirical study of their social, economic, and political environment; and, secondly, a concern to design inquiries so as to contribute to theoretical analysis of the nature of law in society, to a deeper understanding of legal doctrine and institutions in general in the variety of societies and social settings in which legal phenomena exist. Understood in this way sociology of law should take full account of lawyers' perspectives on law. It must claim, nevertheless, to provide a different and broader view of law from that of most participants in law—whether practising lawyers, judges, law reformers, litigants, or teachers of legal doctrine.

The Context of Development of Sociology of Law

At the level of mere aspiration, rather than realized researches, this conception of sociology of law is hardly new. But only recently has it been adopted by a significant minority of legal scholars as the basis of a serious long term commitment defining the objectives and methods guiding their research careers. As will appear below, however, there have been several important antecedents of this development.

Three characteristics of the English common law environment can be identified as having had major long-term effects on the development of social scientific research in Britain. First is the English tradition of empiricism in social research and a long-standing distrust of empirically grounded theorizing in this field. Early social research in England combined emphasis on data collection for social reform as exemplified in the tradition of Charles Booth, Henry Mayhew, and the Webbs, a stress on social statistics (William Jevons, Francis Galton, and Karl Pearson), many scattered developments in a variety of separate research fields, and a background of social philosophy which merged sociological inquiries into ethical and traditional speculative jurisprudential concerns.

A second characteristic is the intellectual tradition of Benthamite rationalism. In its broadest forms it created a general suspicion of claims that analysis of social phenomena cannot be reduced to analysis of individual actions and motivations. Thus it tended to deny the existence of a distinct scientific field for sociology as the study of social phenomena. As Elie Halévy puts it: 'the Benthamites, more or less consciously, conceived of every science as an explanation by reduction, by decomposition into simple elements. Where then, except in individuals, who are the subjects of the egoistic motive, were the jurist and the economist to find the simple elements which were necessary for the organization of their knowledge?' (Halévy 1928: 467). Thus, a number of strands—individualism (or, more precisely, a 'principle of universal egoism': Halévy 1928: 494), a belief in the rationality of human action, empiricism (the belief that empirical study required no aid from theory), and a view of theory as merely rationalistic speculation not requiring the support of systematic empirical study—combined in dominant currents of thought to create a climate generally unfavourable to the growth of sociological study.

The third relevant characteristic of the English tradition is common law pragmatism: a general distrust of legal theory and of the use of broad concepts in legal analysis and a preference for case-by-case lawmaking. In part this stance has been attributed—most influentially through Max Weber's writings (Weber 1978: 785–8)—to the historical conditions of legal professionalization in England which were significantly different from those in other major European countries. But professional attitudes to legal knowledge are not, of course, uninfluenced by more general currents of thought such as those mentioned earlier. So it should be unsurprising that empiricism, individualism, and rationalism are important characteristics of the traditions of legal thought in England, all three of them hostile in one way or another to empirically grounded analysis of law as a social phenomenon.

Reference here has been to English traditions and environments and it is important to stress the different traditions of Scottish thought. The eighteenth century Scottish Enlightenment produced some of the earliest modern sociological treatises, especially Adam Ferguson's *Essay on the History of Civil Society* (1767). In addition, Scottish legal scholarship has benefited from a strong tradition of jurisprudence in legal education, the influence of continental legal ideas, and a relative absence of the traditional English distrust of general concepts. Equally, however, English hegemony has prevented these elements of a more open approach to law and social science from becoming a dominant tradition in Britain.

Despite these circumstances, there has probably always been some concern with systematic studies of law in social context since the nineteenth century beginnings of modern legal education in Britain (see e.g. McGregor 1981). In the second half of the nineteenth century, with the immense success of Henry Maine's *Ancient Law* (1861), historical jurisprudence strongly, if only temporarily, influenced both legal education and legal scholarship towards a 'scientific' concern with the study of law in its cultural contexts (cf. Feaver 1969).

Maine's work was significant in helping to fix the idea that law could provide a valuable focus for anthropological study. Of lasting importance in social science has been the British tradition of anthropological studies of law since the 1920s, with which the names of Bronislaw Malinowski, A. R. Radcliffe-Brown, and Max Gluckman are particularly associated. Until recently, however, legal anthropology has exercised minimal influence on general currents of legal scholarship in Britain. Even today the importance of this tradition of research is not widely recognized in the work of academic lawyers. Equally, anthropology has occupied a somewhat isolated position within British social science so that its concern with law has not strongly influenced sociologists' priorities (cf. Campbell and Wiles 1976: 564).

A further strand of social scientific research in the field of law is represented by criminology, long established as a policy-oriented, interdisciplinary enterprise concerned with the systematic study of crime and of the effectiveness of criminal justice practices and strategies. In Britain the establishment in 1957 of the Home Office Research Unit on the financial basis provided by the Criminal Justice Act 1948 set an official seal of approval on regular sponsored research in this field and so helped to promote what had previously been an area of scattered, albeit quite extensive research, throughout this century and before (Cohen 1974; Cohen 1981).

However, dominant trends in British criminology, certainly until the end of the 1950s, tended to be unsympathetic to sociological theory, and even to the need for empirical research focusing centrally on the bases of crime in social conditions. Powerful currents of opinion in criminology stressed its clinical orientation and its primary links with psychology, psychiatry, and law (Cohen 1981: 222–30). The legacy of this orientation—a stress on pragmatic interdisciplinarity, the marginalization of sociology and a general distrust of broad theory—continued to influence British criminology powerfully at least until the mid-1960s. It is not difficult to see in these orientations of criminology a direct expression of some of the long-standing English attitudes to social research which were identified earlier in this chapter.

Finally, in the field of legal theory it should be noted that there have probably always been countercurrents to the dominant English analytical jurisprudential tradition. Before the 1940s, expressions of dissatisfaction with prevailing orthodoxies of analytical jurisprudence appear repeatedly in the periodical literature. Often the adoption of psychological or sociological approaches in the field of legal theory is advocated. As early as 1917 the prestigious *Law Quarterly Review* published an article strongly arguing the need for a sociological approach to legal analysis (Gupta 1917). Most such critical theoretical literature early in the century reflected the ideas of continental European writers such as François Gény and Léon Duguit and sought to gain a hearing in England for their sociologically tinged theories. Yet it must be said that they achieved little impact until, after the Second World War, a number of new textbooks of jurisprudence—especially those by Friedmann, Paton, Stone, and Lloyd[3]—showed a much more catholic approach to legal theory and helped to break down intellectual barriers between taught jurisprudence and social science.

The 1960s, however, mark the beginnings of sociological study of law in Britain as an important field of development. Some major reasons for this change can only be briefly touched on here. Among them was the expansion of both social science teaching and legal education. A considerable and rapid growth in the number of full-time teachers of law in higher education occurred during this decade, followed by an increase in both the scale and scope of research in law and an assertion on the part of academic lawyers in the universities of their distinct professional role as researchers and teachers rather than as merely the pedagogical branch of the legal profession. Hence a number of academic lawyers began to explore methods of research and analysis of law quite different from those involved in the exposition of doctrine for purposes of legal practice.

Political developments also contributed to the change of outlook, and to an increased interest of social scientists in law, in two major ways. First, a much publicised use of law in social planning, especially in the field of race relations,[4] occurred. As with comparable earlier developments in the United States, this promoted speculation on the social effects of law and the conditions of successful legislative action. Later, the increasing use of law in economic planning raised equally important and far-reaching questions. Secondly, however, there was evidence of increasing avoidance by government of legal techniques and processes familiar to lawyers. Among the matters that seemed to have become more visible and more explicitly promoted by government were the conferring of wide discretionary powers on officials—a practice that had often been passionately denounced by lawyers throughout the century (e.g. Hewart 1929; Keeton 1952), the increasing tendency to entrust adjudication to relatively informal tribunals rather than to ordinary courts, and an emphasis on administration rather than formal legal rights in many developing areas of state welfare provision. Such developments cast doubt on

---

[3] See Friedmann 1967; Paton 1972; Stone 1946; Lloyd and Freeman 1985.
[4] For the background to this legislation see e.g. Lester & Bindman 1972: ch. 3.

important traditional assumptions about the nature of law and of lawyers' tasks and have subsequently become important matters of discussion from many contrasting viewpoints. Thus, at the same time as there appeared to be an expansion of the scope of law and legal policy, there appeared also an undermining of law's exclusivity as a preferred instrument of governmental direction and control.

Among other important factors contributing to the development of concern with sociology of law, changes in the nature of criminological studies in Britain should be mentioned. These changes, no doubt, reflected local political developments as well as new intellectual influences from the United States. From the late 1960s, interactionist and labelling approaches in the sociology of deviance increased the interest of British sociologists in crime and deviance and inspired many criminologists to turn from consideration of criminality as an objective condition towards study of the nature and effects of the criminal law, law enforcement and criminal justice procedures from a sociological viewpoint (see e.g. Cohen, ed., 1971; Cohen 1974). These influences also inspired pioneer sociological research on debt enforcement (Rock 1973). During the 1970s the so-called 'new criminology' or radical (critical) criminology carried these trends further so that many British criminologists and sociologists of deviance turned their attention to law and legal processes as a major focus of study and contributed importantly to the development of sociology of law in Britain (e.g. Hall *et al.* 1978; Fine *et al.*, eds., 1979; National Deviancy Conference, ed., 1980; Carlen and Collison, eds., 1980).

The impetus for these changes in criminology arose largely from political conditions and aspirations, and from a general expansion of the concerns and ambitions of British sociologists. In part, the change in outlook has been attributed to a profound disillusionment in several areas of social science with the pragmatic, empiricist, and reformist traditions of British social research, which were seen as having failed to provide a successful foundation for the rational social planning associated with post-war reconstruction (Campbell and Wiles 1976: 560–3; cf. McGregor 1981: 9). One consequence was a demand for a rigorous theoretical foundation for research, the lack of which was perceived as part of the cause of earlier failure. These impulses in criminology (and in other research fields such as social administration), together with wider political and intellectual concerns, combined in a desire to free the subject from its subservience to governmental definitions of problems and policy objectives. One major ambition was, thus, to make criminology 'intellectually serious, as distinct from professionally respectable', as the sociologist Alvin Gouldner put it in a foreword to one of the key texts of British radical criminology (Taylor, Walton, and Young 1973: ix).

Phases of Development

It is possible to identify three reasonably clear phases in the recent development of sociology of law in Britain. The first phase, during the 1960s and early 1970s, was characterized by the establishment of the legitimacy of socio-legal studies in aid of law. A legal research unit in a social science context was established at London University's Bedford College in 1965, and Birmingham University established an Institute of Judicial Administration in 1969. Pioneer interdisciplinary studies (e.g. McGregor, Blom-Cooper, and Gibson 1970) were undertaken, and the idea began to be widely accepted that social science might have a valuable role in research in legal fields. The emerging assumption was that empirical research drawing on all or any of the social sciences was potentially valuable primarily to solve problems defined in terms of legal or social policy categories. Sociology and other social sciences were proclaimed as 'handmaidens of law'; helpers in the fulfilment of legal tasks.

To this extent, it seemed that the pragmatic, interdisciplinary, policy-oriented, and relatively atheoretical traditions of British criminology might be immediately replicated as a new, instant tradition for social scientific research on law. A major difference, however, was that sociology could not realistically be excluded from this interdisciplinary complex. As a discipline it was, in any event, at the end of the 1960s becoming popular and attracting unrealistically high hopes for its immediate practical utility in contributing directly to the formation of goverment policies. This view of the discipline, largely held by outsiders, was, however, clearly at odds with the ferment of self-criticism and theoretical debate intensifying inside it at the time.

A second phase in the development of sociology of law, especially from the mid-1970s to the first years of the 1980s, was characterized by competition between socio-legal studies, which proliferated from the early years of the 1970s, and an emergent, theoretically guided sociology of law. Sociology of law self-consciously distanced itself from socio-legal studies, which were usually seen—often with justification at the time—as atheoretical, eclectic, pragmatic in approach, primarily reformist in their objectives, and little concerned with the long-term development of a systematic social science of law. Sociology of law, by contrast, was proclaimed as theoretical in aim, not policy-oriented and concerned only to achieve scientific understanding of law as a social phenomenon.[5] It challenged the pragmatic plundering of numerous disciplines and proclaimed the need for a coherent, unified theoretical outlook on law in society. Hence, it stressed the need to locate studies of law clearly within frameworks of inquiry indicated by sociological theory. The rejection of pragmatic interdisciplinarity in favour of sociology was, therefore, motivated (at least for those researchers whose prior background was primarily in law) not so much by a desire to flee to the security of sociology as an established academic discipline as by a recognition that a serious concern with social theory was a prerequisite for any theoretically rigorous study of law as a social phenomenon. As an inevitable first step, adherents of this approach set about re-examining the classics of social theory—especially the writings of Durkheim, Weber, and Marx for insights on law (e.g. Albrow 1975; Clarke 1976; Cotterrell 1977; Hunt 1978; Cain and Hunt, eds., 1979; Phillips 1980).

During the 1970s very important developments occurred. In 1972 the Centre for Socio-Legal Studies was set up at Wolfson College, Oxford. This engaged in a wide variety of interdisciplinary empirical research involving collaboration between legal scholars, sociologists, psychologists, economists, and social historians. In the same year the Socio-Legal Group was formed to provide an enduring forum of regular conferences, allowing discussion between academic lawyers and social scientists. In 1974 the socio-legal *British Journal of Law and Society* (renamed, from 1982, the

---

[5] For an excellent account of the differences between the orientation of socio-legal studies at this time and the orientation of sociology of law see Campbell and Wiles 1976. The paper was, itself, a powerful intervention on behalf of sociology of law in the struggle between the two approaches, though it also perceptively noted the possibility of a future reconciliation between them. For a defence of socio-legal studies against sociology of law see McGregor 1981: ch. 1.

Journal of Law and Society) began publication. In its first issue the journal proclaimed: 'We do not subscribe to the view that the social scientist is to be cast in the role of handmaiden to the lawyer, the lawyer being in the dominant position . . . We reject the notion that "socio-legal" studies is to be an arena in which the lawyer solves problems of social policy on his own terms'.

The introduction of the British-based *International Journal of the Sociology of Law* from 1979 seemed to confirm the recognition in Britain of a distinct intellectual identity of sociology of law and, at the same time, a substantial distancing of its outlook and concerns from those still prevalent in the law schools. While the *Journal of Law and Society* quickly attracted the interest and manuscripts of empirically and theoretically minded legal scholars, the *IJSL*, more uncompromisingly committed to sociology as a distinct disciplinary base, seems, to judge from citations in general legal literature, to have had rather less impact on mainstream British legal scholarship. It has, nevertheless, provided a most valuable international forum for sociological research on law and law-related subjects.

The variety of viewpoints as to how social science should be brought into effective relation with law was hinted at also in book publication policies. Publisher Martin Robertson's 'Law in Society' series, throughout the 1970s, was originally promoted as 'a series of short research monographs and occasional papers in the sociology of law'. It included many valuable empirically grounded studies, for example on drug control (Bean 1974), administration of justice (Baldwin and McConville 1977; Carlen 1976), the emergence of legislation (Paulus 1974), pollution control (Gunningham 1974), legal services (Morris, White, and Lewis 1973), sexism in the legal system (Sachs and Wilson 1978), and criminal justice (Bottomley 1973), as well as more explicitly theoretical works, especially in criminology and the sociology of deviance. At the same time, Weidenfeld and Nicolson's 'Law in Context' series concentrated mainly on new legal textbooks with a 'contextual' slant, drawing on all or any of the social sciences in aid of the lawyer's understanding of the 'realities' of particular legal fields.

By the end of the 1970s a great ferment had occurred and seemed to be growing ever stronger in legal scholarship in Britain. The variety of work being done and the scale of interest in law among social scientists were amply demonstrated by the success of the 1979 British Sociological Association Annual Conference which was devoted, for the first time, to 'Law and Society' (Fryer *et al.*, eds., 1981). Over 400 scholars participated (Harris 1983: 318) and the occasion opened the eyes of many participants to the fact that British researchers in sociology of law and related fields were no longer isolated and marginalized, but part of a very substantial network of activity and interest, transcending several academic disciplines.

The third and present phase of development which dates from the early 1980s is characterized by a complex of conditions which together suggest a consolidation and retrenchment of sociology of law and a discarding of many of the claims of the late 1970s about the need for an explicit separation of sociology of law from socio-legal studies.

Present Conditions and Challenges

What conditions characterize this present phase of development of sociology of law in Britain? First, sociology of law and its intellectual orientations have become sufficiently academically established to defuse some previously militant claims about the need to preserve the scholarly integrity of sociology of law by distancing it from policy-oriented socio-legal studies. Socio-legal scholarship has become increasingly sophisticated, broader in its intellectual concerns, and theoretically informed. It remains the case that it embraces the whole range of social scientific research on law, while sociology of law is characterized by its specific commitment to the problems of empirical social theory and its use of methods and concepts derived from the discipline of sociology. But much empirical socio-legal research is now conducted with an explicit recognition of theoretical orientations that are central to sociology of law.

Courses concerned with sociology of law in some form are taught in a substantial number of law schools (Fielding and Fielding 1983). It seems to have become possible for some law teachers and their students to move between the perspectives of traditional legal scholarship and the broader perspectives of sociology of law, if not easily then at least with a reasonable accommodation to each. The monograph publication of sophisticated empirical research (especially the products of the Oxford Centre for Socio-Legal Studies) has made legal scholars generally aware that theoretically guided socio-legal studies, including empirical sociologically oriented research on legal institutions, are of value. Volumes representing work associated with the Oxford Centre cover a wide range of subject matter. They include several studies of regulatory agencies and their work (Cranston 1979; Richardson 1983; Hawkins 1984; Baldwin 1985), studies of compensation for accidents and illness (Harris *et al.*, 1984; Bartrip and Burman 1983; Genn 1987), of the higher judiciary (Paterson 1982), courtroom interaction (Atkinson and Drew 1979), the professions (Dingwall and Lewis, eds., 1983), and criminal trials (McBarnet 1981). From other sources have come a variety of valuable empirical studies of the administration of justice (e.g. Baldwin and McConville 1979), access to justice (e.g. Byles and Morris 1977), safety regulation (e.g. Carson 1981), policing (e.g. Cain 1973; Brogden 1982; Holdaway 1983), lawyers (Podmore 1980), and women's experience of law (e.g. Brophy and Smart, eds., 1985), among other subjects.

In addition, general textbook-style surveys of sociology of law have been produced (Freeman 1974; Grace and Wilkinson 1978; Roshier and Teff 1980; Cotterrell 1992), as well as various essay collections (e.g. Carlen, ed., 1976; Bankowski and Mungham, eds., 1980; Podgorecki and Whelan, eds., 1981) and a considerable diversity of theoretical contributions reflecting, for example, Marxist (Bankowski and Mungham 1976; Sumner 1979; Hirst 1979a; Collins 1982; Fine 1984), instrumentalist (Allott 1980), legal pluralist (Henry 1983), political pluralist (Hirst 1986), and liberal constitutionalist (O'Hagan 1984) approaches.

A second, more negative factor of change has been that, with a politically right-wing government in power in Britain continuously since 1979, sociology has fallen from official favour, funding for social scientific research has been substantially reduced and financial stringency has affected higher education generally. One developing consequence seems to be increased pressure for research and teaching in legal and other fields with strong vocational or commercial relevance. How this will affect sociology of law in the long term remains to be seen. It may be that, because of the need to attract private funding for research, given the unwillingness of government to support it adequately, empirical studies will again become more explicitly policy-oriented with social science again being cast in the role of handmaiden to legal professional, commercial, and financial concerns. If so, the *rapprochement* between sociology of law and socio-legal studies may be undermined by a distancing of empirical research orientations from speculative orientations in legal and social theory (which, being less dependant on research funding, can remain more detached from financially determined fashions).

A third factor that has contributed to a less confident assertion of sociology of law's independent virtues in the 1980s has been the rise of a variety of other approaches to legal scholarship, equally hostile to traditional approaches but, to some extent, hostile also to important assumptions that underpinned the advance of sociology of law. Economic analysis of law, imported from the United States, has significantly influenced socio-legal research[6] but has so far made only a limited impact on mainstream British legal scholarship, despite the publication of several significant articles (some jointly authored by lawyers and economists) in the major law reviews. In its dominant American forms, however, its fundamental assumptions and objectives are wholly different from and probably incompatible with those of sociology of law as the latter has been discussed in this chapter, in so far as this type of economic analysis of law seeks to find, in theoretical efficiency criteria related to a postulate of ideal market conditions, a new means of rationalizing legal doctrine. Nevertheless, some British writers have explicitly advocated 'neo-institutional' approaches to economic analysis of law which would make it possible to take account of the sociological characteristics and specific social consequences of legal regulation in a more realistic manner than seems to be the case with the hitherto dominant American varieties of economic analysis of law (Burrows and Veljanovski 1981: 22–5).

More immediately significant for sociology of law in Britain is the impact on legal scholarship of a complex of developments focusing on critical legal studies. As in the United States, the emergence of critical legal studies in Britain is associated, to some extent, with a degree of disillusionment, among radical and progressive legal scholars, with social science (perhaps especially in its positivist forms) and a desire to focus attention centrally on the

[6] For a summary of developments see Harris 1983: 326–8.

critical analysis of legal doctrine so as to bring to light its ideological foundations and effects.

Already, however, the theoretical basis of this diverse and loosely structured movement in Britain seems more explicit and, perhaps, more rapidly changing than in the United States. The main collective product so far (Fitzpatrick and Hunt, eds., 1987) of British critical legal scholars includes papers from some writers who have actively championed and promoted the sociology of law in Britain, as well as from others who doubt the theoretical and practical possibility of effectively confronting legal discourse with a distinct sociological discourse, or any other discourse 'external' to it. Some contributors, such as the present writer, see a possibility of 'critique' by confronting the limited perspectives on law of legal participants (for example, lawyers, judges, or litigants) with a necessarily always incomplete but continually broadening, self-critical, sociological perspective on law. Other writers espouse various forms of poststructuralism and postmodernism, emphasizing the impossibility of adjudicating in terms of 'truth' on any confrontation of discourses with each other, and the consequent need for analysis of a discourse in its own terms and in terms of its internal structural lapses or inconsistencies. Closely related to these latter approaches are several important recent contributions to the analysis of law in the light of linguistics and semiotics (e.g. Goodrich 1986; Goodrich, 1987; Jackson 1985).

Developments such as these have forced sociology of law, as a theoretical enterprise, on to the defensive, especially for those who view it as necessarily a branch of the academic discipline of sociology. As noted earlier in this chapter, however, it does not have to be seen in this way and, in many respects, British experience with sociology of law does not justify such a view of it. Recent developments in critical legal scholarship, at least in the particular forms this scholarship is beginning to take in Britain, are, in my view, to be welcomed as forcing a more rigorous development of theoretical ideas relevant to sociological inquiry about law.

So far, the strength of sociology of law in Britain has been largely in the empirical work that has been produced. Although there has been no lack of attention to theory in recent years, most writing specifically on law and social theory has been limited to critical commentary on classic writings or on recent continental

European trends in social theory (e.g. Sugarman, ed., 1983). It may be that the postmodernist challenge will do much good in spurring those scholars who are sympathetic to sociology of law to develop more rigorous theoretical frameworks which address the important insights offered by recent developments in critical legal scholarship. What is essential, now as in the past, is to make sure that empirical research and theoretical analysis remain firmly linked so that sociology of law can fulfil its potential as a rigorous and imaginative science of law in society.

5 Sociological Perspectives on Legal Closure

Western legal thought has shown very strong, relatively consistent tendencies to portray law as a self-sufficient or self-contained sphere of reasoning, practice, or discourse. In part this is an aspect of the characteristics of intellectual disciplines described in Chapter 3. But it also relates to certain conditions of law's legitimacy. The idea of an autonomous legal realm of discourse or normative ordering can be analysed sociologically, in terms of the conditions that allow and underpin this idea. Such an analysis shows most notions of legal autonomy to be extremely problematic. Yet, elaborated in legal philosophy, they are used to support the assumption that legal reasoning can ignore systematic empirical inquiries about social experience.

Legal closure refers to a many faceted but ubiquitous idea: the idea that law is, in some way, radically autonomous, self-reproducing, or self-validating in relation to an environment defined as 'extra-legal'. The idea is multi-faceted because it can be applied to whatever the word 'law' is treated as identifying—an intellectual discipline, a professional practice, a discourse, a normative or communicative system, or a field of knowledge or experience. And it is ubiquitous in the sense that it seems to have embedded itself in many different kinds of legal philosophy and intellectual practice. To adopt an idea of legal closure is to claim that law is self-standing and irreducible or that it has an independent integrity which is normally unproblematic, natural, or self-generated, not dependent on contingent links with an extra-legal environment of knowledge or practice.

Legal closure thus implies diverse but interconnected understandings of law. This chapter sets out to defend the utility of a sociological perspective, or set of perspectives, on legal closure. It distinguishes two approaches to legal closure which I call normative and discursive closure. The aim here is not to show that conceptions of normative or discursive legal closure are misguided in the particular contexts in which these conceptions have been developed, but that they can be reconsidered in a broader sociological perspective. Such a perspective ultimately denies that law is adequately understood as a 'closed' system, knowledge field, intellectual discipline, or discourse. But it recognizes the social conditions that may make law so appear, or which seem to impel the 'legal' to seek to achieve 'closure' in a variety of ways.

Legal Closure and Legitimation

Viewed sociologically, legal closure can be treated primarily as a means by which various forms of legal or political practice attempt to enhance their own legitimacy. Ideas of legal closure are part of the means by which an appeal to 'the legal' provides legitimacy in a variety of empirical settings. First, legal closure helps to support the legitimacy of the office of *judge* as quite other than that of a political or administrative decision-maker. The confident marking off of what is within the enclosure of law from what is outside makes possible a reliable knowledge of what can and cannot properly be said in judgments if judicial authority is to be preserved and enhanced. This is not just a matter of knowing the law—of understanding the criteria that mark particular rules as legally 'valid' and identify precedents as 'binding'. It is also a matter of understanding what kinds of argument and phrasing, and what styles of analysis and connections of ideas will be viewed as proper; as examples of correct and praiseworthy judicial practice. It is a matter of knowing what lines divide imaginativeness from unsoundness, skill and creativity in reasoning from idiosyncrasy, and robustness from carelessness. Of course, these are concerns of all lawyers who wish to have their ideas respected within their professional world. But, for the judge, the arena in which all of this must be done is, in many cases, more exposed than that of other lawyers; and more is at stake since a specifically 'legal' authority is maintained by every sound publicized judgment, and undermined by every unsound one.

Secondly, legal closure may underpin aspects of the *legal practitioner*'s legitimacy, as a kind of pale reflection of the judicial situation. An understanding of what lies within and what is to be considered outside the distinct realm of law provides important elements of the lawyer's professional conception of 'relevance'; of what will count as professional knowledge and good legal arguments. However, it is not necessary to adopt a view of law as radically closed off from an extra-legal environment in order to practise it confidently. Political (or at least policy) arguments, appeals to moral values, emotional rhetoric, and economic calculation may all have well understood parts to play in the construction of forensic arguments and in the interpretation or prediction of judicial decisions. Nevertheless, for certain purposes, professional claims of special expertise are significantly underpinned by the idea that there is a distinctive, autonomous legal knowledge; or a special logic of law to be understood only through specialized training and experience; or, more broadly, that there is a certain indefinable style of thought, a manner of marshalling and of working with ideas that constitutes 'thinking like a lawyer'. Legal closure, the presumed separation of legal ways as radically distinct, irreducible, and self-validating, may provide powerful support for legal professional status and legitimacy. This is so even though it is possible for lawyers to practise law without subscribing to any view that the realm of legal knowledge, legal methods, or legal reasoning is distinctive or autonomous.

Thirdly, legal closure may provide legitimacy for the *academic lawyer's* claim to expertise as teacher and expositor of law. In a relatively vocational environment this may be a direct reflection of the legal practitioners' claims of expertise; a matter of knowing what can be taught to create proper lawyers. Elsewhere, the exposition of law has often been predicated on the assumption or assertion that legal ideas can be organized into an integrated, distinctive, autonomous system of interrelated rules. This system may be treated as gaining much of its intellectual validity from its internal coherence, and the reconciliation of apparent doctrinal contradictions. The most orthodox styles of legal exposition have actually been organized around the effort *to create* legal closure; to portray legal doctrine or discourse as integrated, intellectually and normatively autonomous (at least to a considerable extent), and possessing a self-generated validity though its systematic and logical character. Claims about the autonomy of legal studies are also made on the basis of assumptions about or efforts to demonstrate distinct analytical methods, forms of reasoning, subject-matter, theory, or objectives of legal studies.

Nevertheless, much legal exposition in no way relies upon such models of legal closure. It treats law as open, extremely diverse in its subject-matter and regulatory forms, dependent on moral or political sources of evaluation and validation, often contradictory, implicated in an indeterminate range of extra-legal considerations, and to be taught not as an autonomous body of knowledge, set of skills, or manner of reasoning, but as the focus of broad interdisciplinary endeavour. The law teacher, not necessarily as committed to a distinct legal professional identity as the legal practitioner, and less committed also to the preservation of legal authority than the judge, may have less need than either of them for the aids to legitimation that a conception of legal closure may offer.

Finally, consider the position of an individual *citizen*, a legal lay person. It might be thought that such a person would have least concern for the kinds of legitimating functions that legal closure may offer. This is so, but subject to an important caveat. Legal closure may underpin, to a significant degree, the citizen's perception of security as an inhabitant of a normatively ordered, moral, and political environment free from arbitrariness and uncontrolled discretion, or protected from 'naked politics'. In this setting, legitimacy of the social and political order is provided, at least partly, through *legality* (see e.g. Luhmann 1985: 199–206).[1] It is guaranteed through popular perception of rule-governed, predictable procedures, radically distinguished from extra-legal arbitrariness or unfettered discretion (Tyler 1990). That is, it relies on belief in the Rule of Law; itself dependent on the possibility of firmly distinguishing law from 'non-law' in the organization of social and political relationships. The legitimation that legal closure provides links inseparably the security of the citizen with the legal title to rule held by those who govern.

From a sociological perspective must legal closure be viewed only in terms of these legitimating strategies and functions? Clearly not. It is also necessary to explore the empirical conditions of existence of law (as normative order, discourse, institutions, or practices) that make conceptions of legal closure plausible. A sociological approach should seek to consider what social and political conditions are represented by conceptions of legal closure. From such a standpoint, conceptions of legal closure are most usefully understood as ideological—that is, they represent

---

[1] Cf. Ch. 7, below.

certain partial perspectives on legal experience as if these constituted the totality. Sociologically, law is to be seen as an aspect of social life, implicated in social relations and structures in connection with which 'the legal' refers only to a certain facet or field of experience, variously identified. It is not even useful to think of law as a distinct intellectual discipline, except in so far as this refers to an actual collective allegiance of practitioners or scholars to something that they call 'law'. Its forms of knowledge, methods, and practices are the outcome of a disparate range of demands created by innumerable historical contingencies.

Considered as a field of experience, law in the broadest sense is a myriad of diverse practices loosely arranged around certain continually reformulated practical problems of government and social control. As means of adjustment to ever changing political and social conditions, these practices are contingent and likely to be transient, unstructured, pragmatic, and frequently inconsistent. Yet unending efforts are made to subject many of them to systematic organization and rationalization so as to form the basis of legal professional, bureaucratic, and governmental expertise and codified systems of knowledge and technique. In this way the task of creating law in the more specific sense of a finite body of professional, rationally ordered normative knowledge is pursued. And, as in the case of other fields of intellectual practice, the intimate relationship between knowledge and power may make possible the illusion of closure in this intellectual field of law. Legal practices gain power, influence, and authority to the extent that they appear to be expressions or applications of a unified, autonomous body of knowledge or doctrine.[2]

Normative Closure

Many conceptions of legal closure assume, imply or assert that law is to be radically distinguished from the 'extra-legal' or 'non-legal' by certain identifiable normative characteristics which give it its particular prescriptive character and concerns. *Procedure* is often considered the key. For example, in distinguishing legality from administrative expediency, procedural categories of natural justice or due process of law help to map the terrain of legality

---

[2] See Ch. 3, above.

within administration and informal dispute resolution. More generally, procedure defines the creation of law, allowing the identification of legislation and other new law as the outcome of specific events marking the transition of a bill to an Act of Parliament, or the coming into force of a new order or regulation. In the United States, the once influential 'process' school of scholarship emphasized the essence of legal craftsmanship in processes of legal development rather than in the substance of legal outcomes (Hart and Sacks 1958). Process, as a field of integrity, protected law from being devoured by political partisanship (Wechsler 1959).

Law and non-law may also be considered radically separated by the hallmarks of *legal form*. For Franz Neumann the distinguishing mark of law is found in the fusion of *ratio* and *voluntas*, the insistence that the sovereign's will is to be expressed in the rational form of general rules. To be law, political regulation must assume a form other that of particularized regulation or broad discretion. In Neumann's case this assertion of the radical separation of law from 'non-law' has the political purpose of making possible a clear identification of the legal pathology of the Weimar and Nazi regimes (Neumann 1986: chs. 15 and 16; 1944: 440–58) and, in particular, the pernicious character of *Generalklauseln*. But the emphasis on a fundamental defining form of law is pervasive in much legal philosophy, often introduced with the clear intention of radically separating a realm of 'the legal' from an environment of disorder or unreason.

Thus Lon Fuller's criteria of legality (Fuller 1969: ch. 2), though often referred to as constituting a 'procedural' conception of law, essentially attempt to elaborate what is entailed in the idea of law if it is assumed that law must take the specific form of rules. One aspect of this approach (though ultimately a subordinate one) is to deny the name of law to certain barbaric regulatory systems, such as that of Nazi Germany (Fuller 1958). Even in the case of H. L. A. Hart's model of rules as the core of the legal, a model presented as disinterestedly analytical, the rule form distinguishes law from discretion and helps to ground a belief in the doctrine of the Rule of Law by insisting that a settled core of legal meaning in rules can be securely distinguished from a penumbra of disputed interpretation to be handed over to politics or policy (Hart 1961: ch. 7).

Significantly, all of these types of normative closure are fragile and qualified. Hart's legal rules are only a category of social rules, distinguished from others by relatively flexible empirical criteria of obligation and significance. Fuller insists that the existence of law is a matter of degree and, in his later works, is much concerned to examine the empirical conditions that make specific legal forms and institutions viable. Neumann's examination of legal form is specifically intended to show its contingent historical character; its fragility and changeability in its close relationships with political, economic, and social conditions. Again, an emphasis on process criteria of the legal has tended to lead either to explorations of process in terms of specific empirical conditions or, where process has been claimed to have independent, autonomous merit, the process approach has sometimes been criticized as naïve or sterile.[3] Principles of natural justice may appear in broader perspective not as an irreducible essence of legality, but as moral considerations of fair treatment which for political reasons of good government, social justice, and administrative expediency deserve protection and enforcement in many specific contexts.

In general, therefore, these attempts at normative closure of law appear to fail because the postulates of the distinctively legal ultimately can be demonstrated to depend upon particular historical contingencies or conditions. Thus they appear as a foundation of shifting sands on which the edifice of law is built. Attempts at closure fail because the normative essence of the legal turns out to express or depend upon extra-legal considerations. Certainly the need to designate the legal field for the purposes of analysis and legal practice is not to be denied. But the effort to describe an essence of the legal analytically separate from—rather than empirically dependent upon—specific social environments seems to lead to a reification of law. Legal forms and processes are treated as natural, expressing some essence of the legal; rather than recognized as the consequence of specific, contingent social conditions.[4]

A sociological view cannot be content to dismiss conceptions of normative closure in law as mystification. Law does present itself

[3] See Miller and Howell 1960; and more generally White 1973.

[4] Among modern legal philosophers, Lon Fuller has made the most sustained and serious attempts to recognize and remedy these inadequacies in the analysis of legal forms and procedures. See especially Winston, ed., 1981: sect. 2.

in certain perennial forms, and through certain distinctive procedures. If law is to be understood empirically as a social phenomenon with social causes and effects, the social origins and
consequences of these specific normative characteristics of law
demand analysis. The literature of the sociology of law already
contains important if still inadequately developed resources for
this. In particular, it remains necessary to build on Max Weber's
studies of modern legal formalism, including his analyses of relationships between formal legal rationality and the conditions of
bureaucratic administration, of connections between formal rationality in modern law and the claims to legitimacy made by
modern government, and of enduring tensions between formal
and substantive rationality in modern law.

Much has changed, however, since Weber wrote early in the
twentieth century. Legal positivism, which may be said to provide
the foundation for almost all significant modern claims of *normative* legal closure, was recognized by Weber as the basis of legal
modernity when he wrote of the disintegration of natural law
conceptions as a foundation of law's legitimacy in modern conditions; of modern law having lost its 'metaphysical dignity' and
being revealed as no more than the product or the technical
means of compromises of conflicting interests (Weber 1978: 874–
5). Subsequent writers on law in society have done little to dis-
place Weber's diagnosis of the condition of modern Western law.
But what Weber could not see was the continuing decline in the
consistency of modern rational legal forms as the century has
progressed. Thus, general rules have increasingly been supplemented and supplanted by particularized, mechanical, and discretionary regulation (Cotterrell 1992: 161–6), so that the conception
of formal legal rationality has been reduced to the idea that any
kinds of regulation (orders, precedents, rules, guidelines, technical specifications, authorizations, definitions, broad discretions,
and so on) can be produced within law provided that their official
provenance can be traced to certain formal sources of governmental authority.

Law has lost its metaphysical dignity in a more fundamental
way than even Weber seemed to contemplate. The idea of legal
closure, which makes possible a practical and reliable identification of what is legally valid and binding, now seems to have to
allow law to encompass the most diverse, unrelated, unsystematic

and—in a specific sense—unprincipled regulation, made up of the technical minutiae of innumerable, disparate, and ever-changing governmental directives.

A further major theoretical source for sociological examination of normative legal closure is in Evgeny Pashukanis' now neglected Marxist legal theory, and some of the writings that have built upon it. A major virtue of Pashukanis' work is that it treats an examination of the distinctiveness of legal form as central to a sociological understanding of law; law is to be identified and explained as a social phenomenon in terms of its irreducible form so that a kind of normative legal closure can be explained sociologically. Pashukanis sees the concept of formal equivalence in legal relations—the formal equality of legal subjects or legal persons—as the essence of law. Law is to be understood in terms not of rules but of juridical relations between persons treated as formally identical for the purposes of those relations (Pashukanis 1978: ch. 3).

Unlike Weber, whose analysis of law's contribution to capitalism is highly ambiguous, Pashukanis makes specific and fundamental theoretical connections between legal form and capitalist social relations, in fact treating them as inseparable and thereby creating what many critics have considered a mechanistic and reductive account of law. But, as Alan Norrie (1982) has pointed out, Pashukanis does not confuse form and function of law. His analysis can be seen as an effort to explain the social conditions under which a distinctive modern legal form emerged and the contribution which that form makes to the fundamental structure of social relations in a capitalist society. Pashukanis' analyses do not necessarily require the conclusion, which he himself reached, that legal form is specific *only* to capitalist social formations; nor is it necessary to prejudge the possible variations of legal form and the functions it may serve in contemporary conditions.

The most valuable aspect of Pashukanis' work may be the hints it contains of problems that affect legal forms reflecting capitalist social relations, in circumstances where the state, for various reasons, needs to control, direct, or modify those relations, or intervene in the processes of their reproduction.[5] To this extent, he

---

[5] On this, Pashukanis' (1980) discussion of state controls during the First World War in Britain and other capitalist states contains much of interest.

points to specific tensions in the forms of modern law that are generally less clearly recognized in the Weberian tradition. Claims about the decline of what has been conceptualized, under Pashukanis' influence, as *Gesellschaft* law (Kamenka and Tay 1975) are paralleled by observations of the bureaucratization of the 'autonomous' legal system (Unger 1976) and of the invasion of the legal form of bourgeois law by the political imperatives of corporate society (Neumann 1957).

The most serious limitation of Pashukanis' work, however, is surely its inability to treat legal forms as other than exceptional in so far as they do not reflect the relations of equivalence or the logic of commodity relations that his theory makes central. One might say that he treated legal form *too* seriously, essentializing it, so that the idea of legal closure, instead of being an object of sociological inquiry, came to ensnare his sociology of law.

Discursive Closure

Because normative closure postulates specific features of law that identify and descriptively distinguish it, sociological approaches to law usually have little difficulty in relativizing these claims of closure. But assertions of what can be called discursive closure pose a different order of problems and challenge the explanatory aspirations of the sociology of law in a fundamental way. By discursive closure I mean a conception of law as a distinct discourse, possessing its own integrity, its own criteria of significance and validation, its own means of cognition and of constituting the objects of which it speaks. This conception of legal discourse typically goes along with the claim that discourses are incommensurable; that truth or validity criteria, established by a discourse, function within it without reference to the status of those criteria outside that discourse; that there are no meta-discourses which make it possible to adjudicate on the relative merits of truth or validity claims of different discourses (see e.g. Rorty 1980). Hence, according to this conception, a sociological perspective on legal closure cannot address the significance of legal closure for *law*; that is, for the discourse of law. It can only observe, from a distance, so to speak, the character of another discourse. Sociological characterization cannot be shown to be better or worse than, only different from, the characterization that participants in legal discourse themselves adopt. The challenge for a sociological perspective on legal closure is, thus, to show, first, that a sociological discourse about law is *possible* if law is, itself, a distinct discourse and, secondly, that a sociological characterization of legal closure is *relevant* to participants in any such legal discourse.

Several forms of discursive legal closure are exemplified by modern legal philosophy. Hans Kelsen's pure theory of law is significant in this context for its insistence on the distinctiveness and irreducibility of different modes of cognition. For Kelsen, a science of law constructs its own objects, and presents legal reasoning as a realm of thought and understanding wholly apart from sociological observation: 'in so far as it is the method or form of understanding through which the object (the given) is determined, the antithesis of causal and normative sciences rests just as much on a difference in the direction of understanding as on a difference in the object of understanding'.[6] Kelsen admits that a sociology of law is possible, but this would be a sociology of behaviour in legal contexts and of its ideological determinants, including the ideology of justice (Kelsen 1957: 271). Sociological investigations would be wholly distinct from those framed by a science of law, since legal science is concerned with norms and not with empirical causes and consequences.

The Kelsenian idea of a science of law suggests that the realm of norms remains an object of cognition. The pure theory of law is a means of conceptualizing the normativity of law, of structuring a science of law in terms of a logic of norms. Because law, for Kelsen, can still be described in terms of its form (norms) and their relationships (imputation), his work does not seem to render impossible, and may even facilitate, the adoption of a sociological perspective on legal science; one which would seek to explain the social conditions that make possible the forms of legal thought characterized in pure or ideal form by Kelsen. Again, Weber's examination of the modern conditions of rationality in many spheres of modern experience is highly relevant to such a project. Far from being essentially a theorization of links between law and capitalism, Weber's sociology of formal legal rationality can probably best be considered part of a lifetime study of the fate of

---

[6] Kelsen, quoted by Alida Wilson in Tur and Twining, eds., 1986: 53.

humanity in the modern world (Hennis 1988); a fate bound up with the contradictions of rationality and the complexities of its expression and application.[7]

Weber's conception of diverse value spheres—his diagnosis of the 'ethical irrationality of the world' or the conflicting, independent, and irreconcilable rationalities of different areas of life (see Weber 1948)—mirrors in a significant way Kelsen's insistence on a firm link between philosophical relativism and political pluralism. Kelsen justifies democracy as the device by which continuing processes of tolerant compromise can be made possible in a world of irreconcilable modes of cognition and evaluation (Kelsen 1955). Thus, for him, the 'closure' of law to politics or morality makes possible the preservation of an 'empty', neutral legal science capable of building the autonomous structures of compromise available to mediate between conflicting values and interests. Ultimately, the effort to maintain legal closure through a theoretical project such as Kelsen's can be portrayed as one kind of response to the moral and political conditions of contemporary life, in which, as Weber emphasized, absolute universal values are no longer available to regulate complexity. But Weberian sociology of law seems to indicate that law's structures of reason are always *contingent, timebound, and contested*; there is no warrant to claim that, even in modern conditions, law has actually become an autonomous 'value sphere', despite the powerful impetus that these conditions might give to efforts to secure law's closure.[8]

Because Kelsen discusses law and the possibility of a science of law in descriptive fashion he creates objects which a sociological analysis can locate in some broader context of social existence. Such an analysis does not, in any way, deny the importance of legal science as Kelsen describes it but suggests that the significance and character of this science can be better—because more broadly—understood in a sociological perspective. The situation

[7] The work of the Frankfurt School and, most notably in recent times, Jürgen Habermas can be considered the most direct continuing expression of these concerns.

[8] See Weber 1978: 880–95. The search for 'purity' or closure eventually leads Kelsen to a theory of norms or normativity, rather than of law as such; as though law gets left behind, or the focus is switched beyond the legal to something 'purer'. Cf. Kelsen 1991. It is significant also that in so far as Hart's (1961: 55–6) 'internal aspect' of rules indicates a distinct realm of normative discourse, this discourse is not restricted to law.

is different, however, with an approach such as Ronald Dworkin's which treats law as entirely a matter of discourse and in no way a matter of distinctive normative criteria. Thus Dworkin denies that 'the very meaning of the word "law" makes law depend on certain specific criteria' and that our 'rules for using "law" tie law to plain historical fact' (Dworkin 1986: 31). Law, for him, is best thought of as the conversation of participants in an endless collective enterprise of interpretation; in other words, a discourse. Dworkin does not consider—like the early Foucault or the literary theorist Stanley Fish—that this discourse entirely constructs its own objects of knowledge. For Dworkin, there still remain historical legal materials to be interpreted; so that interpretation must somehow 'fit' what is interpreted. Nevertheless, it is far from clear what the criterion of 'fit' entails in Dworkin's legal theory (see e.g. Cotterrell 1989: 178–80). The whole thrust of his current legal philosophy is to treat law as entirely constituted by interpretation; as a dis- course within which all criteria of the legal are determined by discourse itself.

What is the nature of this Dworkinian discourse of law? It is a discourse in which all participants are engaged in a search for the 'best reading' of legal doctrine, the reading that will make best sense of the patterns of moral and political communication in which participants in legal talk are involved. The search for the best reading presumes that a correct interpretation of legal doc- trine is possible; it assumes the *possibility* of discursive unity and forces all legal participants who wish to challenge this unity to do so only by engaging in the effort to demonstrate it. Law is prop- erly to be understood as having an underlying, immanent, or overall rationality and moral integrity capable of being elaborated through law's own discursive methods. The possibility that law is a field of experience consisting of fragmentary, diverse, and fun- damentally inconsistent forms of talk and practice is marginalized. The Dworkinian idea of 'integrity' as a hallmark of best legal interpretive practice, and the associated idea that there can be 'right answers' to all legal disputes, further symbolize the claim that legal discourse is ultimately coherent and comprehensive, generating resources for a comprehensive legal interpretation of reality. Dworkinian legal discourse generates its own closed world, observing morality, politics, and society only in its own discursive terms.

A legal sociologist is given two choices by this approach: either accept the Dworkinian characterization of law's discursive realm and share in legal knowledge as a participant in this discourse; or else remain an outside observer unable to speak of 'law' as such since law is accessible only as and through legal discourse. If legal sociologists resist being co-opted within this project of exploring the integrity of law's discursive empire, law's closure appears to condemn legal sociology to inhabit an external discourse, unrelated to and unable to embrace, invade, or interact with law.

The dilemma is, however, false. It remains a very open question how far law can be considered an integrated and independent discourse. This is not to deny the specific character and contexts of legal reasoning and the processes by which legal knowledge is generated and validated within the interpretive communities of law. These communities correspond roughly to those categories of judges, practitioners, legal scholars, and teachers, and citizens whose possible interests in legal closure or legal 'integrity' were noted at the beginning of this chapter. It is possible that they might be united, for some purposes and to some extent, in a single legal community as Dworkin seems to suggest (Dworkin 1986: ch. 6). Even so, it seems realistic to recognize numerous sub-communities and that the intellectual practices of law may not constitute a discursive unity. The structure and conditions of existence of law's interpretive communities can be examined sociologically. The question is whether legal discourse and sociological discourse remain distinct, unable to invade each other.

Can the legal discourse of a whole political community as portrayed by Dworkin be thought of as having even *potential* moral or intellectual integrity and autonomy? Or does it, in fact, consist only of diverse, loosely and contingently related rhetorics and rationalities drawn from *Realpolitik*, moral conviction, arguments of economic efficiency, techniques of textual interpretation and criticism, and many other sources? It seems that no convincing reasons for adopting the former view and rejecting the latter have yet been provided by legal philosophers. But if law can be seen sociologically as a field of experience in which actors explain to themselves and others the meaning, structure, or significance of this field and their situation within it in terms of *all or any* of these sources, a sociological perspective on the kind of discursive closure suggested by Dworkin's view of law as interpretation will tend to portray it as mystification.

The claim would be that Dworkin postulates a community that either does not exist or is so loosely conceived that the word 'community' lacks substantial meaning.[9] Such a sociological view might insist that the processes of legal interpretation that lawyers work with can be better illuminated by examining the conditions enabling certain interpretations to prevail over others in law's various interpretive communities, and ordering those communities in hierarchies of social and political significance seemingly unrecognized in Dworkin's theories. These conditions can only be understood in the broad context of empirical examination of legal practices and legal politics.

Autopoiesis

In one recent sociological movement in legal theory the idea of law's discursive closure has been seen as the consequence of the character of law as a communication system. Autopoiesis theory, developed in relation to law by Niklas Luhmann and Gunther Teubner, postulates a form of legal closure as radical as any to be found or implied in the literature of legal philosophy.

In Luhmann's formulation, law as a social system of communication is cognitively open but normatively closed. Law receives communications of information from, for example, natural science (perhaps medical knowledge) or economics (efficiency information) but it attributes or denies significance to these communications in accordance with its *own* system imperatives and only by transforming them into its own normative terms. Closure 'consists in the fact that all operations always reproduce the system' (Luhmann 1988: 15). Teubner declares that 'legal discourse invents and deals with a juridical "hyperreality" that has lost contact with the realities of everyday life and at the same time superimposes new realities on everyday life', and that 'law becomes autonomous from general societal communication' (1989: 742). It has become increasingly a self-referential system. Thus, for example, legal doctrine on the relationship between

---

[9] Cf. Dworkin 1989: 496, where 'political community' is treated as synonymous with 'nation' or 'state'.

corporations and legal personality is neither superior nor inferior to social scientific theory about relationships between organization and collective action. Inhabiting different discourses, these are merely incommensurable knowledges (Teubner 1989: 743–4).

In Teubner's most recent writings the radical autonomy of legal discourse has been expressed, perhaps somewhat confusingly, in terms of law's capacity as a social system or as an institution to 'think' independently from the minds of individual actors. This means that 'law autonomously processes information, creates worlds of meaning, sets goals and purposes, produces reality constructions—and all this quite apart from the world constructions in lawyers' minds' (Teubner 1989: 739). Autopoiesis theory thus accepts the idea of law as a discourse or system of communication creating its own objects, truth criteria, and canons of validity, while receiving information from and transferring information to its environment (conceived as other systems, such as those associated with politics, science, economy, or the psyche). Luhmann's and Teubner's versions of autopoiesis theory seek to conceptualize discursive or system closure sociologically in terms of the conditions of existence of autopoietic systems as well as in terms of their structure and means of self-reproduction. The emergence of self-referential systems is seen as a response to the growing complexity of societies. The separation of social sub-systems makes it possible to reduce, through specialization and differentiation, the organization and information overload problems that otherwise accompany complexity.

At least in Teubner's case, the development of legal autopoiesis theory was inspired by problems in sociology of law. The need to explain the causes of failure to shape society through law and law through social science, or to account for the unpredictability and unintended effects of legal action, led to an attempt to examine legal closure in terms of system imperatives. All of this represents a necessary effort in legal sociology to take ideas of legal closure seriously. But it is significant that Teubner, perhaps more clearly than Luhmann, has recognized that the achievement of self-referentiality or system-closure in law is a relative and even problematic matter. Hence it is appropriate to talk of the *tendency* to autopoietic system reproduction and closure, rather than its achievement. Teubner at least refers to the 'dynamics of social evolution' (in other words, a continuing present process) in which 'self-referential relations are multiplying within the legal process'.[10]

Equally, Teubner's concern is now increasingly with the problem of conceptualizing relations between systems; in particular between law and its environment—that is, its observation of other autopoietic systems or discourses. Given the conception of system self-referentiality and closure to which legal autopoiesis theory holds, the theory seems to adopt a correlative conception of an *absence* of theoretically definable relations between law and its environment. Law does not interact with the environment but is subject to and creates 'interference' in connection with it (Teubner 1992a). The most important problem for autopoiesis theory is now to try to find ways of conceptualizing the extremely complex and varied ways in which this interference may occur.[11]

Autopoiesis theory is the most sophisticated attempt so far to explain, in social scientific terms, such familiar notions in legal philosophy as law that 'regulates its own creation' or law as a 'gapless' system or a legal 'heaven of concepts'. But the theory seems to fuse questions about discursive closure (questions about the nature of ideological thought and practices) with issues relating to the conditions of existence and character of specific social systems of communication (empirical issues about constraints and imperatives arising from dominant interests within organizations and collectivities and affecting the decisions and outlook of members or shaping roles within institutions).

There is no doubt that ideology and organizational interests are closely interrelated. Nevertheless, some analytical separation of them might make it easier to keep in focus the possibility that, even in a formalized, seemingly closed legal system, it is not 'the system' which thinks or communicates, but individual actors (for

[10] Teubner 1989: 742. See also Teubner 1988. Luhmann seems to accept the idea of the functional indispensability of system closure. Thus, he states that legal system 'autonomy is not a desired goal but a fateful necessity' (Luhmann 1986: 112).

[11] Recently, Teubner (1991: 38) has talked in terms of a system having a 'real contact' with its environment, not in the sense of filtering inputs from it, but in the sense that expectations within the system may create a sensitivity to the external environment (*une sensibilité interne au monde extérieur*), impelling the system to ask 'yes/no' questions of that environment. Adjusting itself in the light of the answers, the system then continues to carry on its own processes in its own way. Luhmann (1986: 114) refers to the legal system requiring external 'limitation and guidance—but not determination!—of choice'.

example, lawyers, judges, lay citizens) whose thinking and communicating creates and sustains the system. The constraints upon or conditions and possibilities of their thought and action are capable of being explained in terms of structures of ideology—for example, professional ideologies, legal ideology, and political ideologies. These constraints, conditions, and possibilities also relate to structures of discipline, reward, opportunity, and repression created by dominant interests within organizations, occupational groups, and interpretive communities of many kinds.

In its effort to take discourses or abstract communication systems seriously, a sociological perspective should avoid the temptation to reify them. Even autopoietic metaphors may be dangerous to the extent that they portray a world over which individuals have not only lost control but in relation to which they might absolve themselves of responsibility, so it seems, for autonomous action. It is important to recognize the full extent to which, in modern conditions, subject-centred reason has been confined, repressed, trivialized, and debased in innumerable ways; but it may be possible to do this without actually reducing the sociological status of the individual theoretically to that of a construct or carrier of various social systems, whose human autonomy is retained only as a 'psychic system' (cf. Teubner 1989: 741; Teubner 1991: 37).

Closure and Disclosure

If it is asked what the status of autopoietic legal theory is in relation to the discourse of law which it presupposes and examines, it seems likely that its exponents would claim that it inhabits the discourse of science, which itself is to be understood as an autopoietic communication system. As a form of legal sociology it seeks scientific explanation of a sector of the social world. Hence, this is no challenge to the position seemingly represented by those, like Dworkin, who assert that, from the standpoint of legal discourse, 'external' perspectives such as those offered by legal sociology can offer no elucidation of law itself. Indeed, autopoiesis theory would seem merely to confirm this position in its insistence on the closed character of self-referential social systems of communication. Accordingly, legal sociologists adopting this kind of perspective on legal closure will presumably state honestly that their standpoint is that of social science, offering a different

and distinct knowledge from that of participants in legal discourse; neither better nor worse, stronger or weaker, because
incommensurable.

Whether one can go beyond this limited position in asserting
the power of sociological perspectives on discursive legal closure
is the vital question. Numerous writings in contemporary philosophy and social theory assume or assert the incommensurability of
discourses, the non-existence of any meta-theory or meta-discourse
that could somehow adjudicate between the truth claims of different discourses, the failure of correspondence theories of knowledge, and the survival only of pragmatic relativism (see e.g. Dews
1987; Rajchman and West, eds., 1985). In postmodern conditions
we are said to be fated to engage in endless ungrounded conversation. We can, it seems, only assert knowledge claims lacking and
denying all authority beyond the conditions of argument giving
them 'local' meaning within a discourse. Such claims must be
refused any more fundamental significance as transdiscursive truth.

The possibility remains, however, that discourses are not as self-
sufficient, secure, and integrated as they are sometimes made
to appear. It was suggested earlier that the discourse of law
which Dworkin explores and celebrates may be much more fragmented and morally or intellectually vulnerable than the confident 'empire' he sees. At the same time, the *assertion* that law
constitutes an integrated and autonomous sphere of intellectual
practice serves important legitimating functions and therefore is
strongly maintained.

Sociology, if it takes all social experience as its province, must
also embrace the examination of the social foundations of all
disciplines and discourses, including its own. Thus, its fundamentally reflexive, self-conscious, self-contextualizing character makes
it unlike the political-intellectual practices of law and capable, by
its nature, of examining the social foundations of legal knowledges
and practices; it can even contribute knowledge necessary to participants in legal discourses when, for various reasons, law is forced
by crises of confidence to attempt to become, itself, self-critical
and self-contextualizing.[12] Law, lacking the inherently reflexive
character of sociology and necessarily presenting itself in normal
conditions as authoritative and normatively secure, may, at times

[12] See Ch. 3, above.

of uncertainty, actually need the perspective on its practices that a sociological standpoint can offer.

It would seem that, for Dworkin, the preferred and probably necessary standpoint for understanding law is that of an active participant in legal reasoning. But the claim of legal sociology is that a sociological perspective can be more inclusive and more illuminating than that of such a participant, because it embraces particular participant perspectives but goes beyond them, recognizing their diversity, interpreting and preserving them within a widening vision of law in society.

In relation to conceptions of *normative* closure, sociological perspectives can contextualize the lawyer's claims of closure in ways that further clarify their significance. In relation to *discursive* closure, it is unnecessary, or certainly premature, to conclude that law is a unified discourse in relation to which any sociological perspective on legal practice must remain external. On the contrary, sociological perspectives suggest explanations for the contingency and diversity of law's discourses. The most appropriate strategy for sociological studies of law is to explore the conditions and limitations of the varieties of legal closure; ceaselessly contextualizing and relativizing law's knowledges, exploring the conditions of their truth claims and, through a permanently self-critical, reflexive sociological perspective, attempting to open possibilities for productive confrontations between discourses.[13]

In such a project, sociology is not presented as a meta-discourse or the purveyor of a meta-theory transcending existing divides between discourses. Indeed, it should not be presented as an existing *unity* at all. That would be to mirror the ideology of legal closure. Sociology of law entails only the never-ending effort and aspiration to transcend partial perspectives on legal experience. In my view, the reflexivity inherent in the development of sociological inquiry makes such an effort worthwhile and such an aspiration feasible. There is no 'true' or complete view to be gained by such means; only the possibility of more comprehending and comprehensive ones—capable of incorporating, without denying or trivializing, more specific participant perspectives. Sociology of law should treat legal closure as a significant underpinning of some of these specific perspectives on legal experience.

[13] Cf. Ch. 3, above.

PART II

Law in Social Theory

6 Law, Ideology, and Power: The Marxist Tradition

The writings of Karl Marx and Friedrich Engels on law pose problems which later Marxist theory has not resolved: how seriously is law to be taken as a focus of political concern and as a set of distinctive practices or conceptual forms? Is the character of law ultimately wholly explicable in terms of the logic of economic conditions, or the functional requirements of capitalism? Or does law have some other independent effectivity which justifies treating it as an important object of theoretical analysis in its own right? Marxist theory has not adequately explored or explained ideas of legality. It has, however, properly directed attention towards the ideological significance of legal doctrine, even if legal ideology has been conceptualized in often dogmatic and inflexible ways.

The creation of a literature devoted to the elaboration (and, in part, rediscovery) of a rigorous Marxist analysis of law has been a recent intellectual growth industry. The development is clearly an aspect of wider theoretical concerns in Marxism and it also parallels a general revival of interest in law in social science. Legal theory in advanced capitalist societies has been, for decades, the almost unchallenged preserve of jurists attempting to rationalize and universalize the legal ideology and forms of professional discourse of contemporary Western law. But this restriction of scope was not always characteristic and is again ceasing to be so.

The literature of Marxist legal theory to be considered in this chapter indicates a variety of possible approaches to analysis of law, but it also affirms the intellectual significance of a Marxist tradition in legal theory which until recently was almost forgotten by Western scholars. It points to the significance of law as a focus of social theory and also to those serious ambiguities and silences in theoretical literature that make the development of a rigorous theoretical approach to legal analysis a pressing need.

Legal Theory and Political Strategies

Why was law neglected for so long in Marxist writing? The primary answers lie in the limitations of the kinds of strategic choices indicated by Marxist theory from its beginnings. The limitations are themselves given by theoretical inadequacies which contemporary political conditions have made it increasingly necessary to identify and confront. As Boaventura de Sousa Santos points out in his contribution (Santos 1979) to *Capitalism and the Rule of Law*, an essay collection reflecting recent Marxist approaches to law, the development of a Marxist legal theory was unnecessary as long as a simple reformism/revolution dichotomy characterized apparent strategic choices and the theoretical formulation of them.

If law is seen merely as an ideological form of capitalist social relations or as a part of a repressive apparatus inseparably connected with the maintenance of those relations and immediately redundant with their supersession, a *revolutionary* strategy aims at total destruction of these relations and of this repressive apparatus, and has no concern with analysing any distinctively legal aspects of them. The only appropriate view of law is a wholly negative one. The nature of law is unproblematic since its class character is assumed and it is defined strategically as being incapable of adaption or reconstruction to serve the ends of revolutionary transformation of social relations. The only relevant legal theory would be one that reveals conclusively the necessary functional interdependence of law and capitalist social relations and, thus, the necessary opposition of law to the aims of revolutionary struggle and the impossibility of revolutionary strategy using law as a weapon.

A theory such as that of the Soviet jurist Evgeny Pashukanis, a theory *against* law (cf. Santos 1979: 151), fitting these criteria exactly, thus reveals the capitalist essence of law and helps to explain in a sophisticated manner how law contributes to the structuring and reproduction of capitalist social relations. But because law itself has a theoretically given *function* (the embodiment and guarantee of capitalist social relations) which class struggle cannot change, law tends to appear not as a site of class struggle but as a remote, abstract, structural support of capitalism. Its hidden ideological processes, when once revealed, are seen to work with a structurally determined stability and inevitability which can only be upset by revolutionary transformations entirely bypassing legal forms and processes themselves.

The problem with this view which takes law's functions (repressive and ideological) as given is that, historically, law often appears as a front line of political and ideological struggle. The timeless structures of Pashukanis's *General Theory of Law and Marxism* (Pashukanis 1978) seem to represent uneasily the historical battles over legal limitation of the working day which Karl Marx and Friedrich Engels recount, the history of jury trial in sedition cases (see e.g. Harman and Griffith 1979), recent industrial relations struggles, numerous phases and aspects of the development of the law of property since feudalism, and many other battles on the terrain of legal ideology and legal institutions. How are such developments in legal history and in recent legal practice to be analysed? To conceptualize law merely as class violence is, as Pashukanis clearly showed, inadequate because it is necessary to explain *why* repression takes the form of law. And it is necessary to explain what he did not: under what conditions legal repression and legal ideology serve to support existing patterns of social relations, and under what conditions they offer the opportunity for challenge to these relations.

There is another no less pressing set of questions that are wholly left out of consideration by this tradition of thinking about law. What organizational and administrative forms are appropriate to socialism? It is assumed (on the authority of the classic Marxist texts) that law will contribute in socialism only in a negative and increasingly limited way to the solution of these problems of organization and administration. For too long it has been assumed that the problems would solve themselves since socialist relations of production would give rise to appropriate mechanisms of organization just as capitalist social relations have done. But this utopian thinking has become increasingly untenable after the experience of state socialism in many countries in past decades, and of the varieties of forms of state and legal system that can exist in capitalist societies. The questions of the variability of law's consequences for capitalism and of its relevance for socialist organization now appear as questions of the utmost importance and, given these circumstances, it is unsurprising that the concept of the Rule of Law has reappeared as a serious item on the agenda of socialist discussion.

The concept of revolutionary transformation implies a monolithic uniformity of structures of social relations and their conditions of reproduction which can only be transcended through a total cataclysmic overturning of the structural complex. Conversely, the complementary concept of *reformism* implies a taken-for-granted attitude to social institutions and processes. Reformism implies the inevitable *preservation* of given structures and a failure to see the continuous processes of struggle and change that make the continued existence of established institutional forms always problematic.

Since reformism implies taking existing forms to serve new ends, its theoretical concern is necessarily less with the taken-for-granted forms (for example, law) than with the social and political conditions necessary to transform their functions. Hence, as Karl Renner's Austro-Marxist legal theory indicates (Renner 1949), positivist legal philosophy (of the type most rigorously developed by Renner's compatriot Hans Kelsen), which stresses that legal form can be analysed as a universal form independently of any particular social or political conditions, is not necessarily an inadequate basis for a social democratic analysis of the role of law in social transformation. Legal forms are seen, in a perspective such as Renner's, as substantially unchanging, but accurate analysis of the conditions of evolutionary change is considered to show how these forms are to be used to promote the social and political objectives sought.

What is most important, therefore, about the reform/revolution polarization is that one polarity tends to lead to the assumption of legal form as a given—an unproblematic form which can accommodate any content—while the other tends to treat legal form as an irrelevance in strategic terms and, in theoretical terms, as wholly determined by given structural requirements of capitalism or (in vulgar Marxist conceptions) as the direct expression of the interests of a dominant class. In both of these polarized yet similarly undialectical and rigid approaches the possibility of analysing legal processes, institutions, and discourses in relation to specific historical conditions, of analysing in detail the ideological battles that surround the law and of analysing the conditions under which the forms and contents of legal doctrine develop in all their complexity and variety, is effectively ruled out.

Marx and Engels on Law

The reform/revolution dichotomy is clearly only a particular formulation, in terms of political strategy, of certain fundamental
orientations in Marxist theory, in general, and Marxist legal
theory, in particular, which pose extremely serious problems for
the adequate analysis of law. In presenting their valuable and well-
organized collection of key writings by Marx and Engels on law,
Maureen Cain and Alan Hunt argue that the dichotomy is not
explicitly recognized in these writings (Cain and Hunt, eds., 1979:
xvi, 214, 218). At a certain level of analysis this is undoubtedly
true. In the later writings and particularly in Marx's *Das Kapital*
the relationship between legal form and the fetishized commodity
form is indicated in such a way as to make clear the structural
significance of legal form within the capitalist mode of production. But recognition of the necessarily bourgeois form of law and
the inevitability of its supersession with the transition to socialism
in no way justifies, for Marx and Engels, avoidance of class struggle through the law.

Cain and Hunt make much of this while admitting that Marx
and Engels offer little guidance for a 'theorized distinction between reformist and other non-revolutionary political practice'
(1979: 211). In fact it is Engels rather than Marx who seriously
discusses law as a possible, independently identifiable site of political struggle, and the clearest and most significant illustration of
the differences in outlook between them in this respect is in their
parallel discussions of the struggle for the legally limited working
day.

Marx's analysis of this struggle in *Kapital* is informed by a structural analysis of the capitalist mode of production. Legislative
changes are necessary because of the problem of conservation of
resources, given a certain changing structure of relations of production. Engels, retaining a more or less consistent humanist
position, analyses the legal developments in terms of *political* struggle, in terms of class alliances. Marx, of course, is no less concerned with the consequences of class struggle yet, over all, the
key point is that the legislation 'developed gradually out of circumstances as natural laws of the modern mode of production'
(Cain and Hunt, eds., 1979: 254). Elsewhere, with crushing finality,

he makes a general point about the limits of manœuvre within legal forms: 'Right can never be higher than the economic structure of society and its cultural development conditioned thereby' (Marx 1970: 19). And, significantly, when in 1925 Pashukanis sought to make clear the urgent need for promotion of the revolutionary struggle against the remnants of legal form in the Soviet Union after the October Revolution, he invoked Lenin's writings on the necessity of using 'those "legal opportunities" which the enemy, who was merely broken but not fully defeated, was forced to provide' (Beirne and Sharlet, eds., 1980: 138). But he made no reference to any of Marx's statements on law.

The early Hegelian formulations of both Marx and Engels raise no difficulties, given their relative naïvety, in locating law as a focus of struggle. In these early texts law has an ideal essence which provides built-in criteria for criticism of, and action against, 'misuse' or 'distortion' of legislation and legal processes. The censorship laws and the Prussian law on thefts of wood are central objects of attack in the texts and seen as arenas of conflict in which the weapons of attack and defence are given by law itself. 'Real' law is, by its nature, a 'form of existence of freedom' (Cain and Hunt, eds., 1979: 42). Later, law is seen by Marx to have a very different 'essence': it is a fetishized form, the juridical embodiment of the commodity form, which constructs the legal subject or person (the standardized bearer of rights and duties) as a property owner; that is, as the agent who provides the support of commodity exchange. Although law as fetishized form has the appearance of autonomy, its essence now resides 'outside' itself, outside this form, in the materiality of capitalist social relations which it embodies, and in the conditions of their existence.

Since, in his later writings, Marx offers no systematic analysis of law as such and is only concerned with it as an aspect of the basic structure of the capitalist mode of production it cannot be said with certainty that, for him, law's forms and functions are wholly circumscribed by the mechanisms of the fetishism of commodities. This is, however, the inference Pashukanis draws and it is reasonable given Marx's reluctance to admit any real possibility of using legal struggle as a serious strategy of social transformation. Marx's 1871 letter to Bolte (Cain and Hunt, eds., 1979: 240–1) recognizes the struggle of a class for legislative change as a political action, but the exact significance of such action is not made clear and, while Marx's statements are ambiguous, a reasonable interpretation of them is that this action is important primarily as a means of agitation to gain the maximum rights compatible with 'the existing economic structure of society and its cultural development conditioned thereby' while serving to develop class organization and solidarity.

In general, to the extent that ideological forms, such as law, are seen as expressions or embodiments of particular forms of social relations of production, the reform/revolution dichotomy holds good. Action on and through law alone cannot, as such, achieve or even contribute directly to social transformation of any fundamental kind. Social transformation depends on revolutionary transformation of production relations. Law is the 'form of social stability' of a given mode of production, 'the reflex of the real economic relations' (Cain and Hunt, eds., 1979: 53, 59). 'Revolutions are not made with laws' (Marx 1976: 915) but when forces and relations of production are in conflict it is in the ideological realm that people become conscious of this conflict and 'fight it out', as Marx's 1859 Preface to *A Contribution to the Critique of Political Economy* puts it (Cain and Hunt, eds., 1979: 52). Because law embodies actual social relations it is not 'mere' ideology—it can be a terrain of struggle, but the limits of this struggle are set by the theoretically pre-given functions of the legal institutions and forms.

This relatively consistent position in Marx's later writings is obscured only by the serious divergences between his views and those of Engels which are clearly demonstrated by Cain and Hunt's collation of the relevant texts. Engels's later writings indicate a clear 'relative autonomy' approach to the conceptualization of law. Law emerges, according to Engels, as the 'common rule' governing recurring acts of production, distribution, and exchange. It derives from the 'economic conditions of life' but with increasing societal complexity, a legal system develops its own complexity, and is serviced by professional lawyers who promote special modes of discourse. The link with economic conditions is broken in consciousness and law develops its 'autonomous' ideological self-justification in concepts of justice (Cain and Hunt, eds., 1979: 55). More significantly, Engels notes that in the modern state law must not only correspond to general economic conditions and express them but it must also be an internally coherent expression, lacking serious doctrinal and procedural contradictions (Cain and Hunt, eds., 1979: 57).

In terms not unlike those of Max Weber, Engels consistently stresses the role of legal professionals. The pressure towards internal coherence prevents law acting as the direct expression of economic development or the blunt expression of class interest. The systematic demands of law, promoted in part by its professional guardians, create a tension between legal form and economic relations. Further economic development produces 'repeated breaches' in the systematic structures of legal doctrine, creating contradictions in the body of civil law (Cain and Hunt, eds., 1979: 57). Legal form and economic relations thus exist in a tension which can give law independent effectiveness. In his letter to Bloch, Engels asserts that legal forms and theories exercise their influence in the course of historical struggles and 'in many cases determine their form in particular' (Cain and Hunt, eds., 1979: 56). This is an assertion that goes well beyond anything Marx will allow in these collected writings. For Engels, law as doctrine is the reflection of economic relations, an 'ideological outlook', yet it can influence the economic basis 'and may, within certain limits, modify it' (Cain and Hunt, eds., 1979: 57).

These differences of view between Marx and Engels, specifically related to law, are themselves only reflections of the wider divergence between Marx's and Engels' positions on ideology and the state. Does law constitute economic relations (Marx in *Kapital*), or is it the reflection of them (Engels)? Is ideology a matter of the apparent autonomy of fetishized forms (Marx), or of the relative autonomy of ideas originating in material conditions but developed (in humanistically interpreted processes) to influence action in ways not determined by these origins (Engels)? The extracts from both authors dealing with law as state repression are mainly disconnected items with little or no theoretical content. The theoretical problem of the relation of state and law remains open in these writings.

To say that there is no coherent and comprehensive theory of law in Marx's and Engels' work is to state the obvious. More important perhaps is the point that if Marx's planned work on law and state had ever been completed it would have torn asunder any appearance of unity in the theoretical positions of Marx and Engels and revealed contradictions which the specific problem of the theorization of law focuses with exceptional clarity. Further, it becomes possible to see that the most serious inadequacies of major Marxist theories of law are not the result of distortions or aberrations from the concepts of the classic texts of Marx and Engels. The ambiguities and limitations are written into those texts.

The point applies equally to the rigorous development by Pashukanis of a theory of law from the implications of Marx's writings on the fetishism of commodities, and to the construction of 'relative autonomy' conceptions of law by Nicos Poulantzas and others. In essence, the choice seems to be between some kind of excessively restricting economism (however sophisticated the means of hiding it), or a conception of a genuine sphere of autonomous legal effects which, following Engels, can only be interpreted in a manner that imports problematic humanist assumptions to justify an 'independent' development of ideology in law, as elsewhere. There seems no acceptable solution to the 'really difficult point' referred to in Marx's *Grundrisse*: 'how relations of production develop unevenly as legal relations' (Cain and Hunt, eds., 1979: 122).

Beyond Pashukanis

The essays in *Capitalism and the Rule of Law* (Fine *et al.*, eds., 1979) do not really break out of these difficulties of theorizing law in a manner that seems to reflect its now widely recognized significance as a focus of political action and a site of important political struggles. De Sousa Santos, however, in his paper 'Popular Justice, Dual Power and Socialist Strategy' (Santos 1979), makes a gallant try. In an interesting, but ultimately very inconclusive discussion of instances of popular justice in post-Caetano Portugal and of informal dispute resolution in squatter settlements in Rio (Brazil), he tries to suggest ways in which alternative popular conceptions of legality can be set up in competition with existing 'official' legal concepts and processes. But the conditions under which this is possible and under which such developments could effectively challenge established legal forms are related only to a pre-existing revolutionary situation and no general theory to guide political strategy in relation to legal processes emerges.

Popular justice strategies are no novelty. But what they seem ultimately to involve is a turning of the ideology of justice against itself by confronting the justice of the courtroom with parallel justice concepts, reinterpreting the individualist basis of legal justice between persons in class terms. Class responsibility, rather than the responsibility of the autonomous free and equal subject of law (that is, the individual legal person), is affirmed and the processes of established law are thrown into disarray by consistently reinterpreting the concepts of legal ideology in a manner related to, yet opposite in effect to, orthodox legal interpretations. The effect is a simultaneous *recognition* of law which makes it possible to fight on the terrain of legal ideology, and a consistent *challenge* to the content of this ideology which highlights its inconsistencies and ambiguities and reveals the political significance of 'common sense' techniques of legal reasoning.

Such strategies can only produce, if successful, a collapse of legality in confusion and a reduction of legal ideology to incoherence. They are essentially revolutionary legal strategies which are neither possible nor appropriate in societies where the state obtains powerful legitimation from democratic ideology and so 'popular justice' in confrontation with state justice is seen as a sectarian challenge to democratically sanctioned institutions.

Significantly, Santos' paper, concerned explicitly with special social and political conditions remote from those typical of advanced capitalist societies, stands out from the others in the *Capitalism and the Rule of Law* collection as the only one that specifically emphasizes strategies of political action through law. Several other papers contribute valuable analyses of the contradictions internal to legality as a form of social relations. Phil Cohen's excellent essay on 'Policing the Working Class City' (Cohen 1979) clearly demonstrates the practical dilemmas that are endemic in a police role requiring the promotion of both ideological and repressive aspects of law in social conditions that set these aspects of law in opposition to each other. Cohen clearly shows the variable penetration of legal ideology into working-class culture through specific historical studies and illustrates the tensions of a police commitment to 'law and order' in a context where order and legality (as 'justice according to rule') are not mutually compatible.

Sol Picciotto's 'The Theory of the State, Class Struggle and the Rule of Law' (Picciotto 1979), which is by far the most legally sophisticated of these papers, is also the only one of them to attempt a careful assessment of the limits that legal form puts on the possibilities of political struggle through law. Picciotto rightly stresses the individualism of law and legal processes which, particularly in such fields as industrial relations law, is a powerful means of fragmenting group solidarity. On the other hand (and in apparent opposition to Santos who, at least for short-term strategic reasons, would like to direct a concept of class responsibility against the notion of legal responsibility), Picciotto stresses that the establishment of the concept of strictly limited individual responsibility, especially in criminal law, was genuinely progressive and (presumably) is to be safeguarded.

The tensions in modern law that Picciotto identifies are well known to lawyers. They are tensions between generality and precision in formulation of laws; between, on the one hand, the liberal conception of the Rule of Law which requires that it be applicable to legal subjects in general who are equal before the law, and, on the other, the increasing requirement for more and more detailed legislation, statutory orders, and so on, identifying and specifically regulating particular situations, narrowly defined cases and particular categories of legal actors.

Picciotto relates these tensions to structural problems of advanced capitalism. The liberal Rule of Law provides the basis for the self-reproduction of capitalist social relations since law provides the structure of capitalist exchange. But increasingly this self-reproduction only remains possible because of ever more extensive state intervention to impose equivalence in exchange. This is necessarily particularist in orientation and operates in derogation of the ideological bases of the Rule of Law. The ideological contradictions are only partly cloaked by a kind of 'porosity' in the law enforcement process in which general rules are interpreted with 'a latitude or leeway of indeterminacy which essentially gives scope for the exercise of social or economic power' (Picciotto 1979: 175). As Picciotto notes, police powers in England and Wales today provide a classic example of this phenomenon, although whether there is anything very new about it is extremely doubtful. Nevertheless, Picciotto is undoubtedly right to point to the transformation of general codes of the liberal form of law into 'overblown regulatory systems', to the proliferation of tribunals and 'specific bureaucratic apparatuses', and to the erosion of principles of individual responsibility in certain key areas of private law as indications of very fundamental changes which have occurred in the forms of state regulation of social relations.

Three points need to be made here. First, although Picciotto's concern is to reveal internal contradictions in legal form, which simplistic invocations of the Rule of Law gloss over, these contradictions are not seen as opening up the possibility or necessity of major political strategies focused on law. The argument here, as in several of the *Capitalism and the Rule of Law* papers, is plainly against positions such as E. P. Thompson's which claim that the Rule of Law can be a check on the state and hence a political weapon because of the state's need to obtain the consent of the governed through the maintenance of ideological forms on which it relies.

Secondly, Picciotto's Marxism does not challenge any major formulations in Marx's classic texts and broadly adopts Pashukanis's conception of legal theory as the means of 'unmasking' law. 'Relative autonomy' theories are dismissed as useless to explain the apparent autonomy of legal form (Picciotto 1979: 168). But the problem of what to do about law once it has been unmasked remains. The only answer given is that it must be 'transcended, in forms which challenge the dominance of capitalist social relations' (1979: 177). What this means, or how such transcending is to be achieved, is never revealed. Nor is the matter even addressed. When Pashukanis wrote to broadly similar effect after the October 1917 Revolution he could justifiably believe that the transcending of legal forms was well under way but history proved him wrong. Today, however, there is no excuse for making the same mistakes again.

Thirdly, Picciotto seems to believe that the unmasking of the Rule of Law, as he interprets it, effectively removes questions of legality from the agenda of discussion. It is as though the characteristics of contemporary law in Britain and elsewhere that he identifies, which are undoubtedly of the greatest importance, are nevertheless all that there is in law to discuss. But both the historical phenomena of legal institutions and practices and the political problems of societies to which they are a response are too complex to be swept away in this manner. The question of the relevance of law for socialism remains an important one to be answered. Pashukanis may have authored a theory against law yet he at least reiterated in his writings the need to attack formlessness as well as formalism, to face up squarely to problems of formal political organization and mechanisms of administration and the constraints that the need for form may impose on action. (See Beirne and Sharlet, eds., 1980; Cotterrell, 1980.)

It is appropriate to invoke Pashukanis again here because the shadow of his economism hangs over much of the contents of the *Capitalism and the Rule of Law* collection and helps to explain why, despite frequent protestations of the importance of law by many authors, few propose political strategies centred on the contradictions or 'leeways' of legal form. In the papers by Bob Fine (Fine 1979) and Picciotto, Pashukanis is criticized on less than fundamental points: for concentrating solely on the basis of law in the field of circulation, and not taking note of the particularly significant juridicization of relations of production with the recognition of the unique commodity, labour-power. The general tenor of the criticism is that Pashukanis's position underemphasizes the class basis of law (Fine) or that it obscures important transformations in the development of capitalism by considering the undifferentiated general commodity form while ignoring changes in its application (Picciotto).

Fine's criticism really does not do justice to Pashukanis, whose point is that legal form has as a major part of its function the obscuring of its class basis, and hence contributes to the ideological conditions for perpetuation of class relations. Indeed 'defence of the so-called abstract foundations of the legal system is the most general form of defence of bourgeois class interests' (Pashukanis 1978: 39). Picciotto's point links with some of the important insights contributed by a closely linked series of papers by Richard Kinsey (1979), John Lea (1979), Dario Melossi (1979), and Roger Matthews (1979) which explore aspects of the development of capitalism and the changing nature of capitalist discipline and the agencies available to secure it, and so illuminate changing functions of law in the development of capitalism.

But it is left to Jeanne Gregory in a paper on sex discrimination legislation (Gregory 1979) to note that Pashukanis has little or nothing to say about details of administrative regulation in advanced capitalism where the relation of administrative discretion to legal form becomes a matter of major importance. And none of the authors in this collection faces up to the real problem left for them by Pashukanis and Marx: how to reconcile what appears to be their universally shared view—that law is theoretically important—with theory which appears to demonstrate, often with great sophistication and detailed legal analysis, that it is politically unimportant.

Beyond Althusser

Legal theory must be theory that confronts legal form in all its complexities, variety, ambiguities, and contradictions rather than reducing that form to the 'necessary' expression or embodiment of particular social relations. It must be theory that does not ossify legal analysis through the presupposition that the characteristics of law in all circumstances and conditions are fixed by its unchanging 'necessary' functions, pre-given by social theory. Legal theory requires a different approach from that which has prevailed in Marxist legal theory and which still prevails in the approaches of *Capitalism and the Rule of Law*.

It seemed at one time that the Marxist philosopher Louis Althusser's theoretical advances might contribute powerfully towards the solution of this and other problems in the analysis of ideological forms. As Paul Hirst points out in his *On Law and Ideology* (Hirst 1979a), Althusser's immense popularity as a theorist was based on his 'freeing' of ideology for analysis as a distinct form of social relations. Ideology was held by Althusser to be maintained by, and hence open to the possibility of transformation through, definite kinds of practice that could not be dissolved away theoretically into insignificance by classic economistic arguments. Hirst's articles on Althusser's theory of ideology and related questions of theory, which make up the first half of *On Law and Ideology*, are primarily significant in this context for their demonstration that the political promise of Althusser's theory cannot be fulfilled.

First, the requirements of the theory create a unity out of distinct and varied practices, as 'ideology', which diverts attention from the need for specific and not necessarily uniform strategies and modes of analysis with regard to these diverse practices. Secondly, Althusser's theory promotes a no less negative and politically limited view of appropriate strategies in the field of ideological social relations than do many earlier theories.

Althusser's structuralist conception of ideology presupposes that

a mode of production is a social totality furnishing within itself
the mechanisms of its self-renewal—the means of reproduction of
its structure. Ideology is a necessary 'instance' within this structure. Hence, Althusser's approach does not abolish the conception of 'necessary' functions of ideology; the nature of ideology in
all its forms is pre-given in theory. Strategies of transformation of
ideological social relations are, according to this approach, necessarily revolutionary and are, if progressive, bound to adopt an
oppositional, negative position with regard to the practices encompassed by Althusser's concept. The nature of these practices
and the appropriate strategies in relation to them are legislated in
advance by theory.

Bernard Edelman's often ponderous, sometimes appallingly
obscure, ill-organized and occasionally brilliant essays, translated
as *Ownership of the Image* (Edelman 1979), represent an attempt to
apply Althusserian approaches to the analysis of law. Edelman
struggles manfully with the difficulties of Althusser's conception
of ideology. He asserts that law is the 'site and the stake of class
struggle' (1979: 134), and what this seems to mean is that class
struggle is 'registered within the law' (1979: 130) so that, for
example, industrial relations law is 'none other than the registered, codified, and formalized victories of the working class' (1979:
131). Positive law marks the development of class struggle, but
reflects the process by which it is 'perpetually neutralized' (1979:
135) through the formulation of its results in terms of 'private
right'. Legal struggle thus involves (as with Pashukanis) the unmasking of law as ideological form but, whereas for Pashukanis
this is merely the means of dispensing with law in a society that
has no need of it, for Edelman 'catching out' law is a part of class
struggle itself.

Ideological struggle, in Edelman's view, can show the silences
and incoherences of legal discourse or the confusions and dilemmas of legal doctrinal development when the stark realities of
changing methods of capital accumulation break through the
tranquil, seemingly timeless, legal forms (as in his study of French
law's confrontation with the commercial development of photo-
graphy and the cinema). It can show the mechanisms by which
the relationship of political and private right is organized in law
to register and neutralize class struggle. It does this, for example,
by revealing legal doctrine dealing with a particularly difficult

problem of containment (as in Edelman's study of the problem of the election of Algerian workers to works committees).[1] In this way the calm surface of legal discourse can be disturbed to reveal tension points of capitalism which it seeks to hide, and law is unmasked so that the reality of the struggle to which it contributes is made clear.

Edelman's position is a serious and sophisticated one which, unlike any of the others discussed earlier in this chapter, calls for rigorous analysis of the developing patterns of legal doctrine with a lawyer's sensitivity to its shifting concepts and norms and a theorist's concern for the consistency of its frameworks of analysis. It does not matter that the doctrinal patterns that Edelman traces with regard to the French law of author's right have no direct counterpart in, for example, English copyright law. The example is used to illustrate a mode of analysis that can be applied to legal doctrine in any developed legal system. Nor does it matter particularly that the Althusserian concept of interpellation of subjects through the dual mirror effect (which, as Hirst has pointed out, is in any event merely an unsuccessful strategy to avoid epistemological problems) cannot easily be applied to the constitution of legal subjects. But it is important that Edelman's lengthy and sophisticated discussion of the development of the notion of a universal subject of law is concerned only with *human* legal subjects and, so like earlier Marxist legal theory, reduces law to a uniformity which misrepresents legal history and the complexities of law in contemporary capitalism.

The most important service that Hirst's *On Law and Ideology* performs for legal theory, apart from its immensely important clarifications of the limitations of Althusser's work and its careful explanation of the reductionism[2] and legal nihilism of Pashukanis, is to affirm that the legal subject or person is a more complex and varied component of legal discourse than Marxist legal theory has usually asssumed it to be. Edelman does not, however, *equate* human and legal personality, as Hirst suggests in his introduction to Edelman's book (Edelman 1979: 12). The legal subject in capitalism,

---

[1] For further examples of the application of Edelman's method of analysis see Edelman 1980.

[2] Reductionism, in this context, refers to the idea that the nature of law can be fully explained in terms of some other specific phenomena; e.g., economic processes, relationships, or conditions.

for Edelman, is an abstraction constructed from certain postulated characteristics. These do not necessarily have to be recognized as paralleling actual human characteristics (although they are frequently inspired by humanistic assumptions). For Edelman, the characteristics of the legal subject are given by the ideological functions of law.

In Edelman's sophisticated account the universal legal subject of capitalism possesses the faculties of its human locus, but remains an abstraction separate from them. Hence it can alienate all or any of them (as with the sale of labour power) and yet remain itself—free—as long as it retains the freedom to regain these faculties. 'Everything can be sold, except the subject-in-itself. Man is free' (Edelman 1979: 187). Edelman's conception of the individual legal subject is not given, as Pashukanis' is, by the requirements of the commodity form. It is formed in the transition between modes of production registered in ideology and identifiable, in Edelman's work, through a comparison of ideological developments reflected in Kant's and Hegel's writings on legal right.

To face Edelman squarely with the consequences of Althusserianism, however, we must say plainly that, for him, the legal subject is given by *the functions assigned to legal ideology* by the structure of the social totality of the capitalist mode of production. Thus, despite the real possibilities of sophisticated and critical theorization of legal doctrine which Edelman opens up, fundamental aspects of legal form remain pre-given by theory, which accepts all ideology as having a 'necessary' function and an unchanging universal character. The conception of the legal subject is one of these pre-given elements.

Historically, however, law has recognized numerous kinds of legal subjects with many different statuses. Hirst writes extensively in *On Law and Ideology* of one of the most important legal subjects in advanced capitalism, the joint stock company. The origins of this subject of law, whose significance for advanced capitalism can hardly be exaggerated,[3] are not easily traced to the direct effect of

---

[3] Although neither Hirst nor any of the other authors discussed in this ch. mentions it, there is an extensive literature on the doctrinal theory of corporate legal personality, and the political significance of legal characterizations of corporate entities has long been recognized in this literature. See e.g. Hallis 1930 and Maitland 1900.

changing forms or relations of production, still less to certain 'ideological needs' of the capitalist mode of production. And it is possible to add numerous other legal subjects appearing in the history of legal doctrine—for example, idols,[4] funds, animals, and various types of corporate entities—which are constructed in legal ideology for reasons that deserve analysis and are neither easily reduced to the necessary consequences of economic conditions acting consistently to determine the forms and effects of legal institutions and practices, nor usefully explained away by Althusserian functionalism.[5]

Edelman's legal strategy and its justifications are not to be dismissed. His represents one of the few attempts in Marxist legal theory to treat law seriously as a form of discourse and a set of practices with distinctive characteristics. There are vague but interesting statements in *Ownership of the Image* about the relationship between legal and political ideology and its potential tensions, and also about the distinctiveness of legal ideology. But to the extent that Edelman tries to escape the constraints on legal analysis produced by a conception of necessary pre-given functions of legal ideology derived from Althusserian theory, his analyses tend to be conducted entirely within legal doctrine. The world outside the courtroom tends to disappear. And even the legal agencies through which the doctrine is produced seem to fade from sight.

This is legalism with a vengeance, even if in the service of critical theory. The conditions under which legal institutions exist; the conditions under which law is promulgated and enforced; the conditions that determine how and when particular claims are raised in legal practice; even the realities of courtroom procedures—these are not discussed in any detail. Yet however much legal theory demands attention to the detail of law as doctrine, it cannot isolate law from the conditions that give rise to it, the institutions that support it, and from a careful assessment of the economic, political, and ideological significance of its varied practices in particular historical circumstances.

---

[4] See *Pramatha Nath Mullick* v. *Pradyumna Kumar Mullick* (1925) LR 52 Ind. App. 245.

[5] Functionalism here refers to the idea that particular social phenomena—e.g. ideology—are to be understood in terms of their necessary or constant social functions, which can be deduced theoretically.

Taking Law Seriously in Social Theory

If we seek an approach to the analysis of a set of practices and institutions, such as those centred on law, that sets out to analyse them rigorously with the aim of facilitating strategies of action taking full account of the distinctiveness and possible variety of those practices and institutions and without prejudging them as having 'necessary' functions and effects, there is no doubt that any theory that imports reductionism in any form threatens such aims. Althusser's Marxism is an attempt to minimize reductionism while retaining the ultimate Marxist ontological primacy of the 'economy' within a social totality that is the essential object of analysis for Marxism as science.

But there is equally no doubt that to avoid reductionism in any form, and to open up the possibility of the kind of analysis described above, entails a rejection of Althusserian functionalism and of a whole tradition of Marxist theory. This is the position Paul Hirst has arrived at (Hirst 1979a). A rejection of any concept of 'totality' frees discourses and practices from any theoretical necessity for their interdependence. The need for political strategy and for the means of calculating it, which was in any event the reason for challenging the edifice of Marxist theory in the first place, then becomes the explicitly recognized sole guide for, and test of, the utility of theoretical practice.

It is presumably too soon to assess exactly where such an approach will lead. As a kind of intellectual scorched-earth policy, involving a refusal to fight on the terrain of epistemology at all, it counters all charges of uncontrollable relativism with the answer that these are epistemological attacks on epistemological positions that have been vacated (see especially McLennan 1978; Hirst 1979a: 19–21). Hirst's positions go well beyond what is necessary merely to counter the rigidities of economism and functionalism. But anything less than his radical position on epistemology would leave him open to the charge that his rejection of classical Marxist concepts is made possible only by adopting objectives and perspectives of already existing non-Marxist social theory. His rejection of epistemology allows him to distance himself from the specific problematics of virtually *all* prior theory.

For Hirst, analysis of law means analysis of certain forms of discourse and certain institutionalized practices, their consequences, and their conditions of existence. There can be no quarrel with this. And when he asserts, contrary to what both Marxist and non-Marxist legal theory normally claims, that law has no 'essence', this assertion is justifiable in so far as it denies that there is a universal essential nature and function of law in the sense given by either Pashukanis's economism or Althusserian structuralism (see Hirst 1979a: 111 ff.). But the problem which Hirst's position leaves is that which legal theory has wrestled with throughout its history. How should the object of analysis (law) be conceptualized? Forms of discourse, institutions, and practices need to be theoretically identified as 'legal' unless the needs of political calculation require only a pragmatic labelling of contemporary practices as the basis for conceptualization.

That this latter is not Hirst's position is made clear by his recent clarification (and modification?) (Hirst 1979b: 443–5) of the views on historical analysis set out in *Pre-Capitalist Modes of Production* (Hindess and Hirst 1975: 308 ff.). He recognizes that 'the present' and 'the past' are arbitrary and impossible categorizations for the purposes of theory. The problem of conceptualizing law, in a manner that makes references across legal history (and across societies) possible, remains, therefore, a matter not to be dismissed.

Hirst ridicules the explanatory significance of any concept of 'legality' in *On Law and Ideology*, but the idea of law as the enterprise of subjecting human conduct to the governance of rules entails that rules themselves have certain formal characteristics, canons of interpretation, procedural preconditions, conditions of application, and so on, which, if not present, make the concept of rules of conduct more or less incoherent. In these aspects of rules lies the germ of a concept of legality which is of relevance in theorizing law. Significantly, in a later paper, Hirst has accepted that the idea of rules is a central element of what he considers an appropriate concept of law (Hirst 1980), but the implications of this position, which demand a much deeper analysis than he attempts of fundamental issues explored in the literature of legal theory, are not developed.

Like all approaches to theory, Hirst's must ultimately justify itself in terms of the new methods of analysis and new insights into problems that it offers. *On Law and Ideology* is essentially a polemical, ground-clearing book less concerned with mapping out new paths in detail than with demonstrating that old ones lead nowhere. Hirst thinks there is no reason to believe that the institutions and practices that Althusser calls ideological state apparatuses cannot be changed, by strategies grounded in rigorous theoretical analysis of the nature of those institutions and practices, and in a manner that exceeds capitalist limits. And the 'effect of such reforms and changes on wider social relations is not given and could be very radical indeed' (Hirst 1979a: 15). The reform/revolution dichotomy is finally, and at the cost of a rejection of most of the body of Marxist theory, transcended.

At the level of theory there is clearly no way of testing or justifying Hirst's claim. But equally the Althusserian opposite position reduces to mere assertion. The nature of 'capitalist limits' is, in any event, unclear. Hirst at least opens up again the possibility of a critical legal theory that takes law seriously as an object of analysis. But as the furious controversies surrounding his works and those of his colleagues demonstrate, the exact status of theory that transcends the inadequacies Hirst attacks is far from clear.

Ultimately the limitations and the appropriate conditions of existence of all theory are revealed with brutal clarity by these controversies. Theory exists merely to serve the specific ends for which it is created. And social theory depends for its utility not merely on its capacity to structure analyses of social phenomena in a manner that offers politically relevant conceptualizations of what appear as dominant characteristics of contemporary societies. Its value depends also on its capacity to guide and indicate practical strategies of action in present conditions and to minimize the closing off of avenues of change and influence through excessively rigid theoretical characterizations of the nature and functions of social forms and practices. The history of the development of Marxist legal theory has merely paralleled the history of the process of coming to terms with these conditions of theoretical practice, in the development of Marxist theory as a whole.

7 Legality and Legitimacy: The Sociology of Max Weber

Max Weber's writings from the early years of the twentieth century provide a further tradition of classic social theory related to law. Weber's views on law are best understood in relation to his general analysis of types of political authority. His sociology of law provides essential material for understanding the social and political significance of various types of legal thought even though it does not attempt to develop a general conception and analysis of legal ideology. Weber contributes powerfully to legal theory by examining the social importance of legal formality, but he fails to establish conclusively what the relationship between law and values in contemporary society is, or might be.

Some years ago A. P. D'Entrèves wrote that the relation between legality and political legitimacy—that is, the successful assertion by holders of power of their 'title' to rule and 'right' to be obeyed—'finds no place among the topics normally discussed by jurists' (D'Entrèves 1967: 142). Times have changed, however, and when the authority of law and state seems ever more problematic as a practical matter it presents itself as a theoretical issue not only in the perennial forms of political philosophy but in the changing elaborations in legal reasoning of ideas of sovereignty and the Rule of Law and in increasingly pressing sociological inquiries into the bases of power in society and the structure of the modern state.

Max Weber, 'the greatest of German sociologists' (Aron 1964: 67) and, with Marx, the major founder of twentieth century sociological analyses of capitalist development and its conditions and consequences provided, amongst other elements of his political sociology, a conceptual framework for systematic analysis of the role of law in securing political legitimacy. The significance of this conceptual framework lies partly in the fact that it reflects and promotes a view of legality and legitimacy that has been profoundly influential in the development of sociology of law (cf. Treves 1974: 203) and in modern political and legal theory. But, in addition, its key concept, that of *legal domination*, is elaborated in the context of Weber's important analyses of the character of modern law and of the sociological significance of legal history, as well as his detailed studies of the development of the modern state. Thus, in Weber's writings, the relationships between law and power are analysed with the combination of a lawyer's insights into the character of legal ideas and a great sociologist's synthesizing vision of patterns of economic, political, and social development in history. This chapter examines Weber's theoretical contribution in this area.

Weber's Project

If, as D'Entrèves suggests (1967: 142), the word 'legitimacy' sounds rather obsolete today this is because it is a term associated with the deliberate elaboration of ideologies to support or question the claims of political authority. Today we seek to look at ideology 'from the outside', considering from a sociological point of view the importance of its content in securing the social conditions for the exercise of power. We seek knowledge of the conditions under which ideologies develop, are sustained, and disintegrate because of the sociological and politically practical significance of this knowledge. Hence, while moral and other evaluations of claims to legitimacy are far from unimportant, the conditions of legitimacy are a matter for sociological analysis as well. In modern terms this matter is part of the study of structures of ideology and their social significance.

Weber's analysis of legitimate domination remains one of the most important and detailed *sociological* studies of political legitimacy and, coupled with studies that make up his sociology of law, it provides at least a starting point for modern analysis of the ideological importance of law. For these reasons the concept of legal domination in Weber's writings is one that any rigorous contemporary social theory of law must confront.

Like all Weber's other fundamental concepts for social analysis, legal domination is an ideal type; in other words, a conceptualization that is not a generalization from experience but a logically formulated idea intended as a useful basis for constructing models of socio-historical development and social processes with the aid of which data from experience can be interpreted. The concept of legal domination does not, therefore, imply a description of actual historical circumstances—for example, those in which modern states exist in developed capitalist societies. Nevertheless, in Weber's view, structures of authority in complex industrial societies have come to approximate more and more the type of legal domination. The form of legitimacy that it represents has become the essential meaning content of the sociological fact of acceptance of authority in modern societies.

In essence therefore, the claim that the concept of legal domination allows Weber to make is that political domination, the system of political rule, in modern states obtains its legitimacy from the existence of a system of rationally made legal rules, which designate powers of command exercisable in accordance with the rules. The rules specify also the procedure and the agency by which they may be altered. Authority is recognized in so far as it is exercised in accordance with the requirements of these rules. And, in Weber's view, this form of legitimacy is the essential basis of all stable authority in modern society—in large business enterprises no less than in agencies of state administration. Rationally created and systematically ordered rules officially define the scope of power and provide its legitimacy.

The importance of this conception of legitimacy is in what it deliberately excludes. In Weber's view, in order to understand political legitimacy under conditions of legal domination it is not necessary to evaluate the *content* of the law. The existence of law—in particular conditions and in a particular form—provides its own ideological basis whatever its substantive content. And the action of the state, in accordance with law, derives legitimacy from law. Legal domination does not, therefore, depend on the law's reflection of values to which those who accept its legitimacy are committed. As long as state action conforms to legal requirements it can adopt any policies or reflect any values without disturbing the basis of its legitimacy.

In an important sense legal domination is self-sustaining. Having no dependence on fluctuating value choices it relies only on the formally rational character of its legal basis. Under legal domination, society is governed essentially by technological choices, not ideological ones. Moral criticism cannot shake the fundamental basis of law's legitimacy. Whatever its content, law's rational, systematic character gives it the continuing ability successfully to claim obedience. In modern societies, the relationship between legality and legitimacy is, therefore, one of virtual identity. Law not only provides the technical apparatus for exercise of state power but also the ideological foundation of authority.

The relations of law and legitimacy were far from unexplored when Weber wrote at the beginning of the twentieth century. They are a recurrent theme in the history of legal and political theory and, in particular, in the history of natural law theory, a topic that exerted endless fascination for Weber (see Honigsheim 1968: 53) and one that the elaboration of his concept of legal domination required him to confront. Weber's treatment of the relationship between legality and legitimacy is particularly important because of its sociological, rather than philosophical, treatment of the question of legitimacy and because it is supported by the important insights of his sociology of law which clarify the sociological conditions under which law can provide political legitimacy and the historical conditions that have favoured the particular form of law associated with legal domination.

In considering the relation of law and legitimacy we are considering one aspect of the ideological significance of law, and it will be argued here that Weber's analysis of legal domination takes us some way towards an understanding of the functions of legal ideology even though the conceptual structure of his sociology and the ideal type method could not provide the basis for an adequate analysis.

Legitimate Domination

Power, in the most general sense of the possibility of imposing one's will on the behaviour of others, can exist in the most diverse forms. Within this diversity Weber identifies two broad categories of domination (*Herrschaft*): domination by virtue of a constellation of *interests*, such as that by which a monopolist, or partial monopolist, dominates trading conditions in the market; and domination by virtue of authority, involving power of command and duty to obey (Weber 1978: 943). Although one form of domination can shade into the other and both are inevitably present in social life,[1] their analytical separation is a consequence of the conceptual framework of Weber's sociology. Sociology for him is concerned with the understanding of social action; that is, behaviour subjectively meaningful to the actor and which takes into account experience of, or expectations of, the conduct of others. Weber's sociology is predicated on the ability of individual actors to choose courses of conduct. Power in the sense of market domination can be considered, in Weber's terms, *conceptually* as no more than a cluster of considerations that the dominated actor takes into account in choosing a course of action.

Domination may however operate in a different way. It may operate not merely as part of the calculation on the basis of which actors choose a course of action but as an actual overriding of their independent will so that their 'conduct to a socially relevant degree occurs as if [they] . . . had made the content of the command [addressed to them] the maxim of their conduct for its very own sake . . . this situation will be called *obedience*' (Weber 1978: 946). In so far as the actors' wills are overborne their behaviour cannot be analysed without considering the specific reasons why they submit themselves to the will of another. To the extent that they do so submit themselves voluntarily they recognize the legitimacy of the domination exercised over them. What is involved here is thus a form of relationship in which the behaviour of the dominated is, at least partially, explicable only in terms of the social action of *submission*—and continued submission—of will to the source of command. As Paul Hirst has shown, it is the necessary logical consequence of the structure of Weber's sociology that the behaviour of the dominated becomes invisible to this sociology in so far as domination is accepted by them as legitimate and their conduct is determined by it (Hirst 1976: 87). They cease to be individuals attaching subjective meaning to freely chosen courses of action. Their behaviour choices are made for them.

The concept of *legitimate* domination is thus an essential one in Weber's sociology. Systems of domination, in so far as they are stabilized, depend on effective claims to legitimacy and all such claims, Weber argues, can be analysed in terms of three types: charismatic domination, traditional domination, and legal

---

[1] Weber (1978: 951) explicitly denies the possibility of popular democracy in normal conditions for reasons that are familiar in the tradition of 'élite theory' in political sociology.

domination. The first two are forms of personal authority. *Charismatic authority* 'is the authority of the extraordinary and personal *gift of grace* ... the absolutely personal devotion and personal confidence in revelation, heroism, or other qualities of individual leadership', the leadership of the prophet, the elected warlord, the plebiscitarian ruler, the great demagogue, or the political party leader (Gerth and Mills, eds., 1948: 79). *Traditional authority* is that of 'the "eternal yesterday", i.e. of the mores sanctified through the unimaginably ancient recognition and habitual orientation to conform': the authority of the patriarch and the patrimonial prince (Gerth and Mills, eds., 1948: 79). Obedience is founded on the sacredness 'of that which is customary and has always been so and prescribes obedience to some particular person' (Weber 1978: 954).

In contrast to these personal forms of legitimate domination stands the impersonal authority of *legal domination*. Here the 'validity' of a power of command is expressed:

in a system of consciously made *rational* rules (which may be either agreed upon or imposed from above), which meet with obedience as generally binding norms whenever such obedience is claimed by him whom the rule designates. In that case every single bearer of powers of command is legitimated by that system of rational norms, and his power is legitimate in so far as it corresponds with the norm. Obedience is thus given to the norms rather than to the person. (Weber 1978: 954)

Each of these legitimations of domination is associated with a *structure* of domination: patriarchalism in traditional domination, the rule of the personal charismatic leader in charismatic domination and, under legal domination, the typical structure of domination is *bureaucracy*.

Law as the Basis of Legitimacy in the Modern State

What exactly is the nature of the belief that sustains *law* as the basis of legitimacy under legal domination? What attributes does law possess that enable it to fulfil this role in providing ideological, and not merely repressive, support for domination? We can try to answer these questions, first, by drawing inferences from the logic of Weber's concepts, secondly, by reference to the historical conditions of the development of the state and, thirdly, by examining Weber's analysis of the character of modern law.

The Relationships between Ideal Types

The first of these approaches leads to ambiguities which have engaged the attention of commentators and which are centrally important in the analysis of legal domination. The social action that involves individuals in submitting their wills by accepting a power of command exercisable over them is the basis of legitimate domination. The subjective meaning of this action for the actor who performs it is, presumably, capable of analysis in the manner in which, according to Weber, all social action is understandable: by means of four ideal types of action which underlie the whole of his sociology. Weber explains that action may be *purpose rational*, that is, oriented towards the achievement of the actor's own rationally desired and considered aims. Secondly, it may be *value rational*, that is, undertaken without reference to any aim but because of a belief in the worth of the action in itself, measured against some system of values or ideals. Thirdly, action may be determined *affectually*, by feelings and emotions and, fourthly, it may be *traditionally* oriented, 'determined by ingrained habituation' (Weber 1978: 25).

There is only a partial correlation between the types of social action available for analysis of the act of submission to authority and the types of legitimate domination. The third and fourth types of action correspond with charismatic and traditional domination. But how does legal domination relate to the remaining first and second types of action? Is the act of submission purpose rational, value rational, or a combination of both, or can it be of either type?

This ambiguity is perhaps partly resolved by yet another scheme of typifications which Weber provides in the schematic outline of his fundamental sociological concepts set out at the beginning of his posthumously published work, *Economy and Society*. Here he provides a four-fold typification of the bases of legitimacy of orders (1978: 36 ff.). Legitimacy may be based, first, on *tradition*, secondly, on *affectual* attitudes, thirdly, on a rational belief in the absolute *value* of the order and, fourthly, because the order has been established in a manner recognized to be *legal*. This strongly suggests that, in Weber's view, the acceptance of legality as the basis of legitimacy is to be understood as an act of submission whose subjective meaning for the actor is *purpose rational*, that is, not in any way oriented to acceptance of values but to a calculation of necessary means to the actor's rationally chosen purposes. Although attempts have been made to argue that, in fact, Weber's concept of legal domination implies the acceptance of certain values as he formulates it, the argument seems hard to sustain (see Bendix 1959: 419; Beetham 1985: 265; Mommsen 1974: 86; Habermas 1976a: 99–100).

It seems reasonable to suppose that the final formulation of the three pure types of legitimate domination deliberately excludes the possibility of value rationality as a general basis for acceptance of the legitimacy of domination, not merely because of sociological insights derived from study of the development of the modern state, modern forms of law, and the fate of natural law—all of which we shall consider shortly—but also because the three-fold typification is adequate to cover all forms of submission to authority as legitimate if legal domination is taken to be based on purpose rational submission.

Weber's use of concepts implies that value adherence is, in itself, too vague, variable, uncertain, and scientifically impenetrable to be recognized sociologically as a basis of legitimacy. Ultimately adherence is to the will of persons whose authority is accepted for reasons that may or may not include commitment to the values espoused by or associated with those persons; or adherence is to an order that commands allegiance irrespective of its value orientations and because its structure provides an accepted basis for fulfilment of the purpose rational activities of those subject to it. Weber's sociology of law has as its primary objective the explanation of, first, how modern law *does* provide this basis through its formal rationality and, secondly, what economic, political, and other conditions have promoted a historical development of law that has made this possible.

The Development of the Modern State

Weber defines a state as 'a human community that (successfully) claims the monopoly of the legitimate use of physical force within a given territory' (Gerth and Mills, eds., 1948: 78). Historically, defence of, and forcible dominion over, a territory and its inhabitants have often been maintained not by a single (political) community but by several, for example kinship groups, neighbourhood associations, warrior fraternities, or religious organizations. In

Weber's view, the existence of a separate political community is indicated by communal action, with physical force available to support it, regulating interrelations of inhabitants of a territory in matters not restricted to satisfaction of common economic needs (Weber 1978: 901–2). Various main conditions established the steadily increasing dominance of the political community and created the idea of its legitimacy based in *rational order*. These were the ability of the community to apply coercion (including its power to determine life or death), its gradual permanent institutionalization allowing for the development of a rational order for the administration of coercion, and the constant emergence of new or more complex forms of social and economic interests requiring protection and able to obtain it only through the 'rationally regulated guarantees which none but the political community was able to create' (1978: 904).

This belief 'in the specific legitimacy of political action can, and under modern conditions actually does, increase to a point where only certain political communities, *viz.*, the "states", are considered to be capable of "legitimizing", by virtue of mandate or permission, the exercise of physical coercion by any other community' (1978: 904). The modern state is characterized by the highest development of the rational order on which its legitimacy is based, so that it has broken free of dependence on personal traditional ties of authority as the basis of stability. This state 'in the sense of a political association with a rational, written constitution, rationally ordained law, and an administration bound to rational rules or laws, administered by trained officials' is specifically the consequence of the unique patterns of cultural development of the West (Weber 1927: ch. 29; Weber 1930: 16–17). Legitimacy based substantially on *law* is thus the consequence of particular historical developments.

Of crucial importance is the idea that the legitimacy of the state centres on the *exclusion of arbitrariness* in the exercise of power. While the evaluation of state policies and the advocacy of values and interests that should be reflected in state action may be infinitely various among those whose allegiance the state claims, it increasingly depends for its 'title' to rule on the rationality of exercise of power through formally structured rules. Equally important historically is the fact that the increasing complexity of state administration demands the highest technical forms of administrative organization, and ensures the state's eventual total dependence on a form of administration organized on the basis of a system of formally logical rules. Ultimately the requirements of legitimacy and the requirements of administrative organization combine in the same demand: for a legal order based on what can be called, following Weber's terminology, formal logical legal rationality.

Formal Legal Rationality

Weber's definition of law is in terms of an order (not necessarily a set of rules) guaranteed by agencies of enforcement. Law is *rational* to the extent that its operation is guided by general rules, rather than by subjective reaction to the individual case (empirical law finding) or by irrational formal means such as oracles and ordeals. But legal rationality may be understood in terms of two contrasting types. *Substantively rational law* is guided by general rules determined by the principles of an ideological system other than the law itself: for example, ethics, religion, or political values. *Formally rational law* is guided by general rules in such a manner that 'in both substantive and procedural matters, only unambiguous general characteristics of the facts of the case are taken into account'. Legally relevant characteristics of the case may be formally determined either by reference to rigidly stipulated tangible requirements, for example certain forms of words spoken or written, a signature, and so on, or, in the case of *formal logical legal rationality*, 'the legally relevant characteristics of the facts are disclosed through the logical analysis of meaning and . . . accordingly, definitely fixed legal concepts in the form of highly abstract rules are formulated and applied' (Weber 1978: 657).

In general, the *process* of rationalization in legal development can take two forms: first, *generalization*, the synthetic construction of general conceptualizations of legal relations by determining which aspects of a typical situation or course of action are to be considered legally relevant and in what logical manner the aspects are to be linked in legal analysis; and, secondly, *systematization*, which only appears 'in late stages of legal modes of thought' and, as understood in modern law, involves 'an integration of all analytically derived legal propositions in such a way that they constitute a logically clear, internally consistent, and, at least in theory, gapless system of rules, under which, it is implied, all conceivable fact situations must be capable of being logically subsumed lest their order lack an effective guarantee' (1978: 656).

The important point to note about these processes—generalization of concepts and systematization—is that both can be purely 'internal' orderings and developments of legal material carried out through the use of a logic that does not demand guidance from 'external' interest claims, codes of values, or political policies. This is so even though, historically, the tendencies towards generalization and systematization have, Weber argues, been promoted by the needs of the developing state and also by the demands of particular groups, particularly those interested in the development of the market and in security of economic transactions.

The synthetic construction of legal concepts through generalization does not necessarily produce systematization of law. The two rational processes are essentially separate and, indeed, in many legal systems have been to some extent incompatible. Legal domination depends on a *legal order* that is internally consistent and therefore provides a total, self-sufficient code to specify unambiguous criteria of legitimacy (that is, lawfulness) of action in whatever context legitimacy might be challenged. Ultimately a 'gapless', unambiguous legal order makes questions of legitimacy purely *technical* and politically uncontroversial. Thus, systematization is the key process of rationalization for the creation of such a legal order. And systematization, in such a manner as to create a self-sufficient internally coherent legal order which can be seen as providing its own 'internal' rational justification and hence a self-contained basis for political legitimacy, is only possible when the dominant mode of legal thought utilized in organizing the material of law is formal logical legal rationality.

Alan Hunt remarks that Weber 'makes the leap' of associating formal logical legal rationality with legal domination and adds: 'the danger in so doing is that it obscures the relationship between the two different theoretical constructs which then tend to be used interchangeably' (Hunt 1978: 115). But the association of these concepts is dictated by the logic of Weber's scheme of analysis. For Weber, *substantive* legal rationality—the development and interpretation of law by reference to ethical or other systems of values existing 'outside' the law itself, leads to forms of law which, if they are systematic, are so only because of the common reference points of all the rules in external values. Such law derives the systematic interrelationship of its rules not from their intrinsic logical interconnections but from their common orientation to an outside value source. In such a system it is clear that law itself cannot provide legitimacy for domination. Legitimacy will depend on affectual or traditional attachment to the value source which it reflects.[2] Thus a charismatic basis of legitimacy may ensure the authority attaching to the revelations of a prophet, the natural law invocations of a judge, or the will of a political leader.[3]

Legal domination presupposes the dominance of formal logical legal rationality in the legal order on which it is based. Weber remarks that every system of law is based on either formal or substantive principles of organization of legal precepts (Weber 1927: 342). Formal and substantive legal rationality are ultimately in perpetual opposition to each other. The development of the systematization of law necessary to support legal domination *necessarily* makes it quite impossible for the law to reflect consistently any set of ultimate ethical, political, or other values. Rational order and technical precision are the only values that could conceivably be attributed to modern law as the basis of its capacity to provide legitimacy for the actions of the state. Otherwise modern law exists in an environment characterized by the 'rationally irresoluble pluralism of competing value systems and beliefs' (see Jaspers 1965; Habermas 1976a: 100).

The rational formalization of law which is so important to legal domination has come about in a long process of historical development and through a unique combination of factors arising in Western civilization. Weber stresses the importance of Roman law (not as regards its content but as regards its formal reasoning), the early influence of the Christian church in promoting formalization and a separation of secular law and religion, the intellectual concerns of the jurists of the continental European universities, and the alliance between rulers and jurists to make good the claims of the modern state to power and the suppression

---

[2] In other words, charismatic or traditional domination. Hence attempts to argue for a fourth category of legitimate domination—based on a belief in the validity of ultimate values—seem to miss the point of Weber's analysis (cf. Spencer 1970; and see Albrow 1972).

[3] See the discussion of the 'charisma of reason' in Roth and Schluchter 1979: ch. 3.

of competing sources of authority. The claims of the developing state could only be fulfilled through rational administration which, in turn, presupposed rational, calculable law. Finally, at all times economic interests have pressed for security and they gradually sought calculable law to guarantee the growing complexity of market relations. Hence at a certain crucial historical conjuncture bourgeois interests pressed on law similar demands for formalization and predictability to those that arose from the state's need for rational administration.

The Twilight of Natural Law

The fourth type of legitimation originally mentioned by Weber— orientation to ultimate values—was quite clearly included by him primarily to deal with the historical significance for political legitimacy of the idea of natural law. Weber's discussion of natural law shows that for him its significance was as a unique ideological development in particular historical circumstances and not as an example of a typologically distinct basis of legitimacy. As he makes clear, it is an example of *charismatic* transformation.[4] But the discussion of natural law is important because it leads us towards more general problems of the analysis of legal ideology which Weber's method of conceptualization cannot confront. Also, because of its marginality within the conceptual framework of the analysis of legitimate domination, it shows why the pure types of legitimate domination cannot ultimately provide a sufficient basis for analysis of legal ideology and its sociological significance.

Natural law seemed to Weber to be the only form of consistent value orientation that could be coherently elaborated to provide basic ideals of a system of rational law. To the extent that natural law embodied 'reason' it could be consistent with the demand of reason for consistency and systematization within a legal system. Secular natural law allowed the systematic promotion of values in legal form contributing towards the generalization of contract as a legal concept and uniform conceptions of legal liberties and responsibility.

---

[4] See Weber's closely related discussion of democratic ideologies in terms of the ideal type of charismatic domination (Weber 1978: 266 ff.).

These characteristics allow Weber to draw a distinction between formal and substantive natural law, the former contributing towards rationalization of law through conceptual generalization reflecting individualistic values. Natural law in this form developed from a variety of intellectual sources including religious influences from the rationalistic non-conformist sects, English ideas of inherent rights traceable back to the symbol of Magna Carta, the concept of nature of the Renaissance and, mainly, the rationalistic enlightenment of the seventeenth and eighteenth centuries. But no reference to material sources is made in Weber's general discussion of the origins of this form of ideology. He writes that natural law is the 'specific and only consistent type of legitimacy of a legal order which can remain once religious revelation and the authoritarian sacredness of a tradition and its bearers have lost their force' (Weber 1978: 867). Yet, in his view, it has not remained and positive law has become its own justification.

When Weber wrote, formal natural law had given place to many varieties of substantive natural law making substantive demands for justice through law that were incompatible with the formal, individualistic principles of earlier natural law. Socialist theories contributed in particular to this development. More generally, Weber writes:

In consequence of both juridical rationalism and modern intellectual scepticism in general, the axioms of natural law have lost all capacity to provide the fundamental basis of a legal system . . . The disappearance of the old natural law conceptions has destroyed all possibility of providing the law with a metaphysical dignity by virtue of its immanent qualities. In the great majority of its most important provisions, it has been unmasked all too visibly, indeed, as the product or the technical means of a compromise between conflicting interests. (1978: 874–5)

Thus the 'charisma of reason' has passed and the basis of the legitimacy of the modern capitalist state has approximated more and more to the pure type of legal domination. This is not merely the consequence of the historical development of rational law through the activities of jurists and others combining the satisfaction of professional intellectual needs for systematization and generalization with the accommodation of demands from the state and bourgeois interests. The modern state cannot, in Weber's view, derive stable authority either from tradition or charisma. Natural law, in his analysis, has been an agency of change and development of major significance. Yet its changeability and controversy make it quite unable to provide a stable basis of legitimacy. It infused new ideas and values into the rationalizing Western law, which became stable through processes of formalization with which natural law had only temporarily and incidentally been allied. As it developed in new forms, natural law challenged the formal qualities of law and hence parted company with the essential foundations of legal domination.

For Weber, legal domination is the *essential* foundation of the bureaucratic administration on which not only the modern state but also modern capitalism depends. Bureaucracy is technically superior to any other form of administration and, in Weber's view, it is the only form suitable for managing the complexities of modern societies. Hence Weber's clear opinion is that natural law cannot emerge again as a unified system of values to reshape the law in a manner that sets it free from its ever more formal and systematic qualities and leads it according to systematic value-rational principles.[5] Thus, only at a certain point in history did the substantively rational ideas of 'reason' in natural law coincide with the requirements of systematization in Western law.

Natural law is the only form of 'legal ideology' Weber recognizes. Its historical importance and relatively coherent and systematic value orientation at particular times in Western history tempted him to provide a specific place for it in his typology of legitimacy. Yet its transience convinced Weber quite properly that it could

---

[5] It is relevant to note here that, particularly in the late 19th century, the anti-absolutist tendencies of natural law had been effectively dissolved away in German thought, so that the state was made to appear the guardian of liberties rather than their potential enemy. 'Natural law lost its status as an independent source of social norms. Positive law was redefined as an offshoot or an ally of eternal ethical principles. The idealized state became a moral agent, an educational institution, and the freedom from external restraint was transformed into the inner freedom of the ethically self-directed individual' (Ringer 1969: 114; and see Troeltsch 1934: 214). This view of natural law which sees it *absorbed* into the conception of the modern state rather than discarded, and which was current in Weber's time, suggests why for him the idea of a significant revival of natural law seemed untenable. The modern state, seen from this viewpoint, has superseded natural law and in absorbing it has drawn strength from it. Hence the conception of the German *Rechtsstaat* which is reflected in Weber's concept of legal domination (cf. e.g. Haines 1930: 246 ff.). Compare the idea of the Rule of Law in English constitutional theory which is usually held to import definite *values* governing the exercise of legal authority. See e.g. Finnis 1980: 270 ff. Cf. Kirchheimer 1967, for a typically provocative analysis.

not be representative of a fundamental type of political legitimacy having an explanatory significance similar to that of the other concepts in his typology of legitimate domination. Once natural law had been analysed out of Weber's typology, all possibility of systematically confronting the ideological functions of law disappeared and, with it, all possibility of systematic analysis of the conditions under which legal domination may become problematic.[6]

In Weber's view, escape from the tyranny of the ever more detailed and all-enveloping web of 'value neutral' technical rules can come only from the emergence of a charismatic leader who imposes new values to direct the law according to substantive principles and policies and to lead society into new paths until the inevitable process of routinization sets in again. The role of the citizen is to obey law and perhaps, in periodic elections, to confirm the choice of leaders whose election gives them the power to enact into law whatever policies they see fit. In so doing, leaders are guided only by expediency, personal vision, and the legal restraints of the constitution which, if adhered to, confer unchallenged legitimacy on their acts.

Weber's analysis seems to suggest that it will never be possible to foresee conditions in which tensions in society directly threaten the basis of legal domination. The providential emergence of the charismatic leader is a precondition of change. And such a development—the irrational 'outburst' of charisma—defies theoretical analysis. It is the inexplicable irrationality for which a place is carefully preserved in Weber's rational science.

The only destination of change that is predictable is ever-increasing bureaucratization of politics, economy, and society in a technically rational world which has seen the 'end of ideology' (cf. Parsons 1967: 100). Legal domination is, therefore, not a concept enabling us to reach an analysis of law's ideological functions that could explain their relevance for political action and social change. It sees these functions in a single dimension, that

[6] As David Beetham (1985: 259) suggests, while the static quality of the types of legitimacy prevents such systematic analysis in Weber's sociology, his writings on specific political developments do explore conditions of change particularly in terms of the relations of classes. See J. G. Merquior's extremely negative judgement on the use of Weber's typology (Merquior 1980: 131 ff.) and compare Talcott Parsons' dramatically different assessment (Parsons 1947: 77).

of rationalization. Rationalization is the sole consistent and ubiquitous motor of change, removed from all human choice and struggle.

Thus society becomes, for Weber, an 'iron cage' imprisoning men who increasingly 'need "order" and nothing but order, who become nervous and cowardly if for one moment this order wavers, and helpless if they are torn away from their total incorporation in it' (Weber in a 1909 speech, quoted in Mayer 1956: 127–8). The sociology that begins from the conception of social action as the choices of the free will of individuals leads to a view of society in which, for almost all individuals, there are no politically important choices to be made.

Legal Rationality and Legal Ideology

In this chapter it is appropriate only to consider how far the use of the concept of legal domination and the view of modern law on which it is based provide a acceptable basis for the analysis that leads Weber to adopt this view of present and future society. This will be done, first, by re-examining the idea introduced earlier, that purpose rational submission is the basis of legal domination; secondly, by making some general comments on the nature of legal ideology; and, thirdly, by reintroducing the concept of legal values and relating certain 'ultimate' values to Weber's typology of legal rationality.

It is obvious that in 'normal' circumstances of political stability legal domination usually exists in the form Weber describes. Legal or other rationally established norms do often provide the necessary and sufficient title to power of command and produce sociologically significant ideas of duty in those who are to be influenced towards compliance with the dictates of holders of power who are designated by the norms. Governments change without change in the political system within which they operate. At all levels in structures of political authority officials come and go but the structures remain. Do they become, as Weber suggests, ever more permanent? Is legal domination in important respects self-perpetuating? Contemporary society hardly reflects the 'end of ideology' heralded by some sociologists several decades ago (see e.g. Bell 1961). Competing systems of values and beliefs proliferate yet, as Ernest Gellner has suggested, it is possible to see these ideological currents of Western life today as merely superimposed ineffectually over a technological world with its own dynamics which is too essential for modern life to be fundamentally challenged, whatever the ideological basis of the challenge (Gellner 1974: 192–3).

If, as suggested earlier, in Weber's analysis submission to the authority of law is a type of submission of will corresponding to the type of purpose rational social action, then legal domination exists as legitimate domination because it provides the framework of regulation that is seen as appropriate for the fulfilment of rationally chosen individual purposes. Individuals accept legal domination as legitimate because they consider their interests are best served by the continued existence of a system of rational law in the society in which they seek to fulfil their chosen purposes.

As an analysis of the ideological conditions of social order this is no more adequate than, for example, Herbert Spencer's conception of society as the consequence of the free interaction of self-seeking individual wills. Hence Durkheim's famous criticism (Durkheim 1984) that the Spencerian contract between individuals presupposes a regulation of the contract which is social—supra-individual—and the expression of a 'moral consciousness' within society or, as we might now put it, a certain ideological climate.

Purposes are rationally chosen by individuals within the constraints of what is, for them, *conceivable* as a rational purpose. This conception depends in its turn, to a considerable extent, on how social relations are perceived and on general cognitive and evaluative judgements about the nature of society. These judgements, which involve certain conceptions of justice and social order, enable individuals to define their actual and ideal place in society and thus also their social expectations which provide parameters for the purposes they seek to achieve. Hence, the purpose rational action that takes place within the security of legal domination and so justifies individuals in accepting such domination as legitimate is chosen within an ideological climate that influences the scope of conceivable choices and expectations.

I want to argue here that while Weber is correct in pointing out the partially self-sustaining character of legal domination in certain circumstances, this is not a consequence of the inevitability of rationalization as an unchallengeable necessity removed from influence by human will, but is, to a significant extent, the consequence of ideological effects of law which help to create conditions under which the range of choices of action and the expectations of individuals are normally seriously conceived only within the limits of the conception of society and social relations embodied in legal ideology.

In a recent paper Duncan Kennedy has tried to relate preferences for formalism or substantivism in legal reasoning to particular *value* preferences, centred on, respectively, individualistic and altruistic ethics (Kennedy 1976). His method of doing so is, in some respects, rather impressionistic yet it is vital to affirm that Weber's distinction between formal and substantive rationality is not adequate to parcel value considerations out of formally systematized law. The concept of formal logical law is the essential basis of Weber's claim that legal domination makes no reference to values in law, hence that it sustains itself through its purely technical utility for the fulfilment of purpose rational conduct of those subject to authority. But, in reality, formal and substantive considerations are inextricably related in all legal systems made up of rules intended to influence behaviour; and the development of law, of whatever kind, expresses certain value orientations or, at least, implies certain value preferences reflected in legal rules and principles.

A 'pure' formally rational legal system or a 'pure' substantively rational legal system is realistically an impossibility. A system of fundamental values elaborated according to purely substantive criteria could not produce law (in the sense of rules or intelligible, workable guides for a system of social order) at all but only a private ethical code requiring each situation to which the code is to be applied to be analysed in all its aspects (not just those picked out as relevant by formal criteria in a legal system) and ultimately in terms of a unique subjective determination of how fundamental values may be best realized in all the circumstances. This would involve a process of introspection that could not give rise to a predictable and practical system of legal control.[7] Conversely, a purely formal system making no reference to substantive

---

[7] On the relationship between legal rules and ultimate values in a legal order oriented primarily to substantive rationality in Weber's sense, see e.g. Schacht 1964: 77 ff., 201; Coulson 1964: chs. 3 and 6.

purposes or situations of human beings could only be a system of quasi-mathematical logic, assessing logical relations between concepts bearing no relation to actual experience or human objectives. Such a system could not be a legal system since it would be incapable of connecting its logic with meaningful conduct in social life and hence would be wholly irrelevant to any legal purposes of social control of whatever nature. It is clearly impossible to create a pure formal logic of legal rules (cf. Kennedy 1976: 1724), just as it is impossible to create a system of rules of law on the basis only of a subjective elaboration of substantive values. Formal rationality and substantive rationality cannot therefore represent different types of *legal* thought but only different facets of legal thought. Both are necessarily present in any legal system made up of rules aimed at regulation of social life.

Yet, in Weber's sociology of law, formal logical legal rationality tends to take on a life of its own. In this way it becomes the basis of a 'value free' or 'value neutralized' technology of social order. But even when a rule is applied by mechanical processes of deduction, its meaning is given only by reference to human purposes or human conduct. Even mechanical jurisprudence, as Roscoe Pound called it, which purports to be blind to everything except the logical requirements of formal elaboration of existing concepts, creates value implications by 'unthinkingly' carrying the values embedded in legal rules to new situations by merely applying such rules. Otherwise it alters the value orientations of an area of law by mechanically applying legal concepts or rules to new situations where the substantive effect of application is quite different from substantive effects in areas where the legal concepts or rules have previously been applied. Certainly, these value implications may often be extremely ambiguous. The fact that they may be unrecognized by the judge does not affect their existence for those affected by or having knowledge of the relevant law.

Weber was, of course, well aware of this but he could not analyse it within his framework of ideal types because the value implications of formally systematized and generalized law are necessarily highly complex, historically specific, and often seemingly self-contradictory. They cannot be the subject of a typology. They make up part of a rich tapestry of ideology created in law and developed in modern legal systems to form modes of cognition and evaluation of virtually all important recurrent social relations and of the institutions and processes in which social action is patterned.

Legal ideology in the sense used here refers, therefore, to the structures of values and cognitive ideas presupposed in and expressed through legal doctrine developed by courts and other practical law finding or law creating agencies and in the work of legislators and jurists in so far as these ideas and values serve to influence the manner in which social roles and relationships are conceptualized and evaluated.

Processes of generalization of law which have been referred to earlier are naturally promoted by a legal profession monopolizing the organization and application of law in stable conditions. Thus, although legal ideology in a secular, highly systematized legal order cannot attain consistency in its value orientations, processes of legal development often allow certain value implications in rules or concepts to be developed into quite broad value orientations: partly through 'internal' rationalizing legal processes, particularly those of generalization of concepts and principles; and partly through the effects of identifiable 'external' pressure sources (for example, administrative, order-maintaining requirements of the state, or particular demands of classes and groups) influencing the legal system.

Legitimacy and Personal Values

Legal ideology is sociologically significant in so far as it influences the manner in which individuals conceptualize and evaluate social relations and their place and aspirations within society. In Weber's terms, it is important in so far as it helps to fix the limits within which rational purposes of social action are chosen. Within the limits of this chapter only a few aspects of this matter can be touched upon.

It can be noted that even in the most formally systematized legal orders, two values are regularly associated with law in general. These are the values of 'justice' and 'order'—both of them so ambiguous that they can be supported in some form by individuals espousing the most varied beliefs and ideals. It is unnecessary here to ask what these values 'really' import. Our concern, in analysis of legal ideology, is with recurrent themes in discussion of these values and with the way in which law regularly interprets them and promotes its interpretation as socially significant and essentially definitive.

Order implies the subjection of all phenomena (natural and social) to rational control. The *value of justice* implies fair treatment of individuals, groups, and so on, within this system of rational control. Fair treatment is not necessarily equal treatment. Fairness depends on a judgement of circumstances. Here, then, is a crucial ideological task of the administration of justice: to fix values that determine what circumstances should be weighed in the balance and to promote conditions under which these values are accepted as necessary and sufficient. Part of law's ideological function is to determine the content of justice in social relations: to promote definite conceptions by individuals of what is their 'due'; what is an acceptable return for effort; what obligations can be considered to be attached to oneself and others in the circumstances in which one finds oneself, and in a broad sense, what is to be expected from life.

The *value of order* in law implies consistency, certainty, stability, and, specifically, the maintenance of predictable patterns of action by officials and others (cf. Barkun 1971: 134). Order implies the stability of existing institutions and structures of social relations whatever their substantive content. Order is contrasted with chaos and is thus associated with human capacity to control rationally the conditions of life in its natural and social environment. It is, of course, no coincidence that the deeply ambiguous values of order and justice are related to Weber's categories of formal and substantive legal rationality. Both polarities reflect the essential duality of law which has been recognized as long as legal philosophy has existed.

Weber's primary failure was in not developing a mode of analysis that would emphasize the permanent fusion of these elements in all law and all legal systems. What is understood by values of justice and order varies greatly in different societies and at different times. The content of legal ideology in this sense varies greatly, and the demands made on legal institutions vary correspondingly in so far as these demands are structured by legal ideology. Nevertheless, the tension between these values can, in certain circumstances, determine directions of political change and perhaps also conditions under which political legitimacy based on rational law may be threatened.

In modern societies sophisticated mechanisms are employed to ensure that as far as possible the content of justice and order in legal ideology is accepted as the basis of general social conceptions among members of society. Even in patently undemocratic regimes the consistent appeal to 'the people's will' is used to reinforce acceptance of legal conceptions of justice. In developed legal systems, rigorous formal adherence to legal procedures especially in trial is encouraged, even where—as in political show trials—formal procedures have no relevance to the actual consequences of the trial. The value of order is consistently promulgated in elaborate charades. In many legal systems, the appeal to democratic will and the insistence on procedural propriety are genuine contributions to the safeguarding of legal values. In all systems their ideological significance is not to be underestimated.

How are these matters to be related to the concept of legal domination and to the relationship between law and political legitimacy? Legal ideology, elaborated within legal institutions, and supporting, in so far as it permeates popular consciousness, the view that law is a 'common sense' embodiment of reason and the technically necessary framework for purpose rational social action, exists as a relatively identifiable ideological form only in certain societies. It exists only to the extent that legal institutions possess a degree of autonomy, rather than merely reflecting in a direct manner ideological inputs from political or religious powers. The conditions of this autonomy are partly explored by Weber in his analysis of the development of Western law through the interaction of state interests, the interests of client groups, particularly the rising bourgeoisie, and the professional interests of lawyers seeking to establish a rationally organized body of technical legal knowledge.

Where such conditions are satisfied and a stable development of legal ideas, particularly through processes of generalization, is supervised by an organized legal profession ensuring doctrinal continuity and resistance to rapid uncontrolled change in the content of legal ideology, then legal ideology may well be enabled gradually to permeate a developing society and powerfully to influence more general ideological currents within it (see Cotterrell 1981). To the extent that law can be portrayed as the rational compromise of interests promoted by 'enlightened' rulers or representative democracy, it may come to be seen as a 'harmony of conflicting wills', the necessary regulation that actually *constitutes* and defines all significant characteristics of society itself.[8]

Legal ideology contains detailed elaborations both of conceptions of justice and of conceptions of order. In so far as the former define the 'proper' expectations individuals may have in their relations with each other they purport to fix general conceptions of social relations. In so far as the latter define the range of choice of action available to individuals, they specify in ideology the scope of human personality and its expression, the relation between the individual and 'society', and the nature of individuality.

The connotations of order and justice therefore imply a continuum of values which extend far beyond procedural values directly reflected in the forms of adjudication and application of law. It can be suggested that legal legitimacy depends ultimately on the belief of individual actors that law promotes, within the limits imposed by its 'essential' nature as a consistent and comprehensive rational *system* of regulation, what is most fundamental among the actor's values of justice and order, thought of not merely as procedural elements in law, but *social* values.

Conclusion

Various writers have suggested theories of a 'legitimation crisis' based on particular conceptions of contradictions within modern capitalist societies (see especially Habermas 1976a). To attempt to evaluate such theories would take us too far from Weber's themes and too far from the specific concerns of this chapter. Nevertheless, as Jürgen Habermas and others have noted, the greatly increased scope of state activity in contemporary capitalist societies necessarily produces major changes in the nature of legal regulation and its impact on individuals and their beliefs about the society in which they live. For various reasons differential access to law as between sectors and classes in society has diminished with the development of new forms of legal representation, legal aid, and other institutions. And, with the increase in state intervention, 'taken-for-granted cultural factors which previously were fringe

---

[8] Cf. Weber's criticism of Rudolf Stammler's legal-ideological conception of society (Weber 1977: 98 ff.).

conditions of the political system are now drawn into the administrative field of planning' (Habermas 1976b: 378). Law is brought to the direct attention of individuals in their experience far more extensively and in far more varied contexts than previously. Hence the relationship between the specific content of legal ideology and the detailed experience of individuals and groups is made increasingly apparent to the broad mass of individuals in a wide variety of situations. Consequently, increasing demands are made on the law from all quarters, and established legal conceptions of justice and order are challenged.

This in itself poses no threat to legal legitimacy as long as these demands for particular values can be considered by those making them to be capable of being met without compromising other values of justice or order which provide fundamental justifications of the existing legal system. Even where this is not so there will be no threat as long as law's legitimating values are considered ultimately more fundamental than the values demanded. In such a case demands will not be pressed to the point of challenging the legitimacy of the legal system as a whole.

It may be suggested in conclusion that legal domination begins to become problematic when two conditions are met: first, the values demanded are seen by those demanding them as ultimately more important than values, considered to be embodied in the legal system, that provide the basis of any claim to legitimacy it may have; and, secondly, it is considered that the legal system cannot embrace the values demanded and those that found its legitimacy in a sufficiently rational manner to maintain the systematic character of law on which legal domination depends.

Western law has been dependent on the apparent fusion within a *rational system of rules* of carefully circumscribed values of justice and order. The centring of both of these sets of value orientations primarily on procedural matters and their substantive implications has made this rational harmony possible. And, as Thurman Arnold pointed out many decades ago, the ideological significance of much broader value implications in the law has often depended on the obscuring of practical incompatibilities between them when they are invoked in legal practice (Arnold 1935). To the extent, then, that legal ideology has not actually constrained demands upon the law for satisfaction of values incompatible with the requirements of its systematic rational nature, it has 'neutralized' these demands by continuing to proclaim adherence to broad fundamental values which in fact are not, and cannot be, realized in legal practice. As increasing demands are made on the law and increasingly wide experience of the 'illusion' and 'reality' of its value orientations is made available to individuals, the problem of maintaining the rational order of the legal system and the hegemony of legal ideology may become a particularly serious one.

These considerations do not destroy the utility of Weber's concept of legal domination. They indicate, however, that the highly complex ideological elements of law must be analysed in ways that cannot utilize the ideal type method, if conditions of legitimacy are to be understood in relation to social change. Weber's interpretation of political legitimacy in modern states reflects, perhaps, not only the distinct ideological conditions within which the conception of the German *Rechtsstaat* developed[9] but also a form of legal positivism—the German *Begriffsjurisprudenz*—which, far from being the natural mode of legal thought in modern societies, appears increasingly to have been the product of particular historical conditions and the preserve of a particular tradition of continental European scholarship in law. The combination of formal and substantive considerations in perpetual tension seems to be the continuing legacy of legal history for today's law. In this tension lies both stability and impetus to change in law. And because law's ideological content changes and can be changed, Weber's 'iron cage' is less secure than he thought. Action on and through the law is one of the necessary, though not sufficient, means for breaking out of it.

[9] Cf. Arthur Mitzman's more general judgement: 'At the heart of Weber's vision lies only the truth of his epoch, his country, and his station, the truth of a bourgeois scholar in Imperial Germany' (Mitzman 1970: 3); and see footnote 5, above. Weber's conception of legitimate domination in the modern state reflects what appear to be deep-rooted political assumptions recurrent in German society. Cf. Julien Freund's remarks on a failure of German sociology to confront Weber directly 'as though the author's ideas might prove embarrassing on closer inspection' (Freund 1968: 288). And for detailed discussion of German political reactions to Weber see Roth 1965. On recent German studies, however, see especially the comments in Kalberg 1979: 137, and Kalberg's paper generally.

8 Social Foundations of the Rule of Law: Franz Neumann and Otto Kirchheimer

The theme of historical transformations of legal rationality, introduced in Chapter 7, can be further developed through an examination of the changing social foundations of the idea of the Rule of Law, strikingly illuminated by Neumann's and Kirchheimer's writings. Neumann's view that the Rule of Law reconciles, in specific historical conditions, the contradictory elements of law as sovereign power or will (*voluntas*) and as reason or principle (*ratio*) is important to the arguments in Part 3 of this book. The idea of the Rule of Law recognises centralised political power as the immediate origin of modern law while emphasising certain values that may be asserted against government. But what does that formulation entail in contemporary conditions? Historical evidence suggests why an appropriate reconciliation of *ratio* and *voluntas* may be hard to maintain.

A century after A. V. Dicey's discussion of the Rule of Law in *The Law of the Constitution* was first published there is less agreement than ever about the meaning and significance of the idea. The Rule of Law has been described as a 'concept of the utmost importance but having no defined, nor readily definable, content';[1] as 'a mixture of implied promise and convenient vagueness' (Kirchheimer 1967: 429). Recently renewed attempts to reformulate it precisely have excluded from the concept a wide variety of political value judgements and reduced it, in the manner of the continental formal *Rechtsstaat*, to a specifically technical, or procedural insistence on government through fixed, previously announced rules. These are to be 'general, open, and stable' (Raz

---

[1] Walker 1980: 1093. Cf. Dicey 1959: 187 ('Words which, though they possess a real significance, are nevertheless to most persons who employ them full of vagueness and ambiguity').

1979: 213), interpreted by an independent judiciary, prospective in effect, and, in Joseph Raz's formulation, 'capable of guiding behaviour, however inefficiently' (Raz 1979: 226).

If the German jurist Franz Neumann, whose magisterial mid- 1930s study of the Rule of Law details the political and social origins of all of these elements, were alive today he would prob- ably be surprised at only one aspect of present debates: the extent to which formulations such as the above can still avoid detailed analysis of the fundamental changes in the functions and effects of regulation which he saw as brought about by the development from competitive to monopoly capitalism in Western societies. The publication of Neumann's long-neglected study (Neumann 1986), together with a volume containing new translations of some of the essays that he and his compatriot, Otto Kirchheimer, wrote at around the same time (Kirchheimer and Neumann 1987), is important precisely because these works force attention, in a highly instructive manner, to transformations of the conditions of the Rule of Law. This chapter considers these transformations in the light of Neumann's and Kirchheimer's writings.

The Legal Invisibility of Change

Broader conceptions of the Rule of Law in contemporary British legal scholarship do, of course, suggest substantive problems posed by the development of what can be called corporate society —a society of economic concentrations in giant business en- terprises and groups of enterprises, administrative bureaucracies, and mass organizations having economic, political, or other func- tions. Thus, the Rule of Law has a broader 'political' meaning embracing 'such matters as fair and equitable administrative prac- tices; recognition of the rights of political opposition and dissent; complying with constitutional conventions; adequate means of redress of grievances about government action affecting one' (McAuslan and McEldowney 1985: 11).

Furthermore, recent analyses of constitutional and administra- tive law have tried to take careful account of the consequences, for Diceyan thought, of political practices consistent with cor- poratist theory or developed in conscious reaction to corporatist pressures (e.g. Lewis and Wiles 1984); or of the particular problems of modern state administration which require the structuring aid of law, rather than mere control by law.[2]

Others have addressed the decline in the authority of Parliament and the substantial demise of parliamentary government. They have considered especially the development of administrative regulation and direction by the state in many new or newly important forms. Recently Ian Harden and Norman Lewis (1986), discarding Diceyan approaches, have tried to distill a new understanding of the Rule of Law—emphasizing openness and accountability—from claims or beliefs that they see as implicit in the historical practice of the British constitution. What results from the analysis is, however, essentially a weapon of critique rather than a realized (or even partly realized) constitutional principle.

It seems necessary to stress, nevertheless, that most legal philosophy and much legal scholarship do not register as fundamental these complex social, economic, and political changes. The mainstream of legal philosophy, centrally concerned with rules (and more recently, rights-guaranteeing principles), hardly notices many modern regulatory forms or strategies except to dismiss them, as discretion or policy, from its substantive legal concerns. Much legal scholarship still founds itself on just two core concepts of normative legal theory, the Rule of Law (usually in its narrower, formal senses) and the sovereignty of Parliament, and rarely addresses the problematic character of both concepts.

To some extent, indeed, this is not only understandable but justifiable, since in Britain many of the economic and political changes of the past half century and more have given rise to profound alterations in the regulatory and directive strategies of the state without any substantial recognition in formal constitutional structures (Harden and Lewis 1986: 34; Lewis and Harden 1983), and often with apparently only minor consequential effects on the central structures of positive legal doctrine.

However, if anything more than a formal conception of law divorced from political and social realities is to be adopted, appeals to the Rule of Law can hardly avoid analysis of the social, economic, and political imperatives that have transformed many areas of

[2] See e.g., among many important discussions, Harlow and Rawlings 1984, especially ch. 2.

state regulation and administration in practice. Since a consequence of these regulatory developments has been to blur the
distinction between public and private spheres, such matters concern private lawyers as well as public lawyers. Equally, a rather
different point about the public-private relationship can be made.
The essence of the Rule of Law might be said to be the hope of
subjecting power to the control of reason. If this is so, however,
it has typically been only *public* power which has been addressed
by the concept. The vast concentrations of private (economic)
power that are characteristic of contemporary advanced Western
societies escape it almost completely. But, if a realistic rather than
formalistic view is taken, public and private power appear increasingly intertwined, so that the control of monopolistic private powers
deserves urgent consideration in some way as a constitutional issue.

The 1930s writings of Neumann and Kirchheimer are of special
interest in this context, but since these works have until recently
been scattered and relatively inaccessible they have hitherto attracted little attention in English language legal scholarship.
Neumann, a labour lawyer working in the period of the Weimar
republic in Germany during the 1920s and early 1930s, was faced
as a matter of everyday legal practice with the question of the
meaning of the Rule of Law in an unstable constitutional order
substantially different from the liberal order of competitive capitalism presupposed by Dicey.

Neumann clearly recognized that the Weimar constitution was
a constitution of a new kind, not to be confused with liberal con-
stitutions founded on the theory of the formal *Rechtsstaat.* Weimar's
corporate society required a new kind of legal and constitutional
understanding, and perhaps a reinterpretation of the Rule of Law
in the light of its historical preconditions of existence. One major
aspect of the newness of the Weimar constitution's form was that
it made *explicit* (even if in a confused and ultimately incoherent
way) the new structure of economic and political power that had
arisen in what Neumann recognized as the transition from
competitive capitalism—theorized as an ideal type in the works of
Adam Smith—to monopoly capitalism.

While both Neumann and Kirchheimer can be termed Left
critics of Weimar, Neumann's Weimar writings show him primarily
as a constructive, and even perhaps naïvely optimistic, analyst of
its constitutional structure. He sought to find in it a relatively

stable formal framework, in politically difficult times, for a society made up not of autonomous individual citizens in an ideal-typical liberal polity, but of competing interest groups, social classes, bureaucracies, and monopolistic, cartelized, corporate structures. Kirchheimer, who in his Weimar period exercised, in his own words, 'the trade (*das Handwerk*) of a law trainee (*Referendar*) and a critic of the administration of justice (*Justizkritiker*)' (quoted in Herz and Kula 1969: xvii), was a much more negative critic of the constitution. Kirchheimer saw in Weimar, above all, what so many of its later critics saw: the absence of decision,[3] the lack of a political and constitutional structure that could facilitate and promote rational action to implement the social reforms that had been promised by the revolution out of which Weimar emerged.

The Rule of Law of Competitive Society

For most British students of the Rule of Law and its problems, Neumann's major monograph on the subject, now published under the title *The Rule of Law* (Neumann 1986), will seem both more immediately accessible and of more general interest than the newly translated essays by him and Kirchheimer (Kirchheimer and Neumann 1987). This is because it sets its study of the concept of the Rule of Law in a broad context of Western European history and political thought and has much to say about the foundations of the specifically English version of the Rule of Law in English legal and political history. Neumann's book was originally written as a Ph.D. thesis at the London School of Economics in 1936, under Harold Laski's supervision. Neumann (like Kirchheimer) had fled from Germany in 1933 after the Nazis attained power. He spent three years in London before moving to New York to join the Institute for Social Research. Like Kirchheimer, he spent the rest of his career in the United States. When he died in 1954, in a car accident in Switzerland, he was Professor of Public Law and Government at Columbia University.

Neumann's central thesis about the Rule of Law is simple but the consequences drawn from it are thought-provoking. For him, the essence of the Rule of Law as an ideal in Western legal and

---

[3] Kirchheimer 1969 (the original German version of this essay was published in 1930).

political thought and practice is the demand that the state govern through *general* laws. Law in this sense is 'an abstract rule which does not mention particular cases or individually nominated persons, but which is issued in advance to apply to all cases and all persons in the abstract' (Neumann 1986: 213). Generality should thus be as to both persons and acts, and implicit in the requirement is a prohibition of retroactive laws. Related to it also is the doctrine of the separation of powers in Montesquieu's sense and, especially, the demand for an independent judiciary which applies but does not make law.

Such a familiar conclusion may hardly raise excitement. Neumann seeks to show, however, that while this concept embodies a timeless 'ethical minimum'—a promise of equality, even if only of formal equality before the law—it is a specific product of history inseparable from the historical destiny of a particular kind of economic order, social structure, and political system. His book is thus a sociological study of the Rule of Law which traces the evolution of the doctrine in its particular historical context, and shows its social origins and consequences. The burden of Neumann's thesis is to show that an apparently formal, and extremely limited, principle of legal organization has, in fact, the most far reaching consequences for social, economic, and political organization. But beyond this, the bite in the argument is that if the specific extra-legal conditions of existence of the Rule of Law cease to hold (as in Weimar, or, more generally, in the corporate—not necessarily 'corporatist'—societies of twentieth century Europe) it is futile to seek to preserve it in its liberal, classic form. A new view of law and its destiny is required.

Many of Neumann's arguments are familiar from his previously available work. He summarized in article form the key propositions of his thesis (Neumann 1957), and often restated them in later writings. In *The Rule of Law*, however, they are developed fully in unified form. Written long before modern critical legal scholars discovered the 'fundamental contradiction' (Kennedy 1979) of individual autonomy realizable only within the framework of collective coercion, Neumann's thesis begins with the recognition that the enduring problem of Western political thought has been just such an antagonism. In law and government it has presented itself specifically as the postulated 'dual' character of law as *voluntas* and *ratio*. The former represents the political aspect

166   *Law in Social Theory*

of law as coercion, embodied in a 'pure', wholly unfettered sovereignty. The latter represents 'material law,' or reason expressed in the form of rational norms embodying rights. The history of Western political thought has been an attempt to find a balance between these elements.

Part 2 of *The Rule of Law* consists of a long trawl through the history of political theory from Cicero to Hegel in search of this shifting balance. If some of this, at least, seems arid and unnecessary it is important to understand that Neumann's motivation for it was, as with all other aspects of his book, firmly rooted in contemporary issues. He sought especially to oppose the assertion of the jurist and political theorist, Carl Schmitt, and others, that legal generality was a more or less universally necessary principle, at least in the Weimar context. By contrast Neumann tried to show that the importance of the idea of the generality of law, and more broadly the relationship between the ideas of law as power and law as reason, had varied greatly and crystallized only slowly in Western intellectual and political history, and in specific social and economic conditions.

Hence this history could offer no simple answer to the question of what the Rule of Law could be taken to mean realistically in the modern conditions of corporate society. The crucial claim made in Neumann's long historical analysis of political theories is that the progress of the idea of the generality of law is inseparable from the history of the bourgeoisie. The theory of the state that the idea entailed depended for its coherence on the substantial exclusion of the lower classes from political power. In earlier theories this exclusion is largely taken for granted but, Neumann seems to suggest, it becomes explicit when the matter arises historically as a real issue, as in Hegel's writings (Neumann 1986: 164–5).

The significance of this claim about the social presuppositions of the Rule of Law becomes apparent only when the wider consequences of the demand for legal generality are brought to light. The Rule of Law is the theoretical foundation of what Neumann calls the legal system of competitive society. This system is related to the economic system of free competition expressed in the ideas of freedom of contract and trade (the *material* structure of the legal system). Closely following Max Weber, Neumann argues that the generality of law (which he essentially equates with Weber's

notion of formal rationality) is a vital basis of economic calculability in a society of free competitors. This legal system is also
related to 'a state of affairs in which a working class as an independent movement did not exist, in which therefore the existence of class conflicts was simply ignored' (this state of affairs is
the legal system's *social* structure); and it is related politically to
a system of separation and distribution of powers (the legal system's
political structure) (Neumann 1986: 185–6).

What is especially important about this last point is that it is not
just a reiteration of Montesquieu's thesis on the institutional separation of powers but also refers to a separation (which to some
extent Montesquieu also recognized) between the social groups
or interests that control or have special access to different state
functions or institutions. Though the matter is not particularly
emphasized in *The Rule of Law*, it became a theme that Neumann
stressed in later writings since he maintained the belief that a
factual pluralism in which different sections of society could be
represented through different aspects of state power was at least
as significant, in securing the freedom that the Rule of Law
addressed, as any formal, institutional separation of powers
(Neumann 1949: lviii). The matter is also important, as will appear, in the context of Neumann's Weimar essays.

The Rule of Law elaborates carefully and, on the whole, convincingly the links between the liberal legal order of the Rule of Law
and its specific economic, social, and political conditions. At the
base of Neumann's claims about the impossibility of politically
incorporating the working class in the liberal order is the assertion that liberalism presupposes the possibility of more or less
rational parliamentary discourse within a strictly limited consensus constituency (cf. Cotterrell 1992: 99–102), that is, among those
whose interests are not so fundamentally opposed as to threaten
to tear the constitutional order apart. Neumann assumed (and
Weimar experience seemed fully to justify the assumption) that
the interests of labour and capital were irreconcilably opposed.
Politics in which such antagonistic interests took part could only
be as Carl Schmitt had described all politics—a matter of friend
and foe relations.[4]

---

[4] Schmitt 1976: 26 ff. (the original German version of this text was published in
1927 and revised in 1932). On Schmitt's influence on Neumann and Kirchheimer
see Kennedy 1987.

Of course, against Neumann's assertions can be set the criticism, implicitly made by his later colleagues in the Institute for Social Research (see Jay 1986: ix–x), that he greatly underestimated the extent to which the instruments of influence and mass persuasion, and of administrative control, of modern corporate society could secure the allegiance of the working class to established constitutional structures. But this is not necessarily to deny the profound consequences for the once-liberal institutions of the state that arise to the extent that the most fundamental social conflicts are brought, unmediated, within these institutions in corporate society. Thus Neumann remarks, surely with some justification, writing of Weimar's coalition of class-based parties: 'Parliaments are no longer places where the representatives of the privileged parts of the nation deliberate. They have rather become the stage where compromises are reached between the various partners in the class struggle' (Neumann 1986: 272).

The 'England Problem' and the Rule of Law

Among the most instructive parts of *The Rule of Law* are its detailed comparisons of the continental *Rechtsstaat* and the English Rule of Law. Neumann, relying on Dicey, correctly notes that despite the logical antagonism of the Rule of Law (as the rule of *material* law) and parliamentary sovereignty, they achieved a highly satisfactory sociological reconcilation. That is, in particular political and social conditions these apparently antagonistic doctrines reinforced each other. The two doctrines jointly, and inseparably, underpinned British constitutional theory in the liberal era. Thus they implied substantive values beyond the formal values of the *Rechtsstaat*. While in Germany, the middle classes used the demand for legal generality as a defence against an absolute state which they could not politically control, in England the middle classes secured control of Parliament and could thus combine the ideal of legal generality with the capacity to legislate substantive values of liberal (competitive) society.

Neumann's thesis runs into particular difficulties, however, in his discussions of English law. The thesis asserts that a specific ideal-typical legal order corresponds to the model of the competitive society; that is, the society of free entrepreneurs. Hence Neumann is forced to claim that despite all doctrinal differences there are no significant functional differences between the common law and the continental European code systems, in so far as both correspond to the political, economic, and social order of the competitive society. For example, both kinds of legal order have to be seen as rational in the sense demanded by the Rule of Law. Both consist of general laws, constituting a formally rational and comprehensive system which provides the basis for secure economic calculation, stable rights and duties, and liberal freedoms.

Hence Neumann is apparently faced with the so-called 'England Problem' familiar from Max Weber's sociology of law (e.g. Kronman 1983: 120–4). How can the common law, which in Weberian terms is 'irrational' rather than formally rational—based in empirical law-finding rather than the systematic elaboration of formal concepts, be understood as providing the rational regulatory system that the theory demands? Neumann argues that the *ratio decidendi* of the case takes the place in English law of the general law of continental systems (Neumann 1986: 241) and that 'there must lie at the bottom of the doctrine of the binding force [of] precedent, the conception of the logical closeness of the law' (1986: 245). This is seen as reinforced by the consistent assertion of judges that they find rather than make law, and that the common law is found only in previous decisions. That these assertions have been long recognized as unreliable descriptions of actual judicial practice is, for Neumann, irrelevant to the argument since, in his view, their reiteration reveals the ideal-typical conception of law presupposed, though inevitably not realized, in the common law.

Neumann's arguments here will strike many as odd, but one problem in evaluating them is that there is no clear periodization in his presentation of supporting material. Blackstone rubs shoulders, for example, with early twentieth century cases. Nevertheless, readers sympathetic to Brian Simpson's (1986) analysis of common law thought (let alone Jeremy Bentham's analysis) will find difficulty with Neumann's conception of the common law as a structure of stable rules, even before considering its postulated gapless, logically closed character. In Neumann's defence it can be said that his argument is only that judges and lawyers have tended to see the common law as a complete body of rules (cf. Simpson 1986: 9) (even if by its nature it cannot be). Hence, as he stresses, the fact that the reality is different does not destroy the significance of the ideal-typical image of law. But Neumann's ideal-typical image may reflect a modern positivist view of the common law rather than the view of it that perhaps was strongest when, according to his thesis, it provided the support of developing competitive society.

The difficulties of the argument are highlighted by Neumann's need to date the establishment of *stare decisis* exactly, and to show it as operating significantly as a stable doctrine much earlier than is generally suggested. This may well be a pointless task. It has been suggested in this regard 'that to seek a uniformity of judicial philosophy at different periods may be to seek what never existed' (Baker 1990: 228; and see Simpson 1986: 8); that the idea that accepted principles should outweigh judicial idiosyncrasies is an old one, and expressed in the year books; but that the 'duty of repeating errors is a modern innovation' (Baker 1990: 229).

The doctrine of *stare decisis* was, it seems, probably long significant as legal common sense but not as a rigid prescription for judicial conduct. A better explanation of legal calculability and predictability in the developing common law than Neumann provides (and even, perhaps, a clue to the solution of the England problem) may be found in the idea of the *cultural* (rather than legally logical or authoritatively structured) unity and reflexivity of the common law. On this view the incomplete and unstructured *legal* doctrine of common law could be considered to imply a vast, undefined range of cultural ideas, expectations, values, and attitudes which could be drawn upon to fill its gaps.

Law and non-law were thus not fully differentiated (cf. Simpson 1986: 9–10) and the cultural presuppositions of the law, which might relate—at least to a tolerable extent—to some common sense notions held by the bourgeois consensus constituency, perhaps provided a reasonable potential for predictability in the law even in the absence of specific judicial decisions. The relatively small number of judges, their opportunities for discussion of cases amongst themselves, and their continuing experience of the kinds of demands being pressed on the courts by litigants, are surely relevant factors here. This is not, of course, to deny the Weberian irrationality that no doubt frequently arose from the juxtaposition of incompatible and idiosyncratic ideas in empirical law-finding by the judges.

Since Neumann does not clearly date either the emergence or

the decline of what he identifies as the competitive society, and so makes it difficult to relate specific legal developments to this, his discussion of English law in terms of the thesis of *The Rule of Law* is ultimately confused and unsatisfactory. It might well be accepted that since the late nineteenth century, at least, English law has developed systematic characteristics comparable with (even if not identical with) what Weber saw as the formal rationality of continental code systems. But it seems that Neumann needs to identify such characteristics in English law at much earlier periods.

It might be said finally, in his defence, that *his* 'England problem' is not in fact identical with that associated with Weber's sociology of law. The latter focuses on the compatibility or otherwise of legal form and economic calculation. Neumann, however, is not concerned with the character of legal doctrine itself but with the ideology associated with it. Thus, whether English law did, at a particular time, approximate to the model of formal rationality is not in issue. What is important is whether the controlling ideology of the Rule of Law *asserts* the unity, comprehensiveness, and rationality of the legal order. On this basis the assumed *cultural* cohesion, postulated above, of the common law in its heyday may be sufficient to support Neumann's arguments about the image of the Rule of Law in competitive society, even if his Weberian formulation in terms of logical system and formal rationality is not.

Nevertheless it is extremely unlikely that Neumann could accept such a solution. The 'completion' of the common law by means of its cultural presuppositions was, on the view proposed above, achieved through open standards and implicit values (for example, of economic rationality, morality, propriety, collective self-interest, or custom); these being grounded in conceptions, broadly shared by judges and litigants, of the nature and requirements of the existing social, political, and moral order. But it is precisely these kinds of open-ended standards which Neumann identifies in the Weimar context as *antithetical* to the Rule of Law of competitive society.

The Experience of Weimar

The last thirty pages of *The Rule of Law* which deal succinctly with the experience of Weimar and its immediate aftermath are really

the justification for and final resolution of all the previous discussions in this long, detailed, and rich book. What Neumann
has to say here about the ill-fated Weimar constitution is ampli-
fied in very important respects by the collection of his and
Kirchheimer's Weimar writings published as *Social Democracy and
the Rule of Law* (Kirchheimer and Neumann 1987). For students
of the Rule of Law today these discussions provide much food
for thought.

Two points from Neumann's analysis of the legal transformation brought about by the emergence of the corporate society
seem crucial. First, as mentioned earlier, the incorporation of
the lower classes into the political order eventually produces, in
Neumann's view, a fundamental crisis in the institutions of the
liberal polity—especially Parliament, whose authority declines along
with its rational, law-making capabilities. In *The Rule of Law*
Neumann sees two possible consequences. One is the abolition of
democratic law-making structures, as in Fascist Italy and Nazi
Germany. Another, which he views as a merely temporary, stop-
gap, measure is reliance on bills of rights to restrict the activity
of democratic parliamentary institutions. Neumann's discussion of
Weimar implies two further consequential developments as virtually inevitable: first, the growth of law-making by the executive at
the expense of Parliament; and, secondly, an increasing blurring
of the distinction between legislation and administrative action.

A second crucial point about the emergence of corporate society is that the idea of legal generality ceases in conditions of
monopoly capitalism to serve the ethical, equalizing function which
it served in the competitive society. Neumann writes:

In a monopolistic economic organisation the legislature is very often
confronted with only one individual case or with a limited number of
monopolistic undertakings. The legislature often can and must use individual regulations in order to do justice to these specific circumstances.
Or should it be compelled to veil an individual regulation by having
recourse to a general norm which is avowedly only intended to serve one
particular case? . . . In the economic sphere, therefore, the postulate of
the generality of the law becomes absurd if the legislature is no longer
concerned with equal competitions, but with monopolies violating that
principle of equality on the market which we have found to be essential
to the theory of classical economy. (Neumann 1986: 275)

Thus, while in competitive society formal equality expressed in the idea of legal generality mirrored a substantive equality of competing entrepeneurs, in Weimar's corporate society it was used by hostile critics and interest groups to oppose reformist social policies aimed at promoting material equality through individual regulation. 'By this the generality of law took the place of a natural law. It was in fact nothing but a hidden natural law' (Neumann 1986: 276).

Neumann's claim, therefore, seems to be that while the liberal ideal of legal generality is of great importance and has a 'decisive ethical function' (1986: 256) of providing a minimum yardstick of social and political equality, it cannot be the sole or even the dominant guide for all state action in the corporate society.

Neumann's essays suggest where he hoped other guides might be found during the Weimar period. Weimar's constitution contained an uneasy juxtaposition of *Rechtsstaat* principles (for example, security of property, parliamentary sovereignty, and individual civil liberties) and, especially in its controversial second part, 'social rights' and provisions governing the organization of the economy, social welfare, trade union rights, and obligations of citizens to the community as a whole. Neumann's essays portray the constitution as founded not just on the political needs of the individual citizen in relation to the state, but on actual social contracts (which he identifies as specific historical events) in which the different interest groups, parties, and centres of power (including labour and capital) produced a constitutional structure mediating their conflicting interests and expectations.

One consequence was that the right of property, which liberal theory treats as sacrosanct—being antecedent to the state—was seen as subject to the legal requirements created by this constitution of groups, or 'collectivist democracy' as Neumann calls it (1986: 271). The state was to use private organizations in its tasks and give them a share of political power; it should act as a neutral third party between the negotiating and collaborating groups, interfering only if the 'social opponents' could not reach agreement. And it depended on a balance of social forces which, in the event, was soon upset.

While Neumann's efforts to see in this unstable structure something positive in replacement of the liberal *Rechtsstaat* are interesting, his essays (originally published between 1930 and 1935) can only be a tribute to what might have been. The papers published after Weimar's demise show a more explicit Marxist influence which is also clearly present in *The Rule of Law*. What is most instructive, both from the Weimar discussion in the latter work and from Neumann's and Kirchheimer's essays, is the detailed evidence of the sequence of constitutional collapse.

Not only was the ideal of legal generality used by legal and political critics as a propaganda weapon to paralyse regulatory activity, but the Weimar judiciary invented wholly new powers of judicial review of legislation to protect property rights. The principle of expropriation, analysed in a long essay by Kirchheimer (Kirchheimer 1983), was extended by courts and legal writers from its limited technical meaning to a broad and vague notion used to curtail interference with vested property interests (although provisions of the constitution seemed clearly to authorize redistributive economic policies). Courts, sometimes in support of the executive, began to use open regulatory standards (*Generalklauseln*)— which pervaded Weimar law—and indefinable principles of 'good faith' (*Treu und Glauben*) increasingly to control the consequences of Parliament's legislative activities and to protect monopolies. The doctrines of the 'free law' school, which had been ignored during the era of competitive capitalism, now influenced courts and jurists alike and justified the idea of untrammelled judicial decision to upset or frustrate legislation.

Kirchheimer's essays are almost entirely critical and need to be read in the light of more direct indictments of the whole Weimar constitutional structure contained in his other writings (see Kirchheimer 1969). While, like Neumann, he recognized the Weimar structure as a new constitutional form, he viewed it consistently as a device by which the middle class could maintain economic and social power (Kirchheimer 1969: 41–2). By contrast, Neumann saw real gains in social justice achieved in the Weimar period. Thus, based on his everyday observation of the industrial courts in which he worked, and on statistics of cases, Neumann asserts that: 'In spite of the political weakness of the Weimar democracy, the legal protection of the poor and of the working class reached a very high standard' (Neumann 1986: 283). This was a view he never substantially revised throughout the rest of his career (cf. Neumann 1953: 177).

The Future of the Rule of Law

What lessons are to be learned from this experience and from these analyses? An optimistic view of Weimar would be that, given different historical conditions, something like its constitutional contract for corporate society might work. Neumann is careful to distinguish this arrangement from corporatism, as he understood it, in which the state merely co-opts independent organizations and social groups. But in present British constitutional conditions which lack any clear model to compete with the twin constitutional pillars of the Rule of Law and parliamentary sovereignty it may be more immediately practical to ask directly what lessons relating to prevailing conceptions of the Rule of Law are to be gained from these writings.

Neumann had no doubt that modern corporate society requires active and extensive state administrative activity. Equally, as noted above, much of this activity—in so far as it is aimed at efficient regulation in the general interest—may justify the use of individual directives and particular controls rather than general laws. Further, modern regulation tends to encourage a breakdown of the distinction between legislation and administration. In this regard one can suggest that the attribution of formal legal equality to entities vastly different in power (especially economic power)—for example, giant business corporations and individual consumers or small traders—may be inappropriate,[5] and serve only to undermine the liberty that the Rule of Law in competitive society guarantees. All of these conclusions seem fully justified by the evidence and arguments that these books present. Thus, their analyses point appropriately to a reassessment of the Rule of Law and its necessary modification to prevent the insistence on formal equality before the law from destroying the very possibility of basic liberty of ordinary citizens, as a substantive ideal.

Of course, many problems arise in any such reassessment; and significant risks. Neumann himself assumed that the ideal of legal generality was a necessary guarantee of the minimum liberties of citizens. But, again with some justification, he saw this guaranteed minimum as, in reality, 'steadily shrinking' (Neumann 1953: 189) and, in such a situation, the increasing interpenetration of

---

[5] See further Lustgarten 1988; and Neumann 1953: 171–2, 178.

law-making and administrative powers was not only inevitable but, on balance, desirable. In 1949 he wrote that 'the separation of administrative and legislative functions not only does not guarantee freedom, but hampers the utilization of the state's power for desired social ends' (Neumann 1949: lxiv).

What then of judicial control? No doubt the Weimar experience coloured both Neumann's and Kirchheimer's views of judicial capacities to protect the equal liberties of citizens. Years later, Kirchheimer wrote acidly: 'One does not wish away the reality of the administrative state in mass society by reminiscing on the judge's social role in bygone days' (Kirchheimer 1967: 435). One suspects that, for Neumann, the higher judiciary were the real villains of Weimar's constitutional collapse (cf. Neumann 1987: 72). He notes that the weaker the state, the more likely it is that judges will assert their power (Neumann 1986: 276).

Yet it can be suggested that if wise and expert administration based on sound knowledge of social and economic conditions really is essential in the modern state, judges can hardly do more than rubber-stamp it or restrict it. In policy matters they are, in Kirchheimer's words, 'experts in non-expertise' (Kirchheimer 1967: 435). Thus, if we adopt the kind of outlook suggested by Neumann's and Kirchheimer's writings, the judiciary's role in relation to key administrative tasks remains highly problematic. When, later, Neumann reassessed Montesquieu's separation of powers doctrine he affirmed the need for an independent judiciary (Neumann 1949: lxiv; and see Neumann 1953: 167), without which the minimum guarantees provided by legal generality certainly could not be secured. But he offered no further elaboration of the significance of the judicial function.

One might assume that if none of the traditional structures of the Rule of Law in Neumann's sense—legal generality, separation of powers, and an independent judiciary—offers adequate support of fundamental freedoms in contemporary conditions what must remain high on the agenda for discussion is the difficult question of the forms of democracy appropriate to corporate society. Neither Neumann's *The Rule of Law* nor Neumann's and Kirchheimer's essays in *Social Democracy and the Rule of Law*, however, have much of real value to say on contemporary issues of democracy. Neumann makes the point in his book that the Rule of Law as an ideal of legal form never presupposed democratic structures, and at least in pre-Weimar Germany was a partial substitute for them. Kirchheimer provides, in one of his essays (Kirchheimer and Leites 1987), a discussion of Carl Schmitt's conception of democracy, but this hardly takes the matter further in the present context. While Neumann's later writings, especially, address such issues as popular participation and democratic accountability, they do so in a highly cautious, orthodox, and somewhat contradictory way.[6]

The likely reason, if hardly an adequate justification, is that Neumann (and probably Kirchheimer, too) tended to see real freedom as something that increasingly needed to be created through responsible, state-co-ordinated action serving common interests; and not just treated as a pre-existing attribute of citizens only awaiting expression. But the key word 'responsible' remains substantially unexamined in these writings.

Neumann's and Kirchheimer's works discussed in this chapter provide ultimately no conclusive prescriptions for legal security in corporate society. It would be surprising if—given the context and times in which their analyses were written—they should do so. They are coloured by a specific, disastrous, historical experience. But in trying to come to terms with it they offer useful insights into the modern dilemmas of the Rule of Law. One can surmise that if Neumann were alive today he would probably applaud recent re-assertions in Anglo-American legal philosophy of the need to keep principle and policy separate. At the same time, one can guess, also, that he would express profound doubts about continued declarations of faith in the capacity of judges to do this. And he would surely urge—as many recent writings in administrative law have done—a much more positive view of administration within the scope of law as the necessary centre of governmental responsibility in the modern state.

[6] Cf. the views on popular participation in administration expressed in Neumann 1949: lxiv, and in Neumann 1953: 191–2.

9 Law, Morality, and Solidarity: The Durkheimian Tradition

Émile Durkheim's presently underestimated writings on law are important because of his consistent attempt to find links between law and contemporary moral conditions. While his lack of attention to questions of political power is initially hard to understand, it is explicable in terms of Durkheim's single-minded concern with moral frameworks of social solidarity. A survey of present applications and developments of Durkheimian legal theory and sociology of law suggests that Durkheim's work should be read primarily as a sociologically informed discussion of what law *might be*—what it has the potential *to become* as an expression of solidarity, rather than as an account of law's present moral or political character in complex societies.

Among the classical traditions of sociology of law, that based on Émile Durkheim's work is at once the most problematic and the least developed in modern literature. Indeed, Durkheim's writings, almost symmetrically spanning most of the last two decades of the nineteenth century and the first two of the twentieth, remain the last neglected continent of classic theory in the sociological study of law. Although his major theoretical ideas are part of the common currency of social science as a whole, it is possible for a contemporary sociologist to declare that 'at the present time Durkheim's reputation is the lowest' among those of the classic figures of sociology, and that 'the author of sociology's most powerful manifestos, "Mr. Sociology" himself' is 'probably at his low point in popularity in the seventy years since his death' in 1917 (Collins 1988: 107). If this statement is correct, and if, in this case, general sociological repute carries over to the special field of legal studies, the short term prospects for further development of Durkheimian sociology of law are not good. This chapter is intended to consider how far that bleak view is justified.

Durkheim on Law

Durkheim's writings on law are voluminous, if largely fragmentary, extending far beyond the texts by him that make up Steven Lukes and Andrew Scull's useful reader on *Durkheim and the Law* (Lukes and Scull, eds., 1983). Further, law was always a major focus of interest for the school of followers and colleagues clustered around Durkheim as contributors to the *Année Sociologique*, the prestigious journal of which the first series, under his editorship, appeared in twelve volumes between 1898 and 1913. Some of the Durkheimians produced substantial monographs on law and legal concepts (Davy 1922; Fauconnet 1928). Numerous anthropological, historical, and theoretical studies bearing on the evolution, functions, or organization of law appeared as products of the Durkheim school. Yet many of these works have never been translated into English and accepted into the English-speaking world's recognized canon of pioneer writings on sociology of law. They do not figure as significant influences on the general development of contemporary studies of law in society. Even in France, the school's homeland, 'the vein seems rather exhausted' (Carbonnier 1978: 114) and the writings of the man whose theories inspired so much of this work are not prominent in influential currents of contemporary sociological research on law. Durkheim's thought remains significant through the diffuse influence of his major sociological concepts (Carbonnier 1978: 111), rather than through any of his specific claims about law.

Reasons for the neglect of Durkheimian ideas are easy to find. Lukes and Scull summarize three 'bold and striking hypotheses about law' originally set out in Durkheim's *The Division of Labour in Society* (Durkheim 1984). First, law is to be conceived as an 'external' index, symbolizing the nature of social solidarity in any society in which it exists. Secondly, legal development presents a relatively consistent evolutionary pattern from the predominance of penal law with repressive sanctions (aimed at the punishment of wrongdoing) to a predominance of 'civil law, commercial law, procedural law, administrative and constitutional law' with restitutive sanctions (aimed essentially at the restoration of the *status quo* in social relationships). This evolution reflects the development of societies 'from less to more advanced forms, from an all-encompassing religiosity to modern secularism, and from collectivism to individualism.' Thirdly, crime is to be understood as a violation of collective sentiments, and punishment an expression of them, so that punishment's 'real function is to maintain inviolate the cohesion of society by sustaining the common consciousness in all its vigour' (Lukes and Scull, eds., 1983: 1, 33, 38, 69).

All three hypotheses, or clusters of hypotheses, have been seen as problematic. As Lukes and Scull note in relation to the first, Durkheim's 'index' view of law is 'remarkably narrowly focused'; law and morality are virtually equated so that law is 'treated as an undistorted reflection of society's collective morality' (Lukes and Scull, eds., 1983: 5, 6). Potential moral conflicts are underplayed. So also is the possibility that law and morality may conflict, or that law is often best analysed apart from moral dimensions. Further, Durkheim's focus on law as a constraint 'precluded any systematic inquiry into its positive or enabling aspects' (Lukes and Scull, eds., 1983: 7).

The Durkheimian legal outlook is contrasted unfavourably with, for example, a Weberian one which seriously addresses the question of law's contribution to the formation of economic and political structures. Durkheim also 'was curiously blind to the sociologically explanatory significance of *how* law is organized—that is, formulated, interpreted and applied'. Seeing law primarily as an expression of a diffuse moral condition of social life, rather than as an instrument or expression of power, he paid little attention to the individual or collective interests or strategies of legislators, judges, lawyers, and administrators. Durkheim's writings treat officials and legal professionals, for example, as 'the executive committee, not of a ruling class, but of the moral consensus of society as a whole; they are the authorized "interpreters of its collective sentiments"' (Lukes and Scull, eds., 1983: 7–8, 45).

These positions ensure that Durkheimian legal theory bypasses most modern research on the organization of legal systems and legal practices, and on relationships among law, power, and economy. In these respects, Durkheim's legal sociology reflects broader problems apparent in his ideas on the state and politics generally (e.g. Giddens 1986); ideas that seem consistently to under-emphasize social and political conflict, and thus the role of law in such conflict.

As if this indictment were not sufficient, it is reinforced by critiques of the second and third Durkheimian hypotheses. A substantial literature now challenges Durkheim's proposed general pattern of evolution from a preponderance of penal or repressive law to one of co-operative or restitutive law (e.g. Barnes 1966; Lenman and Parker 1980). Indeed, some critics claim that an opposite pattern of evolution is revealed by the historical evidence (Sheleff 1975). It has proved rather easy to show that restitutive sanctions or processes of some kind are widespread in simple societies (Malinowski 1926; Schwartz and Miller 1964; Wimberley 1973) and that penal sanctions, with the religious overtones that Durkheim associates with them, are much less prominent than he seems to suggest.

Even in ancient societies possessing written legal codes, which Durkheim particularly emphasized as evidentiary sources for his evolutionary hypothesis, legal control of conduct that in modern societies would be the concern of criminal law was often sought through the public regulation of private redress, composition, or self-help. Further, the use of penal sanctions does not seem to conform to the historical pattern Durkheim indicated (Grabosky 1978). Political centralization, rather than being a contingent and subordinate factor as Durkheim suggested, appears to be directly and consistently associated with greater reliance on repressive controls, and with greater punitive intensity (Spitzer 1975; Spitzer 1979; cf. Lukes and Scull, eds., 1983: ch. 4). It has not been difficult to argue that, with the growing power and scope of modern states, the repressive character and functions of law increase and, indeed, that modern types of law characterized by Durkheim as restitutive have significant penal aspects.

Durkheim's third hypothesis or cluster of hypotheses entails, as Lukes and Scull note, three separate claims. First, crime and punishment promote social integration in so far as crime elicits punishment which, in turn, reaffirms collective beliefs and sentiments, and thus social solidarity. Secondly, a certain level of crime is to be considered normal and a crime-free society is impossible. Indeed, if existing types of crime disappeared, society would create new types in order to allow the condemnation of deviance necessary to fulfil the expressive and integrative function of punishment. Thirdly, crime has a generally indirect, but very occasionally direct utility in provoking change in society's moral framework. Durkheim gives the example of Socrates' crime of promoting unacceptable ideas, which perhaps directly helped prepare the way for a new Athenian morality.

With respect to the idea that crime and punishment are functional to social integration, Lukes and Scull argue that the primary difficulty of the thesis is its vagueness. Without clarifying 'which practices, relations and institutions constitute "society" and, in consequence, just what constitutes the "social disintegration" that would *ex hypothesi*, attend the non-punishment (to what extent?) of criminal offences (which? and committed by whom?)' (Lukes and Scull, eds., 1983: 18), the thesis merely serves as a conservative justification for any chosen institution or practice or for the punishment of any activity treated as threatening social integration. Further, the assumed distinction between the normal and the pathological which underpins Durkheim's thinking on crime has long been considered problematic (Lukes and Scull, eds., 1983: 86–90; cf Lukes, 1973: 302–13); and the claim that crime provokes changes in the moral framemork of society remains unproven.

Thus, it is not surprising that, as Randall Collins (1988: 108) points out, few sociologists now defend Durkheim's general analysis of crime (he includes himself, Donald Black, and Kai Erikson as three who do).[1] Yet Durkheim's views remain much discussed. A recent major theoretical study of the social character of punishment devotes much attention to Durkheim's treatment, concluding that, while many criticisms of Durkheim's historical generalizations are unanswerable, these 'fail to strike at the heart' of his work (Garland 1990: 49) and do not destroy the power of his reflections on punishment as a component of the complex moral fabric of social life. Indeed, other recent literature on the Durkheimian tradition in sociology, to be considered later in this chapter, suggests that demonstrations of the empirical inadequacy of many of Durkheim's sociological generalizations do not undermine the value of some of his primary theoretical ideas.

To some extent, the problem of coming to terms with the Durkheimian tradition—in the sociology of law as elsewhere—is an aspect of the broader problem of clarifying appropriate

---

[1] See Collins 1992: ch. 4; Erikson 1966; Black 1976: 96, 98; but cf. Black 1976: 78–9.

relationships between theory and empirical research in social science, and, specifically, of establishing appropriate objectives of any social theory of law. It may be that the Durkheimian tradition can be reinterpreted to show that its theoretical 'essence' retains a significance unaffected by some of the serious empirical criticisms of Durkheim's work. Before looking at these possibilities, however, it is necessary to consider the primary context in which Durkheim's name has been invoked in sociological studies of law.

Sociological Justice

Outside the fields of criminology and the sociology of deviance, Durkheim is probably most frequently relied upon in contemporary law and society studies as a reference point for certain broad research traditions, especially those emphasizing positivist rather than *verstehende* methods in social science, the importance of a rigid separation of social fact and subjective values, or the utility of studying 'macro-level' patterns of social variation independently of the motivations or understandings of individual actors. Thus, a Durkheimian tradition has been claimed to underpin the methodological assumptions and approach of most longitudinal studies of courts (Sanders 1990). The Durkheimian legacy is identified with an emphasis on 'macro processes' or social facts which (as in the case of litigation rates) can be studied quantitatively, relatively independently of the 'micro processes' of human social action by which rates are produced.

In a very different context, Donald Black, championing a behaviouralist approach in sociology of law, invokes Durkheim's authority to claim that 'at the level of social life in its narrow sense' law is merely behaviour, and that if concepts of rule or norm are to be used in sociological analysis they must 'always refer to a behavioural pattern of some kind' (Black 1972: 1091). Black has been called 'one of the cleanest, most exact, and elegant, practitioners of the art of Durkheim' (Stinchcombe 1977: 130), yet he rarely invokes his predecessor except as one literature source among many for specific empirical claims. Black is compared with Durkheim usually because of the positivist outlook on social research that both are held to espouse. Both writers 'consider social facts as things'[2] external to and coercive of individuals, and to be studied without compromising a strict separation of fact and values.[3]

Sociological Justice, Black's recent book on law, is, indeed, Durkheimian in many superficial ways. Like his previous work, it shows a burning faith, like Durkheim's, in the power of sociology as 'science' (Black 1989: 102–3; cf. Lukes and Scull, eds., 1983: 99–100); a similar catechismic style involving the bold statement of general social laws (cf. Durkheim 1982); a comparable belief that ambitious generalizations can properly be grounded in deliberately limited but carefully chosen data (cf. Durkheim 1976: 415–6); and, above all, the Durkheimian view that social control is a central—perhaps *the* central—concern of sociology (cf. Black 1984; Black 1976: ch. 6).

Building on the theses of his *The Behavior of Law* (Black 1976) and subsequent works, Black seeks to show, with a sociological imperialism strongly reminiscent of Durkheim, that all who practise, use, or make law need the resources of sociology; that behavioural sociology of law can show the way law really works; and that no participant in legal processes can afford to ignore sociology's lessons. This powerful modern sociology of law, which reveals the social structure of litigation, Black calls the 'sociology of the case'. This structure refers primarily to clustered criteria of relative social status, relational distance, authoritativeness, and organization that determine which cases, claims, and litigants are 'sociologically' strong or weak. The sociology of the case allows the 'self-conscious application of sociology to legal action' and the possibility of 'sociological justice' (Black 1989: vii).

Lawyers are now in a position to understand, with the aid of the sociology of the case, how law 'as a natural phenomenon' (Black 1989: 4) behaves. In principle, they could choose cases on such a basis (weighing the possibility of success or failure in terms of litigants' and other legal actors' relative social status, relational distance, and collective organization or isolated individual character). They could select witnesses or determine how to handle them

---

[2] Cf. Lukes and Scull, eds., 1983: 152, where Durkheim refers to the consideration of law 'as a set of things, of given realities the laws of which must be sought according to the method of the natural sciences'.

[3] Durkheim 1982: 52, 60, 159–62; Black 1972: 1091, 1094–5, 1098. See also e.g. Griffiths 1984: 38–9.

by taking careful account of 'authoritativeness' criteria related especially to relative social status and associated characteristics of
'powerful' or 'powerless' speech and demeanour; and they could
assess prospects of success before particular judges and juries using
similar criteria. They could fix their fees accordingly and in all
aspects of their work design strategies on sociological as much
as 'technical' legal criteria. 'In theory, an attorney might design
an entire practice from a sociological standpoint' (1989: 26).

Thus, Black fulfils Durkheim's intention, though hardly in the
way Durkheim envisaged, that sociology should provide useful
knowledge for the special field of law. Being value-neutral, the
sociology of the case is not committed to particular interests or
non-scientific objectives. Thus, Black points out that while it should
have special relevance in law schools (*Sociological Justice* is the
product of its author's several years of teaching sociology of law
at Harvard Law School), this knowledge cannot be monopolized
by lawyers. Indeed, litigants could use it in choosing their lawyers.
With no hint of irony but a strong sense of theoretical symmetry,
Black adds that the sociology of the case is available to help criminals select their victims; for sociology can explain which victims
are likely to complain and seek redress and, if they do, which will
be in a potentially strong position in terms of the total social
structure of the case, so as to make it predictable that the offender will be subjected to legal sanctions (1989: 39).

The value-free character of the sociology of the case comes into
its own here, as it does when this sociology provides lawyers with
the technical knowledge for scientific screening of cases and clients. The sociology of the case highlights the relatively poor prospects for legal professional entrepreneurs in representing blacks,
the poor, and the homeless, women in general, and a host of
disadvantaged or relatively 'low status' isolated individuals in
litigation. Indeed, it can help a lawyer calculate whether to demand higher fees when involved in such unpromising cases (1989:
25–6). Sociology, Black reminds us, 'is only a tool, not a theology'
(1989: 33).

Despite the availability in principle of the sociology of the case
to all, Black undoubtedly considers that the best immediate prospects for its career as useful knowledge reside with lawyers. As
he readily admits, many are already aware of some of its findings.
Yet, lacking proper sociological data and theory they frequently

make false assumptions. Thus, the common sense 'theory of deep pockets', which suggests one should sue the most affluent available party, is wrong because the sociology of the case reveals that such action will usually involve 'upward' law, hard to mobilize against relatively high status defendants. Again, the common sense 'theory of the pathetic plaintiff', suggesting that sympathy for the downtrodden can be enlisted to win cases, is sociologically wrong because these litigants are usually the weakest on all sociological criteria of success in legal conflicts.

The most substantial parts of Black's book are certainly its first two chapters which restate, elaborate, and supplement, in the form of the sociology of the case, some of the provocative insights and empirical generalizations established in *The Behavior of Law*, and then present this material as useful to participants in legal processes. Noting appropriately that 'many readers will surely find the idea of sociological litigation unattractive' and that the 'application of sociology to litigation might well shock and disgust anyone who believes in the rule of law' (1989: 39), Black seems to have three answers for such faint hearts. The first is that wishful thinking cannot make the legal realm different from what it is. Secondly, while it is foolish to imagine that changes in law itself could overcome the discriminations that undermine the pretentions of the Rule of Law, there are possibilities for adjusting the social structure of litigation to counter some discriminations affecting litigants, and for insulating legal processes in certain ways from this social structure. Black's third, most radical answer is that if we look at law sociologically and do not like what we see, an appropriate response is to reduce the scope of law to a minimum, rather than to try to do something further about the social conditions that defeat its claims to treat litigants fairly.

Thus, the remainder of *Sociological Justice* speculates freely about ways in which the organization of law, and ultimately the scope of law, might be dramatically changed to escape the discriminations and inequalities inevitable in modern legal systems. First, Black recites the advantages that organizations have over individuals in virtually all aspects of the legal process (1989: 41–4; cf Black, 1976: 91–6). The social structure of the case almost always favours corporate actors as against isolated individuals. A rational response, therefore, would be for individual litigants to organize to redress the structural imbalance. Seizing upon the illustration of the 'dia-paying group' institution apparently found among some Somalian nomads, Black suggests transplanting a version of it to modern Western litigious societies and relabelling the transplant a legal co-operative association, or 'legal co-op'.

Legal co-operatives 'would collectivise the conflicts now defined and handled as the business of individuals' (Black 1989: 50). They would take on the litigation (both claims and defences) of their members, who might join co-operatives voluntarily or perhaps be required to take out membership like a kind of compulsory insurance. The collectivity would act in disputes, civil or criminal, involving its members, holding damages received from their claims, and paying damages for which their members were held liable, though 'the individual directly involved in each case would receive or contribute a disproportionate share' (1989: 50). Co-operatives would also deal with disputes between their members. Black suggests that such a system would reduce economic incentives to sue (since the injured party's co-operative would be the primary recipient of economic redress). It would strongly encourage non-litigious forms of dispute resolution and the use of compensatory remedies and negotiated solutions in criminal cases (since the co-operatives would be able to supervise the whole process of redress). It would also facilitate action against recidivists, who would be far less socially anonymous than at present (since other collectivity members would be directly concerned with their conduct). Recidivists could, if necessary, suffer the penalty of banishment from the association.

These ideas evoke aspects of Eugen Ehrlich's classic theory of the living law of social associations (Ehrlich 1936). Black's co-operatives proposal even calls to mind some of Durkheim's ideas on the delegation of regulation to morally responsible associations intermediate between the state and the individual (e.g. Durkheim 1957: ch. 9). But Black does not relate his proposals to Ehrlich's, Durkheim's, or any other systematic theory. In fact, it is difficult to know what to make of legal co-operatives since almost all important questions about them remain unaddressed. 'How many members legal co-operatives would have, their social composition, how they could be financed, how their activities would be regulated, and other questions remain to be answered, but these details need not concern us here' (Black 1989: 53).

Along with such matters it might be thought essential to consider the major problem of power relationships in these collectivities, the moral or political conditions under which members would actually contribute voluntarily, or be made to contribute to each other's legal welfare, the ways in which grievances and defences would be assessed within the association and disputes between members handled, and the position of those who cannot pay for membership and are likely to be seen as free riders by at least some of those who can. In other words, what remain are almost all of the complex regulatory problems of discrimination, social differentiation, and social structure that Black's proposals are apparently designed to address. His proposals merely enclose these problems within the framework of co-operatives and their interrelations, and remove them from the sphere of responsibility of the legal system of political society as a whole.

From this point on, *Sociological Justice* appears increasingly bizarre. According to Black, the social structure of the case defeats the ideal of the Rule of Law because legal decision-makers (for example, judges and juries) have *knowledge* of such matters as the relative social status, respectability, and authoritativeness of litigants, criminal defendants, and witnesses. Consequently, Black proposes that these decision-makers be denied knowledge, as far as possible, of the social structure of the case. This would entail greatly restricting evidence relating to the circumstances, characteristics, or identity of those involved (Black 1989: 68). Because testimony is coloured by social status and other social structural considerations, witnesses should also be excluded from the courtroom and all evidence presented in documentary form. Litigants and criminal defendants should also be excluded. Cross-examinations would be allowed, but not in court. Only transcripts of the exchanges would be presented (1989: 69–70).

Since lawyers also import their social character into the courtroom they might usefully be excluded as well and reduced to producing arguments to be 'added to the other transcripts submitted to the court for its deliberations' (1989: 70). However, judges and juries are also thoroughly contaminated by social structural determinants of justice. Hence, as far as possible, they too should be expelled from the halls of justice. Admittedly, while 'juries might conceivably be abolished, judges present more of a challenge in sociological engineering'; nevertheless their removal 'would accomplish the final step in the desocialization of courts:

closing the courtrooms themselves' (1989: 71). What would be left would be an embodiment of scientific decision-making immune from the subjective evaluation of social facts: a computer dispensing objective 'technical' legal justice, free of the intrusions of the social structure of the case.

However seriously all this is to be taken (and common law systems today reflect *some* aspects of the tendencies envisaged here[4]), Black's remarkably narrow—and, from a lawyer's perspective, dangerously distorted—perception of law is dramatically demonstrated. It is no longer enough to say that this sociological standpoint is alternative and 'external' to the lawyer's, with which it can co-exist, for now Black's conception of law as governmental social control claims superiority over lawyers' conceptions. What lawyers treat as law is, for him, only a bundle of 'technical' matters, distinct from the 'sociological' aspects of the case (Black 1989: 20–21, 26–7). He shows no recognition that legal participants' views of law might themselves be sociological in an important sense, that legal doctrine itself is, in part, a form of social knowledge, or that processes of creation, invocation, and interpretation of law as doctrine themselves require sociological understanding.

Black sees no substance in legal doctrine and its settings except technicality; it follows that when his behavioural sociology becomes imperialistic in *Sociological Justice*, it *replaces* law, since it treats law as having no social substance, no reality as institutionalized doctrine. In fact, law is invisible to the sociology of the case, which sees only government behaviour. Legality, treated as a hypothesis about behaviour falsified by Black's observations, is dismissed. What the behavioural method makes invisible is the character of the Rule of Law as a fluctuating set of processes, or a cluster of institutional values, professional motivations, and collective aspirations. Seeking the Rule of Law as an observable social fact Black fails to recognize it as a striving towards certain kinds of equality of treatment in governmental activity; a historical tendency dependent on specific social conditions (Neumann 1986); and a complex, ever-changing pattern of regulatory problems and provisional solutions.

---

[4] Examples might be the extension of the use of documentary evidence in trials, the declining practical importance of the jury in the English legal system (including its virtual disappearance in civil cases), and the 'mechanization' of the processing of traffic and other minor offences through the use of tariff systems and administrative, rather than judicial, proceedings.

Another aspect of this myopic perception of law is apparent. The sociology of the case debars itself from understanding what is actually going on in legal arenas. Because it is unconcerned with legal discourses, their effects, and their conditions of existence, it cannot explain *why* the social structure of the case is so difficult for legal processes to cope with. Treating discrimination as an irreducible social fact it has no interest in the balance sheet of law's successes, failures, and possibilities in combating specific discriminations; yet, as will appear, Black draws radical conclusions from an assumption of *inevitable* failure.

Nor can Black's methods recognize the actual constraints on communication and influence among legal, sociological, and other discourses,[5] and the distinctive social characteristics of legal institutions as experienced by those involved with them. Yet these matters are now major concerns in sociology of law, if only because they have a direct bearing on questions about law's regulatory failures and its capacity to provide normative frameworks responsive to social change.

In discussing the authoritativeness and status of judges, for example, Black writes always in terms of general social indicators and gives no attention to the institutional structure, ideology, and organization of judiciaries, which may have as powerful an effect on judges' behaviour as their social origins or allegiances.[6] Yet even thirty years ago, among the legal realists whose collective theoretical contribution is characterized in *Sociological Justice* mainly as something to do with the effects a judge's breakfast has on his decision (Black 1989: 5), Karl Llewellyn (1960) provided perceptive ideas about the influences on judicial work of institutional steadying factors, period styles in judging, and professional 'situation sense'.

The claim that sociology replaces law becomes explicit as *Sociological Justice* progresses. Certainly, the expulsion of most forms of human life from the courtroom is advocated as a way of *preserving* legal processes in improved conditions. But Black makes minimal effort to explore the practicalities, limitations, and consequences of most such proposals. Again, his assumptions that legal decisions

---

[5] See Ch. 3, above, and e.g. Teubner 1989; Nelken 1990.

[6] Compare e.g. Black's assumptions (1989: 32–3) about the relevance of race or ethnic origins of judges and the generally negative research findings reported in Spohn 1990.

can be more fairly and reliably made with less knowledge of the social circumstances in which they arise and to which they are to relate, and that the weight of evidence can be distinguished from assessments of the reliability of its sources are manifestly implausible. All of this suggests that Black's heart is not really in the enterprise of draining law of subjectivity.

The last two chapters of the book confirm this. He proposes that the only real cure for law's failings is to minimize its scope. More explicitly than in his earlier writings (Black 1976: ch. 7), he proposes a kind of supervised anarchy, or perhaps a Nozick-style minimal state, as the way of the future, claiming, in terms reminiscent of Ehrlich, that a 'minimum of law—even a complete absence—is not synonymous with chaos in modern life . . . but may actually bring about a heightened concern with trust, honour, and morality' (Black 1989: 86; cf. Ehrlich 1936: 71).

Black's style never really allows for the expression of irony. Nevertheless, his exploration of radical reforms of legal processes designed to purify law's technical processes may be intended only to show how absurd law's pretentions are. Lawyers and most social scientists typically see discrimination as a cluster of distinct social problems (for example, racism, sexism, ageism) to be addressed, often by means of law. But Black treats as discrimination all patterns of inequality and, therefore, considers it endemic in social life. Thus, in his view, law holds out an impossible dream of equal treatment. Since society cannot be changed by law, it is law which should give way. And, since discrimination, inequality, and disparities of power and influence are natural, it presumably follows—though Black is not explicit—that law as government behaviour should leave the 'natural' social equilibrium of prejudices and dependencies, domination and subordination, privilege and deprivation in peace. Peace may not always be the result, and Black notes that law remains necessary to curb violence. But he believes that law also begets violence, because it reduces the motivation of community members to take responsibility for antisocial acts, and for dealing with offenders in their midst.

Although *Sociological Justice* seeks to be critical, it does not confront the faults and failings of law as a structure of institutions and doctrine. Rather, seeing behaviour divorced from the institutions and ideas that give it meaning in legal contexts, Black's radicalism *avoids* legal issues. His co-operatives are havens of collective self-help against the oppressions of governmental social control. They are not a means of building a more just or legally rational society, as a political project, but of insulating members against the need to participate in such a project. Again, Black's proposals for legal minimalism and his claims about the natural-ness of discrimination suggest that his sociology of law has be-come an excuse to avoid any collective responsibility for promoting a more cohesive society through public institutions of government and law. This is remarkable given the mass of evidence that soci-ological research has presented of the scale of inequality of life chances, and the sense of alienation thereby produced, in mod-ern industrialized societies. Since Black fervently champions the discipline of sociology and its ever-expanding knowledge (1989: 103), it might be asked to what public use he thinks this volumi-nous research should be put.

Ultimately, the question of the supposedly value-free character of behavioural sociology of law reappears. Black's sociology aids lawyers, and litigants in a position to choose their counsel freely. It might also aid criminals in choosing victims. It is employed to show the mythical character of the Rule of Law, and the potential of law as governmental repression. Yet it does not seem concerned to examine rigorously the consequences that would follow for 'have-nots' if law were to be replaced with near-anarchy.

Black's sociology emphasizes public power. Thus, he claims that the poor would not suffer greater victimization if law were reduced, since they are already often victimized by law enforcement agents and processes. But he makes no mention of forms of *private* power which law channels (for example, through contracts and property) and, therefore, to some extent regularizes and makes predictable. Black's sociology does not explore the benefits, for the relatively powerless, of legal formality in this channelling process (e.g. Delgado 1987) or of the ability to invoke legal rights (e.g. Williams 1991: 146–65). Nor does he address old questions of the rep-ressive character of *Gemeinschaft* relationships from which legal distancing provides some escape (Merry 1990: 174–5), the intol-erances of unfettered enforcement of community morality, or the vulnerability of those whose claims as participants in social life depend not on their significant legal status but only on the emotional responses or economic calculations of others.

Indeed, Black's sociology does not give credence to the idea that law itself holds out an important *promise* of non-repressive community or solidarity embracing all citizens, even if the promise seems broken for many. Even if discrimination is endemic in social life, it does not follow that all forms of discrimination have the same essential character, causes, and conditions of existence and raise the same policy issues, nor that all are immune to legal control or influence. In short, behavioural sociology of law, as expounded in *Sociological Justice*, has a no less unbalanced agenda of priorities and preferences than does law itself. This may be because, in ignoring law's character as institutionalized doctrine, it cannot confront distortions in the social vision of legal doctrine but merely substitutes its own.

Rethinking the Durkheimian Tradition

The most significant part of the Durkheimian tradition may be excluded by Black's use of seemingly Durkheimian methods. While subscribing to a view of sociology as the scientific and, in some sense, value-neutral, study of social facts, Durkheim saw it also as a form of enlightenment. Moral concerns could never be far from the centre of a science whose primary object was the study of society as a moral phenomenon. Indeed, the Durkheimian concern to identify moral foundations of modern secular societies that are dominated by instrumental reason is central to a recent revival of interest in Durkheim's substantive work among sociologists.

Whereas, for Black, law and morality compete with and replace each other as modes of social control (Black 1976: 107), for Durkheim they are mutually reinforcing and deeply interpenetrating. Unless treated as behaviour, law, for Black, is merely abstract technicality, almost invisible to sociology. By contrast, Durkheimian law expresses real social bonds as an officially sanctioned form of morality. Thus, law as institutionalized doctrine does not disappear from sociological view. Durkheim's sociology makes questions about law's moral functions and grounding central, whereas for Black these questions are non-existent.

For Durkheim, legal action is necessary to limit gross inequalities (especially of inherited wealth) in the interests of maintaining the balance of moral interdependence that constitutes social solidarity in modern conditions (cf. Pearce 1989: 78). Law is a necessary means of providing the framework for and expressing this solidarity. Black's sociology does not examine whether solidarity could exist in the near anarchy it proposes, nor whether the removal of law's flimsy efforts at promoting justice would only fuel even further the resentment of those excluded from life's benefits. By contrast, for Durkheim and some writers in a renewed Durkheimian tradition, a pressing issue is how to symbolize social unity and create for modern complex societies a moral framework in which regulation is effective, and the regulated are able, in some way, to participate as moral actors in a solidary society which is more than an economic free for all.

Some recent literature shows attempts to reinvigorate these aspects of the Durkheimian tradition. A major hurdle is to overcome, or at least bypass, the perceived defects of Durkheim's political sociology, especially its conception of state and law as largely unproblematic expressions of moral consensus. The various essays in *Durkheimian Sociology: Cultural Studies* (Alexander, ed., 1988) do not address law as such, but their relevance here is in illustrating ways in which modern writers are seeking to advance Durkheimian sociology. Many of these papers use Durkheim's ideas on ritual or the representation of moral unity through the sphere of the sacred. They address such matters as the symbolism of the French Revolution, the political cleansing process of the Watergate affair, the progress of modern revolutions, the sociology of friendship, mass strikes, and the presentation of reality by the mass media. Although the essays canvas many interesting ideas, they frequently give the impression that similar conclusions could have been reached and the structure of argument might not have been very different if no appeal to Durkheim's work had been made. The use of Durkheimian theories or concepts occasionally even seems contrived.

Two papers, by Hans-Peter Müller and Randall Collins, stand out, however, as particularly thoughtful efforts to engage Durkheim's legacy and demonstrate its continuing relevance. Müller uses Durkheim's ideas on civil religion in exploring debates about legitimation crises in advanced capitalism. Like most other contributors, he follows the theme set by editor Jeffery Alexander that Durkheim's later work emphasizing the social functions of religion is fundamental to a renewal of Durkheimian sociology. The 'new understanding of religious phenomena which emerged

after *The Division of Labour'* (Müller 1988: 143) allowed Durkheim
to portray the moral consciousness of modern societies in a new
light. As Müller puts it:

The morality of family, friendship, and professional groups is infused
with a contagious individualism which moves an abstract cultural ideal
into the centre of social life. There is, in short, a shift from rigid regulation via traditional religion and cultural system to open regulation via
the institutional order. There develops a new distribution of moral
competences through the different institutions in modern society . . . Far
from leading to the loss of morality, then, functional differentiation and
secularisation lead in the late Durkheimian perspective to a moral decentralization of social life *and* to an intensive regulation of the differentiated institutions by specific morals (Müller 1988: 144).

Müller thus sees Durkheim as emphasizing complexity and differentiation in modern society and, at the same time, denying that
this makes moral bonds unimportant. On the contrary, modern
individualism presupposes and requires expression through moral
bonds sustained by differentiated institutions, such as occupational
groups. A coherent but complex moral structure of this kind is, in
Müller's view, necessary for the legitimacy of a modern social and
political order. Durkheim sketched the conditions for a modern
society of solidarity: 'a corporative society in which professional
organization overcame economic anomie in the economy, welfare institutions combined economic efficiency with social justice
in the polity, and democracy restructured communication and
restored checks and balances throughout' (Müller 1988: 146).
Essential to such a structure, Müller argues, is the adherence of
individuals to a moral community (1988: 148).

While Müller's argument may seem distant from legal concerns,
it shows a serious effort to argue that Durkheim's conception of
morality in modern societies is more complex and sophisticated
than the idea of an undifferentiated *conscience collective*. Morality is
located in differentiated institutions and therefore linked to many
different kinds of regulation and different types of regulated groups
within society. It is, therefore, less monolithic than is claimed in
many accounts of Durkheim's work. It would seem to follow that
law as an index of morality may also be more complex, more
differentiated, and perhaps more contradictory than the law-as-
index thesis at first proposes.

Collins' essay takes on the seemingly unpromising task of re-vealing Durkheim as a theorist of social conflict. His strategy is the simple one of reading Durkheim's ideas on integration, consen-sus, and shared values as referring not to 'whole societies' such as nation states but to '"society" in its generic sense, as any instance of prolonged sociation, whatever its boundaries in space or in time' (Collins 1988: 109). Thus, Durkheim's ideas on morality and so-cial solidarity can be treated as defining the conditions of unity or cohesion of various collectivities within political societies. The cohesion of social classes can be considered in these modified Durkheimian terms. Collins' development of this idea seems simp-listic, however, when he attempts to contrast middle-class or-ganic solidarity with working-class mechanical solidarity, and it seems a distortion of Durkheim's ideas to suggest that they can provide the basis for a conflict sociology simply by turning their claims about social cohesion into claims about cohesive groups or classes engaged in confrontation with each other. Nevertheless, Collins moves imaginatively in a direction similar to Müller's in suggesting that Durkheim's theories can be used to emphasize moral and social diversity no less than uniformity.

Frank Pearce's recent book *The Radical Durkheim* (Pearce 1989) also tries to save Durkheim from himself by applying his ideas to portray society as a complex of discourses, moral frameworks, and systems of action. Like Müller and Collins, Pearce thinks that Durk-heim's writings provide some warrant for this strategy although he recognizes that Durkheim often treats society as a monolithic 'expressive totality' (1989: 26, 106). Pearce's book is essentially a set of linked essays dealing with such matters as the divergent components of Durkheim's sociological outlook, his politics, as-pects of his study of suicide, the origins and forms of the divi-sion of labour, and the relationships between Durkheim's view of modern society and Marx's. Pearce's avowed aim is to enlist a 'modified Durkheimianism' to develop a conception of a feasible democratic socialist society, which seems to mean here a society combining individualism with reinvigorated democratic traditions and conditions of community, which entail a sense of participation and 'belonging', drawing society's members into a moral commit-ment to each other. The appeal of Durkheim for Pearce (as for Müller) is precisely his stress on the constructive moral founda-tions of social order and his recognition of the complexity of moral conditions in modern Western societies and the need for diverse institutional locations for moral bonds.

The Radical Durkheim returns us directly to law since two of its chapters specifically concern Durkheim's ideas on the subject. Pearce boldly suggests that the relevance of the Durkheimian tradition today must be found in the substance of what Durkheim has to say about links among law, morality, and society, rather than through any generalized appeals to a Durkheimian positivist methodology in social research. Indeed, Pearce shows convincingly that Durkheim's outlook on sociology is too complex and multi-faceted to be appropriately summarized in the package of protocols of research to which the term 'Durkheimian methods' is often attached. Durkheim's work contains, for example, explicit or implicit critiques of empiricism, methodological individualism, positivism, theoreticism, and metaphysical conceptions of society (Pearce 1989: 19). The 'brilliance' of Durkheim's outlook is in its 'feel for the power of the social'; while its fundamental failings are the tendency to treat society as a sentient being, and the belief in a separable social essence and in societies as 'unities of complex wholes' (Pearce 1989: 19, 25). For Pearce, Durkheim's work consists of a variety of 'intersecting discourses,' often mutually contradictory but allowing the possibility of development. Trying to read Durkheim constructively, he does not hesitate to use Durkheim's concepts in ways that might have startled their originator.

Pearce tries to trace Durkheim's earliest views on law. He looks beyond the familiar texts to rely heavily on an 1887 essay on the 'Positive Science of Morality in Germany' which discusses the ideas of the German jurist Rudolf von Ihering (Durkheim 1986). Here Durkheim explains, apparently with approval, Ihering's view of relationships between law and force. 'In origin, law is nothing but force limiting itself in its own interest' (Durkheim 1986: 351). Peace treaties are early forms of law. In so far as the victor could destroy the vanquished but considers it unprofitable to do so, these treaties consist of 'rules which restrain the power of the victor; doubtless, it is the victor who imposes this on himself, but nevertheless law benefits the vanquished' (1986: 352). Thus, force precedes law but becomes subordinated to it and serves it. Law is coercive, but its positive aspects are to be stressed. Further, if law fails to maintain the social balance (the 'peace treaty') that is its ultimate *raison d'être*, 'force, instead of letting itself be regulated by the law, could overturn it to create a new version of it' as in a revolution (Durkheim 1986: 352). In Pearce's view, if Durkheim had followed this 'Hobbesian conceptualization' of the relationship between law and force in his later work and emphasized conflict and power in social change 'he might have developed a more adequate theory of law' (Pearce 1989: 108).

It is, however, by no means as clear as Pearce seems to think that Durkheim accepted Ihering's positions in this early paper. Not much evidence suggests an early Durkheimian position contrasting strongly with that of the later writings. Consequently, Pearce's discussion is more productive when it seeks constructive elements in Durkheim's later views on law, punishment, and legal evolution.

Research now suggests that repressive measures are typically *not* the predominant form of social control in what Durkheim termed *sociétés inférieures*, and that compromises and restitutive measures prevail. But Pearce cites modern anthropological arguments that collective action of a severely repressive kind (expulsion or execution) is used in technologically simple societies against gross violators of community norms or against recidivists (Pearce 1989: 96–7). According to the anthropologist Sally Falk Moore, while Durkheim may have greatly overestimated the scope of repressive law and its significance in the general life of simple societies, 'he was right about the larger picture, the existence of ultimate penalties for that source of group disruption, the trouble maker, the individual who will not conform' (Moore 1978: 124). In some ancient societies possessing legal codes, Durkheim's primary error, Pearce suggests, was in failing to recognize the limited role of law as one form of social control, alongside informal social controls based in the extended household structure (Pearce 1989: 94). But Durkheim was not wrong to believe that the possibility of punishment of gross violators of certain social norms of basic collective concern is fundamental to the moral constitution of early or simple societies.

This conclusion certainly does not vindicate Durkheim's hypotheses about legal evolution. Pearce is right to stress that legal development is related to political and organizational factors which Durkheim considers only to a very limited extent. But Durkheimian sociology did properly draw attention to the general sociological importance of the idea of *responsibility*. 'Every collectivity will impose obligations on its members and impute to them the capacity for responsibility' (Pearce 1989: 97), presumably symbolized most powerfully in the treatment of those who most blatantly reject responsibility. What is most significant in Durkheim's legal sociology is not any claims it may make about the specific character of legal regimes in particular phases of social development but the development of the idea of institutionalized social responsibility, which Pearce calls the 'juridical relation'. The juridical relation 'is endemic to social order itself' and refers 'not so much to formal legal relations but rather to the ways in which individuals are held responsible for their actions' (Pearce 1989: 99). 'It is only if individuals are, on occasion, considered responsible for their actions that they are recognized as personalities; thus punishment can rejuridicalize subjects' (1989: 101).

The idea of the juridical relation remains vague but what Pearce is attempting through its use is the recovery of Durkheim's ideas about links between punishment and the moral constitution of social groups or societies (cf. Garland 1990: 68; Fauconnet 1928: 227) and about the symbolism of the relationship between individual and group provided by the formal attribution of responsibility.[7] The project is to recover these insights without being ensnared by Durkheim's legal evolution thesis, or by his failure to follow through Ihering's insights about relationships between law and power. Pearce's efforts along these lines are in tune with the general emphases of Durkheim's sociology and constructive in opening up important sociological questions about moral foundations of social life, expressed through legal ideas including those of responsibility.

But Pearce does not go far enough since he fails to explain the relationship between these ideas about responsibility and Durkheim's more specific discussions of *law*. He apparently thinks that we can applaud a Durkheimian sociology of responsibility as quite distinct from a Durkheimian view of law which is unacceptable because of its remarkable neglect of questions of power and conflict. Following this approach, however, the dilemma of why Durkheim provided such a seemingly inadequate account of law remains impossible to solve.

---

[7] Pearce does not cite Paul Fauconnet's (1928) Durkheimian study of responsibility which, however, similarly asserts the importance of the attribution of responsibility among the mechanisms by which a society is morally constituted.

Durkheim's view of law, therefore, requires further clarification and elaboration. One method of providing this may be through efforts, such as those of Müller and Collins, to explore the ambiguities of Durkheim's conceptions of moral unity and solidarity, and thereby show their relevance in considering political tensions and conflicts. By this means law might be presented as expressing moral diversity as much as any moral unity of a society.

It is also necessary, however, to rescue Durkheim's concepts of restitutive and repressive law from the mass of critical interpretation and testing they have received. Restitutive law should not be conflated with arbitration or mediation (cf. Schwartz and Miller 1964), the prevalence of which in early and simple societies Durkheim well recognized. Durkheimian law does not need a state, but it does need a guarantee produced by 'the very conscience' of the society in which it exists; in other words, by the fact that members of the society at large 'feel linked together in the struggle for existence' (Lukes and Scull, eds., 1983: 149). Hence, localized dispute resolution, however fundamental to social control, is not enough to satisfy Durkheim's criteria of restitutive law. This law depends upon and reinforces stable relationships between diverse structural components of a society. It requires and expresses a relatively complex pattern of social organization. Georges Davy's (1922) Durkheimian account of the origins of contractual bonds is interesting in this context, since it argues that contract law evolves from public law sources in the constitutional relationships between social groups and family structures. Restitutive law is much more than dispute resolution in specific exchange relationships or local conflicts.

Again, as regards repressive law, it has been claimed that Durkheim mistook the character of early forms of law; in emphasizing the prevalence of penal law and repressive sanctions in simple or ancient societies, he failed to see that 'crimes' in these societies are often dealt with by restitutive measures (Sheleff 1975). But, in fact, Durkheim himself notes this state of affairs (Lukes and Scull, eds., 1983: 64). He sees 'private punishment'—in which the punishment of serious wrongs is left to private initiative—as lying on the boundaries of both repressive and restitutive law (Lukes and Scull, eds., 1983: 66). But he insists that criminal punishment, as such, did not originate in private vengeance or compensation by which many individual wrongs were undoubtedly redressed (Lukes and Scull, eds., 1983: 157). Its wholly different source was in prohibitions presupposing a sense of the social group's moral identity. The redress of wrongs to individuals remained 'on the threshold of the criminal law' (Lukes and Scull, eds., 1983: 127) in early or simple systems. Only later were some of these wrongs pulled into the orbit of a conception of crime established from essentially religious origins.

Thus, Durkheim does not claim that wrongs to individuals in simple or ancient societies are dealt with by penal sanctions. The claim is that penal, repressive sanctions relating to individual, interpersonal wrongs gradually develop as a concern for the integrity of the individual and relations between individuals become matters for society as a whole. Presumably it is at that stage that we begin to observe tariff systems of social control (sometimes specifying exact redress to the victim for wrongs done) as law struggles to assert social control and moral hegemony over matters previously dealt with by feud or negotiated compromise. For Durkheim the eras before these developments are ones in which 'society' exists, if at all, only as the abstract idea of an undifferentiated community, not in complex relations between individuals. Hence, the earliest law, as he understands it, would not be concerned with individual wrongs but with the moral definition of this undifferentiated community.

My aim in making these points about Durkheim's conception of law is not to defend his legal evolution thesis. Rather it is to show that the concepts of restitutive law and repressive law are developed in such a way as to build into them, by definition, the moral components of social solidarity that Durkheim seeks to illustrate through their use. His concepts of restitutive and repressive law are intended to identify generalized legal forms or expressions of certain idealized forms of moral cohesion possible in societies. They are not devised primarily as empirical generalizations about actual legal systems, but are efforts to express, with the aid of legal concepts, certain abstract and elusive moral bonds which are sociologically possible (that is, capable of being experienced as actual social relationships) in particular historical conditions.

In writing about law, therefore, Durkheim is usually searching for material clarifying the character and conditions of existence of these moral bonds. Since his treatment of law serves this purpose

and *not* that of a full account of the political reality of law, his lack
of attention to that wider political reality, including especially the
elements of power and conflict fundamental to law, is less surprising than it otherwise seems.

A further conclusion follows. Because of the way repressive and
restitutive law are conceived by Durkheim, his sociology of law,
in some of its most important aspects, does not allow the kind
of empirical testing that has often been attempted on it. Pearce
(1989: 17) goes too far in claiming that Durkheim's mode of
investigation and explanation is, by its nature, 'unlikely to produce empirical knowledge'. Many important empirical claims
are made in Durkheim's writings on law. But his most important propositions about the general character of law are not set out
in a form that positivist sociology can easily test. Rather, as has
been seen, Durkheim takes from the historical materials of law
suggestive elements relevant to his claims about the moral character
of social life.

Certain aspects of law become, for him, the key to something
that positivist method cannot reach—the condition of responsibility arising from interdependence of individuals or their commitment to a community. When he wrote of treating law as a social
fact he did so because he wished to claim that the methods of
science (as he understood them) could be harnessed to the exploration of moral problems. But after *The Division of Labour*
(Durkheim 1984) was published, the idea of measuring the inci-
dence of types of law in order to observe patterns of social solidarity was largely replaced in Durkheim's work by a more general
idea that legal doctrine and institutions in all their complexity
and variety are integral to the moral life of society, which sociology must understand.

For some critics, the detachment of Durkheim's legal studies
from the ambit of positivist legal sociology might be enough to
condemn them. But Durkheim can be read as a different kind of
theorist of law from the empirical sociologist of legal and penal
evolution that many have tried to find in him. He can also be read
as an empirically minded social philosopher considering what links
among law, individuality, and communal interdependence are
possible, and what the conditions might be for law to function as
an instrument and expression of community or social solidarity,
given the diverse moral milieux of modern societies. Tentative

and inconclusive as any such project of re-reading Durkheim's work on law may be at present, it at least has the merit of keeping to the fore what may be Durkheim's most significant quality: his single-minded search for a sociological grounding for moral bonds in societies that, to many observers, appear to have become far too complex, chaotic, secular, and atomistic for any such moral frameworks to exist.

10 Critique and Law: The Legacy of the Frankfurt School

What conceptual and methodological issues arise in the attempt to develop a sociologically based moral critique of law? In this context, some important ideas of the German scholar Max Horkheimer on the nature of critical theory can be related to theoretical issues presented by the development of the critical legal studies movement in the United States. The conclusion to be drawn is that critical theory and empirical social theory are certainly compatible but critical theory introduces the demand for a 'moral vision' to complete and reformulate the projects of empirical social theory. In this respect critical theory creates certain moral challenges for legal theory which must inform its interaction with the kinds of social theory already considered in previous chapters.

It is not easy for a European, in Europe, to grasp all the important nuances and ramifications of the American critical legal studies (CLS) movement. This is not merely a matter of having to rely on published materials, without easy access to the 'inside dope' of who said what and with what results at summer camp or conference. Much more importantly it is a matter of different intellectual traditions, and traditions of legal and political practice.

At the level of legal traditions, a British writer can rely on common strands which mark a real and important Anglo-American legal style and history. Yet the context (very varied though it may be) of American legal education—a context that informs the problems, practice, and thinking of CLS in the United States so deeply—is very different from the context (cultural, political, professional) of legal education in Britain. This means that some of the specific practical targets of critical legal studies in America may seem rather remote from British concerns. In particular, the sharp divide between the élite law schools and some other sectors of legal (and non-legal) education, which in its acute symbolization of hierarchy (cf. Kennedy 1982) inspires such agonized examination of the nature and possibility of law school radicalism, finds no exact parallel in British legal education.

Coupled with this, but underlining the differences, are contrasts in political culture and practice. In a European context where socialist practice and theory are an established ever-present component of political life and public debate and where socialist thought is an important part of the heritage of political thought, the justification for developing a type of critical thought and practice so centrally focused (as CLS appears to be) on that particular slice of life represented by the law school and the lawyer's practice may seem less than obvious.

The tendency in a European context may be to see the most important avenues of change and influence as quite outside these locales, and indeed to view them as very much less important foci for action than the critical legal studies movement appears to do. The temptation for an outsider is to see CLS as an attempt to offer a substitute for a much broader based (but perhaps presently almost non-existent) movement of social critique; a law school movement pretending to be a radical social movement. Phillip Johnson's hostile comment that critical legal writing 'provides a way of sounding like a radical when you don't know how to be one' (Johnson 1984: 249) needs to be answered.

Equally, however, this in no way alters the fact that CLS has inspired and provided a unifying framework for profound and immensely beneficial changes in the style and scope of much contemporary legal scholarship. Further, it is of the greatest significance that, despite the differences between the European and American contexts just referred to, there seems a developing convergence between the concerns of American CLS and those of the much more fragmentary, and certainly less extensive, literature of critical (or at least 'anti-expository') legal scholarship that has expanded in Britain and other European countries over the past decade or so,[1] despite relatively little direct cross-influence between European and American developments.

The emergence of the CLS movement is of profound present importance for legal scholarship. Whether it can permanently change the nature of legal education and scholarship, whether it

---

[1] For a sample of such material from Britain see Fryer *et al.*, eds., 1981; Sugarman, ed., 1983; Twining, ed., 1986; Fitzpatrick and Hunt, eds., 1987; Cotterrell 1992.

can fundamentally change (or reciprocally influence) legal practice, and whether it will have wider political importance are interrelated and presently unanswered questions. What interests me particularly here is that these questions raise general issues about the nature, rationale, and consequences of 'critique' that are identical with ones faced by the Frankfurt School founders of European critical theory in the 1930s. The most fundamental questions about the epistemology, methods, politics, and prospects of critical legal studies are essentially rooted in ones that the central theoreticians of the Frankfurt School faced and discussed at length.

This chapter seeks to offer a few tentative remarks on some of these general issues about the nature of 'critique'. But it does so in a deliberately limited frame of reference bounded primarily by the writings of Max Horkheimer, the foremost theoretician of critique in the most active period of the Frankfurt School's existence. As such, the concerns of the chapter are part of the more general project of re-exploring the roots of legal theory in social theory.

Questions about Critique

Linking the concerns of Horkheimer with those of CLS is not an attempt to show that there is nothing new under the sun[2] but to explore what to an outsider is a puzzling feature of the American critical legal studies movement: its explicit adherence through its title and frequent citations of Horkheimer, Herbert Marcuse, Jürgen Habermas, and others to the tradition of European critical theory (hereafter referred to, for convenience, as ECT); but its very limited explicit confrontation with the literature of ECT to deal with problems which that literature poses about the ultimate foundations of critical theory and practice.

Peter Gabel's and Duncan Kennedy's (1984) 'Roll Over Beethoven' paper (whose form of presentation no doubt conforms to Kennedy's determination to puncture pomposity and play down abstractions as much as possible) is one of the few CLS papers that confront squarely some of these central 'foundation problems'

[2] Robert Gordon (1984: 102) has, after all, disarmingly suggested that we should accept as an insignificant fact that CLS's understanding of the nature of critique is unoriginal. Interestingly, however, in his personal listing of intellectual antecedents he mentions no Frankfurt School figures.

—about the role and nature of theory as such, about the significance of general concepts in critical analysis, about the philosophy of praxis, about the relevance of utopian thought, about the fundamental aims of critique, and about its epistemological foundations—in a way that shows just how difficult and important they are. Yet the fact that these issues have been faced before in ECT is not adverted to in that paper; let alone is there any mention of the solutions (if any) on offer in ECT literature.

Undoubtedly the critical legal studies movement has a highly ambivalent attitude to social theory—regarding it simultaneously as, on the one hand, the ubiquitous inspiration and context of critical legal studies and, on the other, a reservoir of often unhelpful and even dangerous abstractions and generalizations which ignore or deny the diversity of contexts of critical practice and the 'radical underdetermination' (Gordon 1984: 100–101) of social conditions and legal forms. It seems to me that both views of theory are understandable and in part justifiable but that the ambivalence of their juxtaposition is ultimately stultifying to CLS and that the apparent contradiction between them needs to be removed.

Much is often left unsaid in critical legal studies literature about the exact theoretical foundations of the enterprise, or quite generalized allusions are made to large and often undifferentiated bodies of theory (for example, 'Marx', 'Lukacs', 'Habermas', 'Foucault' or 'The Frankfurt School'). Consequently one is sometimes left with the impression that along with a (proper) rejection of over-broad empirical generalizations and historical laws in social theory, there is also a rejection of any need for a theory of critique. By such a theory I mean a fully elaborated collective view of what the epistemological and ontological foundations of critical legal studies are and what its methods, strategies, and objectives should be.

If, however, the consequence of this apparent lack of theoretical consensus is that CLS is a coalition united only in opposition to legal orthodoxy, it may be that for all its present vitality its long term future is uncertain. Like the Realist 'coalition' in legal thought earlier in this century it may achieve vast success through its explicit organization around experienced discontents of legal practice, education, and scholarship, but be fated for eventual disintegration/absorption because of a lack of an explicit rigorous theoretical foundation from which to withstand the co-optative pressures of legal orthodoxy.

CLS's apparent ambivalence towards theory can, I think, be analysed into five distinct issues which recur in the literature and which can be seen as perhaps its most important theoretical uncertainties.

First, can the relationship between 'law' and 'society' be grasped in general terms at all? Is there any place for general empirical social theory of law which seeks to explain or generalize about law as a social phenomenon? Once 'the constitutive role of law in social relationships' is recognized so that law and society are 'inextricably mixed' (Gordon 1984: 106, 107) and once the need to understand law and legal practices in their specificity is accepted what place remains for general theory about law in society?

Robert Gordon's answer is that there are certainly 'short- and medium-run stable regularities in social life, including regularities in the interpretation and application, in given contexts, of legal rules' but 'none of these regularities are *necessary* consequences of the adoption of a given set of rules' (Gordon 1984: 125). Though this clarifies a particular CLS viewpoint it does not make clear where the limits of social theory relevant to CLS lie or how far CLS depends on such theory. This is important because it raises a larger question of what kind of empirical research on law is useful to CLS (cf. Trubek 1984). David Trubek is surely right to argue that what he calls the doctrinal-empirical dichotomy is false (Trubek 1984: 587). Rejection of the dichotomy is implicit in asserting the constitutive role of law in social relationships. But equally, some clear stance on the nature of empirical research on law and the relationships it constitutes is necessary if we are to begin to understand how, to what extent, and under what constraints law constitutes these relationships.

Secondly, are prescriptions/descriptions of the 'Good Society'— utopian conceptions of a desirable social order towards the promotion of which critique is aimed—necessary or valuable to critical legal studies? A favourite object of attack by critics of CLS is the apparent vacuity and impenetrability of such portraits of the Good Society as are offered in unguarded or visionary moments by CLS writers. But equally the lack of concern apparently shown by CLS for specification of ultimate aims or objectives or desirable future states is an object of criticism as well. There seems to be a lack of

unanimity among CLS writers themselves about the value of utopian prescriptions (cf. Kelman 1984: 343–7). A related though
less abstract problem is whether CLS is necessarily restricted to
negative critique or whether critique can and should be aimed at
positive, constructive ends (which can be defined in some opera-
tional manner), and, if so, what kind of ends.

Thirdly, lying behind both of the above is an even more fundamental issue, addressed directly in the Gabel–Kennedy discussion
(1984), of the value of any general concepts whatsoever. Kennedy
expresses distrust of any concept or idea (including his own 'fundamental contradiction', Gabel's 'unalienated relatedness', and
the notion of 'rights') that can impose (force) meaning on situations other than those in which the concept was formed. On the
one hand is a determination that critique should be of and for
the specific and the concrete and avoid all trace of reifications.
On the other is Gabel's understandable worry that if we take all
this as seriously as Kennedy seems to suggest, we cannot really
talk about anything at all.

Fourthly, how is CLS's agenda of inquiry—its specific choice of
topics for research—to be determined and justified? As Mark
Kelman puts it: 'Surely the objects of our studies of justificatory
micropractices are not *utterly* random (at least, implicitly, I must
have judged that the Model Penal Code's defenders were more
socially significant than phrenologists) but we make little *systematic* attempt to locate precisely our objects of study, whether as
opinion leaders who affect others, fair representatives of a (powerful or not) class, or spokespeople for an epoch' (Kelman 1984:
337).

Fifthly and finally, what is the basis of validity of CLS's central
method—'trashing' (or in ECT terms—immanent critique or ideology critique)? Closely related to this: what is the epistemology
of CLS work? What, if anything, counts as 'truth' here (cf. Trubek
1984: 599–600)? What is the basis of validity of the knowledge
obtained? What sort of knowledge of law and society is it?

Notes from Horkheimer's Agenda for Critical Theory

The rest of this chapter will be concerned with trying to explore
how far these issues about critical theory and practice are

confronted and resolved in some of Max Horkheimer's writings, which seem particularly relevant because of their general concern with the foundations of critical theory and practice.

What is the Relationship between Empirical Social Theory (and Empirical Research) and Critical Practice?

Horkheimer distinguishes critical theory from other forms of theory (which he terms traditional theory) (Horkheimer 1972). It is clear that much social theory (especially of a deterministic or positivistic kind, and including the more deterministic varieties of Marxism) would fall within the category of traditional theory. In essence traditional theory is theory that seeks general or covering scientific laws. Transposed to the human or social sciences it fails to recognize the fundamental involvement of the subject (observer, researcher) with the object studied (society, social relations). Its emphasis on formulating systematically linked sets of propositions is a consequence of the assumption or assertion that ultimately the social world is a finished object awaiting comprehension.

Theory, it is 'traditionally' assumed, must stay close to the facts, relying on 'the gathering of great masses of detail in relation to problems', so that it presents itself as 'stored up knowledge' economically organized (Horkheimer 1972: 206, 208). Equally, however, it tends towards a purely mathematical system of symbols (especially in natural science but increasingly in the social sciences too). Theory seeks prestige from the natural science model— gaining authority (and marketability!), first, from its ostentatious reference to vast amounts of data collected by methods not unlike 'industrial production techniques' (cf. Horkheimer 1972: 208) and, secondly, from the impersonality and objectivity of mathematical models and formulations.

Critical theory *does not deny the utility of traditional theory*, but asserts its radical incompleteness (Horkheimer 1972: 224; Gebhardt 1978: 372). The effect of traditional theory is to deny full recognition of the place of the active individual subject in the seemingly objective social world studied. The individual tends to appear passive; the social object appears active. The essence of critical theory is thus to see subject and object as not identical but inseparable. Therefore, the findings of traditional theory and the empirical researches that are claimed to underpin it have to be reinterpreted continuously. Because subject and object are inseparable there can be no objective standpoint; all viewpoints on social life are partial and limited, reflecting the subject's specific standpoint.

The interesting question is how such partial perspectives are to be overcome. The Hegelian solution is through final transcendence of the subject-object differentiation, subject and object becoming one; the incorporation of diverse perspectives in the unfolding of the universal, absolute Idea—a single perspective which eventually unites all people. 'The closer our knowledge comes to this limit, the closer it is to truth' (Held 1980: 178). The problem of this idealism is that it asserts or assumes that the reconciliation of partial perspectives into universal truth is achievable by some kind of unfolding transcendent reason, above historical contingency. While, for Horkheimer too, critique is to be undertaken in the name of and by means of the yardstick of 'reason', Hegel's idealist critique must in Horkheimer's view be relieved of its complacent tendencies by turning it into materialist critique since 'in genuinely critical thought explanation signifies not only a logical process but a concrete historical one as well' (Horkheimer 1972: 222).

What this involves is highly complex and often obscure but two aspects are important. The first is summed up in Horkheimer's dictum that the overcoming of partial perspectives 'always occurs in the thought of particular historical men' (quoted in Held 1980: 179): in other words, reason cannot fly free of the historical conditions in which people reason. The second aspect, best expressed (much later) by Marcuse, is that if reason is the basis of critique, critique must also drive 'reason itself to recognize the extent to which it is still unreasonable, blind, the victim of unmastered forces' (quoted in Held 1980: 178).

Clearly, 'reason' is being used in two senses here. The reason *of critique* is a reason that seeks to fulfill the interaction and interdependence of individual subject and social object—a reason that sees each individual as a moral person implicated in social life, and all social life as to be judged according to the moral demands of the autonomy and fulfilment of each individual subject. By contrast, the reason *to be critiqued* is, as critical theory later elaborated, above all the instrumental, technological, positivistic, and deterministic forms of reason which imprison the individual subject as a passive observer of 'society'—the object that controls him or her.

Many problems remain with this kind of formulation but it seems clear that in such a view *all* types of existing empirical social theory (and the empirical studies of social phenomena which they organize or attempt to integrate) are relevant to the project of critique. To hold otherwise is to adopt an unnecessarily blinkered view and to debar critique (and CLS) from developing any knowledge beyond isolated studies, with no indication of how far (if at all) possibilities of generalizing from them exist. Critical theory is, however, a special kind of theory, distinct from most social theory. Much social theory falls into Horkheimer's category of traditional theory and serves, at best, as 'raw material' (Gebhardt 1978: 372) for critique. Without it, however, critique is hardly possible, lacking both the necessary basic material and the perspectives with which to work.

My tentative view is that even this conception of the utility of social theory is too limited. Horkheimer's image of empirical social theory and its possibilities was undoubtedly coloured by his view of Marxist analysis as the highest achievement of such theory. As Horkheimer and the other major Frankfurt School theorists came to see the inadequacies and rigidities of orthodox Marxist theory it seems understandable that critical theory appeared to them as the only type of theory that could offer genuine enlightenment about social life. It refused to subscribe to scientific 'laws of history', which experience shows history breaking all the time. It sought different methods which would distance it from the failed gods of social theory's orthodoxies.

Suppose, however, that we do not assume that because social theory offers no wholly satisfactory perspective on social life it consists only of 'failed gods'. Social theory, in its widest sense, can be seen as made up of specific social theories in tension and conflict, each representing a particular partial (though more or less fully elaborated) perspective on social life. These perspectives are not likely to be reconciled in some Hegelian synthesis before the tribunal of transcendent Reason. What is really involved is a conflict between them, fought often bitterly with the weapons of history and experience. The vision of the reconciliation of these perspectives is the vision of *science*; of achieving knowledge that transcends partial perspectives—an aim that is perhaps ultimately unrealisable but certainly necessary. Acceptance of it denies relativism. We can work (struggle) towards what for want of a better term we must call 'truth' even if we shall never attain it. Social theory is essential to this project.

From this standpoint critical theory is a *different* kind of theory altogether. Essentially, critique is the method by which knowledge proclaimed as 'true' is revealed as partial and critical theory is a theory of method. Understood in this way critical theory is a very special kind of social theory or perhaps not social theory at all. Its task is to expound and justify the methods and rationale of critique. Since critique is a permanent task—in my view a necessary responsibility of all serious scholars—critical theory is concerned with what may be relatively timeless matters, including moral and philosophical issues that concern the responsibilities of the individual to his or her society, and the moral worth of a social order judged against the possibilities of realizing the autonomy and authenticity of individuals within it. By contrast, empirical social theory, centrally concerned with the interpretation of continually changing social experience in history, must be in constant flux. Its perspectives are elaborated, challenged, undermined, and reformulated in a constant process according to the judgements of experience.

On Utopian Conceptions in Critical Practice

The second theoretical uncertainty raised earlier in relation to critical legal studies concerns the place of utopian prescriptions or descriptions of the 'Good Society'. How far is it necessary for critique to be organized around explicit conceptions of what is desirable, of some ultimate aims to which critique is addressed in order to build a better future? My conception of critique as essentially method, and critical theory as a theory of method, suggests that critical practice as such cannot, and has no need to, specify particular social arrangements to be aimed at. In so far as critical theory offers prescriptions beyond the narrowly methodological these are likely to be moral prescriptions. As such they cannot be turned by logical deduction into the form of a specification of practical social arrangements. This can be done only by political calculation in specific historical circumstances.

Horkheimer, and most Frankfurt School writers, refused to elaborate any utopian vision of future society, of the possibilities of mankind, or of fundamental human nature. Horkheimer even related this refusal to the traditional Jewish prohibition on naming or describing God and paradise (Jay 1973: 56). It seems to me that a refusal to predict or speculate about the future empirical possibility of particular social conditions is wholly consistent with the position that critical theory is essentially a moral theory and a theory of method. Such predictions could only come, if at all, from empirical social theory.

It seems equally consistent with this position that critical theory should have a clearly elaborated *moral vision*. The difficulties of working towards this are plainly considerable but it can be argued that it is the necessary unifying core of critical theory. ECT failed to develop such a consistent vision. Perhaps this was because the escape from Marxist determinism absorbed so much intellectual energy and because the experience of Fascism and the failure of working class movements was so profoundly demoralizing and induced a pervasive pessimism in so much Frankfurt School writing. Whatever the causes, this failure may account for the fragmented and elusive character of so much of the positive content of ECT.

Concepts, Priorities, and 'Truth' in Critical Practice

The three remaining issues of theory raised earlier in relation to CLS can be discussed together in the context of Horkheimer's version of ECT. This is because most of the central ideas that are relevant have already been mentioned and the remaining aspects that are important here are all interconnected.

It is surely significant that Gabel's and Kennedy's (1984) discussion of CLS ideas largely revolves around the utility and coherence of concepts (especially the 'fundamental contradiction', 'unalienated relatedness', and rights) that are not concepts of empirical social theory (organizing or conceptualizing specific aspects of historical experience) but moral, 'utopian', or transcendental (ahistorical) ideas. In other words they are the kind of concepts we should expect to find at the heart of critical theory on the basis of the arguments earlier stated in this chapter.

Much of the Kennedy–Gabel debate is thus about the utility of utopian prescriptions—the issue discussed in the previous section. In so far as it goes beyond this it seems to me to raise the general questions of the kinds of knowledge that critical practice can create and rely upon, and the kind of principles that should guide the selection of priorities in critical work. Hence fundamental epistemological questions are hinted at. Thus our three remaining

CLS theory issues are closely interrelated, centering on the question of what counts as knowledge (truth?), revealed or created through critique or presupposed by it. The answer to this question surely determines the form (for example, the kind of concepts) in which such knowledge can be expressed and organized. It should also determine how priorities in critical practice are to be set since the choice of priorities depends, first, on what is taken to be reliable pre-existing knowledge and, secondly, on the kinds of knowledge that are sought through critical practice.

For Horkheimer the reason of critique—the reason on which critique relies—cannot be isolated from practice itself. Theory and practice are inseparable (*praxis*) just as object and subject are. Since theory cannot be isolated from practice—action in particular historical conditions—it can never have an existence outside those conditions. There can thus never be a finished picture of reality; there can be no uncovering of immutable truths. The truth of all knowledge is a truth to be judged in the light of the historical conditions in which that knowledge exists. Thus, even ideas that obviously reflect the standpoint of interest groups or historical periods other than our own and which we unhesitatingly consider wrong may have much to teach us—a truth value for their time and for their adherents which is not destroyed but only reinterpreted in the light of other experience or interests.

Critical theory's view that there are and can be no absolute truths—no ultimate reality—but that knowledge can nevertheless progress through the reinterpretation of partial 'truth' in historical experience seems a fruitful one. One of the means of such progress, as Horkheimer and others demonstrated, was through 'immanent critique' or ideology critique involving the critique of a phenomenon or a set of beliefs or ideas by testing the practices associated with them against the structure of truth claims made about them by participants in those practices. Such a strategy provides the implicit or explicit justification also of CLS's 'trashing' strategies (cf. Kelman 1984).

Nevertheless the intellectual legacy of Marxism caused serious problems for this conception of knowledge in ECT. As Martin Jay puts it: 'Critical theory had a basically insubstantial concept of reason and truth, rooted in social conditions and yet outside them, connected with *praxis* yet keeping its distance from it' (Jay 1973: 63). The problem was that the Marxist distinction between true

and false consciousness was retained, which carries with it the
question of which social groups can have privileged access to
true consciousness. Again, in conformity with Marxist tradition,
Horkheimer saw this consciousness carried in the practice of progressive social groups—ultimately the proletariat. The experience
of the 1930s made it harder and harder to maintain such a view
(cf. Horkheimer 1978) and Horkheimer's ultimate position seems
to be that the possibility of enlightenment exists in all mankind,
and depends on the will to realize a rational society.

All this seems a rather unnecessary detour, however, from the
fundamental insight that truth cannot rise above the knowledge
given in specific historical experience. The result of the detour
is, however, apparently to affirm what is in my view an equally important position: that although interests mediate experience and
hence fundamentally influence the acquisition of knowledge, there
is no reason to assume that interests control knowledge, so that
one can read off a person's world view from his or her interests.

If we take the view advanced in this chapter that critical theory
(unlike empirical social theory) is essentially a moral theory and
a theory of method the problem of 'truth' can be stated somewhat differently. While empirical social theory ultimately moves
(should move) towards a vision of scientific truth (albeit such truth
is ultimately unattainable) with its progress tested in historical
experience, critique as method and critical theory as a theory of
method are concerned only with methodological rigour and the
maintenance of a moral vision. The method of immanent critique
needs only the truth claims immanent in the objects (ideologies,
practices) it studies. Beyond that, what critique is concerned
with is not truth as such but moral insight and methodological
appropriateness.

Conclusion

These ideas from critical theory are necessarily at a high level of
abstraction and, in some respects, appear to inhabit a different
world of discourse from much CLS writing with its appropriate
and necessary emphasis on the concrete legal situation. Nevertheless, it seems to me that in their direct confrontation with questions about the nature of theory, the relationship between critical
practice and social theory, and the problem of 'truth' in relation

to critical practice they deal with matters that are (and are recognized to be) fundamental to the enterprise of critical legal studies. Equally the uncertainties that remain in formulations such as Horkheimer's indicate that in various important respects these matters of theory are not entirely settled by any means. If critical legal scholarship is to build the strength necessary to endure and grow such issues of theory deserve continuing attention.

PART III

Law, Power, and Community

11 Law's Images of Society

> Legal thinking makes important assumptions about the general character of society and of social relationships. Indeed, in the Anglo-American context, it has presupposed, in various ways, two sharply contrasting visions of the essential character of the population that law regulates. By exploring these general legal images of society we can identify assumptions about the nature of community and of political power which lie deeply embedded in legal thought. Such an analysis attempts to derive, from legal ideas themselves, elements of a concept of community that may be helpful in constructing a moral vision for contemporary law.

Legal philosophy is more than 'a romp through the clouds' (cf. Graglia 1985: 291). Despite its apparent impracticality, it has, in its most influential forms, frequently made explicit the most abstract level of legal understanding within a legal profession and provided important rationalizations of the lawyer's world. It has helped to give that world an intellectual and moral coherence that has otherwise been quite frail through much of the modern history of legal professionalization in the Anglo-American setting. It has also helped to provide lawyers with images of the society they are supposed to serve and of their place in it. Law students, whether or not they formally study legal theory or legal philosophy, absorb in one way or another, and at many levels of legal discussion and analysis, much of these images of the profession, its role, and its environment. Legal philosophy often does no more than rationalize, at the highest levels of generality, currents of thought that pervade the professional environment of law. Lawyers think legal philosophy in some sense whether they know it or not.

Of course, this claim applies only to certain kinds of legal philosophy. Many contributions to this theoretical literature are no more than personal speculations by writers highly marginal to the professional world of lawyers and to the mainstream of thought and practice within it. But legal philosophers address most of their writing to this professional group and some of it enjoys

sensational success and influence in sections of the legal world of
its time.[1] At least where clear common themes emerge from widely
influential theoretical literature, these themes may be assumed to
be a guide to important tendencies of legal thought of the time
and place. If we seek the most general, abstract self-images of the
legal profession, this literature may be an important place to look
for them.

This chapter uses the literature of English and American legal
philosophy, and other legal materials, for a specific sociological
purpose: to contrast two ways in which the social environment of
law is conceptualized within the professional world of Anglo-American lawyers. The object is to provide a framework within which
practical political consequences of lawyers' acceptance of one or
other of these conceptualizations can be examined. The inquiry
is thus an effort to make explicit some very abstract elements of
legal professional ideology and their possible effects. These elements are general images of the regulated population in its relation to law. While two such contrasting images can be identified
in broad currents of Anglo-American legal thought, this chapter
suggests that one of them has dominated modern English legal
thought. In the following pages I try to develop some hypotheses
about broader important political consequences of this situation.

Although this discussion draws its organizing concepts from legal
philosophy and treats them as abstract rationalizations of lawyers' thought, its concern is equally with practical legal reasoning.
Indeed, the claim is that, in this context at least, legal philosophy
is most instructive for what it reveals about the rhetoric in which
practical legal and judicial reasoning is cloaked. Hence, in what
follows I try to support arguments about a dichotomy between two
legal views of law's social environment and about the significance
of this dichotomy by using illustrations of judicial rhetoric drawn
from recent English and American case law.

The Regulated Population and its Law: Images from Legal Philosophy

Images of law's social environment in Anglo-American legal philosophy fall into two distinct types: on the one hand, the image of

[1] Henry Maine's *Ancient Law* (1861) is a notable early modern example. The
book enjoyed enormous success in both Britain and the USA. See Feaver 1969:
128, 129.

a morally cohesive association of politically autonomous people (*community*) and, on the other, the image of individual subjects of a superior political authority (*imperium*). The first emphasizes a horizontal relationship of natural, spontaneous, or freely chosen association between individuals and between social groups on the basis of values held in common;[2] the second a vertical relationship of domination between a political authority (which may be conceived in concrete, personal terms or highly abstract ones) and each subordinate person. In the latter image, subordinates do not necessarily hold any values in common but may share only their recognition (for whatever reasons) of a common superior authority.

Both images are compatible with a variety of political systems, such as representative democracy. John Austin's nineteenth century legal philosophy founded itself on the sovereign–subject relation—a simple imperium conception, but assumed, despite Austin's personal suspicion of and later hostility to democracy (cf. Rumble 1985: ch. 6), that the sovereign could be the electorate of a democracy. The legislative, administrative, and judicial authorities expressing this sovereign power nevertheless constitute, according to the imperium conception, superior political authorities to which each individual is subject. In the United States, nineteenth-century disciples of Austin applied his ideas to interpretation of the legal order of American democracy (King 1986: ch. 7). The community conception usually, however, sees democracy as an inadequate expression of community values, which are assumed to be more intricate, profound, and enduring than the result of a popular vote.[3]

Conversely, neither the imperium nor the community image necessarily treats democratic participation as essential to the social environment it envisages. Classical common law thought (which I take to be the conception of law made explicit most fully by

[2] The legal images described in this ch. are not necessarily compatible with sociological conceptions of community, which are extremely diverse: see e.g. Hillery 1955 (identifying no fewer than 94 definitions); König 1968; and Taylor 1982: 25–33 (treating shared values, direct and multi-faceted relationships and reciprocity as fundamental elements of community).

[3] See e.g. Dworkin 1971 on the significance of critical principles developed within a community. They exist because most members of the community respect them in the abstract 'but they would serve no function unless it were generally recognized that the majority might be wrong in judging whether they apply in particular cases' (1971: 152). Members of 'a genuine political community . . . accept that they are governed by common principles, not just by rules hammered out in political compromise' (Dworkin 1986: 211).

English seventeenth-century jurists and especially expressed by such writers as Matthew Hale and Edward Coke) typically sees law's social environment in terms of community. The writings of the classical common lawyers consistently invoke communitarian images with their references to the ancient wisdom of law, greater than any individual, and a form of reason distilled from the entire history or ancient origins of the community the judges are considered to represent and speak for (e.g. Postema 1986: 19, 23, 66–76). But classical common law thought in no way presupposes democracy. In England it had to reconcile itself with parliamentary sovereignty from the seventeenth century. But it never ceased to view the law created by democratic legislatures with suspicion (Postema 1986: 15–29) until Benthamite and Austinian ideas in the nineteenth century eventually transformed lawyers' perceptions of the relationship of case law and statute law. And, in classical common law thought, although law is typically seen as the accumulated wisdom or reason of the community or commonwealth, that reason is explicitly an 'artificial' one not available to ordinary people and requiring 'long study and experience before that a man can attain to the cognisance of it'.[4] Classical common law thought justifies a legal and judicial élite, which speaks for the community but has no necessary institutionalized accountability to it.

According to Alasdair MacIntyre, 'the notion of the political community as a common project is alien to the modern individualist world' (MacIntyre 1985: 156). It is not, however, alien to classical common law thought nor to a long progression of writings in modern legal philosophy (including the work of Roscoe Pound, Lon Fuller, and Ronald Dworkin) which can be interpreted, at least in part, as efforts to preserve and reinterpret aspects of the common law outlook. But a great deal depends on the meaning of 'common project'. In so far as this suggests active participation of individuals and social groups in building their community, it does not exactly conform with the associational images present in classical common law thought. The latter tend not to emphasize deliberately building for the future, but remaining true to a heritage of established wisdom. Common law judges, after all, do not make law, but only find it. As the wise

---

[4] *Prohibitions del Roy* (1608) 12 Co. Rep. 63, 65 (*per* Coke LJ).

representatives of the community (past and present generations) they state its law and so help articulate its structure. But, according to this image informing classical common law thought, no one consciously builds community. It is presupposed (Postema 1986: 19, 32).

What of the alternative image—that of imperium? Although this has ancient roots, its origins in modern Anglo-American legal philosophy surely lie in an impatience with what was seen as an essentially fraudulent character of common law's image of community. While the latter prayed in aid all manner of communal virtues to declare the common law 'the most ancient and best inheritance that the subjects of this realm have' (Coke, quoted in Sommerville 1986: 103), it did not provide a rational account of how the common good might be systematically identified and institutionally secured. Hence Jeremy Bentham's attack on William Blackstone's complacency in the late eighteenth century (Bentham 1977). Utilitarianism in the form of Bentham's and Austin's legal philosophies asserted that the common good would result not from the expression of ancient wisdom in common law but from rationally guided legislative action: in other words, through the rational directives of a sovereign power specifically seeking the greatest good of the greatest number of people. Quite clearly, the typical imperium image of the regulated population in modern legal philosophy from the end of the eighteenth century onward is that of a mass of separate individuals (not a group), benefiting individually from their subjection to a rationally directed superior political authority.

In Bentham's late work this goes with advocacy of a form of democracy (Dinwiddy 1975). Austin's picture of the regulated society was, however, at the time of his early nineteenth-century lectures on jurisprudence, that of a mass of subjects rendering submission to an essentially centralized state (Austin 1847), which delegated its sovereign powers through various levels of official decision-making agencies, including courts. The obedience of subjects appears more important than their participation in the polity, but Austin's personal commitment to universal popular education expressed itself in a hope that acceptance of authority could be grounded in informed reason, not mere habit. The subject, informed of at least leading principles of social ethics and economics, and 'practised in the art of applying them . . . would be docile to the voice of reason, and armed against sophistry and error' (Austin 1832: 65).

Later English jurists adopting versions of the imperium conception are generally much less explicit about the nature of the regulated society. Austin's clear image of a society structured in terms of power and authority—continuous obedience to a sovereign, even if reasoned obedience—becomes hazy as the authority of the sovereign is replaced in later theory with the authority of what H. L. A. Hart (1961) calls secondary rules—ultimate legal rules accepted as controlling the manner in which other rules of law are created, interpreted, modified, enforced, or destroyed. But if legal authority is no longer traced back to a sovereign it is still not traced to a community—to the social group conceived as an entity whose values provide law's foundation. The imperium conception tends to develop into one in which, if it becomes difficult to accept theoretically an identifiable sovereign body as the ultimate source of legal authority, the source is nevertheless not identified as the values of the regulated community. *Law itself* is treated as ruling. Legal theory—as in Hart's concept of law—asserts that there is no need to seek legal authority outside law itself. The rule of recognition—a legal rule or cluster of legal rules—provides validity for all other rules of the legal system, and the rule of recognition is valid simply because in a broadly efficacious legal system lawyers, judges, and other legal officials accept it as such or presuppose it.

Thus, while this kind of legal philosophy has gradually stopped talking about law as the sovereign's command, it has not looked to some notion of community to replace the sovereign as author of law. It has given up any concern with the author of law as a theoretical matter, accepting *de facto* that state agencies—legislatures, courts, and administrative bodies—create law but that all that is of interest about this is that these agencies are themselves governed by legal rules. The image of the Rule of Law thus becomes the dominant image. Under law's rule, citizens and corporate bodies engage in transactions as fully autonomous agents. They make use of private power conferring rules, which are now portrayed as of great theoretical significance in the legal system (Hart 1961: 27–41). If there is a coherent image of society here it is that of a myriad of independent, isolated legal persons—such as citizens or corporations—interacting by means of the power-conferring rules which the legal system provides, and being controlled impersonally by a web of obligations created by state agencies, themselves making use of (public) power-conferring rules defining their jurisdictions, procedure, and so forth. The image is the classic image of civil society. The crude and (in a modern democracy) distasteful notion of law as the command of superior to inferior has been replaced with a conception of the relationship between public and private powers. But, in so far as these powers are all given by law, *law* is assumed to rule. Law governs society. The image is not that of society (in the form of a morally cohesive community) controlling and determining law.

American writers have generally been much less sympathetic to these images—so strong in English legal philosophy—of the regulated society in relation to its law. The significant reception of Bentham's and Austin's sovereignty theories in the United States in the nineteenth century inevitably encountered the problems of legal dispersion of authority through the federal system and of a separation of powers doctrine that made Austin's image of centralized and delegated legal authority hard to apply. But it is not so much that the imperium conception is tried and found wanting in this context as that it is often treated as alien. A great deal of modern American legal philosophy clearly relies directly on the image of community. This inspires a search for law's authority in the values of the regulated social group, rather than in formal justifications of hierarchies of political authority among officials or of a combination of official (public) power and citizens' (private) power.

Thus, early in the twentieth century, Roscoe Pound, rejecting Austinianism, tried to explain law's unity and integrity as a system on the basis that it embodied and expressed through rules the values—or postulates—of the time and place. While strongly defending legislation by political authorities against the wrecking tactics of some judges, Pound saw it essentially as an aid to common law methods, a means of putting the natural processes of common law development back into operation when rigid or mechanical judicial reasoning, unresponsive to community need and demand, had made them fail (Pound 1908). More recently, Ronald Dworkin's legal philosophy even more strongly relies on the image of community. What the law is at a given time and in relation to a given issue is a matter of interpretation for the community whose law it is. Legal interpretation is a matter for what Dworkin calls the 'community of principle' concerned to engage in conscientious interpretation of the best current legal meaning of the historical materials—statutes, judicial precedents, and so on—bearing on the issue at hand. Interpretation involves reading these materials in the best light to see them as part of the whole structure of values, principles, and rules that constitute the legal system (Dworkin 1986).

Dworkin's image of community is especially revealing as an expression of many of the same assumptions about community as those embedded in classical common law thought. First, the sociological character of the community is not seriously considered, since Dworkin's perspective is that of someone recognizing himself or herself as a member of the community and not concerned to delimit its boundaries or the conditions under which it can exist. So community is something presupposed rather than explained; a position much like that of classical common law thought. Secondly, while the community is asserted to include not only lawyers, judges, legal philosophers, and other 'expert' legal interpreters (Dworkin 1977: ch. 8) it is very hard to see how, given present institutional structures, non-experts can productively engage in the collective interpretation of law.[5] One senses a new version of Coke's famous dichotomy: while the common law is the embodiment of the community's reason and ancient wisdom, it is an 'artificial' reason which only the highly trained can master. For all the protestations of grass-roots communitarianism, the elitism of professional control of knowledge seems built into the legal image of community. This is explicit in Pound's writings. The reason of law is to be entrusted primarily to the judiciary who, through their special training and experience, understand it. Pound referred to democracy as King Demos (Wigdor 1974: 199, 227, 230); something to be feared as potential tyranny by the ignorant.

The theoretical grounding of law in basic values is, in the American context, frequently associated with the attempt to define enduring constitutional principles or bench-marks of constitutional interpretation (see e.g. Wechsler 1959; Grey 1975; Fiss

[5] Cf. Hutchinson 1987: 655–6 for an assertion of the elitism of Dworkin's image of community.

1979; Brest 1981). But the legal philosophies of Pound, Dworkin, and others suggest that the image of community is both broader and more diverse than a purely constitutional-law image. It is also part of the heritage of classical common law thought, no doubt mediated by powerful traditions of community derived from early American experience (see e.g. Nelson 1976) which gave it a vitality it lost in English legal thought under Benthamite and Austinian hegemony.

But modern legal philosophy also warns against any simplistic demarcation between English and American approaches. Legal realism, in most of its forms, appears as a clear counter-current to the communitarian emphasis in much American legal thought. Joseph Beale wrote of John Chipman Gray, one of the influential early theorists of realism, that 'Gray cannot get far ahead of Austin as exceedingly cleverly corrected by Gray' (quoted in Wigdor 1974: 43). The correction was essentially to treat judges not as delegates of the sovereign, as Austin had, but as sovereigns themselves. Law becomes again the command of sovereign to subject but law—even when its source is in statutes—is what the court finally declares (Gray 1921). The rulers of society are a shifting anonymous body (Fuller 1940: 48) but there *are* rulers. An imperium image of society underpins much American legal realist writing as one would expect from its association with the expansion of activist federal government programmes in the New Deal era. Critics of realism frequently complained of its lack of concern with underlying values of law and its potential as a legitimation of over-powerful government direction (see e.g. Purcell 1973: ch. 9). Realism thus appears as a clear counter-trend to communitarian legal theory.

Again, however, one must avoid over-generalization (see Garlan 1941). Among the leading realist writers in the United States, Felix Cohen forcefully insisted on the need to recognize the importance of legal values while viewing law realistically as an exercise of power rather than abstract logic (Cohen 1960); and Karl Llewellyn devoted much attention to the relationship between law and the regulated social group considered as a community structured by shared needs or concerns (Llewellyn 1944; 1940) and possibly shared values (cf. Cotterrell 1992: 81). Conversely, from the other side of the imperium-community divide, while Lon Fuller's writings defend case law as a means of continuing the search for reason in time-honoured common law methods (Fuller 1946) and defining 'a body of common morality' (Fuller 1940: 137), he also recognizes the essential element of *fiat* in law—its reality as an expression of authority, with a validity founded in the legitimacy of political authorities no less than in the absolute moral imperative of making communication and interaction possible within the regulated community (Fuller 1969).

Some Implications of Legal Philosophy's Images of Community and Imperium

By the 1950s, near the end of his long career, Pound had largely given up his efforts to identify the underlying values of Anglo-American law (Pound 1959 vol. 3: 11–15), arguing that in a time of considerable social change it was impossible to identify them reliably. Later writers have found continuing theoretical controversy in any attempt to postulate particular values underlying either the substance of law as a whole or its procedures. The efforts of these predominantly American writers have, nevertheless, often been sympathetically received in their own country. Dworkin, as the currently most influential jurist continuing this tradition, engages in the task of rationally demonstrating liberal foundations of Anglo-American law at the same time as declaring that the underlying values of a legal order are capable of being established only in the endless process of legal interpretation by those who participate in the legal system's community. Thus, while the community's values inform its law, they are—it seems—intelligible only in the ongoing process of interpreting that law.

Legal philosophy implies problems with both the community and imperium images of law's social environment. With the community conception a fundamental problem lies in the difficulty of identifying unifying values that would make it possible to speak realistically of the regulated population as a community. Pound's search for jural postulates clearly illustrates this problem. Dworkin's view of the principles and values of a legal system being established by interpretation through rational debate among members of the interpretive community, whatever its utility for other theoretical purposes, merely begs the question of what unites or gives coherence to such a community or provides the conditions for it to exist (see e.g. Fish 1982).

Equally serious, the scope of the community often remains ambiguous. Pound's search was for the jural postulates of Anglo-American law as a whole, a narrowing from the German jurist Josef Kohler's earlier conception of the jural postulates of 'civilization' but still presupposing unifying values of a very large and diverse regulated population. Should such postulates be considered those of a single community or of several sharing the same legal values? The matter remains ambiguous. Generally, communitarian approaches in legal philosophy merely assume the community to be co-extensive with the jurisdiction of the legal system of the state, but this seems arbitrary unless a Savignian view of legal systems as full and direct expressions of unique cultures is accepted.

Conversely, the very ambiguity of the extent of community should make communitarian images generally much more compatible with a legal pluralist outlook than imperium images. If law is treated as co-extensive with community it becomes easy and natural to recognize a variety of legal regimes within a single political society or nation, since the authority or legitimacy of these regimes can be seen to lie in diverse communities within a larger political society. The imperium image, stressing a hierarchy of legal authority, generally makes it harder to accept wholeheartedly the idea of diverse and parallel autonomous jurisdictions since it typically insists on a determinate hierarchical ordering of all legal authorities and jurisdictions.

A most important contrast in consequences of adopting a communitarian as against an imperium image of the regulated population is undoubtedly in the conception of the judge's role and, more generally, in conceptions of the source of authority of law and legal institutions. Explicitly in classical common law thought and in virtually all later legal philosophy adopting the community conception, the judge appears as the primary legal representative of the community and the central figure in the legal system. As such, the judge's role is clearly defined as one of considerable freedom (to interpret community values and develop them appropriately in regulatory form) within understood limits (the judge does not have uncontrolled discretion in deciding novel cases, is not empowered to act as a legislator, and speaks only for the community and its established principles and values). The authority that the judge exercises is implied to arise not from the state or any political source, but directly from the community.

By contrast, as noted earlier, legislation may be considered a relatively imperfect expression of community values and in that sense a problematic expression of law.

The imperium conception offers a much less clear view of the specific role of the judge. Because it sees no community but only a hierarchy of authority it can hardly avoid treating the judge merely as a political authority constrained by rules defining that authority as part of the governmental structure of the political order as a whole. In so far as their actions are not wholly controlled by established rules or precedents, judges can be seen only as political decision-makers—legislators. It is, indeed, extremely difficult—following the imperium conception—to explain the nature and origins of this legislative power, unless following Austin, one treats the judge as the sovereign's delegate. The imperium conception, thus, typically provides a much less clear basis of specifically judicial authority and of a specifically judicial role. Judicial creativity is highly problematic in the image of imperium. On the other hand, in so far as it is recognized that judges necessarily make law through their decisions, the imperium conception cannot explain theoretical limits on that law-making. Judges are not seen as constrained to interpret and apply established community values. They merely exercise a decision when the rules do not tell them what to decide.

Thus, more generally, a lawyer adopting the imperium conception is likely to see the policy choices of political authorities (including judges) as relatively unfettered (and so will often be anxious that judges should engage in strict self-limitation of their freedom, in so far as they appear less politically accountable than other law makers). Much scope is recognized for political innovation and policy development[6] but generally judges will not be considered the most appropriate political actors to undertake it. By contrast, in the community conception, the function of legal institutions is to reflect and express the established values of the communities they serve. This may make it difficult to consider sympathetically, in terms of their legal worth, apparently innovative policy-forming and implementing activities of political authorities. But it does remove most uncertainties about the

---

[6] Thus, McDougal and Lasswell 1943 argue that legal education should be a training for policy-making.

decision-making freedom of judges. And if a sceptic should ask how one can tell whether community values are really what courts say they are, the answer of Dworkin and of the classical common lawyers would be that the judge is only a representative of the community and it is the community which ultimately must decide what its values are (Dworkin 1977: ch. 8; 1985: ch. 4; cf. Rawls 1972: 382–90). While the judge's authority may be great it is only as a wise member of the community, not as a delegate of superior political authorities.

These considerations suggest that there is no clear theoretical link between the community–imperium dichotomy and any liberal–authoritarian dichotomy. Images of community can be liberal or authoritarian in thrust, depending on what values are considered to unite the community (a value of individual liberty might be fundamental, for example), how extensive and constraining the system of community values is considered to be, and how the process of establishing and interpreting community values is envisaged.[7] Imperium images may portray a superior political authority as an essential defence of individual liberties against local intolerance or coercion, or—in authoritarian terms—as a means of imposing cohesion and order on a chaos of individual wills. Thus, radical critics of orthodox forms of Anglo-American legal thought have had no difficulty in identifying authoritarian dimensions or possibilities of both imperium-based and community-based legal theories and forms of legal reasoning.[8]

It follows that the value of individuality is not necessarily to be opposed to values of community as the concept of community has been used in this chapter. Individualism—as an assertion of the sanctity of the autonomy and dignity of the individual and of tolerance of individual diversity—can derive from the content of community values, or from an absence of shared values within some imperium conception. The kind of individualism envisaged may well vary depending on whether it is associated with imperium

[7] Dworkin's communitarian theory is thus powerfully liberal in its thrust. Lord Devlin's (1965) enforcement of morals thesis appears relatively authoritarian (e.g. no private sphere of activity theoretically recognized as immune from legal control).

[8] A great deal of critical legal studies literature shows this. Legal liberalism, the most obvious if not always clearly defined target of CLS attack, generally seems to be understood as a broad enough category to encompass forms of legal thought that I would locate on opposite sides of the community–imperium divide.

or community, but an analytical opposition of community values and individualism is not necessarily justified or helpful (cf. Unger 1983: 616 ff.). The same applies to a dichotomy between individualism and altruism (cf. Kennedy 1976) which can be seen as two possible components of community values, or two closely related dimensions of community life if community is understood in the manner outlined above as a social unity capable of being grounded in shared values protecting individual diversity.

The Regulated Population and its Law: Images from Case Law

How does the dichotomy of community and imperium appear in the everyday rhetoric and practical reasoning of law? I have suggested a tendency for American legal thought to be specially sympathetic to the community conception and English legal thought to favour the imperium conception, although very important counter-currents exist, especially in the American context.[9] A sample of legal philosophies taken alone is hardly sufficient to ground such a claim. But, as will be shown in this section, a survey of the rhetoric of community in recent case law seems to lend substantial support to it, as well as helping to clarify the images of community and imperium in law.

The significance of these images cannot be proved but only illustrated. I conducted Lexis searches of all references to community values, community interests, community standards, community morality, and related ideas in United States Supreme Court decisions between 1979 and 1989, and in all cases in English higher courts as contained in Lexis' English General Library for the same period. In addition, all references to public morality and related concepts in the English cases and in United States Supreme Court decisions were examined for the period from 1959 to 1989. The object was to survey the way the image of community appears in these bodies of modern case law.[10] Since what is being considered here is the general use of this imagery, and not the specific legal

---

[9] In Britain, the philosopher John Finnis' (1980) natural law theory has strongly emphasized law's relationship with community. An apparently increasing interest in natural law theory may well reflect a degree of dissatisfaction with dominant approaches in Britain to legal philosophy and legal thought more generally. There is, however, little evidence that this development extends outside the ranks of legal philosophers themselves.   [10] These searches were conducted in Feb. 1989.

contexts, differences in procedure and jurisdiction of the courts
surveyed and in the substantive law are relatively unimportant.
Concern is only with the nature of the images and their possible
consequences in defining a general ideological relationship between the regulated population and its law.

The imagery of community is widespread in recent United States
Supreme Court cases. Probably the most obvious context is the
'contemporary community standards' test of obscenity established
in 1957.[11] In *Miller* v. *California*[12] the court decided that this could
not import a national standard—'our nation is too big and too
diverse'. Community in this context means, for example, 'the whole
State of Illinois'[13] but not the United States. Sometimes it is expressed as 'the adult community as a whole'.[14] Certainly the concept is taken to entail that the people of Maine or Mississippi do
not necessarily subscribe to the same standards as those of Las
Vegas or New York City.[15] Cities as well as states can be a point
of reference in this rhetoric of community.

The apparently uncertain scope of community does not destroy
the resonance of the concept in other contexts. A New York property tax exemption is considered to contribute to 'the community's moral and intellectual diversity'.[16] Reference is made in the
same case to 'the community's well-being', 'the cultural and moral
improvement of the community', and 'the community's cultural,
intellectual, and moral betterment'. The 'whole community' (of
undefined scope) has an interest that children can be safeguarded
and given opportunities to grow to become independent citizens.[17]
In death penalty cases, a judgment may be seen as 'an expression
of the community's outrage—its sense that an individual has lost
his moral entitlement to live'.[18] Further, one of the great virtues
of the jury is its 'ability to reflect the community sense of overall
fairness'.[19] Jurors bring their 'common sense and community

[11] *Roth* v. *United States,* 354 US 476 (1957).   [12] 413 US 15 (1973).
[13] *Pope and Morrison* v. *Illinois,* 481 US 497 (1987).
[14] *Virginia* v. *American Booksellers' Association,* 484 US 383 (1988).
[15] *Miller* v. *California,* 413 US 15, 32 (1973), quoted in *New York* v. *Ferber,* 458 US
747 (1982).   [16] *Texas Monthly* v. *Bullock,* 489 US 1 (1989).
[17] *Prince* v. *Massachusetts,* 321 US 158, 165 (1944), as quoted in *Santosky* v. *Kramer,*
455 US 745 (1982) (dissenting opinion).
[18] *Spaziano* v. *Florida,* 468 US 447 (1984) (*per* Stevens J, concurring in part and
dissenting in part); and quoted in *Cabana* v. *Bullock,* 474 US 376 (1986) (dissenting
opinion).
[19] As quoted in *City of Los Angeles* v. *Heller,* 475 US 796 (1986) (dissenting opinion).

values' to bear;[20] indeed they have the role of maintaining the essential link between contemporary community values and the penal system.[21] The openness of the criminal trial process is justified by its 'community therapeutic value'; it provides 'an outlet for community concern, hostility and emotion',[22] a recognition of the 'community urge to retaliate and desire to have justice done'.[23] Indeed, 'each criminal conviction itself represents a pronouncement by the State that the defendant has engaged in conduct warranting the condemnation of the community'.[24]

The most obvious aspect of these invocations of community is that the community is portrayed as *active*. It thinks, acts, feels, can suffer injury much like an individual ('crime inflicts a wound on the community'),[25] has a conscience,[26] and has views and values represented through judge and jury. Its impact on law is portrayed as direct. Ambiguity as to the extent of community fits conveniently the diversity of legal jurisdictions within a federal system. But, however extensive or inclusive the community, it is consistently seen as the source of moral authority of law, or the constituency to which law must be responsible, or the locus of values to which law must relate.

A significantly different rhetoric appears in the English cases. There are frequent references to the interests of the community or of the whole community,[27] in contexts in which these phrases clearly mean the same as the public interest. References to community values or standards are, however, very rare by

[20] *Parklane Hosiery* v. *Shore*, 439 US 322 (1979) (dissenting opinion).

[21] *Witherspoon* v. *Illinois*, 391 US 510, 519–20 (1967), as quoted in *McCleskey* v. *Kemp*, 481 US 279 (1987).

[22] *Richmond Newspapers* v. *Virginia*, 448 US 555 (1980); and see *Press-Enterprise Co.* v. *Superior Court of California for the County of Riverside*, 478 US 1 (1986).

[23] *Press-Enterprise Co.* v. *Superior Court of California, Riverside County*, 464 US 501 (1984).   [24] *Missouri* v. *Hunter*, 459 US 359 (1983) (dissenting opinion).

[25] *Flanagan* v. *United States*, 465 US 259 (1984).

[26] *Witherspoon* v. *Illinois*, above, at pp. 519–20 (jury to 'express the conscience of the community on the ultimate question of life or death'), as quoted in *Lowenfield* v. *Phelps*, 484 US 231 (1988).

[27] See e.g. *Tomkins* v. *Commission for the New Towns* (1989) 58 P & CR 57 (CA, Civil Div.) ('the wider interests of the community' as justification of compulsory purchase of land); *Ketteman* v. *Hansel Properties Ltd.* [1987] AC 189 (HL) ('interests of the whole community' in efficient administration of justice); *Banque Keyser Ullmann SA* v. *Skandia (U.K.) Insurance Co. Ltd.* [1987] 2 WLR 1300 (QBD Comm. Ct.) ('greatest value to the whole community and especially the commercial community'); *Fayed* v. *Al-Tajir* [1988] 1 QB 712 (CA, Civil Div.) ('direct interests of the community in the United Kingdom').

comparison with those in the American cases. By contrast, in the United States Supreme Court, community interests are not commonly referred to but, as has not been noted above, the community is frequently mentioned in relation to its values. The difference is surely significant. A group of people trapped in a lift between floors has a common interest, though not necessarily any common values. Community in the English cases often refers merely to the group, or society, or the public at large, with no specific indication of the regulated population as united by and organized around shared values. Sometimes community in these cases means no more than locality as in 'the character of a community' in a land use planning decision.[28] Significantly, the term is often used to refer specifically to subgroups having special interests or problems. Thus, cases explicitly identify the maritime, banking, business, commercial, shipping, mercantile, farming, and Lloyd's (insurance) communities and the black, Jewish, Bengali, Sikh, Asian, and gypsy communities. In these cases the concept of community identifies occupational or ethnic groups which may indeed be united by shared values but are to be differentiated from the public at large. Conversely, in one of the very rare cases in which values are attributed to the regulated population in general as a community ('the generally accepted standards of the community') this formulation is invoked against the claims of an immigrant seeking to avoid deportation.[29] It seems here that society is given values as a community in order to declare limits on its moral pluralism and assert absolute values against a foreigner. In another case, the interest of the Anglican Church in a locality is set against that of 'the wider community',[30] and in others the need is recognized for the judge 'on behalf of the community' to weigh a professional person's duty of confidentially to the client against 'the ultimate interest of the community in justice being done'.[31] These cases suggest that the imagery of community is invoked where there is a need to recognize special divisions of interest or localized moral unities within the regulated population, or to assert

[28] R. v. *Westminster City Council ex p. Monahan* [1990] 1 QB 87 (CA, Civil Div.).
[29] R. v. *Immigration Appeal Tribunal ex p. Florent* [1984] Imm. AR 109 (QBD).
[30] *Re St. Thomas's, Lymington* [1980] 2 All ER 84 (Winchester Consistory Court).
[31] *Att.-Gen.* v. *Mulholland* [1963] 2 QB 477, 490, quoted in *British Steel Corporation* v. *Granada Television Ltd.* [1980] 3 WLR 774 (HL), *Att.-Gen.* v. *Lundin* (1982) 75 Cr.App.R 90 (QBD, Div. Ct.) and *Re an Inquiry under the Company Securities (Insider Dealing) Act 1985* [1988] BCLC 76 (CA, Civil Div.).

a special unity of the society as a whole, specifically to distinguish it from what are treated as morally distinct or problematic elements within or around it.

In some cases a concern with the 'spiritual, moral, mental, and physical development of the community'[32] or community interests is dictated by statutory provisions which the court must construe. Generally it can be said, however, that English courts refer to the community in discussing the public interest without invoking any idea of an active community or of community values of the regulated population as a whole. Only in relation to relatively distinct subgroups of the population may there be a recognition of community values—often in a context where these values may be seen as in some way posing a regulatory problem for the legal system.

If we turn to the concept of public morality, the cases show that in the period since 1958 the United States Supreme Court has hardly ever used this concept as a deliberately invoked element of its own reasoning. Where public morals or public morality are referred to this is almost invariably in quoting from earlier and often old cases[33] or old statutes or legislative debates.[34] The court hardly ever chooses the language as its own. In English cases, by comparison, the concepts are familiar and appear relatively frequently. Many decisions are concerned with statutory or treaty provisions referring to public morals.[35] Elsewhere, in assessing prison conditions, there is reference to an 'irreducible minimum below which the court, reflecting public standards of morality, will not allow society to sink';[36] in an important restraint of trade case the validity of covenants against competition on the sale of goodwill of a business is defended on the ground that it 'offends public morality if he [the seller] can filch back what he has sold';[37] and Lord Atkin's famous statement in *Donoghue* v. *Stevenson* on the moral foundations of negligence liability ('a general public

[32] Education Act 1944, s. 7. See e.g. *R.* v. *Birmingham City Council ex p. Equal Opportunities Commission* [1988] 3 WLR 837 (CA, Civil Div.).

[33] See e.g. *City of Eastlake* v. *Forest City Enterprises Inc.*, 426 US 668 (1976), quoting *Euclid* v. *Ambler Realty Co.*, 272 US 365 (1926).

[34] See e.g. *Bolger* v. *Youngs Drug Products Corp.*, 463 US 60 (1983).

[35] Especially Treaty of Rome, art. 36, and European Convention of Human Rights, art. 9.   [36] *Williams* v. *Home Office (No. 2)* [1981] 1 All ER 1211 (QBD).

[37] *Petrofina (Great Britain) Ltd.* v. *Martin* [1966] Ch. 146 (CA).

sentiment of moral wrongdoing for which the offender must pay')[38] is cited in several cases.

The general character of many of these invocations is, however, significantly different from the American imagery of community. The protection of animals as a charitable object in English law is explicitly justified[39] as 'calculated to promote public morality by checking the innate tendency to cruelty' (that is, because it helps to *create* a moral climate in some educational manner, rather than expressing existing community values). Lord Atkin's moral foundation of negligence in *Donoghue* v. *Stevenson* is treated merely as a moral backdrop against which the state defines rules to prevent individuals interfering with each other's freedom. Although courts emphasize that heads of public policy recognized in law are 'grounded on incontestable and fundamental moral considerations'[40] or 'on general principles of morality',[41] the point is that, even if grounded in morality, these are matters of law *because public institutions have so made them.* In other words, the notion of public *policy* puts state agencies between the public and the law. The state, not a community, is author or source of law, and morality is merely a resource on which state regulation can draw where appropriate. This imagery explains the otherwise odd expression 'the interests of society and public morality' as a factor for the court to take into account.[42] Public morality is an interest or factor for the state to consider. It would be harder to envisage community values being discussed as 'factors' or 'interests' in the American cases, because these terms suggest the passivity of an object rather than the active community subject which the United States Supreme Court so frequently assumes.

In one important cluster of English cases public morality appears in something like the role of community values in the American ones. These are the decisions of the 1960s and 1970s beginning with *Shaw* v. *DPP* (1962) in which the common law crime of conspiracy to corrupt public morals was resurrected and

[38] [1932] AC 562 at p. 580.
[39] *Re Green's Will Trusts* [1985] 3 All ER 455 (Ch.D).
[40] *Mitsubishi Corporation* v. *Aristidis I. Alafouzos* [1988] 1 All ER 191 (Comm. Ct.).
[41] *Lemenda Trading Co. Ltd.* v. *African Middle East Petroleum Co. Ltd.* [1988] 1 All ER 513 (Comm. Ct.).
[42] *Webber* v. *Gasquet Metcalfe and Welton*, transcript of case 1980 W No. 3345 (Ch.D, 7 April 1982).

elaborated by the courts.[43] In *Shaw*, the House of Lords declared itself *custos morum* of the people, adopting the ancient expression of Lord Mansfield. Morality is, in the context of *Shaw* and the cases following it, assumed to mean sexual morality and the common law conspiracy offence is invoked as an aid or supplement to statutory anti-obscenity provisions. It is necessary only to note here the intensely controversial character of these decisions[44] and the widespread opinion both within and beyond the legal profession that they are anomalous, archaic, or an unsatisfactory use of judicial authority. While the legislative definition of public morality in various forms is relatively unexceptional in English law, the classical common law (communitarian) idea of judges as custodians of popular morality is sufficiently controversial to make its explicit adoption generally counterproductive. And, unlike the American situation where an appeal to the jury's role seems easily to admit references to community values into legal rhetoric, the presence of a jury in *Shaw*-type cases does little to quell disquiet. Indeed, the rapidly declining role of jury trial in the English legal system may be further evidence that any suggestion of an American-style link between law and community maintained by the jury seems remote and unpersuasive in the English context. No accepted imagery of community is now available to be linked to English law. Public values are invoked but they are what political institutions declare them to be. The image of the regulated population is an image of imperium.

Image and Reality

This final section will suggest reasons why these components of legal professional ideology matter, primarily with reference to law, politics, and social conditions in contemporary Britain. Both community and imperium, as described above, are ideological conceptions. That is, they fuse general unexamined assumptions as to what and how society actually is with normative evaluations as to how it should be regulated. Although grounded in some respects

[43] See especially *Shaw* v. *DPP* [1962] AC 220 (HL); *Knuller* v. *DPP* [1973] AC 435 (HL). See also *R.* v. *Anderson* [1972] 1 QB 304 (CA, Criminal Div.) (jury acquitted on count of conspiracy to corrupt public morals); and *R.* v. *Quinn* [1962] 2 QB 245 (Ct. of Crim. App.).

[44] See Smith and Hogan 1992: 291–3, and literature cited therein.

in historical experience, they present, as general *truths* about social experience, perspectives that are merely partial and limited. The question of the significance of law's images of community and imperium is thus an aspect of the more general issue of the social and political effects of ideology.

No claim is being made here that the judicial rhetoric identified earlier produces or explains specific decisions or even influences them in determinate ways. Neither can it be assumed that this rhetoric reflects in any direct way popular (lay) opinion, attitudes, perceptions, or values. The courts in which the rhetoric is presented are typically appellate or superior courts rather than low-level trial courts. Whatever the situation of the latter, the language of the former seems best thought of as derived from and largely addressed to the world of legal professionals (Cotterrell 1992: 239). On the other hand, the combination of imagery from judicial rhetoric and legal philosophy does suggest persistent conceptions of law and its social environment that are present in the professional world of law. And since this professional world has important links to the wider world of politics and many lines of influence in a wide variety of social spheres it seems reasonable to suggest that law's images of community and imperium may, like all ideological ways of thought, help to define the general limits within which debate and disagreement take place in many diverse social or political contexts.

If this is so, the dominance of one or other of these images is significant. Each encourages a different outlook on legal institutions and processes in general, including especially such matters as the role of legislatures and courts, popular participation in law, and the significance of bills of rights and similar constitutional documents. The imperium image encourages a belief that law is purely instrumental in character, with no necessary value content; that almost anything is legislatively possible since no value constraints are built into the substance of law; that law provides direction and order for isolated individuals not linked by any necessary moral bonds. Yet in modern times, as has been seen, the imperium image also makes central a concern for the Rule of Law, for calculability and predictability flowing from the idea that law is to be expressed in rules created by distinct authorities using rational procedures. It rejects the vagueness of an appeal to immanent community values as a means of determining what the law is.

In Britain, where the imperium conception seems dominant, any notion of a bill of rights, or of legally entrenched values, has been extremely difficult to accept since the time of Bentham. Under the slogan 'law regulates its own creation' (cf. Kelsen 1967: 71, 221) the dominant imperium outlook on law and society has offered no obstacles to tendencies for the power of governments to grow, unfettered by any constraints except the need to follow procedural proprieties in creating, applying and enforcing law. And in *political practice*, at least, it has defined the proper role of the judiciary, in default of any better theoretical formulation, as that of Austinian delegates of the sovereign; underworkers in the task of making governmentally formulated law an efficient tool of direction and control. Perhaps it has also contributed to a current climate of thought in which it is possible for governmental authorities in contemporary Britain explicitly to reject social consensus as an appropriate justificatory basis of legislative action.

In the perspective provided by the imperium image the dangers of communitarian thinking are highlighted, and no doubt properly so. An imperium perspective notes the problem—perhaps fatal to Pound's legal philosophy—of deciding what the unifying values of community are or should be for regulatory purposes. This problem raises the spectre of authoritarianism: the imposition of values, on those who do not share them, by institutional or self-appointed definers of a postulated shared morality of the community. Literature on the use by American courts of communitarian imagery stresses this danger (Chesler 1983; Newton 1976). Much sociological literature has claimed that shared values uniting complex modern political societies are, if they exist at all, extremely limited in scope (Durkheim 1984). Those who have argued otherwise (e.g. Devlin 1965) are confronted with a lack of empirical evidence in support of their case (see e.g. Mann 1970; Cotterrell 1992: 99–102). Thus, the communitarian appeal to shared values often appears fraudulent. Bills of rights appear in this perspective as essentially manipulable instruments used by legal and political authorities not to express the shared values of an active community but to cloak with legitimacy the claims of various sections of a divided population. And because, for those who cannot subscribe to a communitarian conception, the actual condition of the regulated population is not that of a united and integrated moral entity but of a vast diversity of interests and needs, an appeal through legal institutions (as, for example, in the use of lay juries) to popular legal attitudes and perceptions frequently appears merely irrational.

Could one say that the imperium image reflects an essentially realistic view of modern law and society? Reduced to a partial perspective it contains much that is plausible. But the image of imperium, as elaborated in this chapter, is no less ideological than that of community in so far as it purports to present a complete image of the relationship between law and its regulated population. The top-down image of law's authority presented in the imperium conception typically ignores complex questions of the 'bottom-up' or 'grass roots' sources of that authority. Why and under what conditions is law accepted and acceptable? Law's typical image of imperium as developed in modern analytical jurisprudence is of a legal authority unproblematic because it arises in purely formal sources. Sociological questions about the social foundations of law's legitimacy are not seriously addressed. Thus, determination of the existence or validity of laws is not seen as a matter within the competence of ordinary citizens. Equally, the responsibility for making appropriate and effective regulation is assumed to be wholly that of state authorities and not at all that of the regulated general population as such.

Thus, in the image of imperium the notion that law *dominates* is taken for granted. The possibility of spontaneous or consensual regulatory forms whose legitimacy derives from active participation by the regulated in the regulatory process tends to be ignored. So does the possibility that law's authority is relatively weak or problematic unless social sources of that authority are nurtured as the real foundation of the acceptance of purely formal sources (that is, of lawyers' formal criteria of law in what Hart terms secondary rules). Equally, the image of law-as-domination as the natural order of things obscures the possibilities for pluralistic structures of regulation; for extensive diversity, flexibility, and fluidity in regulatory arrangements in different local, social, and cultural contexts that reflect the variety of the regulated population.

It might be assumed that an imperium image emphasizing hierarchies of legal authority would at least make it possible to view realistically actual social patterns of power and authority. But the modern form of the imperium conception in legal philosophy has, as noted earlier, ceased to rely on the idea of such social patterns (having rejected the concept of sovereignty). Instead the dominant image is that of an interplay of public and private legal powers structured by rules. The modern imperium image is ideological not least because it emphasizes the significance of the Rule of Law—the idea that law controls and structures power by means of rules—without putting corresponding emphasis on the wide range of conditions under which the power of particular actors is used to form rules, interpret them, exercise discretion under them, avoid, or negate them.

Thus from a communitarian position the dangers and inadequacies of the imperium conception seem obvious. This conception appears to take no serious account of (and may even promote) tendencies for state authorities and their regulatory processes to become increasingly remote from and alien to the regulated population. It seems to encourage the arrogance of political authorities—especially legislators and administrators. It leaves the role of judges unclear so that they are likely to lurch between, on the one hand, timid subservience to the legislative will in disregard of other values, and, on the other, improper (from a communitarian perspective) policy-making behaviour not distinguishable in essence from that of legislators or governmental administrators. Finally, it ignores and may encourage inadequate provision for popular participation and opinion in the processes of social regulation.

It seems clear, therefore, that law's images of community and imperium matter because they define parameters within which possibilities for the promotion and realization of practical ideals for legal regulation can be set. They define what is 'obviously' true of law and society, requiring no evidence or justification beyond the stating. And they define these obvious characteristics of law and its social environment in mutually contradictory ways.

From this writer's perspective, formed in a British legal and political environment in which the English image of imperium dominates, it is tempting to look for elements from the contrasting communitarian image suggesting possibilities for mitigating political tendencies identified as dangers inherent in the imperium conception. Is it possible then to confront imperium with community as an aspiration while avoiding the dangers and inadequacies that the image of community, in its turn, is seen to contain?

A primary issue must be that of the conditions under which community becomes a realistic empirical possibility. Anglo-American legal philosophy hardly addresses this issue,[45] typically presuming the existence of community when it invokes communitarian images. Indeed it may often be the very frailty, uncertainty, and elusiveness of the empirical conditions for community which provoke the intensity with which communitarian images are invoked. It seems to be assumed, however, in law's images of community that, while the community shapes or even creates law and law expresses the values of community, law cannot *itself* shape, create, or define community. The role of law in contributing to the conditions of existence of community seems highly problematic. Indeed, a strong theme in the literature of sociology of law is that of law's incompatibility with community. In Richard Schwartz' famous *kibbutzim* studies, law is absent in the Kvutza *kibbutz* as long as community thrives and it appears in the Moshav *kibbutz* to compensate for the relative lack of community controls (Schwartz 1954). 'Law seems to bespeak an absence of community, and law grows ever more prominent as the dissolution of community proceeds', writes Donald Black (Black 1971: 1108). But, for Black, law is simply governmental social control (Black 1976), and the image of the regulated population is clearly an imperium image. Indeed, in much sociology of law, an imperium image of the regulated population in modern complex societies is treated as self-evidently realistic. The idea of community rejected in the literature of sociology of law is usually that of a comprehensive, all-embracing or very extensive system of shared values as in Ferdinand Tönnies' (1955) concept of *Gemeinschaft*; an idea of community that is, understandably, typically seen as irrelevant to modern legal systems. To consider conditions under which community could be a basis of modern law it is necessary to specify more clearly what kind of community is being sought.

This chapter has noted criticisms that the image of community allows authoritarian pronouncements by courts and others about shared values of the community in modern conditions where few shared values can be reliably assumed to exist. Consequently, if an appeal to community values is to be anything other than manipulatory, repressive, or mystificatory, the appeal must be limited to the *minimum* that makes possible a social bond

---

[45] Some of Karl Llewellyn's strongly sociological writings bear directly on the matter. See e.g. Llewellyn 1940; 1944; 1957.

of mutual concern. The problem, which Durkheim (1984) recognized clearly but did not solve, is that of expressing solidarity in conditions of social and cultural diversity. As a practical basis of contemporary regulation an ideal of community must surely entail both individualism and altruism. These concepts cannot realistically be opposed as ideals in modern conditions (cf. Kennedy 1976; Kelman 1987: 54–63), but need somehow to be fused. To avoid its authoritarian tendencies, community as a practical ideal might be viewed productively, in part, as entailing a commitment to public altruism in regulation—that is, the promotion of a sufficient degree of sharing of the resources of social life to ensure that all members of the regulated population can benefit from the collective wealth, cultural and material, as full members of the society as a morally united entity. At the same time, in another part, it might be taken to entail a commitment to maximum facilitation of collective participation in determining the regulation and direction of the society and of any subgroups within it to which the individual adheres; so that individuality and autonomy are asserted in the right of each person to have his or her voice and actions taken account of as fully as those of any other.[46]

Thus, all that can be suggested here about the conditions of community in general is that community is possible only when all members are free and able to participate as fully as they wish in the life of the entire group, and when the shared values of the group express a collective concern to ensure the full inclusion of each member in the group's collective life.

Karl Llewellyn (1944), considering the concepts of in-group and out-group, notes that communities or in-groups typically define themselves through their exclusion of outsiders. Hence the existence of communities within political societies may act against the unity of the whole society. But surely the essence of this problem is the frequent arbitrariness or irrationality of the dividing line established between insiders and outsiders, which makes outsiders unconvinced that they are properly excluded; no more so than where (as in the problem that most concerns Llewellyn) the line is one of race. Llewellyn asserts the importance of values defining the identity of the 'wide we-group' within which smaller groups can see themselves as a part (Llewellyn 1944: 462). He

[46] See Ch. 12, below.

further suggests education and the promotion of personal contact across subgroups may help. But in my view law's images of community imply that all members of a regulated population are to be presumed to be part of the same community, unless they deliberately choose to exclude themselves. And the scope of the regulated population is usually defined historically in terms of pre-established common culture, language, economic interests, territory, political traditions, or other criteria. Further, the legal pluralism implicit in the communitarian view suggests that law can and should include regulation at many different levels within a political society; regulation expressing the values of subgroups—communities within the wider community—to the fullest extent compatible with the maintenance of a bond of common commitment by all individuals and subgroups to the whole society as a moral entity.

A further problem in drawing upon law's images of community concerns forms of institutional expression or representation of community values. As has been seen, the problem is not in defining the scope of proper *activity* of institutions representative of the community (the communitarian image seems, for example, to remove many doubts about the scope of judicial activity which remain acute in the imperium conception). The uncertainty is as to the limits of the *authority* of institutions, such as courts, as representatives of the community and its values. The community often appears, in both judicial rhetoric and legal philosophy, as the source of legal authority or even, in a sense, the author of law. The authority of legal institutions such as courts or professional judges is thus limited and may be properly subject to popular challenge. That is, for example, explicit in Ronald Dworkin's theory of civil disobedience, or in common law acceptance of jury nullification of law (see e.g. Green 1985). But the popular basis of regulation and of its authority would seem to need clearer institutionalization. The privileging of judges as special representatives of the community seems archaic and insupportable, a relic of classical common law thought and a reflection of the special professional biases of Anglo-American legal philosophy. Why should not political and moral philosophers, and teachers and leaders of thought of a variety of kinds have a claim to be the authoritative repositories or oracles of community values? And if they do, then why should not all members of the community have such a claim? There is no reason to assume that a popular conversation on community values could conform to some model of undistorted communication or unhindered understanding (cf. Habermas 1981: 69–70, 94–5). The distortions produced by conflicting interests and limited knowledge and experience seem all too obvious. But a communitarian conception might properly entail such popular debate which (extending beyond immediate instrumental issues) would be potentially deeper and richer than the discussion of short-term considerations and interests associated with the usual deliberations of democratic law-making.

Clearly, as a practical matter a communitarian approach would require institutions to provide working authoritative definitions and applications of community values in relation to law, and state courts would surely have a role in doing so. But a communitarian conception should, as has been suggested earlier, recognize the plurality of communities within the 'wider community' and the corresponding need for decentralization of regulation and of regulatory institutions in an extensive legal pluralism. It would thus also recognize that the moral demand for collective participation at these many levels would give rise to a wide range of institutions (not just ones having the form of courts) engaged in defining, for the moment and for the purposes of everyday regulatory practice, the meaning of community values and their applications in particular contexts. Perhaps, subject to conditions and qualifications of these kinds, law's images of community might yield non-utopian practical ideals worth serious consideration, at least in a legal environment hitherto dominated by images of imperium.

12 Feasible Regulation for Democracy and Social Justice

Currently dominant views about law's appropriate functions are revealed as problematic if careful account is taken of the character of contemporary regulation. Like the images of society considered in Chapter 11, these views about law's functions are components of legal ideology—in this case, the ideology that defines law's general character. Analysis of them leads to the question: what are the inherent limits of law as a means of building social solidarity or structures of community? My argument is that although law cannot directly create these structures it can support them in important ways; at the present time, however, its resources in this respect are hardly tapped.

A puzzling ambiguity attaches to presently influential views of the functions of law in many contemporary western societies. Law and state regulation—what can be collectively termed, following Karl Llewellyn, law-government[1]—are being expected to do more and more to bring about major social changes and economic restructuring at a time when those who make use of law in this way proclaim its capacity to do less and less. This chapter seeks to explain this ambiguity and, in doing so, to derive some conclusions about the limits which contemporary legal ideology sets on efforts to rethink the role of law in society.

The Dominant Ideology of Law's Functions

Present political rhetoric asserts, on the one hand, that among the most important tasks of law and state is to 'get off the backs' of the people and free them from restriction by greatly reducing the coercive reach of regulation. On the other hand, law-government is being used in Britain on a most extensive scale with the explicit aim of directing the recreation of a *laissez-faire* economic

[1] On Llewellyn's usage of the term, see Twining 1973: 179–80.

order, or a rational framework for competition (cf. Hayek 1944: 27 ff.), in conditions shaped by the existence of large-scale, transnational, and often semi-monopolistic economic enterprises. It is also being used ostensibly to create an individualistic society of independent, self-reliant citizens in the conditions of late twentieth century 'mass society'.

By this latter term I mean to indicate a society in which the population is addressed *en masse* by powerful communications media—television, popular newspapers, and so on—which simultaneously shape and reflect mass tastes and opinions;[2] is extensively organized in mass collectivities—for example, large business enterprises, political parties, and trade unions; and is subject to a previously unparalleled technical development of centralized state surveillance and administrative or regulatory controls on the everyday life of citizens.[3]

It is necessary to recognize, then, two faces which law seems to present as a functional instrument of government. Law's current 'official' face presents it primarily as *negative*, cumbersome, intrusive, and even potentially destructive in social and economic life, except as an absolutely necessary regulatory minimum by which basic order is maintained. Law and order are thus, in much political rhetoric, treated as synonymous or interdependent. Law's 'unofficial' face, much less emphasized in currently dominant political attitudes in Britain, is that of a *positive*, powerful, and indispensable directive instrument of government policy, actively used on an extensive scale to reshape social and economic conditions and even popular attitudes.

As recent examples of this active use of law the following can be mentioned: the Education Reform Act 1988 introducing a radical restructuring of the national education system in Britain and a national curriculum for schools; legislation aimed at restructuring industrial relations by severely restricting closed shop arrangements, imposing trade union democracy in particular forms, and deterring and controlling strikes by new means; rate-capping

---

[2] Cf. Sumner 1906: ch. 1, para. 57 ('The Common Man'), eloquently summarizing the 'mass orientation' of the popular press (as opposed to any conscious reflection of social diversity) in terms that need only minor modification for application eight decades later.

[3] See e.g. Poulantzas 1978: 217–31; and, from a different perspective, Donzelot 1980.

legislation intended to curb severely the financial expenditure of local government, and legislative prohibition of political advertising by local authorities; legislation strengthening the position of the private sector in education, health care, and in the supply of local government services; and provisions aimed at increasing the influence of parents in the operation of schools and in the shaping of patterns of local educational provision.[4] All of these examples, and many others which could be mentioned from recent British experience, show considerable governmental faith in the capacity of law to play a major part in social and economic restructuring. The fact that so many of these illustrations relate to education seems to indicate also that the capacity of law to play its part—at least indirectly (see Dror 1959)—in the shaping of attitudes, values, and knowledge is also not in doubt.

These developments are reinforced in Britain by a vigorous use of legal and administrative measures to control certain flows of information or ideas. The Contempt of Court Act 1981 restricts press reporting of trials, and the law of contempt was used in the *Harman* case[5] against a defendant who had shown official documents relating to prison control units to a journalist, even though these documents had previously been read out in open court. Although the British Government was subsequently found to be in breach of the European Convention on Human Rights, it seemed unlikely that the matter would be allowed to rest with this finding.[6] Attempts in 1979 to replace the Official Secrets Act 1911

---

[4] See e.g. Employment Act 1980 (secondary industrial action); Employment Act 1982 (closed shop practices, unions' funds liable for illegal strikes); Trade Union Act 1984 (secret ballots before strike action); Local Government, Planning and Land Act 1980 (requirement of private tendering for certain local authority works); Local Government Finance Acts 1982 and 1987 (local authority financial controls); Rates Act 1984 (central government power to limit local authority rates; local authorities' duties to consult representatives of industrial and commercial ratepayers with regard to expenditure proposals and financing of expenditure); Local Government Act 1986 (prohibition of political publicity); Education Act 1980 (assisted places at independent schools); Education (No. 2) Act 1986 (redefined powers of school governors; increased influence of local business communities in school government); Health Services Act 1980 (raising funds in National Health Service from private sources; treatment of private patients in NHS hospitals); London Regional Transport Act 1984 (provision for transfer of services to independent companies).

[5] *Harman* v. *Secretary of State for the Home Department* [1983] AC 280.

[6] Cf. *Bibby Bulk Carriers* v. *Cansulex Ltd.* [1988] 2 All ER 820, interpreting RSC Ord. 24, r. 14A, introduced as a result of the 'friendly settlement' of the application to the European Commission on Human Rights.

252   *Law, Power, and Community*

with a more specific Protection of Official Information Act failed, but since then the 1911 Act has remained a major legal weapon in the governmental armoury of information control.[7] It has been used against civil servants revealing sensitive information; and, for example, it has enabled searches to be made of the premises of those connected with the making of a BBC film alleging that the Government had broken an undertaking to inform Parliament about a defence project, the Zircon spy satellite. The law of confidence has been extensively used recently to restrict the circulation of allegations about unlawful or unconstitutional activities of the British security services, including alleged plots to undermine an elected British government. In addition, the Public Order Act 1986 strengthens the state's ability to control public expressions of opinion by virtue of its provisions giving the police extensive new powers to restrict public demonstrations.[8]

What these illustrations suggest is that law is extensively used today not only for controlling behaviour but also for controlling influences on attitudes. Law's relation to ideology has long been recognized as fundamentally important. This relationship, however, takes at least three different forms. First, as has often been stressed, legal doctrine embodies, reflects, or strengthens currents of ideology—systems of ideas and assumptions in terms of which social life is understood as a matter of 'common sense'. Ideology in this sense is *expressed* in the content of law. Secondly, however, as is suggested by the above illustrations of positive uses of law to encourage a certain climate of thought and negative uses to control access to information, law seems presently to be used as a means of controlling the contexts in which ideas and attitudes are developed by facilitating this development in some respects and restricting it in others. In this way law contributes to the shaping of a climate of opinion by indicating what kinds of conduct and opinion have the support of state authority—exercised through the allocation or withholding of benefits as well as through

[7] The Official Secrets Act 1989 has now repealed and replaced s. 2 of the 1911 Act.

[8] Bonner and Stone 1987. An unsuccessful attempt has recently been made to use the Act to prosecute the display of a poster critical of the British Prime Minister, as an insulting representation under s. 5(1)(b) (see *The Guardian*, 2 December 1987). See also, on government action to restrict and control research on social issues and the publication of research results, Caudrey 1987, and 'Don't publish, and awkward truth be damned', *The Guardian*, 8 January 1988.

coercive control (cf. Daintith 1982)—and what kinds are viewed with less favour. There is, however, also a third relationship between law and ideology which is suggested by the opening comments of this chapter with regard to law's 'two faces'. It seems to be possible in some conditions, at least, and apparently in Britain and some other Western countries at present, to maintain a particular, relatively consistent ideological conception of law's functions. That is, a particular ideology *about law itself* exists. It is the foundations of this ideology and its consequences that this chapter seeks to examine.

The term 'ideology' is often used with a variety of meanings. I use it here, in referring to an ideological conception of law's functions, to mean a set of taken-for-granted, largely unexamined, common sense, and highly generalized assumptions about the nature of law which inform political and legal practice and popular attitudes to law and regulation. A fundamental characteristic of ideology in this sense is that limited, *partial perspectives* on experience—based, as all knowledge must be, on incomplete evidence and understanding—tend to be treated as complete, total 'truths'. Consequently, to term ideas 'ideologies' is not to declare them 'wrong' but to assert that they represent a particular, partial perspective which is, however, often treated as a total perspective on the particular matter addressed—as unchallengeable *truth* (see Cotterrell 1992: 114–15).

One major consequence of the dominant conception of law's functions is that the extensive use of law in social and economic restructuring is, on the one hand, accepted implicitly as possible and even inevitable. Yet, on the other hand, such a use of law to plan a more egalitarian economic welfare, or to direct economic or other activity in the communal interest even on a relatively limited scale, is often seen as illegitimate, pointless, and even disastrous. The conception is *ideological* in so far as it sees no serious need to address, through systematic analysis of actual legal experience, the justification for and logical coherence of its general view of law as, simultaneously, on the one hand, a positive, legitimate, and necessary instrument of social and economic restructuring (in what Friedrich Hayek (1944: 31) has called 'planning for competition') and, on the other, a negative, obtrusive, and destructive intrusion upon economic and social freedoms (in planning a more egalitarian society).

Very extensive positive and directive use of law to recreate a climate of free enterprise appears largely unquestioned as a matter of *legal* legitimacy, even if it is viewed as highly controversial politically. Debate is about the merits of the policy to be pursued, not usually about law or its techniques, as such. By contrast, the use of law in shaping social relationships in pursuit of some egalitarian ideal of social justice is often viewed as fraught with problems phrased in terms of the legitimate functions of law—what law can properly be used *for*—and the 'limits of effective legal action' (Pound 1917)—what law is technically capable of achieving. Debate is frequently not about the merits of policy, but about the legal mechanisms themselves and their utility (see also Allott 1980: ch. 6). In this regard, even quite limited legal initiatives in this area aimed at substantive and not just formal legal equality (for example, sex and race discrimination law) have had to struggle for acceptance and are readily ridiculed whenever they lead to anomalies.

The dominant ideology of law's functions thus asserts that law can, by its nature, properly do some things but not others. In particular, it can create conditions to allow certain kinds of enterprise and initiative to flourish; but it must not direct people in the exercise of that enterprise or initiative. This ideology seems to attach to law-government as a whole. Thus, administrative and regulatory bureaucracies within the central state and outside it could probably be arranged in a hierarchy of worth according to this ideology; those of low value would tend to be seen especially as self-serving bureaucratic empires, as in the often-invoked image of a race relations 'industry'.

Four Supporting Ideologies and the Conditions They Obscure

There are, undoubtedly, many difficult technical and other problems that arise in the use of law to achieve any kind of significant economic redistribution (see e.g. Bettelheim 1976), or some major alteration of the balance of social power between different groups within a population.[9] The partial perspective that is the germ of

[9] The best cautionary tale is probably Massell 1968. For issues closer to Western experience see e.g. Greene 1985.

the dominant ideology of law's functions is not unfounded in legal experience.

Nevertheless, the ideology of law's incompatibility with substantial egalitarian policies is not based on specific experiences of regulatory failure alone. It is grounded more fundamentally in what may be termed supporting ideologies of property, liberty, the minimal state, and the Rule of Law. These are, themselves, reinforced by certain generalized sociological claims and philosophical assumptions about the nature of Western law. The supporting ideologies are far from unchallenged, although they are more powerful than any opposing currents of ideas. But the sociological and philosophical ideas that seem to underpin them have been widely shared by observers of law from all parts of the political spectrum. Unless the supporting ideologies can be shown to be, at best, partial 'truths', and unless the sociological claims and philosophical assumptions about law can be seen as providing inadequate support for them, they stand as fundamental barriers to the use of law to promote socialist ideals.

Before examining these ideologies and assumptions, it is necessary to ask what the ideals just referred to might be. When Dicey tried to define 'collectivism' (which was the term he used for the broadly developing socialist currents of the late nineteenth century) he could find only a negative unity to it, as the antithesis of individualism (Dicey 1905: 64 and *passim*). But modern conceptions of socialism tend to see it as the aspiration to *fulfil* individualism and thus make it possible for every individual to exist as a whole being, fully autonomous, and not repressed and alienated from herself or himself by conditions that prevent human fulfilment.[10]

Two closely related aspects of this aspiration can be identified. The first is the promotion of a *public altruism* that recognizes the collective and individual obligation of all members of society to contribute to the welfare of each other, and, correspondingly, the claim of each individual to a reasonable share of the human fulfilment available within society (which can be termed 'social justice'). The second aspect, inseparable from the first, is the promotion of *collective participation* in social life and particularly in the collective decisions and understandings that are essential to

---

[10] One major source of these ideas is Marx 1963.

its maintenance (which, for want of a better term, must be described by the ambiguous and inadequate word 'democracy'). For the purposes of this chapter I treat the aspirations of social justice and democracy in these senses as fundamental moral ideals and, since this chapter is concerned solely with questions about regulatory frameworks for pursuing them, no discussion will be offered here of wider economic, sociological, or political consequences that their pursuit may entail.

What, then, are the ideologies that support the dominant ideology of law's functions and oppose the use of law to realize these aspirations? They are, above all, ideologies of property, liberty, the minimal state, and the Rule of Law. All are ideologies in the sense used in this chapter since they obscure dilemmas, contradictions, and complexities with regard to the subject-matter they refer to (the inevitable incompleteness of all partial perspectives) in abstractions that imply a total, complete, all-embracing 'truth'.

The *ideology of property* asserts the 'sanctity' of private property rights. This is because property is seen as antecedent to the state[11] and, therefore, the right of private property is more fundamental than any state claims. Thus, property can, at best, only be taken by the state with just compensation,[12] and then only for strictly limited purposes (cf. Kirchheimer 1983). Taxation—the compulsory taking of particular property—is justified, if at all (cf. Nozick 1974: 169–72), only to provide the state with the means to protect property of individuals generally. According to this ideology, property is always private, and the state's control of property is always problematic and must never be more than temporary. Hence tax evasion, while condemned, is not violently condemned since it is seen as a matter of property owners' seeking to protect their property from the state, whose claim to it is not 'natural' but based only on specific positive legal provisions. By contrast, social security fraud is forcefully condemned since it involves people with no entitlement (legal or natural) taking property belonging 'naturally' to tax-paying citizens, even though—as a matter of positive law—the property of the latter (as revenue from taxation) is in the custody of the state.

---

[11] Although attempts to theorize this tend to run into well-recognized philosophical problems, especially that of the difficulty of deducing from such a starting point any property right of historically unlimited validity. See Steiner 1980: 251–7.

[12] Cf. United States Constitution Amend. V, cl. 4.

The contradiction which this ideology hides is that, in fundamental respects, property—in modern conditions at least—cannot be seen realistically as antecedent to the state but is defined by law and the creature of state power. Thus, many of the most economically significant forms of property in modern society are 'intellectual'—consisting of resources of knowledge, expertise, and creativity embodied in copyrights and other legal forms—or are promises, commitments, notional shares of future profit, and so on, embodied in commercial paper and numerous legal devices of financial and commercial security. All of these property forms exist only because of their definition and recognition in legal form and because of their guarantee by the state. In modern conditions they exist because the policy that supports their recognition and encouragement is embodied in law. In many cases the maintenance of their value as property depends directly on the policies and actions of the state. They are not antecedent to state and law as 'natural rights', but are specifically creatures of law, governed by such terms and conditions as law attaches to their existence, and which can be changed, on the basis of state policy, at any time. Whether similar arguments should be made in relation to other forms of property today—for example, rights in land—cannot be discussed here (see, further, Cotterrell 1986). It is enough to note that the ideology of property obscures fundamental characteristics of property and its relation to law in modern society.

A second supporting ideology is the *ideology of liberty*. Because this has been so frequently discussed it is necessary here to refer only briefly to its claims and contradictions. Liberty, in this ideology, is negative;[13] it is freedom from interference with the person or property. Like property, liberty is seen as antecedent to the state in the sense that the state can interfere with it only to protect the equal liberty of all. As it stands, such a principle could justify the most extensive state action to promote economic equality so as to create equal liberty of all to share in the benefits of life. However, the principle adopts a partial, limited idea of liberty as freedom of the person and of property *only* from interference by the state and law. This legal freedom can be abrogated only if the individual's actions deny the equal legal freedom of others.

---

[13] For its comparison with other conceptions of liberty see e.g. Neumann 1986: 31 ff.

Following the characteristics of all ideology, the ideology of liberty treats its limited, partial perspective on liberty as a total, comprehensive conception of freedom. Recent active use of law in social and economic restructuring is justifiable, in terms of this ideology, as destroying pre-existing legal or regulatory restraints on personal freedom, especially in relation to private property. The contradiction obscured by the ideology, however, is that while liberty is treated as freedom from legal interference, this liberty is merely what it is defined to be by law.

The conception of liberty thus becomes empty of substantive content. The effect of the other supporting ideologies is such, however, that it can be assumed that law should define liberty in general as freedom from arbitrary repressions of public power but not from those of private economic power or natural misfortune. The ideology of liberty does not see liberty as the general absence of constraints on legitimate activities or as freedom for fulfilment (Neumann 1986: 31 ff.). It treats one particular constraint (that of law-government) as the only one deserving serious notice.

A third supporting ideology is that of *the minimal state*. The state is to be seen as the servant of civil society and as having legitimacy only as such. It exists to preserve the spontaneous mechanisms of civil society—the free interaction of citizens by means of contract and property. The state does not create order and cohesion in society; it merely exists to prevent interference with the spontaneous processes of interaction between citizens which create this order and cohesion. Hence state action must not interfere with these processes. Extensive recent state activity and legal direction is justified only as a temporary measure by which pre-existing legal and administrative interferences with liberty and property are removed.

The contradiction hidden by this ideology is that the 'spontaneous' mechanisms of civil society seem to depend extensively on active state regulation and direction of social and economic life. The demarcation between public and private spheres, between state and civil society, seems increasingly problematic (see e.g. Cotterrell 1992: 295–8). Thus, without controls, competition tends to give way to monopoly; and free contractual interaction seems to lead to capital accumulations which ultimately diminish the bargaining power of many in maximizing that of others. Increasing economic concentration (see e.g. Aglietta 1987: ch. 4) creates greater risks of serious social disruption as a result of economic failure or lack of economic co-ordination.

Hence, the state is forced to intervene extensively in most Western nations to regulate financial markets, banking, insurance, international trade, foreign investment, commercial and industrial monopolies and semi-monopolies, and trade unions. The state also intervenes to organize and regulate welfare provision, land use planning, and environmental control, monitoring of national economic performance, and the direction of regional and national economic development. The ideology of the minimal state ignores the reality of an increasingly powerful, extensive, and centralized state apparatus; it also ignores the increasing difficulty of coherently conceptualizing the distinction between state and civil society and the apparent necessity in present conditions of very extensive activity by the former, ostensibly as servant of the latter. But the ideology does, at least, sense the present inability of the modern nation state to secure stable conditions within which civil society—as classically conceived—can maintain itself (see e.g. Beetham 1984).

A fourth supporting ideology is that of *the Rule of Law*. To refer to this as an ideology is not to disparage a fundamentally important aspiration and principle of government but to indicate that, as in other ideologies, a partial and limited view of reality is presented as a complete summation of a particular matter.[14] The Rule of Law is taken here to refer to the idea that law's most important contribution to liberty is found in the notion of the generality of law, as to acts and as to persons, and the associated ideals of clarity, prospectivity, and stability in law (Neumann 1986; and e.g. Raz 1979: ch. 11). Thus, law controls the powerful equally with the powerless. It prevents favouritism, prejudice, and arbitrariness in government. Law rules in the sense that whatever it stipulates it should stipulate for all concerned.

This ideology makes it possible to see the judiciary as a protection against the state, despite the fact that the judiciary is clearly *part of* the state in the sense of the total structure of centralized government of a modern society. This is because the real 'enemy' of the Rule of Law is not the state as such, which in the absence

---

[14] Cf. the half-ironic description of the Kantian *Rechtsstaat* as 'a splendid edifice for freedom and equality' in Berolzheimer 1912: 285.

of limiting constitutional provisions is free to enact any content
into law and is, therefore, hardly constrained by law if formal rule-
making procedures are followed. It is the administrative activity of
the state which is identified as problematic, because particularized
or discretionary regulation challenges the ideal of equality before
the law which is the ethical foundation of the demand for legal
generality.

The ideology of the Rule of Law, however, like all ideology,
hides the fact that it is based on a partial perspective—the recognition of equality before the law as something inherently valuable
in regard to particular, even if fundamentally important, aspects
of the experience of citizens and *under certain conditions*. Thus,
legal equality is obviously a most fundamental bastion of liberty
when legal subjects are not greatly unequal in economic power
and have roughly equal chances in the market-place. In such circumstances, law's great contribution is to reinforce that approximate equality through the recognition of all legal subjects as having
equal rights. It is also fundamentally important in so far as it
protects the relatively powerless from the effects of economic,
political, or other power by insisting that the legal rights of the
powerless are no less than those of the powerful.

As ideology, however, the ideology of the Rule of Law turns an
important but partial and limited perspective into a universal,
total perspective, proclaiming equality before the law as the fundamental and essential guarantee of equal liberty in all social and
economic conditions. However, as Franz Neumann, in particular,
has shown,[15] the Rule of Law can have other consequences in
modern conditions. Here, economies are typically dominated not
by numerous roughly equal small entrepreneurs but by huge, semi-
monopolistic business corporations, often multi-national in their
operations and resources, which, however, are treated according
to the Rule of Law as legal persons, presumptively 'equal', in
general terms, with the individual citizens who confront them—
for example, as consumers or employees.

In this case, as Neumann demonstrated, insistence on the
generality of law may be less significant for its refusal to recognize

[15] Neumann 1986. See also Friedmann 1971, one of the few discussions since
Neumann's that tries rigorously to examine the practical dilemmas that the development of monopoly capitalism poses for the Rule of Law as a principle of legal
generality. See further Lustgarten 1988.

any special claims of the powerful (who can often bring sufficient informal pressure to bear on the powerless without law's aid, and in a way that defeats the citizen's formally equal right).[16] Instead, its primary significance may be its wilful blindness to the need for special protection by law for the powerless, and special control of the powerful. Effective protections and controls may require quite particularized regulation taking detailed account of special circumstances and needs, or the exercise of broad administrative and regulatory discretions (Neumann 1986: 275; Offe 1984: 280; 1985: 306–7). All of these, however, are condemned by the ideology of the Rule of Law in so far as they detract seriously from the ideal of legal generality. Yet these kinds of regulation are already used on a most extensive scale as indispensable instruments of government. They challenge the ideology of the Rule of Law 'in a manner that has now become quite spectacular' (Poulantzas 1978: 218).

If these supporting ideologies—of property, liberty, the minimal state, and the Rule of Law—are all founded on limited, partial perspectives on the conditions of contemporary society and regulation, how is it that they remain powerful? It is necessary to stress again that such perspectives are not 'wrong'—each of these ideologies reflects important lessons from experience. But they are radically incomplete, so that, as ideology, they oversimplify a complex reality. Perhaps the main reason they prevail in popular consciousness is that, in general, the aspects of legal experience that most strongly justify the four supporting ideologies are the ones that most directly affect the immediate personal interests and consciousness of a majority of citizens.

Thus, in advanced Western societies it is traditional forms of property which are most familiar to most individuals. And negative legal liberty provides for most citizens a meaningful basis for individual effort (though the visibility of large numbers of the unemployed, the homeless, the poor, and the derelict may make significant numbers of even the relatively fortunate pause to consider the meaning of a 'free' society). Equally, bureaucratic incompetence and governmental interference in everyday life are sufficiently irksome for a self-reliant majority, relatively unaware

---

[16] Neumann 1986: 282; and for numerous modern illustrations of the point see Nader, ed., 1980.

of the full complexities of central and local government responsibilities, to justify its strong support for the idea of the minimal
state. Finally, since public power and public disorder appear as
greater immediate threats than private power—in the view of a
majority of citizens who hope for, or possess, some private power
of their own—the Rule of Law in its traditional sense is an 'un-
qualified human good' (cf. Thompson 1975: 266), understood
not as a positive means of creating equal rights but as the general
virtue of 'law and order'.

The tenacity of these ideologies is, thus, understandable but
nonetheless harmful to any widespread realistic assessment of law's
potentialities and responsibilities in modern conditions. The ideals
enshrined in these ideologies are not unambiguously served by
the legal strategies they approve and, in practice, these ideologies
obscure the complexities of modern experience of law-government.

The Element of Freedom of Decision Presupposed by the Form of Law

The dominant ideology of law's functions is also reinforced by
particular sociological claims and philosophical assumptions about
law which are widely accepted by lay and professional observers
of law. The general burden of the sociological claims is that law
is a relatively ineffective means of positively directing behaviour
towards specified objectives. Many modern empirical studies in sociology of law on 'legal impact' or legal effectiveness reach some
such conclusion. Much earlier, Adam Smith remarked on the limited information and wisdom of the legislator and the superiority
of the 'invisible hand' of private interests (within the limited constraints of law) in securing the common good.[17]

In modern times this claim is echoed in debates on the possibility of replacing the 'value form' of the market or commodity
categories by some other economic regulatory mechanisms (e.g.
Bettelheim 1976; Nove 1991: 22 ff.). It is also paralleled by some
Marxist arguments, especially grounded in Evgeny Pashukanis'
(1978) work, that legal form and perhaps, more generally, the
form of the Western state are, in themselves, merely reflections

[17] Smith 1784: 456 (vol. 1, bk. 4, ch. 2); and see the discussion of Smith's social
theory in a legal context in Neumann 1986: 188–9. On 'competition as a discovery
procedure' see Hayek 1982 vol. 3: 65–70.

or direct expressions of the logic of spontaneous market relations (Holloway and Picciotto, eds., 1978). From a quite different
standpoint the claim is reflected indirectly also in the recent application to law of autopoiesis theory. The latter suggests, among
other things, that a legal system should be seen as one of many
different social systems in a society, each having its own independent mode of internal communication and information selection.
This relative system-independence, or autopoietic self-sufficiency,
makes law's relationships with other systems (economic, scientific,
and so on) indirect and problematic—perhaps a matter of 'interference' (as with an electrical circuit, radio waves, or a nervous
system) rather than direct influence (see Teubner 1992a).

Many of these sociological positions suggest limitations on all
law's techniques and not just on those that could relate to attempts to promote social justice and democratic participation and
commitment by law. Beyond that, some positions (such as Pashukanis') presuppose a particular form as essential to law. Adam
Smith's claim, reduced to the assertion that individuals know their
own interests better than do distant legislators or administrators,
has much plausibility. But Smith restricted his thesis of the 'invisible hand' to the conditions of free competition rather than of
monopoly or semi-monopoly, and saw the need for government intervention if the conditions of competitive society ceased to hold.[18]

Further, if individuals are the best judges of their own interests,
they may not (if they lack the ordinary capacities and social advantages of Smith's typical bourgeois citizen) have the chance to realize these interests without the interventionist aid of government.
Even if they can do so, the knowledge on the basis of which they
judge both the nature of their interests and the best strategies for
realizing them may not, in all respects, be superior to that on
which the modern state—with its vast potential resources for data
gathering—can rely. The remoteness of the state from the conditions of everyday life must be balanced against the difficulties for
individuals in gaining a broader view of social and economic
conditions beyond their immediate situation.

Nevertheless, all of these sociological positions suggest either
that the form of law necessarily presupposes autonomous patterns

[18] See the discussion in Neumann 1986: 193–4 ('wherever monopolies exist, the
principle of freedom of contract and of non-intervention ceases to be applicable').

of individual action and decision anterior to itself (as, for example, Pashukanis argues) or that law-government can only operate effectively in partnership with these patterns.

Discussions about the form of law often involve philosophical assumptions which, in important respects, parallel the sociological claims. Legal thought typically invokes a range of concepts such as 'responsibility', 'intention', and 'fault' which presuppose the active will of the legal subject. While law presupposes this realm of will it cannot, as a practical matter, inquire very far into it. Hence, it frequently uses 'objective' tests of mental state such as those of 'reasonableness' and typically tries to distinguish intention from motive, usually ignoring the latter and interpreting the former as a minimum mental element required to make sense of an act as 'voluntary'. Although law usually makes no judgment about the nature of the element of will that it presupposes (for example, whether it is 'free' or 'determined'), any exclusion of the will element from law's presuppositions seems problematic, as is shown by the controversial character of absolute liability offences.

The importance of these considerations here is that law is thought to frame the subject's will but not to 'replace' it. Its operation is thought to presuppose the possibility of choice—even if, as the rejection in English law of the general doctrine of necessity shows,[19] that choice may sometimes be realistically very limited. It is probably chiefly because of this that the use of law to *direct* specific actions often seems less compatible with assumptions about the typical form of law,[20] than the use of law to *constrain* or to *facilitate* them.

Why should this be so? Clearly, legal directions to act in one way can usually be rewritten as prohibitions against acting in another.[21] As a theoretical matter of legal categories the distinction between acts and omissions is often unclear and usually relatively

[19] See Brudner 1987; and cf. *Perka* v. *The Queen* (1985) 13 DLR (4th) 1.

[20] Hints of this incompatibility—manifested in various ways—are common. See e.g. Hughes 1958: 636 ('conventional attitudes to *mens rea*, particularly with respect to ignorance of the law, are not adequate tools to achieve justice for those accused of inaction'). The absence of a clear 'defence of impossibility' in English law has been seen as most serious in relation to regulatory offences involving failure to perform specific actions: see Smart 1987. See also Glazebrook 1960.

[21] See e.g. Stone 1964: 196; and, in the context of causation questions, Hart and Honoré 1985: 138–9.

unimportant. In practice, however, the important issue is how much freedom of manœuvre is left for the citizen by a legal provision.[22] A rule *prohibiting* or penalizing a particular kind of act, such as theft or deliberate killing, may leave untouched a theoretically infinite range of possible lawful actions (that is, acts other than those identified by law as theft or murder) which could legitimately be the object of the individual's will. A rule *requiring* positive action of a particular kind might, however, be thought of as removing all legitimate possibility of other action as regards the particular time, situation, and so on, when the specified legal action is required.[23] If the legal direction specifies action in minute detail it can perhaps be regarded as even requiring that the law's direction should *replace* the individual's will.

This contrast between legal prohibition of a specified action and legal requirement for a specified action points to differences of degree, not of kind, since the apparent scope left by law for the individual's 'expression of will' depends on the content of the legal provision and the environment of actual conditions of action and other legal provisions within which it operates. But a legal provision that appears to limit the formally free exercise of will oppressively—beyond an unspecifiable threshold—is likely to meet strong psychological resistance, as empirical studies have shown (e.g. Muir 1967).

Something comparable seems to arise with regard to moral attitudes. There is a common tendency to consider immoral acts as somehow worse, other things being equal, than omissions to act in ways dictated by morality. For example, 'killing' is often thought to be worse than 'letting die' (Thomson 1986: 95–6). Yet, as Judith Jarvis Thomson has shown, such a general position is very hard to justify logically when many specific circumstances are considered (Thomson 1986: ch. 6; Glover 1977: ch. 7). We may guess that the 'incoherent' general idea that an immoral act is worse than an immoral omission is, nevertheless, related to general assumptions about a necessary balance between regulation, on the one hand, and a realm of unexamined, uncontrolled 'freedom', on the other

---

[22] e.g., Allott (1980: 48) notes 'pragmatic and socio-psychological differences' in effects of regulatory forms which may make it highly misleading to think of prohibitions as ways of restating requirements for positive action.

[23] Cf. Glover 1977: 104, discussing implications of the fact that 'actions take time, while omissions do not'.

(see also Glover 1977: 104–5). These assumptions are expressed in many ways in relation to law. Thus, law can act only on the 'outside' and not the 'inside' of people and things (Pound 1959 vol. 3: 353); it can impose duties but not aspirations (Fuller 1969); and it is concerned 'with the minimum and not with the maximum' (Devlin 1965: 19).

These philosophical images of law should force us to recognize not that law is unable to direct conduct or positively mould social conditions in conscious pursuit of social justice but that it can— according to prevailing Western legal conceptions—do so only in partnership with the elements of 'will' that are ascribed to the individual citizen. These elements can be described in terms of individuals' recognition and pursuit of self-interest and personal conscience and of their interpretation of social, moral, economic, and political realities.

Thus, the philosophical assumptions and sociological claims about law's nature seem to reinforce and parallel each other. While the former stress the moral inappropriateness of certain kinds of positive direction by law, the latter stress its likely ineffectiveness and inefficiency. Together, these assumptions and claims indicate an undefined but very important realm of 'free' action and choice —a kind of 'no-go' area of individuality—presupposed or required by the form of law.

Self-interest and Community

What should we conclude about the relationship between the dominant ideology of law's functions, the four supporting ideologies, and the sociological claims and philosophical assumptions about law's nature? As regards the supporting ideologies, this chapter has sought to show that they are seriously undermined by the complexities of actual experience, as to both their cognitive assumptions and the plausibility of their prescriptions. It is not possible, however, responsibly to deny the importance of the *partial* perspectives on which these ideologies are based. They are grounded in certain important aspects of experience.

Equally, the sociological claims and philosophical assumptions about law point to an important characteristic of Western legal form which cannot be denied unless that form is itself discarded. It is not possible to deny the element of freedom of decision—the 'no-go' area of unregulated individuality—presupposed by this legal form, and implied in sociological claims about the regulatory capacities of law.

None of these observations, however, serves to support the dominant ideology of law's functions, though they indicate the main elements from which that ideology is constructed. They also suggest primary general considerations that should attach to the pursuit of the ideals of public altruism and collective participation by means of law. One such consideration is that law must respect the element of freedom of decision presupposed by its form.

Roscoe Pound noted one aspect of this in declaring that law 'depends for its efficacy chiefly upon the extent to which it can identify social interests with individual advantage or interest' (Pound 1959: vol. 3, 373). Up to a point, self-interest or 'individual advantage' clearly justifies state activity. Self-interest requires a certain guaranteed minimum of security of the person and property. Hence, it clearly supports state activities guaranteeing this security. What is less often emphasized, however, is that the pursuit of self-interest usually requires more than just this minimum if it is to be satisfying or self-evidently worthwhile.

Thus, self-interest presupposes an environment in which, at the least, it is worthwhile to the individual to find interests to pursue. The pursuit of personal fulfilment presupposes a context which helps to define what that fulfilment could be. For most people, at least, that context is largely a social one, in some sense. Thus, status is worth seeking if status, in a particular social context, is worth having; power is worth pursuing if, in the relevant context, it is worth exercising; wealth is a desirable objective if it can, in a given social context, actually buy a desirable life. The pursuit of self-interest becomes meaningful and fulfilling to individuals if many intangible contextual prerequisites are present. For different people, and for different perceptions of 'individual advantage', these prerequisites vary greatly. In general, they are taken so much for granted, referred to in such opaque terms as 'quality of life', 'civilisation', or 'civilised values', that their importance passes unrecognized by most individuals at most times.

Probably the term 'social solidarity', which Émile Durkheim made an enduring part of the sociological vocabulary (Durkheim 1984), best describes the context within which these prerequisites are most fully met for the members of a society, as a whole. Indeed,

Durkheim was right to identify social solidarity as a *moral* phenomenon. But while he understood it as, in modern society, primarily a condition of interdependence between individuals and between social groups, it is more appropriately seen as a positive *recognition* and *affirmation* by citizens of this interdependence; a recognition and affirmation that can be expressed, among other ways, through law and legal institutions.

In this chapter I take the term to express a condition in which the individual's gain is also the community's gain; and social welfare is expressed not only in overall levels of economic well-being of citizens but of community commitment and concern for the total 'quality of life' of its members. In this context, then, the term 'community' itself refers to a collectivity of individuals who feel this solidarity and who recognize a strong common commitment or moral involvement in the welfare of the collectivity as a whole and all its members.

What has this to do with the functions of law? It suggests that the dominant ideology of law's functions is profoundly wrong in so far as it separates the (permissible) use of law to facilitate the pursuit of self-interest from the (impermissible) use of law to promote actively the wider common interest which socialist ideals seek to identify. Individual self-interest requires collective co-operation to build the solidarity without which many of the intangible benefits of individual life are undermined or lost. Not only are these intangible but they are also often unnoticed until they begin to disappear in a serious decline of social morale, 'community spirit', public order, and civic responsibility.

Because of this one can amend Adam Smith's claim that individuals know their own self-interest better than does the legislator. If lawmakers really do represent the collectivity as a whole and not just an élite that dominates it, law may identify self-interest *in some respects* better than the individual can, because it expresses a collective judgement of the members of the collectivity as a whole (informed by their experience of all the varied circumstances of social life) as to the conditions which self-interest requires for its pursuit within the security of a community.

Such a claim would be merely arrogant unless the limited knowledge of lawmakers as regards the interests of individuals and social groups, and as regards the particular circumstances in which those interests are pursued, were remedied by 'democracy' in the widest sense—by collective participation. This is a complex concept. At root, however, it can be taken to involve commitment of citizens to a community and its processes and organizations, and an active involvement in and moral responsibility of citizens for decisions and actions in pursuit of the common welfare.

Present democratic processes, whatever their virtues, seem seriously inadequate to frame collective participation. This is, perhaps, the primary reason why lawmaking ostensibly in pursuit of social justice has, indeed, often been seen as arrogant (cf. Allott 1980: 175), as well as inefficient and ignorant of citizens' actual needs and demands. Public altruism, as the effort to make the pursuit of self-interest (or, in this context, the full realization of individuality) meaningful for all individuals as members of a society worth living in, is inseparable from collective participation. Thus, social justice and democracy, as the terms have been used in this chapter, are not separate ideals but two aspects of the same aspiration.

What Can Law Do?

What, then, can and cannot law do to further this aspiration? It seems to follow from the idea that law presupposes a realm of legally uncontrollable 'will' anterior to itself, that it cannot, itself, *create* a commitment of will or a moral motivation. Attempts have often been made to analyse law itself as being an expression of will—the will of the legislator, the state, or the people.[24] But these attempts are merely ways of trying to conceptualize the realm of control that law creates, by analogy with the way that it conceptualizes the realm of freedom it presupposes. If law cannot create commitment it cannot create solidarity or community. But it can aim to create conditions for human existence that *symbolize* a moral commitment of the community in its care for its members as individuals.

It does seem, however, that current legal policy in Britain assumes law can directly influence motivation in a variety of ways. The illustrations with which this chapter began—of the use of law to influence attitudes, to shape the content of education, and to

[24] On these 'will theories' see Olivecrona 1971: 73–7 and *passim*.

encourage a free market climate of life in various ways—surely suggest this. But law is being used here not to create motivations but ostensibly to release existing ones; to remove constraints from the pursuit of self-interest as intuitively grasped by many individuals in the short-term and limited considerations of immediate everyday experience. One primary means of doing this is by changing power relationships—in the workplace, in educational systems, in local politics, in the market, and so on—so as to free motivations that are favoured and constrain those that are not. Thus, law approves some motivations, purports to reinforce and reward some attitudes, 'officially' confirms some assumptions about what counts as merit and demerit, and potentially discourages, deters, and disconfirms other motivations, attitudes, and assumptions.

This present use of law holds important lessons. It assumes that law is a potentially important instrument in influencing the climate of thought in a society. Thus, law might equally be used to create conditions under which a broader conception of self-interest—as the fullest realization of individuality in the conditions of solidarity—could flourish.

One means is the adjustment of power relations specifically so as to free motivations towards solidarity and community, and to constrain antagonistic motivations. But this is only a part of what law might do, and no more than a matter of playing the existing socially divisive game of favouring, through the use of power, some people's values and attitudes at the expense of those of other people.

Much more importantly, law-government could, amongst other things, create conditions that would make it possible for citizens to obtain a clearer, broader, less distorted view of the society they live in. For example, in Britain it could promote a freer press, independent of narrow proprietorial interests (see e.g. Curran and Seaton 1991: ch. 16), perhaps by establishing the necessity of trust arrangements guaranteeing editorial freedom and encouraging editorial and journalistic responsibility for the accurate and balanced presentation of news, in the interest of all sections of the community. It could, in various ways, actively facilitate and promote both the expression of opinion from sections of society whose voices are otherwise rarely heard, and also the dissemination of knowledge about the varied cultures, conditions of life, and experienced needs of social groups. It could, equally, establish wide principles of open government in legal form, so that to a far greater extent than at present citizens could judge for themselves where their 'security' lies, and where threats to it lie.

Another lesson needs to be learnt from present state actions to influence the prevailing climate of thought and activity. Law (in the sense of general laws, approved by the ideology of the Rule of Law) and discretionary or particularized regulation are, at the present time, almost invariably used in combination to achieve chosen governmental purposes. Although rule and discretion, and general law and particular order, are usually clearly distinguished in legal philosophy, in practice they form merely a continuum of devices available for modern regulatory strategies. This is why it has become increasingly appropriate to speak of law-government rather than law. Such a situation would be unlikely to change should serious attempts be made through regulation to further social justice as public altruism.

The ideal of legal generality and equality before the law—as envisaged in the ideology of the Rule of Law—remains a most important ideal, to be promoted and realized to the greatest possible extent to minimize governmental arbitrariness, and to ensure that law and regulation do not explicitly favour the powerful more than the powerless. But in modern conditions it has become an increasingly empty ideal in many areas of regulation (cf. Poulantzas 1978: 218–9). As a result, perhaps, administration as a necessary responsibility of the state—but always problematic within the ideology of the Rule of Law—has tended to lack legitimacy in the eyes of citizens (cf. Neumann 1949: lxiv).

Again, if there is a solution for this it is probably to be found in the extension of democracy as collective participation. The commitment and moral involvement of the regulated population is necessary in order to legitimize modern administration (see further Harden and Lewis 1986; Prosser 1982). The distinction between law and administration has been transformed into a matter of degree: how much specific direction and how much freedom of manœuvre of the regulatees is implied in the form of regulation? How far is the citizen seen as an object of regulation and how far seen as a 'freely acting' subject within regulatory structures? In essence, collective participation of citizens in public decision-making and organized public action appears as the only means by which, given present and (likely) future regulatory forms, citizens

—in so far as they are necessarily *objects* of regulation—can also become *subjects* in the creation of regulation.

This requirement suggests another as essential if there is to be any possibility of its fulfilment. Law-government in the service of social justice cannot be thought of merely as the combination of state law and centralized regulation. Durkheim recognized the inadequacy and remoteness of the centralized state as a mechanism for providing regulation compatible with the requirements of social solidarity. He advocated, as have many later writers, regulation at many 'levels' and in different functional environments within society (Durkheim 1957; Durkheim 1984: xxxi–lix). This pluralistic approach to regulation necessitates a considerable decentralization of regulatory power within the overall co-ordinating structure of the state.

Without it, regulation is likely to remain—as now—frequently inefficient and remote from experienced needs and social and economic conditions, since it is created in processes that are themselves remote, and which produce regulation usually too inflexible to take full account of variations in those conditions. Equally, without this decentralization, regulation cannot acquire the legitimacy that might be provided by the collective participation or concern of citizens in the processes of its creation, and by a conception of regulation as expressing the active moral commitment of the community.

Thus, the ideal of the 'minimal state', which properly asserts the need for individual citizens to be able to control as far as possible their own destinies, should not lead inescapably to the myth that social life would be made free by dismantling regulation and administration. It should lead instead to a recognition that the necessary regulation and administration ought to be as far as possible removed from the centralized state to structures more amenable to popular control and influence. On this view the role of centralized law-government is primarily that of *co-ordination* of regulation, and enforcement of certain foundation conditions for social co-operation—primarily the protection of citizens from physical harm caused by others, and the general specification and protection of property rights.

The ideologies of the minimal state and the Rule of Law both need to be replaced with conceptions that recognize and seek to preserve the important ideals these ideologies frame, while taking full account of the complexities of modern regulation and of the conditions of social and economic life. A further reorientation of legal thought is, however, equally necessary in the attempt to make law available to promote public altruism and collective participation. The 'sanctity' of private property, which the ideology of property assumes, is undoubtedly justifiable in so far as property provides *security* for the individual. But, from the perspective adopted in this chapter, it cannot be justifiable in so far as it makes possible the extensive manipulation and control of others. History has shown repeatedly how potent the legal claim of absolute sanctity of property can be against attempts to achieve egalitarian social reforms (Kirchheimer 1983). Thus, all property beyond certain (generous) limits of scale should, on the basis of the viewpoint developed in this chapter, be held subject to a recognition that it is held on trust for the common good and that its use can be subject to control by law in the public interest. Between the concept of private property, which the ideology of property sanctifies, and that of state property which—for many good reasons—it condemns, there ought to be re-established a concept of community rights in property, asserted not to defeat the vital security which private property provides for the individual, but to supplement and extend it.

These replacements of the threadbare ideologies of property, the minimal state, and the Rule of Law would pave the way for legal structures which firmly recognize the important virtues these ideologies seek to express, but which address contemporary regulatory problems realistically. In doing so they would help to transform the fourth and most important ideology—of liberty—into a principle that recognizes liberty as the conditions of maximum autonomy of all citizens within a free society.

13 Legal Theory and the Image of Legality

What kind of legal theory is needed to take account of changes in the nature of regulation discussed in Chapter 12? It must be theory focusing on the complexity, diversity, and indefinite boundaries of contemporary legal regulation, and on the variety of its sites and settings. It must recognize legal doctrine and practices as instruments of coercive power but also, potentially, as frameworks and expressions of integrated communities. Contemporary legality is a matter of fragmented regulation, diverse regulatory regimes and jurisdictions, piecemeal legal rationality, and policy-driven law. In such conditions moral foundations for law are not impossible to find but the moral milieux in which legal principle can be rooted will be relatively local and specific. The resources of both legal philosophy and sociology of law are necessary in conceptualizing a morally meaningful legality.

Legal theory ought not to be esoteric, though it too often seems so. Theoretical studies of law become remote when law itself seems academically remote, as though it can be analysed and understood without constant reference to the specific empirical social conditions of its existence. Legal theory maximizes its vitality and relevance in a rapidly changing social world by remaining permanently sensitive to the specific historic and social contexts, causes, and consequences of legal experience. And to do this it needs to adopt a broad, open, and self-critical sociological perspective on law; a perspective continually and consistently informed, reformed, and challenged by social theory and empirical social research, and shaped by an overriding aspiration to extend systematic knowledge of the social world.

This chapter considers some vital challenges which theoretical studies of law presently face if they are, indeed, to take proper account of law's changing character and conditions of existence. It will be necessary first to say more about the outlook on legal theory that informs discussion here, and then to suggest how changing ideas about legal regulation are posing fundamental problems which legal theory must address. These changes amount to the emergence of what I shall describe as a new or altered image of legality. Finally, it will be necessary to ask how legal theory is responding, and should respond, to the challenges posed by these changes.

The Scope of Legal Theory

Legal theory is the enterprise of trying to explain systematically and generally the nature of law—as legal ideas, legal institutions, and legal practices. This is often a matter of philosophical inquiry: about the general nature of legal doctrine, reasoning, argument, or interpretation; about general relationships between legal concepts, rules, or principles; and about essential moral or rational foundations of legal authority, or general determinants of legal validity. Because of the apparent centrality of these kinds of inquiries, legal theory is sometimes considered synonymous with legal philosophy, which focuses on them as well as on other philosophical questions surrounding law.

But theoretical inquiries about law are not just of this philosophical character. They necessarily include studies of the changing historical character of legal regulation and assessments of the social (including legal professional) significance and sources of these changes. Legal theory must address the social origins and effects of law, the conditions of change in the character of regulation, and the social consequences of legal ideas and institutions. It must be historical and sociological in orientation because it must operationalize empirically, and not treat with lip-service, the proposition that law is a social phenomenon—an aspect of social experience. Legal philosophy's efforts to analyse the character of legal doctrine, to identify law's moral implications, or to construct theoretical accounts of legal interpretation or legal logic, gain practical significance in the context of lawyers' and lay citizens' specific experiences of law. And these experiences change with the changing historical conditions of the societies in which law exists. Philosophical speculations on the nature and significance of legal ideas are essential to legal theory. But they must be subordinate to enquiries examining the very conditions that make such speculation possible and shape it. Only thus can the relevance of legal philosophy in contemporary conditions be assessed and guaranteed.

Legal theory can most usefully treat law in its broadest sense as an *aspect or field of social experience*. Law in this sense is a very diverse set of practices loosely arranged around and related to tasks of government and social control. Since knowledge and practice interact and reinforce each other, legal practices give rise to and are shaped by normative and cognitive ideas; in other words, doctrine. Thus, law in a narrower and more specific sense is *institutionalized doctrine*: rules, regulations, concepts, principles, and modes of reasoning with these, all of which are, in some way, rationalized from practices of government and social control and serve, in varying degrees and with varying effectiveness, as guides for, orderings of, and legitimations for these practices.

Law is thus the doctrine, rhetoric, and reasoning that legal philosophers study. But its broad patterns of ideas also contribute to and reflect the ideological structures that social and political theory examines; the general, taken for granted frameworks of evaluation and understanding of social and political life. Equally, law's processes of dispute resolution, its roles, and institutions (such as courts, police, legal professions, regulators, administrators, complainants, and disputants) are illuminated by anthropological and sociological literature. Some of its problems and practices of textual interpretation relate to those addressed by literary theorists. Law in all of these guises and aspects cannot be the preserve of a specific academic discipline. It is a field of experience whose complexity challenges the student to ignore or reject the assumed prerogatives of disciplines in search of better understanding. If law is an important aspect of social experience this importance must be reflected in the range and ambition of legal theory.

Equally, this theory has to be aware of the social and professional conditions of its *own* existence and the constraints and challenges that those conditions pose. Legal theory in modern Western societies has been fortunate to have lacked a certain kind of official sponsor. In less favoured environments it has sometimes been harnessed deliberately to serve ideological functions dictated by state or church. In another sense, however, much modern legal theory has seemed to presume as its sponsors, lawyers themselves, in so far as lawyers have felt an intellectual need to make explicit the assumptions entailed in the idea of law as a learned profession, an intellectual discipline, and a cultural possession.

Much—but certainly not all—modern legal theory has been addressed in one way or another to lawyers. John Austin spoke of jurisprudence as providing a 'map of the law', a sound underpinning of theory and an ordering of legal ideas which would make it possible for students to learn law as a science, a systematic body of knowledge (Austin 1863: 379–80). Modern legal philosophy has generally been concerned to portray law as rational, principled (that is, embodying certain consistent values), or systematic; or unified by distinctive forms, procedures, or discourses. It has supplied general theories of legal reasoning, argument, or interpretation and general explanations of such fundamental notions as legal system, legal rule, legal obligation, and legal authority. At least indirectly it has often presented lawyers with images of an ordered and sophisticated system of professional knowledge (cf. Abbott 1988: 52–7), a scholarly practice founded on a coherent, finite, and systematic body of learning or a principled and creative interpretive practice (see generally Cotterrell 1989).

Yet I shall argue in a moment that legal theory itself is being forced to recognize that this imagery of legality—in terms of unity, system, and principle—is not enough and may even be misleading. Legal regulation seems to be changing its character. And lawyers, let alone ordinary citizens, are not best served by presenting law in ways that romanticize a complex reality. A related point is about the place of power in law and its theory. The effort to portray law as a system of reason, a model of rules, or as collective practices of interpretation, may sometimes obscure law's aspect as an instrument of power. The significance of law's complex, ambiguous, and varied relationships with power is highlighted by treating law in the broadest sense as a set of diverse practices related to government and social control—while recognizing that these are not restricted to the government of states or to public control and order but that they also embrace structures of power and control in private and group relationships of many kinds.

Law has been portrayed appropriately by some jurists as a

combination of reason and power or fiat (Fuller 1946), a balance of *ratio* and *voluntas*, rational order and imposed will (Neumann 1986: 45–6; Neumann 1944: 440 ff., 451–2). Recently Michel Foucault has taught us to see disciplinary power and expert knowledge as intertwined and reciprocally reinforcing. For Foucault, power is dispersed and omnipresent, the means by which everything in social life gets done—neither to be regretted nor celebrated (see e.g. Foucault 1980). But it is necessary to emphasize that power in modern law means the exercise of coercion or the ability to call on others to exercise coercion on one's behalf. As Robert Cover put it dramatically, legal interpretation takes place in 'a field of pain and death' (Cover 1986: 1601). In modern legal systems power is concentrated through structures of government, but also delegated to subordinate agencies and individuals; it rests in some indeterminate measure on the consent or acquiescence of the governed (cf. Cassinelli 1959; Vollrath 1976) so it is also a matter of negotiation and compromise. Law expresses and channels power. Yet, seeing the law of the contemporary state as reasoned doctrine, it is easy to ignore the social consequences of its practice as the allocation, application, diversion, and negotiation of force, actual or potential.

Legal philosophers have properly sought to theorize the elements of system, regularity, and reason with which law achieves this channelling and makes it productive. Yet to some extent modern legal philosophy in this country has neglected power, having rejected as simplistic Austin's conception of laws as the commands of a sovereign power. The tendency has been to talk not of power but of rule-governed powers, with the emphasis on the rules that govern rather than on the power of legal practices themselves (Hart 1961: ch. 3; Hart 1982: ch. 8). Legal philosophy's concern with law as reason or *ratio* has tended to obscure the *voluntas* or power element in law. But by remaining relatively silent about the latter legal philosophy reflects power in its own practice, a Foucauldian practice of knowledge which may divert attention from law as coercion while enhancing and celebrating intellectual techniques of legal control. I want to argue that changes in legal regulation itself, or at least in the image of the nature of legality which lawyers and others recognize, are bringing the issue of the relationship between law and power, and the many diverse forms that both can take, back to the agenda of legal theory.

Images of Legality

What are these changes? I will merely outline three themes relating to United Kingdom law which provide some important undercurrents of the literature of legal commentary in this country, and are paralleled in discussion in many foreign jurisdictions.

Most obvious to lawyers and lay citizens alike is that of the *increasing bulk of legal doctrine*—legal rules, regulations, and prescriptions of all kinds. The American lawyer, Grant Gilmore, once tried to explain the development in the United States in the first half of this century of what he saw as a temporary crisis of confidence in the idea of law as a coherent body of knowledge and as a principled practice of decision-making. Gilmore's explanation was partly in terms of the massive growth of case law and the proliferation of published reports of judicial decisions, which had made it difficult to rationalize and organize into a systematic and consistent body of knowledge a vast, ever-growing bulk of legal doctrine (Gilmore 1961).

But, at least in Britain, we look in the wrong place if we see the operation of courts as posing the main problems of proliferation of regulation. Reporting practices limit the number of cases selected for inclusion in published reports and in relatively small jurisdictions, such as those of the United Kingdom, the number of decided cases is limited by the constraints of court loads, just as the amount of legislation produced by Parliament is limited by parliamentary time. The proliferation of case law in courts is certainly significant (see Schuchman 1988), as is the expanding size of the statute book (see generally Galanter 1992: 6–7; Engle 1987), but taken alone these developments give an incomplete picture of the growing bulk of doctrine.

More generally important in this context are ways of creating regulation that make it possible to escape constraints of time and manpower affecting ordinary legislative or judicial processes and so allow legal doctrine to expand seemingly without limits. Sites of adjudication are created outside formal court structures, for example through tribunals of many kinds, which may establish doctrine of their own. More fundamentally, modern statutes frequently sketch frameworks of regulation while allowing details to be filled in or adopted from other sources, through subordinate legislation, the creation or adoption of various kinds of codes of practice,[1] and the provision of broad ministerial powers or of jurisdictions for regulatory or standard-setting agencies. Sometimes the coming into force of legislative provisions and of regulations created under their authority is phased over a considerable time so that an Act of Parliament may appear less as the presentation of a structure of legal doctrine than as a rolling programme of policy implementation.[2] In this and other ways law-creation can be made a very open-ended process. It is misleading to consider the words of many statutes separately from the trail of orders, regulations, and codes required to complete their meaning, but which may frequently be changed by processes that appear as much administrative as legislative.

Thus, the theme of the increasing bulk of doctrine merges with a second theme, that of *the fragmentation of the form of law*. A statute such as the Shops Act 1950—recently the most celebrated piece of dead-letter law thanks to the non-enforcement of its Sunday trading provisions—contains, in schedules, classifications that read more like the contents of a manual of bureaucratic practice than a body of legal rules or principles. The striking, though hardly exceptional, Nightwear (Safety) Order 1978 made under consumer safety legislation then in force, is almost entirely made up of definitions of items of children's nightwear in terms of chest, sleeve, and inside-leg measurements.[3]

More broadly significant is the interdependence or fusion of legal forms and scientific standard-setting (see e.g. Livock 1979). Current British consumer protection regulations require, with startling precision, that in a particular chemical compound used in cosmetics: 'The ratio of the number of aluminium atoms to that of zirconium atoms must be between two and ten'.[4] The Food

---

[1] As e.g. under the Employment Act 1980, Transport Act 1982, and Police and Criminal Evidence Act 1984. And see e.g. McCrudden 1988; Fennell 1990.

[2] A notable example is the Consumer Credit Act 1974 specifying that much of the statute would come into force on 'appointed days' to be determined for particular parts of the legislation by commencement orders made under s. 192 and Sch. 3. The first commencement order under these provisions was made in 1975. The most recent dates from 1989.

[3] The current statutory instrument is the Nightwear (Safety) Regulations 1985 (SI 1985/2043). See also the 1967 order (SI 1967/839) which this replaced and which contains similar definitions.

[4] Cosmetic Products (Safety) (Amendment) Regulations 1987 (SI 1987/1920) Sch. 1. Numerous examples of the attachment and incorporation of scientific standards in regulation can be found in the many statutory instruments issued under the authority of Consumer Protection Act 1987 s. 11.

Safety Act 1990 gives broad powers to ministers to create regulations in the light of scientific advice and after consultation with interests likely to be affected by regulation of food production and distribution. A recent commentator describes the regulation intended to evolve within the broad framework of the Act as 'the product of a process of scientific negotiation'. It is 'to be determined by a policy bargaining process, mediated by expertise' (Scott 1990: 800).

One can debate at length in these contexts what is legislation or quasi-legislation (cf. Ganz 1987), law, or non-law, and the topic is familiar to public lawyers. But this uncertainty about the limits or the specific hallmarks of 'the legal' is part of the point. Legal form is ever more clearly in these instances the instrument of governmental power or the means of negotiated compromises between interest groups. It has fragmented into regulatory regimes with indeterminate limits and very varied normative components.

The shifting boundaries between legal and extra-legal controls are illustrated also by reliance, in fields such as financial services (see Bagnall 1990) and some other business contexts, on structures of governmentally organized self-regulation, monitored, invaded, and shaped by legislation. In some such contexts: 'Where do we stop speaking of law and find ourselves simply describing social life?' (Merry 1988: 878). It is possible to talk, as some writers have, of a re-establishment and intensification of legal pluralism[5]— that is, the complex interplay of different, relatively autonomous, regulatory systems whose interactions constitute legal order. This development is apparent not just within the borders of municipal legal systems but internationally in such contexts as the European Union with its intersection of régimes or planes of state and supranational legality. In such circumstances it is still useful and appropriate to think of law as institutionalized doctrine: institutionalized in the sense of being created, interpreted, or enforced in governmentally co-ordinated patterns of official activity (cf. Cotterrell 1992: 41–3). But the concept of law has necessarily been loosened considerably from that assumed in much legal literature.

My third and last theme is that of the *enhanced visibility of policy in law*. There is some evidence that British judges—once reluctant to discuss policy issues publicly—are becoming more willing to talk about legal policy, in the sense of social, economic, or other

[5] See e.g. Teubner 1992b, and many references therein.

282 Law, Power, and Community

goals of laws (see Bell 1983: 1–7; Stevens 1979: Part 4; Atiyah and Summers 1987: 349), and to do so both within and without the courtroom. But policy issues have been brought more generally to the forefront of discussion about law by the proliferation of legislative and regulatory forms referred to above, the introduction of which is often explicitly justified in policy terms. Equally, the growth of a cadre of academic lawyers willing to assume the role of professional commentators on legal policy[6] has been important.

A particularly significant further development has been the recovery of the idea that legal interpretation is not a matter only for lawyers. Modern pressure groups of many kinds, and such occupational groups as journalists, police, social and public administration specialists, regulators, and social scientists, have contributed, for very varied reasons, to policy critique of law in a dialogue with government and legislators. It seems that much more is said about law, and by much more diverse groups of commentators, than in the recent past (cf. Galanter 1992: 14–15).

These developments around policy have encouraged a generalized instrumentalist view of legality (see e.g. Daintith 1988; Posner 1987). Law's formal rationality, its consistency as a unified body of doctrine, and its coherence as a principled structure of ideas seem less vital considerations than they once did. The main value of a particular legal precept is in its usefulness for the specific goal or goals it is thought to serve. It may seem less appropriate to view regulatory precepts as exemplifying principles applied across broad areas of legal doctrine. Discussion of implementation is hard to isolate from interpretation of policy (Hill 1981). An instrumental view may be impatient with questions about the technical forms of legal argument or reason applicable to particular legal precepts, or even, indeed, about whether regulation should take a particular form; for example, that of rules allowing a degree of generalization. Policy arguments provide substitutes for those kinds of legal reasoning made less persuasive by the fragmentation of legal form discussed earlier. An instrumentalist outlook may require that each legal precept be coupled with specific social or economic goals, however difficult this coupling sometimes is to achieve (see Summers 1977). Such an approach sometimes obscures the point that legal doctrine can fulfil a role merely by contributing a

---

[6] On the earlier reluctance of academic lawyers to assume this role see Sugarman 1986: 46 ff.

predictable framework of regulation, however insignificant, contradictory, or indeterminate any particular rule may be when judged in policy terms.

An increased emphasis on policy does not promote the moral or even political coherence of legal doctrine. In fact, the opposite is true. An emphasis on policy will tend to treat all substantive values as foreign to law, so that law appears essentially as mere technique or instrument. Policy imports values into legal institutions and doctrine only temporarily from a wider world of politics.

Instrumentalism largely replaces the image of law as *ratio* with one of *voluntas*. It is often remarked that policy-dominated regulatory practices are potentially incompatible with the ideal of the Rule of Law—regarded as a set of specifically legal values of predictability and consistency in rules, and coherence, equality, and fairness in adjudication.[7] Traditionally, British judges during most of the nineteenth and twentieth centuries have considered policy an 'unruly horse' to be seen to ride[8] primarily because of the fear that policy argument might lead to abandonment of the search for principle—broad value consistency in legal doctrine—in favour of a mechanical or subjective implementing of specific political aims. But in practice—that is, in the practices of law creation and legal decision-making—principle often seems subsumed in or subordinated to policy. Efforts to preserve the former as something distinct from the latter increasingly appear as a romantic hankering for a form of legal reason no longer viable. Perhaps, indeed, legal principle analytically separable from policy was never more than an illusion created in the ceaseless effort to present the intersection of inchoate social practices and norms, on the one hand, and the pragmatics of state government, on the other, as stable, professionally controllable knowledge.

The themes sketched above embrace matters that seem increasingly significant to many legal observers. They relate to a changed *image of legality*, whatever the complexities of assessing the character of regulatory change. And this altered image of legality requires a change in traditional orientations of legal philosophy and legal theory. The very idea of the (at least potential) unity of law, or of its systematic character is put in issue. So is the idea of law's

[7] The *locus classicus* is probably Hayek 1944: ch. 6.
[8] See *Richardson* v. *Mellish* (1824) 2 Bing. 229 at 242, *per* Burrough J; Winfield 1928; Knight 1922.

intellectual or moral autonomy, and its integrity as a discipline or practice. The notion of law as a species of rules, distinguished from official discretion, is problematic (cf. Galligan 1986: ch. 2), because the dichotomy of rule and discretion seems an unsatisfactory way to refer to a *continuum*: an immense array of standards, prescriptions, and modes of interpretation and decision in modern regulatory systems. Discretions may harden into rules (see e.g. Pattenden 1990: 19). Elsewhere rules appear undermined or dismantled by discretion in their application.[9] The idea of a specifically legal form of argument, reason, or interpretation is challenged by the range of modern state regulation with its varying methods, diverse sites of practice, and indefinite boundaries. Equally, the tendency to think of law instrumentally creates tensions with the idea of law as *ratio*, unless we find new ways of relating the elements of *voluntas* and *ratio* in theoretical analyses of law.

It is certainly not the case that these newer views of legality have superseded older ones. The traditional views have not been invalidated or discarded. Law still appears, and is made to appear as rule and principle, concept, and system. But it now appears as both more and less than these categories suggest; and the newer views cast doubt on their adequacy as presupposed in the traditional imagery. One might see the older image of legality as attaching to a 'core' of legal thought in which 'law feels natural, secure (unchallenged), unadulterated by incompatible paradigms or rationalities'. The newer imagery relates to a legal periphery where 'everything is opposite: law feels awkward, bureaucratic and challenged both by other forms of thought and other kinds of experts'. Yet, at the core, law seems 'abstract, socially inconsequential, obsolescent; while the periphery seems modern, relevant, substantive, powerful' (Clune 1989: 189).

The traditional imagery no longer represents the experienced reality of law. The problem is to find a means by which the older and newer views of legality can co-exist; to find theoretical structures that will make it possible to interpret the full complexity of contemporary legal regulation.

Legal Theory and Legal Experience

In a sense modern legal philosophy in this country began with John Austin's London lectures on jurisprudence from 1829, built

[9] For instructive examples in the law of trusts see Moffatt 1992: 128–9.

on Jeremy Bentham's then largely unpublished analytical legal theory. Austin recognized modern law unequivocally as the instrument of the modern state; the expression of sovereign power. He may have misunderstood or (as I prefer to think) underemphasized much that is important about it but—in his discussions of centralization and delegation of authority, his insistence on law's lack of dependence on any moral basis of validity, and his essentially sociological conception of sovereignty (Austin 1847; Austin 1832: 191 ff.)—he recognized some of the changes in legal thought demanded by the growth of modern legislation. Treating law as an expression of governmental power, he suggested an outlook on law that would not have been dumbfounded by the proliferation of regulatory forms through which state power now expresses itself; nor by the increasing difficulty of distinguishing rule and discretion; nor by the emergence of particularistic regulation hardly conforming to a model of general rules.

Austin emphasized *voluntas* so much that he said relatively little about the rationality of rules and all that their interrelationships involve. Modern legal philosophy, however, has sought ways of celebrating and exploring law's *ratio*, the possibility of a rule of reason, the very ideal of the Rule of Law or the *Rechtsstaat*, in ways to which Austin was largely insensitive. Nevertheless contemporary theory has to address the consequences of the modern legal era which his ideas heralded—such as the unclear limits of regulation, the fragmentation of legal form, and overt legal instrumentalism.

In important respects Austin's most direct heirs were the American legal realists of the early decades of the twentieth century.[10] They readily accepted the idea of law as *voluntas*, considered it obvious that law should be viewed instrumentally, and often claimed to attach relatively little significance to abstract doctrinal reason in law. Some even tended to treat the judge as a 'little sovereign' (cf. Fuller 1940: 29) in place of Austin's sovereign. But realism failed to make clear that law could no more be considered *voluntas* without *ratio* than it could be understood as *ratio* alone.

Citizens demand more of law than that it be an instrument of power; it is to be predictable, reasoned and connected with popular

---

[10] On Austin's powerful influence on Oliver Wendell Holmes Jr., the inspiration of much later realist thought, see the succinct discussion in Cosgrove 1987: ch. 4.

notions of fairness in some way (see e.g. Tyler 1990). As an instrument of government, it must at least be intelligible and non-arbitrary. Yet its acceptability may depend on it appearing less as an instrument than as an institution embodying cultural values and supporting stable but diverse social structures (Habermas 1986). For many lawyers, too, an instrumentalist view is inadequate. If law is considered only in terms of governmental power, the lawyer cedes place as an expert to others, for example political scientists, who are specialists in the practices by which governmental power is gained, exercised, or negotiated.

Recent legal theory shows more sophisticated efforts to come to terms with the problem of understanding relationships between *ratio* and *voluntas*. In general, modern economic analysis of law wholeheartedly accepts legal instrumentalism while attempting to argue that policy itself must be guided by theoretical principles. The principles of legal theory, on this view, are to be imported from outside law, itself a mere technical instrument, in the form of economic theory. But economic approaches can be criticized on the grounds that legal policy—like legal form—may be too untidy and varied to rationalize consistently in this way. This kind of theory at least illustrates the fact that legal instrumentalism presupposes an interdisciplinary view of law. Thus, the newer imagery of legality has also inspired research in socio-legal studies and some theoretical writings in sociology of law that are less tied to assumptions about the usefulness of models of rational choice in analysing action.

Very different strategies appear in contemporary postmodernist legal theory. While it is hard to generalize it seems that an important part of what postmodernism in law has to say is this: here is the chaos of contemporary legal thought. Let us give up the hopeless attempt to philosophize about its ultimate coherence. We will merely observe the rhetorical devices by which people, including lawyers, try to convince themselves of the law's continuing rationality, and of its principled unity. Let us recognize that what law has become is regulation without grounding in principle or in any grand systems of reason. Law is *merely* regulation; it reflects nothing grander than its own resounding rhetoric. It provides the masks that we wear in relating to each other in conditions in which society has lost moral certainties, or beliefs in absolute truths (see e.g. Goodrich 1990). Let us accept that moral meaning, if it is to be found at all, must be found outside law's false claims to rationality and principle.

Postmodernist legal theory appropriately highlights the contingent, fragmented, and morally unguided character of much contemporary regulation. It is important also in so far as it stresses legal doctrine's ideological, rhetorical or symbolic power, despite (or even, perhaps, because of) its unsystematic, ungrounded, contradictory, and piecemeal character as a form of knowledge. But this is not a warrant for saying—as some postmodernist writings do—that, having properly rejected the idea that law can be understood in terms of 'some single principle, form or meaning' (Douzinas and Warrington 1991: 18), we should discard systematic efforts to understand it theoretically.

Certainly, theoretical study of modern law cannot achieve 'a coherent totality of meaning' (cf. Douzinas and Warrington 1991: 20). Explanatory theory is subject to permanent revision and challenge, in confrontation with historical experience. Meaning lies in context and 'context is boundless' (Douzinas and Warrington 1991: 21), but this is only to say that theoretical understanding is always a process and never a final destination. Perhaps the fact that postmodernist legal thought has emerged contemporaneously with the collapse of Marxism as dogma—as a plausible 'totality of meaning'—has led to an overreaction: the tendency to reject not just ideological total visions of the world, but also the utility of provisional general explanatory theories relating to the field of legal experience.

The most promising recent legal philosophy has tended to abandon the idea of law as a distinctive form or a finite system. For example, some modern institutional theories of law claim to combine philosophical and sociological approaches by emphasizing certain kinds of (apparently quite varied) institutions—rather than particular legal forms as such—as central to law's identity. Institutions are recognized as normatively structured but the implication is that the structuring may allow more diversity or flexibility in regulatory forms than was generally recognized by earlier positivist theories centred on a model of law in terms of rules.[11] Institutional theories may offer insights into the intricate

---

[11] Ota Weinberger, a major exponent of modern institutionalism, notes somewhat obliquely that 'what is constitutive of any institution is practical information (norms, goals and values)': see Weinberger 1991: 48.

interdependence of *voluntas* and *ratio* in law in so far as they portray governmental power as both normatively structured and irreducible as a part of social experience (Weinberger 1991: 47).

A philosophy seeking to demonstrate and enhance components of *ratio* in law is necessary. Indeed, one cannot think of doctrine at all, in any strong sense, except by presupposing and elaborating *ratio* components of regulation. But this is not enough. Much legal philosophy continues as though nothing had happened to the traditional imagery of legality in legal experience: as though law could be considered only as the reasoned, integrated, and hierarchically ordered interpretation of norms and not also as the diverse, fragmented, and dispersed practices of power. The most influential contemporary theory of legal interpretation, that of Ronald Dworkin, is almost entirely a theory of interpretation by courts—centred on the image of a fictitious, perfectly wise judge (Dworkin 1977: ch. 4). Dworkin portrays a community of legal interpreters in which judges—and above all, appellate judges— are central. But the newer images of legality which highlight the growth, diversity, and complexity of regulation, unified only by the governmental strategies that inspire it, imply also a proliferation of sites or settings of adjudication, interpretation, and application of legal doctrine. In this sense regulation is *decentred.* The ideas of unifying, hierarchical structures or sites of doctrine that are often associated with legal philosophy fit uneasily an image of centrifugal tendencies in regulation. Paradoxically, they make it harder to see the complexity and power of contemporary governmental strategies and practices.

It may also be misleading to think in terms of a single, vast enterprise of legal interpretation—a unitary interpretative community of lawyers, or even of legally knowledgeable citizens, with judges at its centre. It hardly seems surprising that Dworkin, trying to maintain the idea of a single community of legal interpreters engaged in elaborating coherent legal values, advocates excluding policy argument as far as possible from the specifically legal discourse of this community. But policy has invaded modern regulation so that questions about the interests that law serves are made explicit. Legal interpretation has become a matter for all kinds of informed, organized groups pursuing interests considered to be enshrined in or affected by legal doctrine. Their concern is not necessarily to engage in a common search for the best meaning of law. It is often merely to persuade the deciding authority to adopt, for whatever reason, regulatory policies favourable to or favoured by the group concerned.

A sociological perspective is necessary to examine contexts of interpretation of regulation, and the way in which legal interpretive communities (within legal professions and judiciaries, but also outside them) are established and maintained. This is part of what is necessary to understand how the elements of *ratio* in regulation can be and are produced, and what types and limits of legal rationality exist. And these inquiries lead back to questions about power, because the significance of legal interpretations depends not only on the *ratio* of doctrine which interpretation reveals, but also on the *voluntas* that guarantees the judicial or other interpreter's authority to speak, and capacity to get interpretations adopted or decisions enforced. Law's community of interpretation is not one but many. Legal theory must explore both the possibilities for rational interpretation within such communities, and the sociological factors that determine their structure and hierarchy—indeed their very conditions of existence.

Prospects for Principled Regulation

Ratio in law requires not just consistency and predictability, but also that doctrine be intelligible in terms of generalizable values. But the image of legality I have suggested as emerging today implies that, increasingly, principle in law appears localized and contingent. An enduring task for legal theory is to find ways of infusing legal regulation with moral meaning. Even in the conditions outlined above, this is a far from hopeless task.

It cannot be done, however, by simply ignoring the contemporary imagery of legality. It is not possible to retreat to a kind of pre-modern legal world in which law appears as an expression of community morality, or in which legal interpreters are merely exhorted to engage in a quest for the best interpretation of the values of the political community (see Dworkin 1986)—which, like mystical visions, are to be believed in even if experience of them is rare and interpretations of what was seen are always controversial. An important current of contemporary German legal theory, especially expressed in the writings of Niklas Luhmann, has suggested that in modern conditions, law as discourse should be expected to do no more than map *technically defined* fields of 'right' and 'wrong' with certainty and clarity. We should expect of law only that it produce yes/no decisions—determining a matter as either legal or illegal—according to its own criteria (Luhmann 1986). According to this view the effort to find foundations of contemporary regulation in moral experience is naïve. Law has become a self-referential system of communication: a necessary, specialized means of coping with, and facilitating, social complexity.

Luhmann's conception of law strongly reinforces the idea of law's autonomy and independent identity. In this sense it seems to deny the newer imagery of legality outlined earlier. But it is precisely because Luhmann sees the predicament of modern regulation that he insists on this identity of law. He views legal regulation as overloaded and overblown. Dragged this way and that by policy demands, it is faced with tasks it cannot fulfil. In order to see what is essential in law, Luhmann argues that we should clearly distinguish its specific modes of reasoning from, for example, an administrative language of policy implementation and goal achievement. By doing this it becomes possible to understand why legal regulation so often seems ineffective to achieve particular policy goals, for example in promoting and controlling the development of economic activity. Law's methods of reasoning are different from those of economic analysis. It is not possible to use one of these discourses to substitute for, control, or direct the other. Criteria of legality are fundamentally different from criteria of efficiency, though common elements of experience may be reflected in both.

Ironically, therefore, Luhmann recognizes the complexity of modern regulation only as a prelude to differentiating law from much of it and asserting the autonomy and self-sufficient character of legal discourse. Like Dworkin, he suggests that, even in modern conditions, law can retain its integrity as a distinctive discourse. Dworkin's interpretive community is able to engage in a shared and distinctive enterprise only because policy is held, as far as possible, outside this enterprise. Correspondingly, Luhmann's portrayal of law depends on clearly distinguishing the discourse of legality from the discourses of instrumentality or efficiency. Viewing law as a certain kind of communication system which produces only decisions—rather than, for example, inputs of efficiency in economic life—makes it possible to assert that law's *raison d'être* is not just a matter of its policy-relevance. But, unlike Dworkin, Luhmann firmly denies that legal communication is permeated by moral or political values: the question of the general grounding of law in values is an old-fashioned question, naïve in the complex regulatory conditions of modern societies. To pose it in the typical forms of legal philosophy shows a lack of necessary sociological perspective.

Luhmann's and Dworkin's theories illustrate state-of-the-art efforts to explore in rigorous theory the predicament of contemporary law as an autonomous intellectual field. Yet they assume, despite the contemporary complexity and fragmentation of regulation, that law is, at least potentially, unitary and cohesive; that it is characterized by standard intellectual features or components of some kind—whether defined as components of discourse or discursive practices, methods, or aims of interpretation. For Dworkin a debate about unifying political values underpins this assumed cohesion of the legal world. For Luhmann the narrowly specialized scope of legal communications, wherever and whatever they may be, achieves the equivalent effect. But, just as the first approach must ultimately appeal to an almost theological belief in a value core uniting the political society, so the second must appeal to a belief in a 'purified' legality distinct from its diverse political and cultural contexts of practice. Contemporary legal theory often shows a much more sophisticated view of the complexity and diversity of legal ideas and practices than did the writings of earlier periods. But what seems still inadequately recognized is the diversity of sites and contexts of regulation and interpretation and, partly related to this, the diversity of methods and strategies of regulators and interpreters.

Law's relation to values can be understood only by examining the particular settings in which regulation is developed and applied and the interaction of interpreters in those settings. Regulatory diversity may reflect, to some extent, the actual variety and complexity of moral experience in contemporary societies. At the same time, principle in contemporary law is often an invention of doctrinal interpreters, impelled by the need for system and order in legal doctrine, rather than a direct importation of local values from the regulated milieu. Regulation created as an instrument of specific governmental policy may yield principle—stable values enshrined in legal doctrine—through the conscious effort of interpreters to infuse elements of *ratio* in legal doctrine. Interpretation in this sense fulfils a desire to generalize beyond what legal instrumentalism has to offer and to seek more enduring doctrinal foundations of regulation than policy provides. Possibilities for creating principle out of policy may exist not only in courts but in many fora of interpretation and application of doctrine.

As always, however, it would be misleading to neglect the theme of power in legal regulation. Governmental power (and, in contexts such as the European Union, this may be supranational power) underlies most of whatever unity exists in the continuum of regulation of complex modern societies. Regulatory regimes are structured partly by the simultaneous centralization and delegation of governmental power. But they are also structured in part by pressures from local moral or social milieux, on particular jurisdictions or regulatory regimes operating within them, to maximize the possibilities for independence of these jurisdictions or regimes.[12] Centralized governmental controls tend to mediate or curtail direct influence from local moral milieux on regulation created or interpreted in these milieux. Thus, attempts to link particular forms of regulation directly with the moral conditions of their sites and contexts of development and interpretation are potentially limited by these controls. On the other hand, as regulation itself assumes diverse forms, interpreted in diverse sites and contexts and by widely varied categories of interpreters, possibilities exist for a loosening of standardizing governmental structures.

Legal theory's task in these conditions is not to search for the ever more elusive grounding of reason or principle in law in general. Neither is it to provide abstract characterizations of legal doctrine, legal discourse, legal communications, or legal interpretation as though these could be uniform and somehow freestanding from the specific contexts of government and social control practices. Nor is it to condemn or celebrate contemporary regulation's character as an instrument or medium of governmental and private power. Instead, theory should consider and compare the ways in which doctrinal reason and regulatory power interrelate

---

[12] Recent research by members of the Amherst Seminar in the United States has been concerned with empirical study of local and popular 'legal consciousness' and the possibilities for its interaction or confrontation, in various settings, with 'official' understandings and practices of law. See e.g. Merry 1990; Sarat 1990.

in varied sites and settings of regulation. It should examine possibilities for maximizing *ratio* given the diverse conditions in which
voluntas is expressed through regulation.

Thus, the unstable relationship between, on the one hand, the
controlling, co-ordinating and unifying tasks of state regulation
and, on the other, the struggle for autonomy, identity, or integrity
of local cultures and normative systems must be a prime concern
of legal theory today, exemplifying legal theory's character as an
integral part of social theory. The newer images of legality, emphasizing law's character as *voluntas*, reflect ever more ambitious,
comprehensive, and intricate modes of exercise of governmental
power in modern states faced with increasingly complex and
unavoidable problems of social and economic co-ordination and
control. But equally, these forms of government action, their
perceived inadequacies, weaknesses, and lack of moral resonance,
and the irksome or sometimes brutal constraints they involve may
be among the most important spurs to contemporary demands
for local regulatory autonomy—in such forms as regionalism, na-
tionalism, ethnic and religious separatism, among many other
manifestations.

Non-esoteric Legal Theory?

Lawyers and other occupational groups concerned with law are
having to adjust to the contemporary imagery of legality. If legal
theory seeks to address students and practitioners of law it may
be that its audience is now relatively unconcerned with the idea
of law as an autonomous, distinctive, intellectual discipline, or a
unique profession with distinctive knowledge or methods. It may
be that what has become much more important is the idea of law
as a heterogeneous yet not chaotic field of practice, a loose cluster
of disparate skills, and a manageable compendium of instruments,
mechanisms, and sources of 'know-how' for solving disputes, exercising power, or achieving security. The 'skills' revolution with
its implications of interdisciplinary and pragmatic approaches to
legal doctrine has arrived in legal education in Britain. The transformation of law from learned profession to trouble-shooting
business operation is a theme in the literature in this country as
elsewhere (see e.g. Abel 1989; Glasser 1990).

Images of system, unity, cohesion in law, together with the idea of law's intellectual distinctiveness as doctrine and practice, seem less plausible than even in the quite recent past. In so far as legal theory seeks to address an audience of those occupationally concerned with law (which now necessarily includes not just lawyers), it will confront their practical experience and intellectual needs most directly, I think, partly by explaining the nature, origins, consequences, and conditions of existence of the diverse forms of regulation that contemporary images of legality suggest. Such inquiries will be historical and sociological. In part, also, legal theory will address lawyers' (and citizens') concerns by continuing to examine the nature and conditions of *ratio* in law, including the tendencies to uniformity, cohesion, principle, and consistent modes or objectives of interpretation which the practical application of legal doctrine encourages and, up to a point, requires. But it must recognize the very nature of *ratio* as dependent on context and therefore variable, disputed, and contingent.

Just as law is too important to be left to lawyers, so in contemporary conditions it is too important to be left to the diverse occupational and interest groups directly and regularly concerned with specific legal outcomes or legal interpretations. The search for *ratio* in law appears to citizens generally as the promise of the Rule of Law, a government of fairly interpreted, uniformly applied, and mutually consistent rules. Legal philosophy's search for system and coherence in legal doctrine, and for principle in legal interpretation, partially addresses cultural demands for a morally meaningful legality. But such a legality also requires, as legal philosophy must consistently recognize, a dignified existence under law for all citizens and all social groups, and governmental action to achieve this. The recognition that law's community is not a matter of unproblematic unity but of complex diversity puts the nature and consequences of this diversity at the heart of legal theory's concerns.

Equally, the effort to explain law sociologically—as a complex, intricate, and often disordered field of social experience—is part of the continuing effort of science to lift human beings to vantage points from which they can see beyond immediate experience, so as to put that experience in a broadening perspective, illuminating it through the distillations of many observations and reflections. In legal studies a sociological perspective is a necessary corrective to legal romanticism. It alerts us to the fact that the search for a morally meaningful legality will be unproductive without rigorous empirical study of the complex and varied conditions in which legality is to be sought. It is all too obvious now how problematic the methods and achievements claimed for science often are. But the aspiration to broaden perspectives on experience through systematic comparative observation and theoretical reflection will remain fundamental as long as we insist on trying seriously to understand the social world and refusing to acquiesce willingly in prejudice or mystification.

14 Socio-legal Studies: Between Policy and Community

Although contemporary law's dominant character is as a policy-instrument of centralized government, social studies of law should not necessarily adopt the policy-maker's agenda, nor, indeed, the policy-maker's view of law's scope and nature. An appropriate focus is on the diversity of regulatory forms and requirements arising directly out of experience in particular social fields. Socio-legal studies might include within the scope of 'the legal', alongside state law created by the agencies of centralized government, many other forms of institutionalized doctrine constituting socially significant regulation. In this way social science might point towards new understandings of law's relations with community.

All the centuries of purely doctrinal writing on law probably have produced less valuable knowledge about what law is, as a social phenomenon, and what it does than the relatively few decades of work in sophisticated modern empirical socio-legal studies—social scientific studies of the nature and consequences of legal practices and institutions. They extend a vital tradition of theoretical, historical, and sociological study of law. The pioneer social theorists who concerned themselves with legal studies—scholars such as Montesquieu, Marx, Maine, Weber, Durkheim, Ehrlich, Petrazycki, Gurvitch, and Geiger—helped to make law a vital subject for analysis, rather than a field of casuistry, dogma, and hypocrisy produced from endless efforts to reason about society's norms in relative ignorance of society's character. Socio-legal scholarship still pursues this necessary task of illumination: showing through systematic behavioural studies what law as institutionalized doctrine means in the varied local contexts of social life, where its ultimate value and significance must be judged.

Yet the field of socio-legal studies is undoubtedly in a transition phase in which there is much radical rethinking to do. This chapter is intended as a contribution towards that rethinking. It involves trying to set the tasks of socio-legal research in the context of the changing general character of legal regulation today. It also involves trying to view those tasks in the light of the kinds of general demands that can properly be made on law and regulation in contemporary conditions by individual citizens and diverse social groups.

Law, Policy, and Community

Evidence of present ferment in socio-legal studies is not hard to find. The law and society movement in the United States is presently experiencing a period of major internal reassessment, spurred partly by contributions from members of the movement who have been also involved in or influenced by the project of critical legal studies (see e.g. Trubek 1984; Silbey and Sarat 1987; Abel 1980). Similar influences are at work in Britain.[1]

A recurring criticism has been that socio-legal 'law and society' researches have paid insufficient attention to legal doctrine and its ideological, rhetorical, or symbolic power. The line between socio-legal study of behaviour in legal contexts and lawyers' study of legal doctrine has been too rigidly drawn. Further criticisms have focused on the supposed insufficient theoretical foundations of modern law and society studies, their sometimes naïve epistemological assumptions, the scientistic or positivistic outlook that has often informed law and society work (Trubek and Esser 1989; and see Unger 1987: 16–17), or a too close, comfortable, and unquestioning relationship between the law and society movement and policy makers and their concerns (Sarat and Silbey 1988). Awkward questions have sometimes been asked about who socio-legal research is really addressed to and what its objectives, in terms of influence and the advancement of knowledge, ultimately are (see e.g. Abel 1980).

An especially pressing general underlying question is, can socio-legal research say anything about justice? Can it engage directly and effectively with contemporary legal debates, in the sense of debates about what legal doctrine and practices *should be* rather than what legal agencies in fact do? The felt need to give a clear affirmative answer to this last question underlies many of the criticisms referred to above.

[1] See generally Fitzpatrick and Hunt, eds., 1987; and the post-modernist critique in Douzinas and Warrington 1991: 20–1.

Social studies of law have sometimes appeared marginalized because they have not seemed to provide essential (rather than background or context) material in legal debates. The old idea of social science as subsidiary to legal analysis, as 'on tap rather than on top', has sustained both an exclusion and a hierarchy. Lawyers have operated with the idea of a stable, autonomous, exclusive, and integrated realm of legal analysis and reason in relation to which socio-legal studies are peripheral. Equally, the idea that legal doctrinal analysis can treat systematic knowledge of social behaviour in legal contexts as optional, as relatively unimportant, rather than essential in making sense of the character of law as doctrine and practice has also been widespread. The consequence is that much socio-legal writing has had to be addressed to the policy-maker, the concerned citizen, or the professional social scientist, rather than directly to the lawyer or legal scholar.

Perhaps this is appropriate. But socio-legal studies cannot be satisfied any longer with remaining 'on tap' in the world of law. The most pressing legal issues today are *issues about the social character of law itself.* As lawyers wrestle with more and more regulation in an ever wider range of legal areas, they try to cope with continuous regulatory change, and negotiate relationships between many different types of regulation. The problem of making sense of the changing structures of legal regulation and of their overall significance becomes increasingly acute. Law seems a much less secure, well-defined, autonomous regulatory realm than it has often been assumed to be in the relatively recent past. It is hard for lawyers to deny that policy is a pervasive element in the creation and interpretation of legal ideas. Indeed, Karl Llewellyn's composite term 'law-government'[2] is useful to refer to the whole cluster of governmental strategies and techniques focused on and through legal doctrine and institutions. This doctrine is created and applied in top-down fashion by agencies representing or responsible to the centralized state. It is the product of relatively centralized policy-making or policy-co-ordinating processes.

Political and social experience—in the form of a contradictory, chaotic jumble of contemporary social tensions and demands— has invaded legal logic in new, blatant ways. It has done so through the recognition of policy as an inevitable, central element in legal

---

[2] On Llewellyn's use of the term see Twining 1973: 179–80.

thought, and the focusing of techniques and strategies of government in legal doctrine. It inspires also regulatory forms whose diversity reflects the wide variety of social contexts to which they relate, and complex relationships between regulation and self-regulation which point to a wide-scale blurring of the specific boundaries of legal control.[3]

Yet, as all this happens, law as doctrine seems no less opaque to the sociological gaze. The technicality and specificity of legal doctrine increase and its bulk and complexity become more intimidating to the non-specialist. As legal thought is invaded by the challenges of social complexity and its autonomy and identity are questioned and threatened it spins increasingly intricate networks of doctrine. Its rationality becomes piecemeal and localized in special jurisdictions, or policy-shaped fields. Generalization in terms of broad legal principle seems increasingly inappropriate. Thus, ironically, as legal doctrine's relations with the contexts of its social existence become more important topics for lawyers and legal scholars, this doctrine seems to retreat further into moral and social obscurity. It is as though, while society presses in on law, dissolving it into a diversity of regulatory practices, law hides from society's gaze behind dense webs of proliferating technical detail.

These conditions of law have important consequences for empirical socio-legal research. Socio-legal studies have sought to engage in debate around law-government primarily by contributing to policy formulation or policy implementation. The dominant image of law with which modern empirical socio-legal scholarship has worked (indeed, on which it has been founded) is an *instrumental* image; an image of law as a mechanism of centralized government intervention. But I want to suggest that the fundamental debates around law to which socio-legal studies must contribute are no longer ones that can be framed in traditional terms of policy. It is not so much that socio-legal scholarship must free itself from what has been called 'the pull of the policy-audience' (Sarat and Silbey 1988). It is that the very idea of policy as a focus of socio-legal concern needs reconsideration. Policy-makers and their research sponsoring agencies have been and will probably remain some of socio-legal research's primary funding sources and ultimately its most powerful audiences. But they may need to

[3] See Ch. 13, above.

revise fundamentally some assumptions about how far and in what ways law is to be considered a policy instrument.

Many common lawyers seek ways of retrieving elements of principle in a continually shifting mass of regulation. Their concern is to adjust to a recognition of legal doctrine as a transient expression of governmental will or power, of law as *voluntas*. But they seek to do so without undermining their professional commitments to the idea of legal doctrine as a structure of reason or principle, of *ratio* (cf. Neumann 1986: 45–6). For many socio-legal scholars the problem may be quite different. Socio-legal scholarship typically has no difficulty understanding law as a policy instrument, as *voluntas*. It needs to hold on to important elements of this realistic focus. But it also needs to adjust to a pressing requirement to think about law sociologically in different terms. Its task of adjustment may be almost the reverse of that which faces many lawyers lacking a socio-legal perspective.

Socio-legal scholarship needs to understand law's relationship with particular social contexts in other than instrumental ways. It needs, to some extent, to shift its focus from law-government's particular interventions in social life and the agenda of intervention that law-government follows. It needs to ask what kinds of regulation (whether or not appropriately provided by law-government) exist, and should exist, to express requirements of order, efficiency, integration, and solidarity appropriate to particular social fields. But the concept of 'social field' will, deliberately, not be further refined here. It refers to networks of social interaction very varied in scale, scope, and character. The focus is thus on *understanding the specific character of particular social fields* and the forms of regulation existing within those fields. Regulation in this sense typically includes much more than what law-government provides. Sometimes regulation is spontaneously developed through social interaction within a particular field. Regulation in this sense is part of the structure of that field. The need is to understand and assess that structure, and to evaluate law's place in it. And in such a context law-government's present interventions may often appear in far from favourable light.

This kind of approach is mirrored in more moralistic, philosophically framed inquiries. Can law help to express community bonds and values, in some sense? Indeed, what would this entail? I take community here to refer to an ideal of social life in which all actors[4] interacting within a social field are able to participate effectively in shaping the conditions of collective life within that field and in which the secure, autonomous existence of all actors within it is guaranteed by operative principles of social justice.[5] But expressing bonds or values of communal life is not a policy like any other policy that government may adopt. Enabling institutions and values of community to develop and flourish may be quite different from government-led social engineering through law. At the same time, the framing of law to support structures of communal life in various ways requires the kind of information and insight about law's place in social life that socio-legal studies can provide. And it needs planning and a deliberate development of law. The issue is not the familiar one of de-regulation. It is one of *re-regulation* to refashion or strengthen structures of social interaction, but with a sharp sensitivity to their diversity and intricacy. The task, if we express it in terms of values, is to explore sociologically the conditions under which law can become a principled component of social life, a direct expression of community interests, structures, and concerns.

Lawyers are having to adjust their outlook to contemporary conditions in which legal doctrine is dominated by policy, and in which principle is hard to find on any significant scale. But socio-legal scholars, with their wider insight into the effects (and failures) of law as a policy instrument and into the social conditions in which regulation must exist, should be in the forefront of trying to find ways of *rethinking the nature and role of legal regulation of social life* and examining and enhancing law's possibilities for becoming a vital factor in the rebuilding of structures of community. The task is that of maximizing possibilities for *ratio* in law. That means, in sociological terms, building values and principles into law that reflect and express the requirements of a well-integrated and well-ordered but also very diverse society. This cannot be done as some legal philosophers seek to do it, by rationalizing legal interpretation as a kind of philosophical conversation about postulated community values (e.g. Dworkin 1986). Those approaches give little reliable knowledge of the values that inform life outside the

---

[4] The term actor rather than individual is appropriate here because there is no reason in principle why an ideal of community should not govern relations between collective actors (e.g., social groups or associations of various kinds) as well as between individuals.   [5] See Ch. 12, above.

courtroom, or of the relationship, if any, between the values and
principles lawyers may invoke in legal argument and the regulatory needs experienced in social life. It is necessary to study the
specific political, social, and cultural conditions under which regulation is interpreted, shaped, and applied in particular social fields.
Empirical socio-legal research, examining these fields in relation
to their regulatory requirements, is essential to this task.

Moral Distance and the Limits of Law

The rethinking of law's relations with policy is well under way
in social studies of law. Much recent writing in sociology of
law and in sociologically oriented legal theory points to the dangers of assuming that law can be unproblematically accepted as a
policy-instrument. Autopoietic legal theory has sought to explain
why law-government's attempted communications of norms into
economic life or social welfare contexts often seem distorted, or
misunderstood, as they reach the intended arenas of regulation.
Equally, great significance is attached to the fact that interpretations in lawyers' professional legal discourse of the character
of these arenas are often very different from the perceptions of
lay citizens who operate within them. Gunther Teubner reiterates
what he calls the 'regulatory trilemma': law is sometimes merely
ineffective, sometimes it disrupts sensitive mechanisms of social
or economic life, and sometimes law is itself weakened or loses
authority through its perceived inadequacies (Teubner 1987:
21–7).

General claims about law's ineffectiveness in steering society
have often been used to justify wholesale de-regulation, but some
recent writing has resisted these negative conclusions. It has argued that the role of law should be to provide 'regulatory signals',
rather than positive direction, in social and economic spheres
that depend on substantial autonomy. Desirable legal frameworks
will, according to this view, often be those of guided or co-ordinated
self-regulation. What is sought, in Teubner's words, is 'the well-
considered design of internal organizational structures which make
the institutions concerned—companies, public associations, trade
unions, mass media, and educational institutions—sensitive to the
social effects which their strategies for the maximization of their

specific rationality trigger'. The main object, as he puts it, is 'to replace interventionist state control by effective internal control' (Teubner 1987: 38).

Other writing, reflecting similar worries about law as a policy instrument, stresses law-government's intrusiveness in spheres of social life in which values and patterns of social interaction may otherwise be spontaneously developed. Jürgen Habermas emphasizes that law as medium or policy instrument can threaten the structures of what he has called the life-world, the realm of spontaneous interaction and value formation in social life (Habermas 1986). It may smother the necessary autonomous moral conditions of social existence. Policy-directed legal doctrine cannot substitute for values formed in social interaction and communication. But law as a policy-instrument may certainly disrupt sensitive networks of community in so far as these exist.

I do not think that this literature in general should be read as advocating the withdrawal of legal controls from fields of social life that cry out for rational and fair regulation. It demands a rethinking of the nature of legal intervention in the light of better understanding of the nature of the fields that law-government attempts to regulate, or of fields where law-government should intervene but which it presently fails to regulate. The emphasis, in various ways, in much writing on law's ineffectiveness, is on the *remoteness* of law-government, its isolation from many particular local conditions of life to which it is supposed to relate.

Various conditions seem powerfully to foster this remoteness. One of the most important is the increasingly *transnational* character of law-government. Government policies, translated into legal regulation, are increasingly dominated by international obligations and transnational interests. Regulation in economic and financial fields is significantly dictated by national needs to compete in transnational marketplaces, by the requirements of transnationally organized industries dominated by multinational corporations, and by transnational banking and financial systems. Legal doctrine and legal practice itself is increasingly transnational in character. This is most obvious in the United Kingdom in the growing importance of European Community law but the tendency is manifested in many other ways as standardized regulation, or regulation arising from powerful political sources, is enforced across national boundaries.

In Britain, at least, other conditions go along with this. The perceived need for firm legal direction and control in relation to national finance and economic competitiveness seems to inspire, in everything related to these concerns, an unrelenting *centralism* which devalues local democracy and diversity and severely restricts the creation and adaptation of regulation at local levels in society —for example, in the context of local government or regional devolution. The culture of market freedom, seen as the necessary underpinning of unfettered transnational dealing and ultimate national prosperity, is not only the dominant basis of policy but also limits concern with local variation and diversity, and with specific social consequences at local level of regulatory policies designed to ensure free and market-efficient economic and financial relations at national and transnational levels.

If socio-legal scholarship focuses attention primarily on policy-formation in national government without reconsidering the nature of policy as a basis of legal regulation what will be the consequence? Socio-legal scholarship is likely to appeal ultimately, even if indirectly, to processes of policy-formation that are increasingly remote from (and, to some extent, relatively unconcerned with) many specific social situations in which law is applied. These specific social situations are, however, often a main focus for socio-legal research itself. Clearly not all central government policy is shaped by macro concerns such as those mentioned above. Policy is always a balancing of macro and micro concerns—the broad view set against local requirements, but the tendency may often be to see the broad view more clearly than the local one from the vantage point of central government and national or transnational lawmaking agencies.

Apart from these abstract determinants of law-government, policy is often a response to social problems as perceived by the particular political constituencies of policy-makers. Where policy-making is highly centralized it may reflect, sometimes in very direct ways, values grounded in social experience wholly different from that of the particular populations affected by policy-guided regulation. Where these values are part of more general ideological outlooks they may make policy priorities in law-government highly resistant to arguments raised by empirical socio-legal research.

The fundamental problem for law-government is, thus, the frequent remoteness or separation of its normative expectations from many of those current and familiar in the fields of social interaction that it purports to regulate. I shall call this a problem of 'moral distance', using the term 'moral' in a Durkheimian sense to refer to a wide variety of social bonds of integration, order, communication, and interaction. Moral distance in this context has at least five dimensions. First, government often lacks and fails to acquire knowledge of the specificity of the circumstances to be regulated; its knowledge may be too *generalized*. Secondly, it often applies or presupposes values at odds with or insensitive to those of regulated populations; its values may appear *absolutist* to the regulated. Thirdly, techniques of regulation, often shaped without reference to local conditions of their use, may seem crude, limited, or poorly adapted to regulatory conditions; regulation may seem *inflexible*. Fourthly, governmental receptiveness to and possibilities for obtaining feedback information about the consequences of regulation may be limited; in these circumstances, regulation will seem *impressionistic*. Finally, direct influence from regulated populations on the shape of regulatory policy may be limited; popular or lay participation in the structuring of regulation may be *democratically weak*.

Considerations such as these seem to demand a different view of law and its appropriate relationship to government from that of simple legal instrumentalism. For example, Habermas insists that law be considered primarily not as a policy instrument but as an institution, an expression or framework, in some sense, of existing structures of social life (Habermas 1986). This idea becomes something more than a truism when we adopt a view of law that treats it as comprising very varied types of social regulation, with their sources and characteristics not just located in governmental activities and processes of the state, or in formal, official, and relatively centralized lawmaking processes, but in a wide variety of social and cultural contexts.

This is in no way to deny that modern legal doctrine is an expression of the power of the state, channelled through complex hierarchies of jurisdiction. But it is to emphasize that legal ideas are formed, interpreted, applied, and enforced in many, diverse social sites and settings; and that law encompasses a wide range of forms of regulation. It is to claim that, from a sociological point of view, law as institutionalized doctrine does not necessarily appear as a unified system but might be better thought of as a complex interweaving and overlaying of different patterns of regulation. It is to suggest that law's meaning and significance are not definitively given either by the imperatives of policy-makers or by the official legal interpretations of judges or other decision-makers, but vary in different social contexts, in many different arenas of interpretation. In other words, we should think of law as a social phenomenon *pluralistically*, as regulation of many kinds existing in a variety of relationships, some of them quite tenuous, with the primary legal institutions of the centralized state.

Legal Pluralism and the Contemporary State

Early sociology of law established a strong tradition of pluralistic conceptions of law. Almost a century ago Eugen Ehrlich distinguished living law in social life from lawyers' law in the state courts (Ehrlich 1936). Leon Petrazycki taught that law might be more or less 'official' in terms of state recognition (Petrazycki 1955). Legal anthropology has almost always worked with pluralist conceptions of law. But the modern harnessing of much socio-legal research to policy concerns and to a conception of law as an instrument of centralized government has tended to sideline the implications of these kinds of views of law. Sociology of law in the twentieth century typically came to embrace an instrumental view of law—treating law most often as the behaviour of legal officials of various kinds—because it properly recognized the asserted power and scale of activity of the modern state. It saw the weakness, if not disappearance altogether, of links between legislation and everyday moral conditions of social life. It recognized law as a policy instrument because seeing law in any other way seemed profoundly unrealistic.

By contrast, Ehrlich had thought that the informal living law of social life, existing more or less independently of the norms for decision (*Entscheidungsnormen*) recognized by and applied in state courts, was of overriding importance. His sociology of law underplayed the significance of the state and of centralized agencies of government in producing and applying law. It may be appropriate to think of classic legal pluralism in this form as a kind of intellectualized nostalgia for a fast disappearing or already lost local autonomy in regulation; a nostalgia for the neighbourhood norms and customs of a pre-modern world being replanned out of existence by the lawmaking activities of modern states. In this sense classic pluralist approaches in sociology of law tended to divert attention from the *predominant* character of modern law as law-government. In the main they seemed to provide no adequate guide to the problems of dealing with the political realities of contemporary law.

Modern interpretations of law should incorporate a pluralistic outlook which recognizes in some way the actual and potential variety, complexity, and fragmentation of contemporary regulation. But they must not deny that contemporary legal regulation is *structured and co-ordinated by centralized governmental power*.

Why is it important to re-emphasize pluralistic visions of legal regulation in socio-legal studies? It is primarily because there is now an urgent need to examine how far and in what ways legal doctrine and its use can be linked more closely to the demands and requirements of individual citizens arising from their everyday social experience. We need to ask how far law, considered as deliberately constructed regulation, can be reclaimed from a kind of social isolation as an instrument of abstract policies only indirectly reflecting the individual moral experience of many citizens. We need to consider law not only in 'top-down' terms, in terms of the perceptions, aims, and vocabulary of governmental policymakers, but also in terms of the localized needs of particular populations for appropriate, sensitive, and intelligible social regulation and in terms of possibilities open to those populations to express their needs in the formation, interpretation, and application of regulation. We ought, in brief, to stop thinking of legal regulation primarily as something imposed on the rest of social life; and to think of it equally as something that might grow spontaneously out of everyday conditions of social interaction, and might provide a part of the cement that gives moral meaning to social existence.

Today, the capacity of governments to steer society through law is far from obvious and frequently explicitly denied. Yet that capacity was typically assumed in the literature of sociology of law through much of the twentieth century. Again, the fact that many citizens have only severely limited access to and a wide incomprehension of state-supervised legal processes seems clear. Again, policy sometimes seems to be set by forces that are treated, by government no less than by citizens, as beyond legislative control. In these circumstances the empirical and theoretical study of law in society surely needs to consider how legal regulation can acquire the qualities of being simultaneously rationally planned and purposeful and also deeply rooted in social and cultural life. The task now may be to examine how modern regulation can *build afresh* some of the qualities that writers have long associated with pluralistic law and regulation.

Longstanding theoretical traditions have some bearing on this reorientation of concerns. Among the writings of the classic social theorists of law those of Émile Durkheim seem most useful in this respect although his legal theory has so far exerted least influence on modern social studies of law. Durkheim's ideas have been adopted usually only as a model of positivist methods in social science. His claims about links between law and social solidarity, about the interpenetration of law and morality, and about sociological conditions for this interpenetration have received, in the main, polite dismissal. But Durkheim is the only one of the classic theorists who insists, in one way or another, in almost all his legally oriented writings on the importance of the task of finding moral grounding for modern law. He declares that if law lacks moral content it withers; it becomes a mere abstraction rather than an effective discipline of wills (Durkheim 1975: 277). And he wrestles with the problem of how to identify and enhance its moral content.

Durkheim was profoundly wrong to suggest that modern law is actually a reliable index of the moral life of society; and he was misleadingly off-centre in his lack of attention to the nature of modern law as an expression of governmental power. But at the same time, if we re-read Durkheim as explaining, in sociological terms, what law in modern society *needs to be* in order to be an effective discipline of wills and a meaningful regulatory structure of social life, many of his ideas acquire new relevance.[6] In particular there remains much of value in his sketchy but provocative discussions of decentralization of lawmaking, and of possible corporate structures for participation and representation in the formulation of regulation. There is importance also in his insistence that processes of creating, interpreting, and applying regulation must reflect local moral settings and be designed to express, in

[6] See Ch. 9, above.

regulatory practice, principles grounded in the moral experience
of the relevant regulated population.

Modern political philosophy also emphasizes the need for values to guide law. Ronald Dworkin sees legal interpretation essentially as interpretation of the values of the political community.
Modern communitarian thinkers seek the underlying values of
polity and society and often criticize liberalism for its failure to
put sufficient emphasis on shared or necessary value commitments
as the cement of social and political life. But much of this philosophy seems to hanker naïvely for a pre-modern condition of society,
in which underlying social values appeared relatively unproblematic
or consensual rather than mired in permanent dispute and controversy. Durkheim struggled with the problem of how complex,
diverse modern societies can realistically be seen as grounded in
any identifiable shared values. His effort to explain the problem
of value consensus sociologically and his analysis of individualism as the sole foundation of moral consensus in diverse, complex modern societies, remain useful. They offer at least partial
foundations for socio-legal inquiry about moral foundations of
contemporary regulation.

By contrast, contemporary legal and political philosophy seems
to provide relatively little useful guidance for socio-legal studies in
considering the possibilities for moral groundings of regulation
because this philosophy generally takes no serious account of
empirical evidence about the existence of value consensus in
contemporary complex societies,[7] and it usually lacks a sociological sensitivity to the empirical conditions that limit possibilities
for value consensus. Often it considers values solely as reflected
in lawyers' discourse or philosophical speculation. If law is to link
directly with moral conditions of social life, these will usually be
localized conditions. This is why law needs to be rethought in pluralist terms, as many levels and regions of regulation, linked with
many diverse moral milieux. In this way the effort to make regulation meaningful in social life moves in opposite directions to
most of the dominant pressures of contemporary law-government.
These seem to be towards centralization and uniformity in regulation. But socio-legal studies may help to show the need for

[7] The most convenient general discussion of this kind of evidence is still Mann
1970.

diversity and devolution in state regulation, and for more specificity and responsiveness to particular demands arising in relatively local contexts.

None of this is to deny the importance of socio-legal studies in helping to influence the directive power of the centralized state as channelled through law. Law-government is vitally important especially in controlling power within particular social fields and between them, and in ensuring the integration of particular social fields with others. Socio-legal scholarship must continue to address many of its conclusions to the agencies of centralized law-government which, in any event, control most prospects for translating these conclusions into rapid regulatory change.

But a pluralistic view, seeing the conditioning influences on regulation as not wholly centralized but located in diverse social contexts, suggests that socio-legal scholarship might also address other sources or agencies of regulatory change beyond those of the centralized state and located in the distinct social fields to which regulation relates. It might aid agencies and interest groups within particular social fields that seek to shape, alter, or preserve regulation so as to enhance conditions of solidarity, integration, efficiency, and order specific to the relevant field.

Rethinking the Legal Field

Thus, socio-legal studies today should stand, in a sense, between policy and community, providing necessary knowledge about law's effects in society which can be used to show how law's significance and relevance in the lives of ordinary citizens might be enhanced. As has been argued above, this requires that law itself be reconceptualized. Rethinking law in pluralist terms involves recognizing the diversity of forms of regulation and exploring the variety of settings and methods of creation, interpretation, and application of legal doctrine. It also involves focusing on possibilities for devolving lawmaking activities and for easier and more effective participation by citizens in legal processes presently controlled by agencies of the state. Legal ideas and practices need to be understood as wider and much more diverse than those typically encompassed by the professional knowledge of lawyers. Regulation is a continuum in which lawyers' law—the law of the statute book and the appeal court—coexists with many other forms of regulation emerging or powerfully shaped within many different specific social contexts beyond the professional control of lawyers.

Contemporary law-government shades into self-regulation and into informal normative systems which, with varying degrees of effectiveness, it supervises or frames. It exists in tension with itself, in occasional conflicts of jurisdiction, disagreements between lower and higher levels in judicial hierarchies reflected in appeals, or in relatively autonomous decision-making—sometimes reflecting conditions local to the particular field or context of regulation—in circumstances where appeals are impracticable for one reason or another. Socio-legal scholarship, in setting its own agendas, can see law in all its complexity as a structure of governmental power confronting, interacting with, and blending into an immense array of normative systems and controls located in different localities, industries, ethnic groups, social classes, business associations, commercial communities, administrative systems, family structures, marginalized social groups, organizations, professions, and even criminal subcultures.

Some of this is clearly visible in existing socio-legal work. Much current empirical research does not tie itself to law-government's policy concerns in any obvious sense. But an appropriate ambition for socio-legal studies also frees it from lawyers' typical visions of law and its priorities. A wider view of the field of regulation—and a willingness if necessary to extend the term 'law' to embrace regulation far beyond the lawyer's usual gaze—gives socio-legal scholarship its own field defined by its own priorities. Treating law in this broadest sense as a field of social experience structured by problems of government, social control, and social order provides standpoints from which socio-legal studies can contribute to debate about the very nature of law and about the values legal regulation should serve.

What kinds of researches might be particularly central to the agenda that has been sketched? Up to a point the literature on 'unmet legal needs', representing one of the founding traditions in modern socio-legal empirical research (see e.g. Carlin and Howard 1965; Morris, White, and Lewis 1973; Abel-Smith, Zander, and Brooke 1973), exemplifies the effort to examine particular social fields in terms of their regulatory requirements. But the thrust of much of this research was towards examining need in relation to access to law-government's regulation, rather than in exploring the nature of appropriate regulation more broadly. More recent work on alternative dispute resolution, conciliation, mediation, and negotiation comes closer to this broader concern. But not everything to be considered in relation to regulation is a matter of resolving disputes, and the very idea of 'alternative' measures suggests that law-government is still held too unquestioningly as a model against which other regulatory devices are compared.

Studies of so-called private or informal justice emphasizing relationships between formal law and other social norms are important here (see e.g. Henry 1983). Especially significant also is the example of some recent American work on 'popular legal consciousness'. This seeks to show how legal ideas, elaborated by lawyers and courts, feature in sometimes surprising ways in the consciousness of lay citizens. These legal ideas serve as a focus for conflict, negotiation, moral discourse, and disputing. Some of this literature shows how lay citizens negotiate law's social meanings in ways quite different from those of lawyers or develop popular understandings and expectations of legal processes which are significantly different from lawyers' professional interpretations. When law-government acting through courts and represented in lawyers' offices confronts citizens they may bring to the confrontation important perceptions of law rooted in their own social experience (see e.g. Merry 1990; Sarat and Felstiner 1988; Sarat 1990). Other recent writing, extending familiar traditional themes in sociology of law, shows how citizens do without law or, in a sense, devise their own law to suit the circumstances of their social relationships and disputes (see e.g. Ellickson 1991; Greenhouse 1986).

Particularly thought-provoking, in terms of this chapter's concerns, is Mary Pat Baumgartner's recent study of social control in American suburban life (Baumgartner 1988). It portrays a chilling moral vacuousness coupled with an exclusion from the consciousness of suburban residents of any significant need to rely on law in the lawyer's sense. Baumgartner sees this as the dominant moral regulation of the future (by the 1980s some 45 per cent of Americans were living in suburbia and the percentage is rising steadily). But the moral order of the American suburbs, even if as uniform and generalized as she suggests, is surely based on the confidence that society's 'haves' assume in their privileged, unproblematic, and secure protection by law-government. As is well known, this suburban social order exists in parallel with the disintegration of the moral order of inner cities. Here, such structures of urban regulation as exist—which seem urgently to require law-government's control—are best understood as based on a shared powerlessness to build social integration, and a largely unlimited power of victimization flourishing in urban ghettos.

Other themes in this American literature seem important. Kristin Bumiller has stressed the ideological effect of anti-discrimination law in disempowering those whom ostensibly it is intended to help (Bumiller 1988). The point is that, unless we know the moral structure of social relations in the social fields in which law-government intervenes, its effects may be disabling. Those whom law-government seeks to help may not recognize the message that the law of the state purports to give. Equally, law-government may not correctly identify either targets or methods as it attempts to adjust social conditions. And it may fail in this not merely because of inadequate information, legal techniques, or enforcement powers, but also because in intervening it displaces social expectations and perceptions in ways that disrupt rather than support. Regulation should appear as an aspect of social life, a representation of the context that gives meaning to it. But law-government too often appears as an alien force in relation to this context.

It is important not to deny the need for policy-driven law, but to explore the vacuum between policy and community; or, more generally, between policy and the local moral conditions of its implementation. As Sally Merry has shown, people do not inevitably see regulation by lawyers' law as alien or unwelcome. Those seeking to escape from stifling urban communities with ever-present possibilities of violence may strongly welcome the distant, peaceful, arm's-length, individualistic relationships which state law seems to promise and encourage (Merry 1990: 176). The provisional picture that the popular legal consciousness literature offers is of an ambiguous and complex situation of lawyers' law located within a regulatory continuum. Within this continuum that law is sometimes resisted, sometimes applied or invoked (even if with different understandings and expectations of it from those that lawyers may have), and sometimes welcomed or urgently demanded as a means of escape or protection from intolerable social environments.

It is appropriate to end with the theme from which this chapter began. Socio-legal scholarship in the broadest sense is the most important scholarship presently being undertaken in the legal world. Its importance is not only in what it has achieved, which is considerable, but also in what it promises. I believe that its importance has not been sufficiently widely recognized, either by lawyers and legal scholars working outside the socio-legal enterprise, or by policy-makers in shaping legal strategies. There is a profound sense of malaise in the legal field: a sense among some lawyers that law has become hopelessly unprincipled, a disorganized mass of transient and mindlessly technical regulation. There is also surely a profound sense among citizens at large as well as professionals in law and politics that much law-government does not work in the ways intended, or in the ways it should. Yet there are also urgent demands from those who know the conditions of specific social fields for effective regulation within them to control power and ensure fair life-chances, efficient co-ordination of activity, and appropriate integration of individuals within these fields. The overriding demand is surely that intervention be sensitive, knowledgeable, flexible, responsive to opinions emanating from participants in the relevant field, and responsive to values deeply rooted in it.

Socio-legal scholarship is well fitted to stand between policy and community. It should set its own agenda in relation to both. In this way it can address felt needs for responsive regulation. It can play an indispensible role in increasing understanding of the nature of social regulation and perhaps of helping to reshape in radical ways the policy agenda in law, and perceptions of law itself.

15 Conclusion—Imagining Law's Community

The purpose of this final chapter is to draw together some main themes that have arisen earlier in this book and to present them as different aspects of a single complex problem. The problem lies in a paradox—a package of unresolved tensions or contradictions—at the heart of law's character. One way of expressing this paradox is to say that law's political authority depends ultimately on a certain kind of moral authority; yet the extension of law's political authority has a seemingly inevitable tendency to weaken or deny this moral authority and hence, in an important sense, to undermine law itself. The difficulties of the paradox seem to bedevil attempts to characterize contemporary law's relationship with social values and to specify the general nature of legal authority. In what follows I try, first, to link systematically some fundamental analytical dichotomies that previous chapters have associated with law. Together, these map the contours of the paradox just referred to. An analysis of relationships between these dichotomies leads specifically to a recognition of the importance of the concept of community for theoretical analysis of law. In the final sections of the chapter an attempt is made to develop a particular conception of community as an element in legal theory, and to suggest why this concept is indispensable in addressing fundamental problems about the nature and tasks of legal regulation.

Law's Polarities

In previous chapters the nature of some of contemporary law's social characteristics has been expressed in terms of various dichotomies or polarities. Reconsidering each of these in turn it becomes possible to see that they relate in different ways to a complex analytical problem about the nature of law. They highlight this problem as it relates to different facets of legal regulation. The dichotomies to be reconsidered here are between order and justice as legitimating values, between *voluntas* and *ratio* as components of legal doctrine, and between imperium and community as images of society that are presupposed in legal doctrine and rhetoric.

Order and Justice

In Chapter 7, the bases of the legitimacy[1] or acceptance of law were considered in terms of a dichotomy between personal values of *order* and *justice*, themselves indirectly linked with Max Weber's contrast between formal and substantive rationality in law.[2] Justice, however defined, is typically a desired value. Order is often considered in juristic thought merely as a state of affairs; at least, compared with justice, it does not typically attract such an automatic positive evaluation. Nevertheless, treated as the conditions of security, stability, and predictability in social, moral, or political life, order is certainly recognizable by citizens as a value. As such it is separable from any idea of justice—of the fair distribution of benefits, burdens, and expectations—which they may also approve. A stable socio-political system, even if considered unjust, may retain a legitimacy grounded in the valued security and stability that it provides. On the other hand, a widespread perception of a system's injustice may, in certain circumstances, undermine the conditions under which it can offer stability and security. In Chapter 7 an attempt was made to sketch the dichotomy between order and justice as values, recognizing that their content may be interpreted by individual citizens in widely varying ways, typically mediated by ideology, and that the balance of importance between them varies for different people, contexts, and times.

The balance and interplay of these interpretations of justice and order determine the level of legitimacy accorded to legal doctrine and the agencies involved in its institutionalization. Ultimately, order might be considered the generally stronger of the two value elements determining legitimacy, if only because judgements of whether justice has been realized or is capable of being realized within the legal system can seem more controversial, variable, and indeterminate than judgements of whether order and security exist within the framework of law. Order and justice are interrelated. Yet order is the more basic value. There may be no point is seeking justice without an assurance that one can rely

---

[1] To accord legitimacy to law is here taken to mean to recognize no higher authority as cancelling or removing for practical purposes the authority of law.

[2] See pp. 154ff., above.

securely on retaining what justice provides; in other words, that conditions of order make the pursuit of justice meaningful. If justice seems unobtainable perhaps one may settle for order, adjusting stable, predictable relationships around a resignation to or resentment of predictable injustices. Further, because the meaning of justice is permanently controversial in secular and pluralistic societies, the existence of formal mechanisms of representative democracy is often seen as a main contribution to satisfying the justice dimension of legitimacy in so far as democratic procedures may be recognized as the only available means of compromising radically conflicting and otherwise irreconcileable demands for social justice (cf. Cassinelli 1959).

It should also be noted that a powerful way in which legal doctrine promotes *its own* legitimacy through its formal qualities is by radically *narrowing* and ultimately substantially *merging* values of justice and order in technical legal interpretations through the doctrine of the Rule of Law: a doctrine that, in its most widely accepted versions, tends to equate (legal) justice with order, predictability, security, and stability in the uniform application of known legal rules. This narrowing of justice and order to substantially technical or procedural values, shorn of wider social considerations, can be effective in promoting the acceptance of legal processes (see e.g. Tyler 1990). But it may not ultimately prevent wider social values of order and justice being applied in evaluation of law. Nor can it control controversy as to the meaning of these wider values.

Voluntas and Ratio

A further dichotomy, developed especially in Chapters 8 and 13, is between *voluntas* and *ratio* (or fiat and reason) in legal doctrine. *Voluntas* is the element of sovereign will, coercive power, or unchallengeable political authority that shapes legal doctrine and is expressed through it (in this context, authority can be regarded as power that is treated as legitimately exercised). By contrast *ratio* is the element of reason or principle that structures and presents doctrine in patterns of ideas whose strength to bind and convince the citizen (and the lawyer or official) comes from their logical persuasiveness, normative consistency, or rational coherence.[3]

---

[3] See generally, pp. 165–6, 278ff., above.

Voluntas identifies and represents the co-ordinating and hierarchical characteristics of law as a system of *political* control. When legal doctrine seems rationally fragmented or inconsistent as between different legal fields, or where divergent legal decisions or interpretations of legal doctrine are produced in different institutional settings within the state legal system, it is ultimately the political authority of law—channelled through legislative, administrative, or judicial hierarchies and using the currency of appeal and review, of delegated orders and supervisory functions—that holds the elements of the state legal system together. When inconsistencies in doctrine develop, the inconsistencies are ultimately removed by fiat—by the imposition of higher authority which *requires* that subordinate authorities (judicial or administrative) discard the interpretations or rules (whatever their rational merit) that are held to be inconsistent with those favoured by politically superior agencies of the legal system.

The search for reason and principle impels legal scholars to systematize doctrine, to tease out connections between rules, to generalize, extend, or distinguish principles, and to construct concepts and categories around which regulation can be rationally organized and justified. Thus, while *voluntas* represents the political authority of law (its power to decree), *ratio* expresses its moral authority, unity, and integrity (its power to persuade). And it is easy to see that these elements are often in tension. If the *voluntas* element increases in importance in law it tends to substitute political control and co-ordination of institutionalized legal doctrine (and of the agencies of its production and application) for the rational unity of doctrine (which its decrees may actually frustrate). In the legal systems of contemporary Western states, for example, law's substantive rationality—the structure of principle or moral reason underlying the content of regulation—tends to be 'piecemeal' and localized (cf. Cotterrell 1989: 223–8). In Chapter 13 it was noted that this rationality is continually 'disrupted' by infusions of policy into doctrine through legislation and judicial lawmaking. It is fragmented by the sheer complexity of the circumstances to be regulated as well as by the detail, intricacy, and ever-growing bulk of regulation.

It was suggested earlier that as between the legitimating values of order and justice, the former may be thought of as generally dominant. In present conditions of the creation and development of legal doctrine in the legal systems of contemporary Western states, the element of *voluntas* may similarly be thought of as dominant, in important respects, over the element of *ratio*. The fact that policy-driven legislative, judicial, and administrative law-making continually disrupts the tendencies to *ratio* in law, so that lawyers are engaged in a permanent repair job on law's edifices of doctrinal reason, is proof enough of this.

But it is very important to note that the theoretical relationship of *voluntas* and *ratio* is not to be defined solely by the way this relationship appears in complex, politically centralized, contemporary Western legal systems. *Ratio* and *voluntas* combine in all systems of legal regulation, whether these are more or less extensive and intricate than the typical legal systems of contemporary Western states. *Ratio* and *voluntas* co-exist in law in unitary or federal systems, or sub-systems of legal regulation of whatever size or scope, whether identified by geographical locality, by regulatory function or field, by defining characteristics of particular regulated populations[4] or by a particular level of jurisdictional authority within or beyond the scope of a state legal system.

Just as order and justice are interdependent values, so too *voluntas* and *ratio* are interdependent elements in legal doctrine. Law's authority as *voluntas* can promote peace, order, and security, but usually only when it is constrained and channelled by doctrinal principles that make it sufficiently predictable and rational in operation. Conversely, the elaboration of *ratio* in legal doctrine can provide intelligible principles of justice in social relationships, yet these have only limited practical significance unless they can be imposed by authority on those for whom the general reasonableness or moral persuasiveness of principle is an insufficient motive for compliance in the face of conflicting specific interests. The element of *voluntas* is required eventually to terminate debate about *ratio*, and to prevent irreconcilable demands for social justice, focused on legal interpretation, reaching the kind of levels of uncontrolled controversy that threaten social or political order.

How then, in general theoretical terms, do the legitimating values of order and justice relate to the dichotomy of *voluntas* and

---

[4] To take random examples: business corporations, banks, social welfare recipients, juveniles, criminals, prisoners, aliens, or mental patients.

ratio? The most appropriate analytical linkage seems to be between these legitimating values taken together and the *ratio* element in law. The values of order and justice provide legitimacy for
law through their appropriate expression—and the appearance of
their reconciliation—in the *ratio* of legal doctrine. If all of this is
done successfully—that is, if the combination and reconciliation
of values generally seems appropriate to citizens[5]—the values embodied in law's *ratio* provide legitimacy for the coercive power of
law as *voluntas*. They underpin legal doctrine's political authority.
It follows that if there are, in contemporary conditions, important
limits on the extent to which legal doctrine can develop qualities
of *ratio*—of consistent, integrated, rational coherence and principle—across the entire present regulatory range of state legal systems, there may also be limits on the extent to which the coercive
power of the centralized state can retain recognition as legitimate
legal authority. This is a matter which will be analysed in the light
of the third dichotomy to be reconsidered here.

Imperium and Community

This third dichotomy is between contrasting images of the general
nature of society that are implicit in legal rhetoric and legal doctrine. As discussed in Chapter 11, the image of *imperium* is one of
hierarchy—of a society structured by sovereign authority imposed
on individuals or other legal persons who stand before law as its
subjects. The contrasting image of *community* is that of a morally
cohesive collectivity linked by its members' agreement on or acquiescence in values that bind them.[6]

In contemporary Western societies and their legal systems there
is a clear link between the image of imperium and law's *voluntas*,
and between the image of community and *ratio*. The image of
community presupposes a moral grounding of principle which is
considered to unite society and which finds its expression in legal
doctrine as *ratio*. If *ratio* is the element of unifying moral authority

---

[5] It can be assumed that the various currents of legal ideology discussed throughout this book, for example with regard to legal closure (Ch. 5) and the appropriate functions of law (Ch. 12), are important in influencing the kinds of judgements that citizens will make on these matters. There seems no particular reason
to separate officials of the legal system as a special category of citizens for this
purpose.   [6] See generally pp. 222ff., above.

in law it implies social arrangements in which principles of justice are derived by elaborating a substantive rationality justified as grounded in shared moral experience. The idea of law's *ratio* suggests the image of a regulated population united by a shared rationality which makes agreement on principles of justice feasible. It assumes some shared moral outlook and code as the necessary foundation of the social bond linking autonomous members of a community. Imperium, by contrast, expresses the implications for social organization of the specifically *voluntas* element in law, elaborately institutionalized. As has been noted, *voluntas* highlights the element of political authority in law, the element of hierarchical ordering and deliberate normative prescription. In the legal structures of contemporary Western states the organization of *voluntas* in political arrangements for lawmaking—in the production and promulgation of policy, in judicial and administrative systems of appeal, supervision, and review, and in the co-ordination, control, and delegation of processes of interpretation and application of doctrine—implies the more general social structure of imperium.

Law's images of community and imperium are ideological images of society produced specifically in the context of the complex legal systems of contemporary Western states. They suggest how the *voluntas* and *ratio* elements in law tend to work themselves out in legal doctrine and rhetoric in this kind of social and political context. And they suggest some of the limitations of existing legal arrangements in complex contemporary states when judged against the need for an appropriate reconciliation of the elements of *voluntas* and *ratio* in law.

For example, in Chapter 11, it was suggested that images of community produced in the rhetoric of contemporary law in Britain and the federal jurisdiction of the United States seem attractive in certain ways and yet also dangerously mystificatory. In the legal rhetoric of these jurisdictions the values of community are often postulated *ex cathedra* by judicial elites or legal philosophers. The link between the idea of community and mechanisms for democratic expression of the interests, values, and judgements of the regulated population seems often obscure or even non-existent. In the absence of adequate democratic means of developing and registering the shifting values and aspirations of specific communities, courts (or legal philosophers) take it upon themselves to express these values in authoritative form. Yet it is not obvious that the authority by which they do this is derived directly from any specific community for which they may purport to speak.

Nevertheless, American judicial rhetoric, which elaborates legal ideas of community more fully than does equivalent judicial discourse in Britain, shows a clear and important recognition that within the borders of the territory of the state *many* communities of different kinds must be held to exist.[7] The specification of community values leads to a recognition of the diversity of these values as well as the complexity of relationships between contrasting communities, in so far as these communities are seen as sources of regulation or of ideas and beliefs relevant to the interpretation of regulation. Thus, even judicial rhetoric from relatively unified legal systems of contemporary states suggests that a concern for relationships between law and community is a concern with legal and moral *pluralism.* The issues that emerge as central are how to express in regulatory form the values of *numerous* communities and how to develop regulation to co-ordinate, integrate, and respect the experiences of social existence characteristic of different communities.

An emphasis on community values is thus, in contemporary conditions, an emphasis in some sense on the *localized* as against the centralized, and on *diversity* as against uniformity. The reason is that any emphasis on a shared underpinning of values as a defining element of community becomes unrealistic unless accompanied by a corresponding recognition that the scope for agreement on values, or even for significantly shared social experience, is necessarily limited in contemporary conditions of social complexity. To postulate, with some sociological sensitivity, the utility of a concept of community is necessarily to recognize diversity in social arrangements and radical pluralism in moral life as the essential conditions of existence of those areas of moral agreement that can underpin social solidarity today.

By contrast, law's image of *imperium* implies political centralization but neither moral cohesion nor moral diversity. Individuals, as portrayed in the image of *imperium*, have no necessary moral links with each other. They have only parallel individual allegiances to a superior authority (for example, to the sovereign or to

---

[7] See pp. 235–6, above.

law as a system of doctrinal authority). Consequently, they appear uniform merely as citizens or subjects. They need no special allegiances to each other and hence have no need of the particular moral groupings that might otherwise be conceptualized as communities. They are neither united nor divided by moral ties. But the *political* ties that link each of them to a central authority are fundamental. As was noted in Chapter 11, the image of imperium suggests no significant limits on the political authority that controls citizens or subjects. Hence the expansion of this authority allows the extension and elaboration of state law's *voluntas*. This expansion encourages the incorporation of independent or semi-independent regulatory jurisdictions and their replacement with complex systems of delegated authority co-ordinated within a centralized state structure (cf. Austin 1847).

If, in Britain at least, the image of *imperium* seems dominant (just as the element of *voluntas* in law seems to dominate) this seems in turn to reflect a general, though not necessarily still continuing, line of political development of the modern state towards the accumulation of more extensive governmental powers and functions (Beetham 1984), towards political centralization (Nisbet 1962: ch. 7) and towards the corresponding subjection of independent or competing regulatory authorities (see e.g. Arthurs 1985).[8] The dominance of *voluntas* over *ratio* celebrates political authority at the expense of moral authority in legal doctrine. Hence, whatever might be wished, the effort to promote reason and principle in doctrine is best seen as an effort to *limit* what seems to be an inevitable moral and intellectual fragmentation of legal ideas through the expansion of the political *voluntas* element in law. Today, substantive reason and principle in legal doctrine are most likely to flourish not in a monolithic state-wide and court-focused system of normative control but in the interrelation of forms and structures of regulation developed and morally grounded in diverse social spheres. Thus, in Chapter 14 it was argued that an important task of sociologically oriented studies of

[8] This line of development, it should be noted, is not necessarily challenged in fundamental ways by the growth of such transnational legal and political regimes as that of the European Union. Such regimes can be viewed, at least on some contemporary interpretations, as co-operative instruments of state policy rather than replacements for or even significant modifications of existing state structures. See e.g. Milward *et al.* 1993.

law is now to explore the nature and conditions of regulation (and demands for regulation) that develop within the local moral milieux of these particular spheres.

In a sense therefore, a recognition of the conditions for and limitations of *ratio* in law, like the image of community with which it is closely related, points towards pluralism and diversity, rather than towards aspirations to unify doctrine within the national legal systems of contemporary states. The question is *how much* unification, rationalization, and systematization is possible if doctrine is to be able to ground itself in the diverse common-sense moral understandings that inform individuals' everyday experience—and that provide the basis of intelligible legal principle. To ignore this problem and to assume that ultimately the doctrine of state legal systems is a principled, moral unity—that it has an underlying, consistent, and complete (even if imperfectly expressed or understood) substantive rationality which lawyers must continue to seek— is to think ideologically. It is to treat as complete and unified that which in contemporary conditions cannot be. Lawyers' tendencies to think in this way ensure that the interpretation of legal doctrine continues to fuel and sustain legal ideology. The diversity and fragmentation of legal doctrine are transformed in thought and aspiration into the familiar moral certainties and intellectual self-sufficiency of legal ideology.

The paradox of law is revealed by the interrelationships between the dichotomies of order/justice, *voluntas/ratio* and imperium/ community. The law of the contemporary state, typically centralized and hierarchically organized, spreads through its diverse jurisdictions by means of lines of delegated authority and intricate supervisory and appellate controls. Yet as its political authority is extended to cope with the regulatory complexities that confront the state, law's rational integrity seems to decline. So does its moral authority. Justice seems, on most understandings, to require principled judgement. Yet as legal regulation becomes more particularized and technical (see Cotterrell 1992: 164–6) the possibilities for broad principle seem reduced. Correspondingly, the value of order suggests the importance of regulatory precision which is served, up to a point, by increasingly specific and detailed legal interventions yet is also threatened in some degree by increasing regulatory complexity, by rapid regulatory change, and by the growth of regulatory discretion (Cotterrell 1992: 162–4).

Thus, the image of imperium seems in important respects more powerful than that of community; *voluntas* dominates over *ratio*; and the conditions of order seem more attainable than those of justice. The complex question of the links between law and community seems marginalized. Even where, as in American legal discourse, the image of community seems to be evoked strongly, its theoretical implications remain highly problematic, raising the suspicion that this particular image cannot easily be detached from its specific setting in legal ideology.

Indeed, it is vital to remember the precise way in which law's image of community, elaborated in Chapter 11, *is* ideological, and what is necessary in order to progress towards a rigorous, empirically informed concept of community. Like all ideology, the image of community (no less than the image of imperium) treats as complete that which is partial. It emphasizes a certain side of experience and treats this as if it were the whole. Thus, while the image of community seems to represent exclusively law's *ratio*, a wider empirical perspective on law in society recognizes that since *ratio* and *voluntas* are inseparable components of legal doctrine, any actual social arrangements that might be called 'communities' will, to the extent that they require doctrinal frameworks of regulation, embody and express both *ratio* and *voluntas* in these frameworks. Furthermore, in so far as the image of imperium portrays the social setting of *voluntas*, it follows that any actual social arrangements for community will also involve elements of imperium. Thus, it must be stressed that law's images of community and imperium are *merely* images. They do not represent the complexity of actual social systems or arrangements. They are ideological presentations of certain partial aspects of social and political life. They present these aspects as totalities. Hence, while they highlight aspects of the relationship between legal ideas and social structure, they obscure the need to work out how political authority and moral agreement are to be reconciled in the regulation of actual societies.

The Concept of Community

The need to retrieve *ratio* from its seemingly subordinate position in contemporary law is what creates the motivation to rethink the nature of legal regulation on what might be termed a 'community basis', as well as retaining the realistic idea of law as the law of the centralized contemporary state.

This reason for appealing to ideas of community is different from, though not unconnected with, those encountered in a variety of intellectual fields beyond legal theory. Invocation of the idea of community has been 'intermittently fashionable' (Walzer 1990: 7) in political philosophy mainly as a counter to dominant liberal theories. Thus, recent communitarian political philosophy has insisted that the autonomous freely-choosing individual, which liberalism puts at the centre of its concerns as the source and *raison d'être* of all worthwhile political and moral structures, is actually a socially or culturally constituted being. The individual cannot be conceptualized apart from society. Hence the nature of the community in which individuals exist is fundamental in determining their character as rational beings and what moral and political choices they can make. As the philosopher Michael Walzer notes, the enduring appeal of communitarianism also 'reflects a sense of loss, and the loss is real'; a rootlessness in a world of increasing mobility, a part of the experience of living in 'a profoundly unsettled society' (Walzer 1990: 11, 12). Thus, communitarianism also suggests the idea that social life in contemporary Western societies could be made more in tune with needs, perhaps rooted in the very nature of human beings, for satisfactory bonds of communal existence.

The literature of sociology also contains important theoretical traditions of writing about community, some of which reflect a similar sense of loss and longing. In the late nineteenth century the German social theorist Ferdinand Tönnies wrote of the relatively enduring and multi-faceted moral bonds of community (*Gemeinschaft*) associated with family and kinship, friendship, the rural village, and the neighbourhood. He contrasted these bonds with the looser, more fleeting and instrumental interactions of modern society (*Gesellschaft*) in which, despite all links between individuals, 'everyone is by himself and isolated, and there exists a condition of tension against all others' (Tönnies 1955: 74). For Tönnies, the bonding element of *Gemeinschaft* is love or easy adjustment to others when people 'speak together and think along similar lines'; hence, mutual understanding links people who 'remain and dwell together and organize their common life' (1955:

55). By contrast, the typical social bond of *Gesellschaft* is the contract or the short-term association. Social interaction revolves around money, credit, and commodities, including defined and limited service obligations, all of these operating in relation to specific and limited transactions premised on the peaceful calculated exchange of equivalents (1955: 80–90).

Tönnies sees the increasing dominance of *Gesellschaft* over *Gemeinschaft* social organization not only as the extension of modern capitalist relationships but also as a reflection of social mobility, the increased scale and pace of social interaction, urbanization, and broadly based currents of individualism. The relationship between *Gemeinschaft* and *Gesellschaft* also reflects the permanent interplay of two states of mind, which Tönnies calls natural will and rational will, and which are present in all forms of social life and in all eras (Tönnies 1955: 119 ff.). These claims helped to inspire a sociological literature on the 'loss of community' (see e.g. Nisbet 1962: 7–22) brought about by the development of modern society. Particularly in Émile Durkheim's work, Tönnies' sense of social change was transformed into the idea of the morally problematic character of modern society resulting from a transition from a pre-modern social system founded on shared values, beliefs, understandings, and experiences to a modern one founded mainly on differentiation, reciprocity, and functional interdependence between individuals and groups.[9]

Much of the 'loss of community' literature is flawed by the difficulty of operationalizing empirically anything like Tönnies' *Gemeinschaft* concept, given that he himself treats it as an abstraction and not as an empirical description. Indeed, the concept of community has been highly problematic in sociology, with a host of attempted definitions (Hillery 1955) and a pervasive vagueness in most attempts to give it theoretical significance (see e.g. König 1968: ch. 3). What lies behind many of the difficulties is a tendency to fuse subjective evaluation and empirical observation in characterizing particular kinds of social patterns as those of community. Tönnies' writing, for example, suggests a longing for idyllic social forms which the ideal type of *Gemeinschaft* evokes but which empirical inquiry cannot easily identify as distinct social phenomena. Hence the 'village' or the 'neighbourhood' easily

---

[9] See Ch. 9, above.

become symbols, mere foci for nostalgia, rather than rigorously defined concepts identifying specific social phenomena. Modern sociology uneasily avoids these problems, mainly by equating community with locality. It defines as 'community studies' the analysis of social structures and patterns of social interaction in limited geographical areas such as towns or rural neighbourhoods which are treated pragmatically as relatively distinct from their wider social environments.

The American sociologist Talcott Parsons tried to cure the imprecision of the *Gemeinschaft* and *Gesellschaft* distinction by isolating four distinct variables which he saw as confused within it (see e.g. Rocher 1974: 36–40; cf. Parsons 1937: 686–94). These are different kinds of judgements (or orientations) on the basis of which social action takes place and social relationships are established, varied, or ended. For example, first, social judgements may be *universalistic* (other people or things are judged according to general criteria) or *particularistic* (unique or specifically personal characteristics are the basis). Secondly, judgements of persons or things may be on the basis of their *performance* (their usefulness or achievement) or of their inherent *quality* (their essential nature or value). Thirdly, judgements may be *affective* (emotionally based or influenced), as typically in family and friendship relationships, or *affectively neutral*, as often in occupational relationships. Finally, judgements may be *specific* (where relationships are limited to the pursuit of specific purposes, as in a contractual relationship) or *diffuse* (where relationships are many-sided, as in a marital relationship or relationship of parent and child). Particularism, emphasis on inherent quality, affectivity, and diffuseness might be seen as combined in *Gemeinschaft* relationships, but these characteristics can more usefully be treated separately as distinct orientations interacting in highly complex ways in patterning an infinity of social relationships.

Parsons' four 'pattern variables', whatever their theoretical utility, illustrate two important points. First, the concept of *Gemeinschaft* is unsatisfactory because it combines elements that, empirically, interrelate in an infinite variety of ways. Secondly, a community cannot be understood as a specific, empirically identifiable social phenomenon but only as a variable combination of types of social interaction. It is characterized, nevertheless, by certain predominant patterns or tendencies in the orientation of those interactions.

In other words it may not be useful to search theoretically for a sociological object which can be called a community. It might be more productive to identify basic orientations of social interaction which, in very varied combinations, produce the kinds of social patterns which are typically associated with the idea of community.

This is the approach to imagining law's community which the rest of this chapter seeks to follow. It differs significantly from more orthodox approaches to the conceptualization of community. Thus, the political theorist Michael Taylor, noting that neighbourhoods, villages, towns, cities, nations, and ethnic groups are often seen as communities, suggests three general attributes of community, possessed in some significant measure by all specific communities (Taylor 1982: 25–33). First, community members have beliefs and values in common. Secondly, relations between members are direct (for example, unmediated by political or other authorities) and many-sided (diffuse, if we use Parsons' term). Thirdly, relations between members are reciprocal in a strong sense, with a relatively high degree of sharing, generosity, uncalculated help, and mutual aid. The conditions of existence of these characteristics of community are such that, in Taylor's view, communities are only possible in so far as they are relatively small and stable. As the social unit increases in size the characteristics of community necessarily become diluted.

The difficulty with this approach is that it presents a model of community which, like the compendium of elements in *Gemeinschaft*, is almost guaranteed to seem inapplicable in the complex conditions of contemporary societies. If, on the other hand, the idea of community is built from the interplay of certain general orientations of social interaction it becomes possible to see how far those orientations are possible and present in various contexts in contemporary complex societies.

Adopting this approach, the basic building block of community—the fundamental orientation of action that makes it possible—can appropriately be considered to be interpersonal trust (cf. Cotterrell 1993). The judgement by which a person decides to trust another combines many aspects of the *Gemeinschaft*-promoting orientations to social action that Parsons usefully identifies. Thus, trust typically involves a judgement of quality of the person trusted, and a particularistic judgement. Interpersonal trust is a relatively open-ended commitment; one necessarily trusts the other person to exercise discretion (Baier 1986: 240) in one's interests in a range of unknown and possible unforeseen eventualities, which could involve disappointment of the trusting person; trusting someone invariably involves taking a risk (cf. Luhmann 1979: 26). So the relationship is necessarily diffuse in at least some respects. And often, though certainly not always, trust is specially characteristic of affective relationships. Certainly, its existence tends to promote the affective (emotional) element in social relationships.

Trust implies power and dependence; the person trusted has power over the one who trusts, as long as trust lasts (Cotterrell 1993). But community is not a matter of 'one way' trusting relationships. Taylor's emphasis on reciprocity is important since it emphasizes a fundamental mutual orientation of action in a community. Trusting relationships in a community are necessarily reciprocal. The essence of community is *mutual interpersonal trust*. Hence, in conditions of community, people are in dependency relations with others in certain respects and so must trust those others in those respects, while the relations of power and dependence may be opposite in other respects and so trust flows in the 'opposite' direction.

On this understanding, therefore, power as an element in social relationships is neither excluded by community nor opposed to it, but is at the heart of it. The creation and maintenance of patterns of social interaction that express mutual trust depends on principles of regulation that limit, direct, diversify, and formalize the power and dependence relationships that pervade networks of community. The failure to recognize the centrality of this problem of power in the organization of communities and to control it can be seen as the key reason why repression is no less often a feature of small scale or highly moralistic societies than is solidarity (see e.g. Coser 1956).

Viewing communities in terms of the conditions of mutual interpersonal trust makes it possible to understand the real significance of the criterion of size emphasized by Taylor. Interpersonal trust is hard to maintain when social relationships become remote—separated by substantial *moral distance*. Yet geographical distance is not necessarily the key determinant. Relationships of community can exist within extremely dispersed groups (an international network of scholars might be an example). What is important is the real possibility of personal communication and interaction between members which allows them freely to establish, affirm, or adjust their judgements of trust in relation to other members. Communities are possible, therefore, where 'human scale' in social networks or systems of social activity can be maintained.

Niklas Luhmann has helped to explain some of the social developments that seem to make the maintenance of interpersonal trust a less obviously dominant feature of contemporary life than it may have been in certain social contexts in the past (Luhmann 1979: ch. 7). Social complexity—which is not just a matter of the size of networks of social activity in advanced Western societies but more particularly of their detail, intricacy, fluidity, and specialized discourse—makes reliance on face-to-face relationships increasingly inadequate in many contexts. Active interpersonal trust is largely replaced in many situations by a more passive confidence in impersonal systems (for example, financial, economic or political systems; or systems of activity represented by large business corporations or other organizations). Many of these social systems are defined, stabilized, and guaranteed by the law of the centralized state. Hence the transfer of reliance from specific interpersonal trusting relationships to more general impersonal social systems also entails a shift from reliance on largely moral understandings between individuals in relationships of trust towards a stronger reliance on the ultimately politically guaranteed authority of state law.

The matter can be expressed in other terms. Contemporary capitalist development seems to promote larger concentrations of capital (see e.g. Aglietta 1987: ch. 4). These concentrations are often in organizations—such as business corporations or groups of corporations—of increasing size, complexity, and geographical reach in their operations. Sometimes, however, capital is held in financial organizations (for example, merchant banks) that are relatively small in terms of numbers of staff employed but control very extensive national or even international networks of economic power and influence. It should be stressed that market relations as such are not antagonistic to or incompatible with the existence of mutual interpersonal trust relationships. Nevertheless, the increased size or power of organizations and their increasingly global operations tend to promote moral distance[10] in the social relationships controlled or shaped by them. This is a major factor creating the appearance of society's domination by remote systems of the kind Luhmann describes. The tendency towards greater moral distance in important social and economic networks is inimical to the extension of relationships of community. Thus, the search for community seems to run counter to some important tendencies of contemporary capitalist development. In advanced capitalist societies it remains an open question how far and with what consequences the communitarian counter-tendency can extend.

The Regulation of Communities

Communities can be understood as patterns of social interaction that involve a relatively high degree of mutual interpersonal trust. The claim made, for example, by Michael Taylor that acceptance by members of shared values and beliefs is a fundamental characteristic of communities needs to be reinterpreted in the light of this understanding. Shared values or beliefs are necessary to the extent that mutual trust requires these. They are instrumental rather than essential to the idea of community. What is fundamental is a regulatory structure that fosters and supports relations of mutual trust within communities.

In Chapter 12 some elements of this structure were sketched in terms of the twin requirements of what I have called *public altruism* and *collective participation*.[11] Public altruism—the provision by a community of sufficient material and cultural resources for each of its members to ensure their ability to participate as members in the collective life of the community—fosters the sense of mutual support and of shared destiny which expresses itself in trust between members. Collective participation—the opportunity and freedom for all members to be involved fully and actively in determining the nature and projects of the community as a whole—is a means of stabilizing and reinforcing mutual trust through the continuous ongoing negotiation of its consequences and its conditions of existence.

[10] See Ch. 14, above, pp. 302–5.   [11] See pp. 246, 255–6, above.

Thus, collective participation serves the value of order by stabilizing the conditions for continuance of mutual trust. But also it facilitates discussion and debate, the sharing of experience and the development of collective understandings. In this way it contributes to the evolution of principles of justice and their elaboration in the *ratio* of community regulation. Equally, public altruism serves the value of justice by infusing a calculated moral content of mutual concern into social relations. But also it guarantees the inclusion of all members in the collective welfare. Hence it helps to foster the motivation and, up to a point, the obligation of each member to participate in developing and promoting the interests and values of the community as a whole. In this way it stabilizes the community and serves the value of order in it.

Nevertheless, the translation of these regulatory aspirations into practical structures raises serious problems. The convincing reconciliation of elements of principle in the *ratio* of regulation in contemporary conditions is, as was noted earlier, hard to achieve except on relatively 'local' levels or in relatively specific social fields. It follows, therefore, that the focus of regulation must become, increasingly, these levels or fields, rather than the purportedly all-embracing unitary jurisdiction of the contemporary centralized state.

This is not, however, to deny the importance of state-wide regulation. Indeed, the logic of the analysis here suggests an *extension* of state regulation in certain respects. The value of order, as has been noted, is, for individual citizens, perhaps more basic and more susceptible to uniform interpretations than the value of justice. It is also one that can in some respects be better served by centralized state legal regulation than can the value of justice. It was noted earlier, for example, that relatively particularized state regulation is not, as such, necessarily incompatible with the value of order. Justice, however, tends to be thought of in terms of general principles and their application—principles which are often elusive in the context of the technical minutiae of state legal regulation.

Hence, as regards its direct impact on individual citizens, state regulation in present conditions seems suited best to the securing of certain basic conditions of order and security in society. Nevertheless, treating the nation as, itself, in some sense a 'community of communities', national state regulation is concerned also with ensuring the collective participation of specific communities within what can be thought of as the national community as a whole, as well as with the organization of conditions of social justice between communities co-existing within the nation. It is also concerned with adapting the life of the national community in certain respects to its international environment. Thus, the appropriate primary regulatory role of the centralized state may be that of co-ordinating communities within the political society as a whole, guaranteeing peace and security for all citizens, and promoting the welfare of the whole political society within a larger international environment.

Viewing matters in this way, an emphasis on community regulation does not lead to the emasculation of state legal authority or to wholesale state de-regulation. The task of co-ordinating relationships between communities is a more complex task and puts a heavier responsibility on state legal agencies than is implied by the more orthodox liberal view of the state as merely the facilitator and regulator of the interactions of individual citizens. The appropriate concern of state regulation is to be seen not as largely restricted to the facilitation of individual political and economic freedoms but as embracing the overall cultural wellbeing of a complex of diverse and interacting moral communities.

In addition, the devolution of substantial regulatory powers from the state to communities loosens state controls in certain ways but necessitates stronger controls in others. Ultimately, as Eugen Ehrlich argued, the nation as a community (or, in Ehrlich's term, a social association) embraces the members of all sub-national communities (cf. Ehrlich 1936: 68). Individuals who are threatened with exclusion from these latter communities (or, indeed, forced inclusion in them) should be able to appeal to the law of the nation state for a guarantee of certain mimimum principles of collective participation and public altruism from which they can benefit within appropriate communities. Thus, either alongside— or, more usually, working through—subordinate communities, the state has the task of ensuring the appropriate inclusion of individuals, at least as full members of the national community and more generally within other specific communities in which they seek and are qualified for membership.

Where the devolution of regulation to communities occurs it is especially important that state law is seen not to relax those powers which it must properly retain. In practice, the *de facto* withdrawal of legal controls and the failure to use state coercion to ensure basic order and security of individuals is viewed as 'impunity' (see e.g. Dahrendorf 1985: ch. 1) and as a symbol of regulatory weakness. It fosters not the orderly division of regulatory powers between communities but the creation of 'no-go areas' in which rational structures of community regulation are absent. It promotes not the extension of a plurality of intersecting realms of social solidarity, but a regulatory vacuum.

The devolution of regulatory power to a range of communities within the national political society as a whole carries a risk of increased moral distance and conflict between these communities. The prevention of open conflict depends, in large measure, on the state's regulatory commitment to coercive order maintenance. The prevention of increased moral distance depends equally on community members' perception of themselves as members also of a larger national community in whose welfare they share. In this context, public altruism and collective participation as guiding themes of state regulation are likely to play a crucial role in fostering the sense of national community. But, since the limitations on pursuing these themes through state regulation beyond a certain point were noted earlier, additional elements of national solidarity are likely to be achieved, if at all, by means of ideology; in other words, by the ideological portrayal of diversity as unity. Thus the unity of the national community is typically represented through constitutional and political symbols (e.g. Arnold 1935; Edelman 1964), in the rhetoric of patriotism or in the rituals of civil religion (e.g. Müller 1988), and—not insignificantly— through the various aspects of legal ideology considered in earlier chapters.

Thus the valuable *partial* perspectives that are hidden in law's ideological images of *imperium* and community finally appear. In *certain* respects, legal regulation needs to retain the qualities of the familiar hierarchical, centralized, co-ordinating regulation provided by contemporary state law (including the regulation of individual conduct to provide fundamental guarantees of security and autonomy for individual citizens). In *other* respects, legal regulation needs to evolve through processes of radical differentiation and devolution as the diverse, pluralistic expression and support of the collective understandings of different communities, premised on the importance of fostering conditions of mutual interpersonal trust and hence solidarity within and between these communities.

The implications of these general ideas about law and community cannot be adequately elaborated here. But something further can be said about the variety of communities. Approaching the idea of community in terms of orientations of social interaction implies that communities can be extremely varied in size and character. They may be unified by locality (for example, town, region, or nation), or by function, interests, outlook, or needs (for example, professional, industrial, commercial, religious, cultural, ethnic, political or other groups). Often the unifying elements are diverse and fluctuating. It might well be asked how regulation could be devolved to such nebulous groupings. But it is a matter for specific legal and political analysis, rather than for general legal theory, to answer this question in relation to many particular contexts. The primary role of legal theory in highlighting the relationships between law and community that are revealed by a reconsideration of law's polarities of order and justice, *ratio* and *voluntas*, and community and imperium is to point to a necessary and urgent reordering of legal thought and legal priorities. The law of the centralized state remains and will continue to remain fundamentally important in regulating the complex conditions of contemporary advanced Western societies. Yet, as the discussions in this book have attempted to show, the regulatory task that faces this law is currently too great for it alone to discharge, and threatens to undermine the moral foundations that are ultimately necessary for effective and legitimate legal regulation.

The devolution of regulation in various ways from the centralized state to functionally, locally, or otherwise defined specific communities is hardly a novel proposal. It was advocated, for example, by Durkheim precisely on the basis of the need for law to retain a moral authority that in contemporary conditions it seemed in danger of permanently forfeiting. I have tried to argue in this book, however, that this necessity must be understood partly as a consequence of the very character of law as the combination of *ratio* and *voluntas* and partly in terms of changes in the character of the modern state that have led to the over-extension of state law's regulatory responsibilities. One of the most important effects of legal ideology—as discussed in different aspects in previous chapters—has been to obscure the processes of change taking place in the character and conditions of legal regulation, as well as to obscure law's fundamental paradox which is intensified by transformations of the character of legal regulation and its contexts. As has been seen, the paradox of law lies in its permanent dual appeal to moral and political authority, and in the fact that while political authority is ultimately grounded in moral authority, the former tends to divorce itself from the latter. One of legal theory's most important present tasks is to analyse in sustained fashion the conditions that have encouraged this divorce and to explain its consequences. Another task, the dimensions of which have been merely sketched here, is to set out possibilities for the emergence of regulatory innovations that can contribute significantly towards restoring moral authority to law in contemporary society.

Bibliography

ABBOTT, A. (1988), *The System of Professions: An Essay on the Division of Expert Labor* (Chicago: University of Chicago Press).

ABEL, R. L. (1973), 'A Comparative Theory of Dispute Institutions in Society', 8 *Law and Society Review*, 217–347.

—— (1980), 'Redirecting Social Studies of Law', 14 *Law and Society Review*, 805–29.

—— (1981), 'Conservative Conflict and the Reproduction of Capitalism: The Role of Informal Justice', 9 *International Journal of the Sociology of Law*, 245–67.

—— (1989), 'Between Market and State: The Legal Profession in Turmoil', 52 *Modern Law Review*, 285–325.

ABEL-SMITH, B., ZANDER, M., and BROOKE, R. (1973), *Legal Problems and the Citizen: A Study in Three London Boroughs* (London: Heinemann).

ABERCROMBIE, N., HILL, S., and TURNER, B. S. (1980), *The Dominant Ideology Thesis* (London: Allen and Unwin).

ABRAMS, P. (1968), *The Origins Of British Sociology 1834–1914* (Chicago: University of Chicago Press).

—— (1981), 'Visionaries and Virtuosi: Competence and Purpose in the Education of Sociologists', 15 *Sociology*, 530–8.

—— (1985), 'The Uses of British Sociology 1831–1981' in Bulmer (ed.) (1985), 181–205.

ABRAMS, P., DEEM, R., FINCH, J., and ROCK, P. (eds.) (1981), *Practice and Progress: British Sociology 1950–1980* (London: Allen and Unwin).

ADLER, M., and ASQUITH, S. (eds.) (1981), *Discretion and Welfare* (London: Heinemann).

AGLIETTA, M. (1987), *A Theory of Capitalist Regulation: The U.S. Experience*, transl. by D. Fernbach (London: Verso).

ALBROW, M. (1972), 'Weber on Legitimate Norms and Authority: A Comment on Martin E. Spencer's Account', 23 *British Journal of Sociology*, 483–7.

—— (1975), 'Legal Positivism and Bourgeois Materialism: Max Weber's View of the Sociology of Law', 2 *British Journal of Law and Society*, 14–31.

ALEXANDER, J. C. (ed.) (1988), *Durkheimian Sociology: Cultural Studies* (New York: Cambridge University Press).

ALLOTT, A. (1980), *The Limits of Law* (London: Butterworths).

ANDERSON, P. (1968), 'Components of the National Culture', 50 *New Left Review*, 3–57.

ARATO, A., and GEBHARDT, E. (eds.) (1978), *The Essential Frankfurt School Reader* (Oxford: Basil Blackwell).

ARNOLD, T. W. (1935), *The Symbols of Government* (New York: Harcourt Brace and World, 1962).

ARON, R. (1964), *German Sociology*, transl. by M. and T. Bottomore (Westport: Greenwood Press reprint, 1979).

ARTHURS, H. W. (1985), *'Without the Law': Administrative Justice and Legal Pluralism in Nineteenth-Century England* (Toronto: University of Toronto Press).

ATIYAH, P. S. (1978), *From Principles to Pragmatism* (Oxford: Oxford University Press).

—— (1987), *Pragmatism and Theory in English Law* (London: Stevens).

ATIYAH, P. S., and SUMMERS, R. S. (1987), *Form and Substance in Anglo-American Law: A Comparative Study of Legal Reasoning, Legal Theory, and Legal Institutions* (Oxford: Oxford University Press).

ATKINSON, J. M., and DREW, P. (1979), *Order in Court: The Organisation of Verbal Interaction in Judicial Settings* (London: Macmillan).

AUBERT, V. (1963), 'The Structure of Legal Thinking' in J. Andenaes *et al.*, *Legal Essays: A Tribute to Frede Castberg* (Oslo: Universitetsforlaget), 41–63.

—— (1966), 'Some Social Functions of Legislation', 10 *Acta Sociologica*, 98–120.

AUSTIN, J. (1832), 'The Province of Jurisprudence Determined', reprinted in J. Austin, *The Province of Jurisprudence Determined and the Uses of the Study of Jurisprudence* (London: Weidenfeld and Nicolson, 1955), 1–361.

—— (1847), 'Centralization', 85 *Edinburgh Review*, 221–58.

—— (1863), 'The Uses of the Study of Jurisprudence', reprinted in *The Province of Jurisprudence Determined and the Uses of the Study of Jurisprudence* (London: Weidenfeld and Nicolson, 1955), 363–93.

BACHRACH, P., and BARATZ, M. S. (1970), *Power and Poverty: Theory and Practice* (New York: Oxford University Press).

BAGNALL, G. (1990), 'The Regulation of Financial Markets' in S. Livingstone and J. Morison (eds.), *Law, Society and Change* (Aldershot: Dartmouth), 33–50.

BAIER, A. (1986), 'Trust and Antitrust', 96 *Ethics*, 231–60.

BAKER, J. H. (1990), *An Introduction to English Legal History* (3rd edn., London: Butterworths).

BALDWIN, J., and MCCONVILLE, M. (1977), *Negotiated Justice* (Oxford: Martin Robertson).

—— (1979), *Jury Trials* (Oxford: Oxford University Press).

BALDWIN, R. (1985), *Regulating the Airlines: Administrative Justice and Agency Discretion* (Oxford: Oxford University Press).

BANKOWSKI, Z., and MUNGHAM, G. (1976), *Images of Law* (London: Routledge and Kegan Paul).

—— (1981), 'Laypeople and Lawpeople and the Administration of the Lower Courts', 9 *International Journal of the Sociology of Law*, 85–100.

—— (eds.) (1980), *Essays in Law and Society* (London: Routledge and Kegan Paul).

BANKS, J. A. (1967), 'The British Sociological Association: The First Fifteen Years', 1 *Sociology*, 1–9.

BARKUN, M. (1971), 'Law and Social Revolution: Millenarianism and the Legal System', 6 *Law and Society Review*, 113–41.

BARNES, J. A. (1966), 'Durkheim's *Division of Labour in Society*', 1 *Man. (n.s.)*, 158–75.

—— (1981), 'Professionalism in British Sociology' in Abrams *et al.* (eds.) (1981), 13–24.

BARTRIP, P. W. J., and BURMAN, S. B. (1983), *The Wounded Soldiers of Industry: Industrial Compensation Policy 1833–1897* (Oxford: Oxford University Press).

BAUM, L. (1976), 'Implementation of Judicial Decisions: An Organizational Analysis', 4 *American Politics Quarterly*, 86–114.

BAUMGARTNER, M. P. (1988), *The Moral Order of a Suburb* (New York: Oxford University Press).

BEAN, P. (1974), *The Social Control of Drugs* (London: Martin Robertson).

BEETHAM, D. (1984), 'The Future of the Nation State' in G. McLennan, D. Held, and S. Hall (eds.), *The Idea of the Modern State* (Milton Keynes: Open University Press), 208–22.

—— (1985), *Max Weber and the Theory of Modern Politics* (2nd edn., London: Allen and Unwin).

BEIRNE, P., and SHARLET, R. (eds.) (1980), *Pashukanis: Selected Writings on Marxism and Law*, transl. by P. B. Maggs (London: Academic Press).

BELL, D. (1961), *The End of Ideology: On the Exhaustion of Political Ideas in the Fifties* (Revised edn., New York: Free Press).

BELL, J. (1983), *Policy Arguments in Judicial Decisions* (Oxford: Oxford University Press).

BENDIX, R. (1959), *Max Weber: An Intellectual Portrait* (Berkeley: University of California Press, 1977).

BENTHAM, J. (1977), *A Comment on the Commentaries and A Fragment on Government*, edited by J. H. Burns and H. L. A. Hart (London: University of London Athlone Press).

BEROLZHEIMER, F. (1912), *The World's Legal Philosophies*, transl. by R. S. Jastrow (Boston, Mass.: Boston Book Company).

BETTELHEIM, C. (1976), *Economic Calculation and Forms of Property*, transl. by J. Taylor (London: Routledge and Kegan Paul).

BLACK, D. J. (1970), 'On Law and Institutionalization', 40 *Sociological Inquiry*, 179–82.

—— (1971), 'The Social Organization of Arrest', 23 *Stanford Law Review*, 1087–111.

—— (1972), 'The Boundaries of Legal Sociology', 81 *Yale Law Journal,* 1086–100.

—— (1976), *The Behavior of Law* (New York: Academic Press).

—— (1984), 'Social Control as a Dependent Variable' in Black (ed.) (1984), 1–36.

—— (1989), *Sociological Justice* (New York: Oxford University Press).

—— (ed.) (1984), *Toward a General Theory of Social Control, Vol. 1: Fundamentals* (Orlando: Academic Press).

BLACK, G. S. (1974), 'Conflict in the Community: A Theory of the Effects of Community Size', 68 *American Political Science Review,* 1245–61.

BONNER, D., and STONE, R. (1987), 'The Public Order Act 1986: Steps in the Wrong Direction?', *Public Law,* 202–30.

BOTTOMLEY, A. K. (1973), *Decisions in the Penal Process* (London: Martin Robertson).

BOTTOMORE, T., and NISBET, R. (1978), 'Introduction' in T. Bottomore and R. Nisbet (eds.), *A History of Sociological Analysis* (London: Heinemann), vii–xvi.

BRAMSON, L. (1961), *The Political Context of Sociology* (Princeton: Princeton University Press).

BREST, P. (1981), 'The Fundamental Rights Controversy: The Essential Contradictions of Normative Constitutional Scholarship', 90 *Yale Law Journal,* 1063–109.

BRODERICK, A. (ed.) (1970), *The French Institutionalists: Maurice Hauriou, Georges Renard, Joseph T. Delos,* transl. by M. Welling (Cambridge, Mass.: Harvard University Press).

BROGDEN, M. (1982), *The Police: Autonomy and Consent* (London: Academic Press).

BROPHY, J., and SMART, C. (eds.) (1985), *Women in Law: Explorations in Law, Family and Sexuality* (London: Routledge and Kegan Paul).

BRUDNER, A. (1987), 'A Theory of Necessity', 7 *Oxford Journal of Legal Studies,* 339–68.

BULMER, M. (1984), *The Chicago School of Sociology: Institutionalization, Diversity, and the Rise of Sociological Research* (Chicago: University of Chicago Press).

—— (ed.) (1985), *Essays on the History of British Sociological Research* (Cambridge: Cambridge University Press).

BUMILLER, K. (1988), *The Civil Rights Society: The Social Construction of Victims* (Baltimore: Johns Hopkins University Press).

BURIN, F. S., and SHELL, K. L. (eds.) (1969), *Politics, Law, and Social Change: Selected Essays of Otto Kirchheimer* (New York: Columbia University Press).

BURROWS, P., and VELJANOVSKI, C. G. (1981), 'Introduction: The Economic Approach to Law' in P. Burrows and C. G. Veljanovski (eds.), *The Economic Approach to Law* (London: Butterworths), 1–34.

BYLES, A., and MORRIS, P. (1977), *Unmet Need: The Case of The Neighbourhood Law Centre* (London: Routledge and Kegan Paul).

CAIN, M. E. (1973), *Society and the Policeman's Role* (London: Routledge and Kegan Paul).
—— (1974), 'The Main Themes of Marx' and Engels' Sociology of Law', 1 *British Journal of Law and Society*, 136–48.

CAIN, M., and HUNT, A. (eds.) (1979), *Marx and Engels on Law* (London: Academic Press).

CAIN, M., and KULCSAR, K. (1982), 'Thinking Disputes: An Essay on the Origins of the Dispute Industry', 16 *Law and Society Rev.*, 375–402.

CAMPBELL, C. M. (1974), 'Legal Thought and Juristic Values', 1 *British Journal of Law and Society*, 13–30.

CAMPBELL, C. M., and WILES, P. (1976), 'The Study of Law in Society in Britain', 10 *Law and Society Review*, 547–78.

CAPPELLETTI, M., MERRYMAN, J. H., and PERILLO, J. M. (1967), *The Italian Legal System: An Introduction* (Stanford, Cal.: Stanford University Press).

CARBONNIER, J. (1978), *Sociologie juridique* (Paris: Presses Universitaires de France).
—— (1988), *Flexible droit: textes pour une sociologie du droit sans rigueur* (6th edn., Paris: Librairie Générale de Droit et de Jurisprudence).

CARLEN, P. (1976), *Magistrates' Justice* (Oxford: Martin Robertson).
—— (ed.) (1976), *Sociology of Law* (Keele: Sociological Review, University of Keele).

CARLEN, P., and COLLISON, M. (eds.) (1980), *Radical Issues in Criminology* (Oxford: Martin Robertson).

CARLIN, J. E., and HOWARD, J. (1965), 'Legal Representation and Class Justice', 12 *University of California at Los Angeles Law Review*, 381–437.

CARSON, W. G. (1981), *The Other Price of Britain's Oil: Safety and Control in the North Sea* (Oxford: Martin Robertson).

CASSINELLI, C. W. (1959), 'The "Consent" of the Governed', 12 *Western Political Quarterly*, 391–409.

CAUDREY, A. (1987), 'Whose Research?', *New Society*, 23 October, 12–13.

CHESLER, M. A., SANDERS, J., and KALMUSS, D. S. (1988), *Social Science in Court: Mobilizing Experts in the School Desegregation Cases* (Madison: University of Wisconsin Press).

CHESLER, R. D. (1983), 'Imagery of Community, Ideology of Authority: The Moral Reasoning of Chief Justice Burger', 18 *Harvard Civil Rights–Civil Liberties Law Review*, 457–82.

CLARKE, M. (1976), 'Durkheim's Sociology of Law', 3 *British Journal of Law and Society*, 246–55.

CLUNE, W. H. (1989), 'Legal Disintegration and a Theory of the State' in

C. Joerges and D. M. Trubek (eds.), *Critical Legal Thought: An American–German Debate* (Baden-Baden: Nomos Verlagsgesellschaft), 187–208.

COHEN, F. S. (1935), 'Transcendental Nonsense and the Functional Approach', reprinted in L. K. Cohen (ed.) (1960), 33–76.

COHEN, L. K. (ed.) (1960), *The Legal Conscience: Selected Papers of Felix S. Cohen* (New Haven, Conn.: Yale University Press).

COHEN, P. (1979), 'Policing the Working-Class City' in Fine *et al.* (eds.) (1979), 118–36.

COHEN, S. (1974), 'Criminology and the Sociology of Deviance in Britain: A Recent History and a Current Report' in P. Rock and M. McIntosh (eds.), *Deviance and Social Control* (London: Tavistock), 1–40.

—— (1981), 'Footprints on the Sand: A Further Report on Criminology and the Sociology of Deviance in Britain' in M. Fitzgerald, G. McLennan, and J. Pawson (eds.), *Crime and Society: Readings in History and Theory* (London: Routledge and Kegan Paul), 220–47.

—— (ed.) (1971), *Images of Deviance* (Harmondsworth: Penguin).

COLLINI, S. (1979), *Liberalism and Sociology: L.T. Hobhouse and Political Argument in England 1880–1914* (Cambridge: Cambridge University Press).

COLLINS, H. (1982), *Marxism and Law* (Oxford: Oxford University Press).

COLLINS, R. (1988), 'The Durkheimian Tradition in Conflict Sociology' in Alexander (ed.) (1988), 107–28.

—— (1992), *Sociological Insight: An Introduction to Non-Obvious Sociology* (2nd edn., New York: Oxford University Press).

CONKLIN, W. E. (1989), *Images of a Constitution* (Toronto: University of Toronto Press).

CORWIN, E. S. (1936), 'The Constitution as Instrument and as Symbol', 30 *American Political Science Review*, 1071–85.

COSER, L. A. (1956), *The Functions of Social Conflict* (London: Routledge and Kegan Paul).

COSGROVE, R. A. (1987), *Our Lady of the Common Law: An Anglo-American Legal Community 1870–1930* (New York: New York University Press).

COTTERRELL, R. B. M. (1977), 'Durkheim on Legal Development and Social Solidarity', 4 *British Journal of Law and Society*, 241–52.

—— (1979), 'Commodity Form and Legal Form: Pashukanis' Outline of a Materialist Theory of Law', *Ideology and Consciousness*, No. 6, 111–19.

—— (1980), Book Review, 7 *British Journal of Law and Society*, 317–21.

—— (1981), 'The Development of Capitalism and the Formalisation of Contract Law' in Fryer *et al.* (eds.) (1981), 54–69.

—— (1983), 'English Conceptions of the Role of Theory in Legal Analysis', 46 *Modern Law Review*, 681–99.

—— (1986), 'The Law of Property and Legal Theory' in Twining (ed.) (1986), 81–98.

—— (1989), *The Politics of Jurisprudence: A Critical Introduction to Legal Philosophy* (London: Butterworths; Philadelphia: University of Pennsylvania Press).

—— (1992), *Sociology of Law: An Introduction* (2nd edn., London: Butterworths).

—— (1993), 'Trusting in Law: Legal and Moral Concepts of Trust', 46 *Current Legal Problems*, 75–95.

COULSON, N. J. (1964), *A History of Islamic Law* (Edinburgh: Edinburgh University Press).

COVER, R. M. (1986), 'Violence and the Word', 95 *Yale Law Journal*, 1601–29.

CRANSTON, R. (1979), *Regulating Business: Law and Consumer Agencies* (London: Macmillan).

CURRAN, J., and SEATON, J. (1991), *Power Without Responsibility: The Press and Broadcasting in Britain* (4th edn., London: Routledge).

DAHL, R. A., and TUFTE, E. R. (1974), *Size and Democracy* (Oxford: Oxford University Press).

DAHRENDORF, R. (1985), *Law and Order* (London: Stevens).

DAINTITH, T. (1982), 'Legal Analysis of Economic Policy', 9 *Journal of Law and Society*, 191–224.

—— (1988), 'Law as a Policy Instrument: A Comparative Perspective' in T. Daintith (ed.), *Law as an Instrument of Economic Policy: Comparative and Critical Approaches* (Berlin: De Gruyter), 3–55.

DAVIS, K. (1959), 'The Myth of Functional Analysis as a Special Method in Sociology and Anthropology', 24 *American Sociological Review*, 757–72.

DAVY, G. (1922), *La foi jurée—étude sociologique du problème du contrat: La formation du lien contractuel* (New York: Arno Press reprint, 1975).

DELGADO, R. (1987), 'The Ethereal Scholar: Does Critical Legal Studies Have What Minorities Want?', 22 *Harvard Civil Rights–Civil Liberties Law Review*, 301–22.

D'ENTRÉVES, A. P. (1967), *The Notion of the State: An Introduction to Political Theory* (Oxford: Oxford University Press).

DEVLIN, P. (1965), *The Enforcement of Morals* (London: Oxford University Press).

DEWS, P. (1987), *Logics of Disintegration: Post-Structuralist Thought and the Claims of Critical Theory* (London: Verso).

DICEY, A. V. (1905), *Lectures on the Relation Between Law and Public Opinion in England During the Nineteenth Century* (London: Macmillan).

—— (1959), *An Introduction to the Study of the Law of the Constitution* (10th edn., London: Macmillan).

DINGWALL, R., and LEWIS, P. S. C. (eds.) (1983), *The Sociology of the Professions: Lawyers, Doctors and Others* (London: Macmillan).

DINWIDDY, J. R. (1975), 'Bentham's Transition to Political Radicalism, 1809–10', 36 *Journal of the History of Ideas*, 683–700.

DONZELOT, J. (1980), *The Policing of Families: Welfare Versus the State*, transl. by R. Hurley (London: Hutchinson).

DOUZINAS, C., and WARRINGTON, R. (1991), *Postmodern Jurisprudence: The Law of Text in the Texts of Law* (London: Routledge).

DREYFUS, H. L., and RABINOW, P. (1982), *Michel Foucault: Beyond Structuralism and Hermeneutics* (Brighton: Harvester Press).

DROR, Y. (1959), 'Law and Social Change', 33 *Tulane Law Review*, 787–802.

DURKHEIM, É. (1957), *Professional Ethics and Civic Morals*, transl. by C. Brookfield (London: Routledge and Kegan Paul reprint, 1992).

—— (1975), *Textes. Tome 2: religion, morale, anomie* (Paris: Les Éditions de Minuit).

—— (1976), *The Elementary Forms of the Religious Life* (2nd edn., transl. by J. W. Swain, London: Allen and Unwin).

—— (1982), *The Rules of Sociological Method and Selected Texts on Sociology and its Method*, transl. by W. D. Halls (London: Macmillan).

—— (1984), *The Division of Labour in Society*, transl. by W. D. Halls (London: Macmillan).

—— (1986), 'The Positive Science of Morality in Germany', transl. by F. Pearce, 15 *Economy and Society*, 346–54.

DURKHEIM, E., and FAUCONNET, P. (1982), 'Sociology and the Social Sciences' in Durkheim (1982), 175–208.

DWORKIN, R. M. (1971), 'Philosophy and the Critique of Law' in R. P. Wolff (ed.), *The Rule of Law* (New York: Simon and Schuster), 147–70.

—— (1977), *Taking Rights Seriously* (London: Duckworth 1978 reprint with new appendix).

—— (1985), *A Matter of Principle* (Cambridge, Mass.: Harvard University Press).

—— (1986), *Law's Empire* (Cambridge, Mass.: Harvard University Press).

—— (1989), 'Liberal Community', 77 *California Law Review*, 479–504.

EDELMAN, B. (1979), *Ownership of the Image: Elements for a Marxist Theory of Law*, transl. by E. Kingdom (London: Routledge and Kegan Paul).

—— (1980), 'The Legalisation of the Working Class', transl. by E. Kingdom, 9 *Economy and Society*, 50–64.

EDELMAN, M. (1964), *The Symbolic Uses of Politics* (Urbana: University of Illinois Press).

EHRLICH, E. (1936), *Fundamental Principles of the Sociology of Law*, transl. by W. L. Moll (New York: Arno Press, 1975).

ELDRIDGE, J. (1980), *Recent British Sociology* (London: Macmillan).

ELLICKSON, R. C. (1991), *Order Without Law: How Neighbors Settle Disputes* (Cambridge, Mass.: Harvard University Press).

ENGLE, G. (1987), 'The Legislative Process Today', 8 *Statute Law Review*, 71–6.

ERIKSON, K. (1966), *Wayward Puritans: A Study in the Sociology of Deviance* (New York: Wiley).

EVAN, W. M. (1962), 'Public and Private Legal Systems', reprinted in Evan (1990), 123–37.

—— (1977), 'Administrative Law and Organization Theory', reprinted in Evan (1990), 86–108.

—— (1990), *Social Structure and Law: Theoretical and Empirical Perspectives* (Newbury Park, Cal.: Sage).

FAUCONNET, P. (1928), *La responsabilité: étude de sociologie* (2nd edn., Paris: Alcan).

FEAVER, G. (1969), *From Status to Contract: A Biography of Sir Henry Maine 1822–1888* (London: Longmans, Green).

FENNELL, P. (1990), 'The Mental Health Act Code of Practice', 53 *Modern Law Review*, 499–507.

FERGUSON, A. (1767), *An Essay on the History of Civil Society* (Edinburgh: Edinburgh University Press reprint, 1966).

FERGUSON, R. B. (1980), 'The Adjudication of Commercial Disputes and the Legal System in Modern England', 7 *British Journal of Law and Society*, 141–57.

FERRARI, V. (ed.) (1990), *Developing Sociology of Law: A World-Wide Documentary Enquiry* (Milan: Giuffrè).

FEYERABEND, P. (1975), *Against Method: Outline of an Anarchistic Theory of Knowledge* (London: New Left Books).

FIELDING, N., and FIELDING, J. (1983), 'Teaching the Sociology of Law: An Empirical Study', 10 *Journal of Law and Society*, 181–200.

FINE, B. (1979), 'Law and Class' in Fine *et al.* (eds.) (1979), 29–45.

—— (1984), *Democracy and the Rule of Law: Liberal Ideals and Marxist Critiques* (London: Pluto).

FINE, B., KINSEY, R., LEA, J., PICCIOTTO, S., and YOUNG, J. (eds.) (1979), *Capitalism and the Rule of Law: From Deviancy Theory to Marxism* (London: Hutchinson).

FINKEL, N. J. (1988), *Insanity on Trial* (New York: Plenum).

FINNIS, J. (1980), *Natural Law and Natural Rights* (Oxford: Oxford University Press).

FISH, S. (1982), 'Working on the Chain Gang: Interpretation in Law and Literature', 60 *Texas Law Review*, 551–67.

FISS, O. M. (1979), 'The Supreme Court 1978 Term—Foreword: The Forms of Justice', 93 *Harvard Law Review*, 1–58.

FITZPATRICK, P. (1983a), 'Marxism and Legal Pluralism', 1 *Australian Journal of Law and Society*, No. 2, 45–59.

—— (1983b), 'Law, Plurality and Underdevelopment' in D. Sugarman (ed.), *Legality, Ideology and the State* (London: Academic Press), 159–82.

FITZPATRICK, P., and HUNT, A. (eds.) (1987), *Critical Legal Studies* (Oxford: Basil Blackwell).

FOUCAULT, M. (1972), *The Archaeology of Knowledge*, transl. by A. M. Sheridan Smith (London: Tavistock).

—— (1977), *Discipline and Punish: The Birth of the Prison*, transl. by A. Sheridan (Harmondsworth: Penguin).

—— (1980), 'Two Lectures' in C. Gordon (ed.), *Power/Knowledge: Selected Interviews and Other Writings 1972–1977 By Michel Foucault* (New York: Pantheon), 78–108.

FREEMAN, M. D. A. (1974), *The Legal Structure* (London: Longmans).

FREUND, J. (1968), *The Sociology of Max Weber*, transl. by M. Ilford (London: Allen Lane).

FRIEDMANN, W. (1967), *Legal Theory* (5th edn., London: Stevens).

—— (1971), *The State and the Rule of Law in a Mixed Economy* (London: Stevens).

FRYER, B., HUNT, A., McBARNET, D., and MOORHOUSE, B. (eds.) (1981), *Law, State and Society* (London: Croom Helm).

FULLER, L. L. (1940), *The Law in Quest of Itself* (Chicago: Foundation Press).

—— (1946), 'Reason and Fiat in Case Law', 59 *Harvard Law Review*, 376–95.

—— (1958), 'Positivism and Fidelity to Law—A Reply to Professor Hart', 71 *Harvard Law Review*, 630–72.

—— (1969), *The Morality of Law* (2nd edn., New Haven: Yale University Press).

GABEL, P., and KENNEDY, D. (1984), 'Roll Over Beethoven', 36 *Stanford Law Review*, 1–55.

GALANTER, M. (1974), 'Why the "Haves" Come Out Ahead: Speculations on the Limits of Legal Change', 9 *Law and Society Review*, 95–160.

—— (1992), 'Law Abounding: Legalisation Around the North Atlantic', 55 *Modern Law Review*, 1–24.

GALLIGAN, D. J. (1986), *Discretionary Powers: A Legal Study of Official Discretion* (Oxford: Oxford University Press).

GANZ, G. (1987), *Quasi-Legislation: Recent Developments in Secondary Legislation* (London: Sweet and Maxwell).

GARLAN, E. N. (1941), *Legal Realism and Justice* (New York: Columbia University Press).

GARLAND, D. (1990), *Punishment and Modern Society: A Study in Social Theory* (Oxford: Oxford University Press).

GEBHARDT, E. (1978), 'A Critique of Methodology: Introduction' in Arato and Gebhardt (eds.) (1978), 371–406.

GELLNER, E. (1974), *Legitimation of Belief* (Cambridge: Cambridge University Press).

GENN, H. (1987), *Hard Bargaining: Out of Court Settlement in Personal Injury Actions* (Oxford: Oxford University Press).

GERAS, N. (1981), 'Classical Marxism and Proletarian Representation', 125 *New Left Review*, 75–89.

GERTH, H. H., and MILLS, C. W. (eds.) (1948), *From Max Weber: Essays in Sociology* (London: Routledge and Kegan Paul reprint, 1991).

GIDDENS, A. (1977), *Studies in Social and Political Theory* (London: Hutchinson).

—— (1984), *The Constitution of Society: Outline of the Theory of Structuration* (Cambridge: Polity).

—— (1986), 'Introduction' in A. Giddens (ed.), *Durkheim on Politics and the State* (Cambridge: Polity), 1–31.

GIERKE, O. von (1900), *Political Theories of the Middle Age*, transl. by F. W. Maitland (Cambridge: Cambridge University Press).

—— (1934), *Natural Law and the Theory of Society*, transl. by E. Barker (Cambridge: Cambridge University Press reprint, 1958).

—— (1977), *Associations and Law: The Classical and Early Christian Stages*, transl. by G. Heiman (Toronto: University of Toronto Press).

GILMORE, G. (1961), 'Legal Realism: Its Cause and Cure', 70 *Yale Law Journal*, 1037–48.

—— (1974), *The Death of Contract* (Columbus: Ohio State University Press).

GINSBERG, M. (1956), *On The Diversity of Morals* (London: Heinemann).

GLASSER, C. (1990), 'The Legal Profession in the 1990s: Images of Change', 10 *Legal Studies*, 1–11.

GLAZEBROOK, P. R. (1960), 'Criminal Omissions: The Duty Requirement in Offences Against the Person', 76 *Law Quarterly Review*, 386–411.

GLOVER, J. (1977), *Causing Death and Saving Lives* (Harmondsworth: Penguin).

GOODRICH, P. (1986), *Reading the Law: A Critical Introduction to Legal Method and Techniques* (Oxford: Basil Blackwell).

—— (1987), *Legal Discourse: Studies in Linguistics, Rhetoric and Legal Analysis* (London: Macmillan).

—— (1990), *Languages of Law: From Logics of Memory to Nomadic Masks* (London: Weidenfeld and Nicolson).

GORDON, R. W. (1982), 'New Developments in Legal Theory' in D. Kairys (ed.), *The Politics of Law: A Progressive Critique* (New York: Pantheon), 281–93.

—— (1984), 'Critical Legal Histories', 36 *Stanford Law Review*, 57–125.

GOULDNER, A. W. (1971), *The Coming Crisis of Western Sociology* (London: Heinemann).

GRABOSKY, P. N. (1978), 'Theory and Research on Variations in Penal Severity', 5 *British Journal of Law and Society*, 103–14.

GRACE, P., and WILKINSON, P. (1978), *Sociological Inquiry and Legal Phenomena* (London: Collier Macmillan).

GRAGLIA, L. A. (1985), 'The Constitution, Community, and Liberty', 8 *Harvard Journal of Law and Public Policy*, 291–7.

GRAY, J. C. (1921), *The Nature and Sources of the Law* (2nd edn., Boston: Beacon Press reprint 1963).

GRAY, K. (1991), 'Property in Thin Air', 50 *Cambridge Law Journal*, 252–307.

GREEN, T. A. (1985), *Verdict According to Conscience: Perspectives on the English Criminal Trial Jury, 1200–1800* (Chicago: University of Chicago Press).

GREENBERG, D. F. (1983), 'Donald Black's Sociology of Law: A Critique', 17 *Law and Society Review*, 337–68.

GREENE, L. S. (1985), 'Twenty Years of Civil Rights: How Firm a Foundation?', 37 *Rutgers Law Review*, 707–54.

GREENHOUSE, C. J. (1986), *Praying for Justice: Faith, Order, and Community in an American Town* (Ithaca: Cornell University Press).

GREGORY, J. (1979), 'Sex Discrimination, Work and the Law' in Fine *et al.* (eds.) (1979), 137–50.

GREY, T. C. (1975), 'Do We Have an Unwritten Constitution?', 27 *Stanford Law Review*, 703–18.

—— (1980), 'The Disintegration of Property' in Pennock and Chapman (eds.) (1980), 69–85.

GRIFFITHS, J. (1984), 'The Division of Labor in Social Control' in Black (ed.) (1984), 37–70.

GUNNINGHAM, N. (1974), *Pollution, Social Interest and the Law* (London, Martin Robertson).

GUPTA, A. C. (1917), 'The Method of Jurisprudence', 33 *Law Quarterly Review*, 154–60.

GURVITCH, G. (1947), *Sociology of Law* (London: Routledge and Kegan Paul).

HABERMAS, J. (1976a), *Legitimation Crisis*, transl. by T. McCarthy (London: Heinemann).

—— (1976b), 'Problems of Legitimation in Late Capitalism', transl. by T. Hall, in P. Connerton (ed.), *Critical Sociology: Selected Readings* (Harmondsworth: Penguin), 363–87.

—— (1981), *The Theory of Communicative Action. Vol. 1: Reason and the Rationalization of Society*, transl. by T. McCarthy (Boston, Mass.: Beacon Press).

—— (1986), 'Law as Medium and Law as Institution' in Teubner (ed.) (1986), 203–20.

HAGAN, J. (1982), 'The Corporate Advantage: The Involvement of Corporate and Individual Victims in a Criminal Justice System', 60 *Social Forces*, 993–1022.

HAINES, C. G. (1930), *The Revival of Natural Law Concepts: A Study of the Establishment and of the Interpretation of Limits on Legislatures with Special Reference to the Development of Certain Phases of American Constitutional Law* (New York: Russell and Russell, 1965).

HALÉVY, E. (1928), *The Growth of Philosophic Radicalism*, transl. by M. Morris (London: Faber and Faber).

HALL, S., CRITCHER, C., JEFFERSON, T., CLARKE, J., and ROBERTS, B. (1978), *Policing the Crisis: Mugging, The State, and Law and Order* (London: Macmillan).

HALLIS, F. (1930), *Corporate Personality* (Oxford: Oxford University Press).

HALSEY, A. H. (1985), 'Provincials and Professionals: The British Post-War Sociologists' in Bulmer (ed.) (1985), 151–64.

HARDEN, I., and LEWIS, N. (1986), *The Noble Lie: The British Constitution and the Rule of Law* (London: Hutchinson).

HARLOW, C., and RAWLINGS, R. (1984), *Law and Administration* (London: Weidenfeld and Nicolson).

HARMAN, H., and GRIFFITH, J. (1979), *Justice Deserted: the Subversion of the Jury* (London: National Council for Civil Liberties).

HARRIS, D. R. (1983), 'The Development of Socio-Legal Studies in the United Kingdom', 3 *Legal Studies*, 315–33.

HARRIS, D., MACLEAN, M., GENN, H., LLOYD-BOSTOCK, S., FENN, P., CORFIELD, P., and BRITTAN, Y. (1984), *Compensation and Support for Illness and Injury* (Oxford: Oxford University Press).

HART, H. L. A. (1961), *The Concept of Law* (Oxford: Oxford University Press).

—— (1982), *Essays on Bentham: Studies in Jurisprudence and Political Theory* (Oxford: Oxford University Press).

—— (1983), *Essays in Jurisprudence and Philosophy* (Oxford: Oxford University Press).

HART, H. L. A., and HONORÉ, A. M. (1985), *Causation in the Law* (2nd edn., Oxford: Oxford University Press).

HART, JR., H. M., and SACKS, A. M. (1958), *The Legal Process: Basic Problems in the Making and Application of Law* (Cambridge, Mass.: Harvard Law School).

HARVEY, L. (1982), 'The Use and Abuse of Kuhnian Paradigms in the Sociology of Knowledge', 16 *Sociology*, 85–101.

HAWKINS, K. (1984), *Environment and Enforcement: Regulation and the Social Definition of Pollution* (Oxford: Oxford University Press).

HAWTHORN, G. (1987), *Enlightenment and Despair: A History of Social Theory* (2nd edn., Cambridge: Cambridge University Press).

HAY, D. (1975), 'Property, Authority and the Criminal Law' in D. Hay *et al.*, *Albion's Fatal Tree* (London: Allen Lane), 17–63.

HAYEK, F. A. (1944), *The Road to Serfdom* (London: Routledge and Kegan Paul).

—— (1982), *Law, Legislation and Liberty* (Corrected composite edn., London: Routledge and Kegan Paul).

HELD, D. (1980), *Introduction to Critical Theory: Horkheimer to Habermas* (London: Hutchinson).

HENNIS, W. (1988), *Max Weber: Essays in Reconstruction*, transl. by K. Tribe (London: Allen and Unwin).

HENRY, S. (1983), *Private Justice: Towards Integrated Theorising in the Sociology of Law* (London: Routledge and Kegan Paul).

HERZ, J. H., and KULA, E. (1969), 'Otto Kirchheimer: An Introduction to His Life and Work' in Burin and Shell (eds.) (1969), pp. ix–xxxviii.

HEWART, LORD (1929), *The New Despotism* (London: Benn).

HILL, M. (1981), 'The Policy-Implementation Distinction: A Quest for Rational Control?' in S. Barrett and C. Fudge (eds.), *Policy and Action: Essays on the Implementation of Public Policy* (London: Methuen), 207–23.

HILLERY, G. A. (1955), 'Definitions of Community: Areas of Agreement', 20 *Rural Sociology*, 111–23.

HINDESS, B., and HIRST, P. (1975), *Pre-Capitalist Modes of Production* (London: Routledge and Kegan Paul).

HINKLE, R. C. (1980), *Founding Theory in American Sociology 1881–1915* (London: Routledge and Kegan Paul).

HIRST, P. Q. (1976), *Social Evolution and Sociological Categories* (London: Allen and Unwin).

—— (1979a), *On Law and Ideology* (London: Macmillan).

—— (1979b), 'The Necessity of Theory', 8 *Economy and Society*, 417–45.

—— (1980), 'Law, Socialism and Rights' reprinted in Hirst (1986), 15–68.

—— (1986), *Law, Socialism and Democracy* (London: Allen and Unwin).

—— (ed.) (1989), *The Pluralist Theory of the State: Selected Writings of G. D. H. Cole, J. N. Figgis and H. J. Laski* (London: Routledge).

HOBHOUSE, L. T. (1906), *Morals in Evolution: A Study in Comparative Ethics* (New York: Johnson reprint, 1968).

—— (1966), *Sociology and Philosophy: A Centenary Collection of Essays and Articles* (London: Bell, London School of Economics and Political Science).

HOEBEL, E. A. (1954), *The Law of Primitive Man* (Cambridge, Mass.: Harvard University Press).

HOLDAWAY, S. (1983), *Inside the British Police: A Force at Work* (Oxford: Basil Blackwell).

HOLLOWAY, J., and PICCIOTTO, S. (eds.) (1978), *State and Capital: A Marxist Debate* (London: Edward Arnold).

HONIGSHEIM, P. (1968), *On Max Weber*, transl. by J. Rytina (New York: Free Press).

HORKHEIMER, M. (1972), 'Traditional and Critical Theory' reprinted in P. Connerton (ed.), *Critical Sociology: Selected Readings* (Harmondsworth: Penguin, 1976), 206–24.

—— (1978), 'The Authoritarian State' in Arato and Gebhardt (eds.) (1978), 95–117.

HUGHES, G. (1958), 'Criminal Omissions', 67 *Yale Law Journal*, 590–637.

HUNT, A. (1978), *The Sociological Movement in Law* (London: Macmillan).

—— (1983), 'Behavioural Sociology of Law: A Critique of Donald Black', 10 *Journal of Law and Society*, 19–46.

HUSBANDS, C. T. (1981), 'The Anti-Quantitative Bias in Postwar British Sociology' in Abrams *et al.* (eds.) (1981), 88–104.

HUTCHINSON, A. C. (1987), 'Indiana Dworkin and Law's Empire', 86 *Yale Law Journal*, 637–65.

JACKSON, B. (1985), *Semiotics and Legal Theory* (London: Routledge and Kegan Paul).

JASPERS, K. (1965), *Three Essays: Leonardo, Descartes, Max Weber*, transl. by R. Manheim (London: Routledge and Kegan Paul).

JAY, M. (1973), *The Dialectical Imagination: A History of the Frankfurt School and the Institute of Social Research 1923–1950* (London: Heinemann).

—— (1986), 'Foreword: Neumann and the Frankfurt School' in Neumann (1986), ix–xiv.

JOHNSON, P. E. (1984), 'Do You Sincerely Want To Be Radical?', 36 *Stanford Law Review*, 247–91.

KALBERG, S. (1979), 'The Search for Thematic Orientations in a Fragmented Œuvre: The Discussion of Max Weber in Recent German Sociological Literature', 13 *Sociology*, 127–39.

KAMENKA, E., and TAY, A. E. -S. (1975), 'Beyond Bourgeois Individualism: The Contemporary Crisis in Law and Legal Ideology' in E. Kamenka and R. S. Neale (eds.), *Feudalism, Capitalism and Beyond* (London: Edward Arnold), 127–44.

KEETON, G. W. (1952), *The Passing of Parliament* (London: Benn).

KELMAN, M. G. (1984), 'Trashing', 36 *Stanford Law Review*, 293–348.

—— (1987), *A Guide to Critical Legal Studies* (Cambridge: Harvard University Press).

KELSEN, H. (1945), *General Theory of Law and State*, transl. by A. Wedberg (New York: Russell and Russell, 1961).

—— (1955), 'Foundations of Democracy', 66 *Ethics*, 1–101.

—— (1957), *What is Justice? Justice, Law and Politics in the Mirror of Science* (Berkeley, Cal.: University of California Press).

—— (1967), *Pure Theory of Law*, transl. by M. Knight (Gloucester, Mass.: Peter Smith reprint 1989).

—— (1991), *General Theory of Norms*, transl. by M. Hartney (Oxford: Oxford University Press).

KENNEDY, D. (1976), 'Form and Substance in Private Law Adjudication', 89 *Harvard Law Review*, 1685–778.

—— (1979), 'The Structure of Blackstone's Commentaries', 28 *Buffalo Law Review*, 205–382.

—— (1982), 'Legal Education as Training for Hierarchy' in D. Kairys (ed.), *The Politics of Law* (New York: Pantheon Books), 40–61.

KENNEDY, E. (1987), 'Carl Schmitt and the Frankfurt School' 20 *Telos*, 37–66.

KING, P. J. (1986), *Utilitarian Jurisprudence in America: The Influence of Bentham and Austin on American Legal Thought in the Nineteenth Century* (New York: Garland Publishing).

KINSEY, R. (1979), 'Despotism and Legality' in Fine *et al.* (eds.) (1979), 46–64.

KIRCHHEIMER, O. (1967), 'The *Rechtsstaat* as Magic Wall', reprinted in Burin and Shell (eds.) (1969), 428–52.

—— (1969), 'Weimar—And What Then?' in Burin and Shell (eds.) (1969), 33–74.

—— (1983), 'The Limits of Expropriation', reprinted in Kirchheimer and Neumann (1987), 85–129.

KIRCHHEIMER, O., and LEITES, N. (1987), 'Remarks on Carl Schmitt's *Legalität und Legitimität*' in Kirchheimer and Neumann (1987), 148–78.

KIRCHHEIMER, O., and NEUMANN, F. (1987), *Social Democracy and the Rule of Law*, transl. by L. Tanner and K. Tribe (London: Allen and Unwin).

KNIGHT, W. S. M. (1922), 'Public Policy in English Law', 38 *Law Quarterly Review*, 207–19.

KÖNIG, R. (1968), *The Community*, transl. by E. Fitzgerald (London: Routledge and Kegan Paul).

KRONMAN, A. (1983), *Max Weber* (London: Edward Arnold).

KUHN, T. S. (1970a), *The Structure of Scientific Revolutions* (2nd edn., Chicago: University of Chicago Press).

—— (1970b), 'Reflections on My Critics' in Lakatos and Musgrave (eds.) (1970), 231–78.

—— (1974), 'Second Thoughts on Paradigms', reprinted in Kuhn (1977b), 293–319.

—— (1977a), 'Objectivity, Value Judgment, and Theory Choice' in Kuhn (1977b), 320–39.

—— (1977b), *The Essential Tension: Selected Studies in Scientific Tradition and Change* (Chicago: University of Chicago Press).

KURTZ, L. R. (1984), *Evaluating Chicago Sociology: A Guide to the Literature, with an Annotated Bibliography* (Chicago: University of Chicago Press).

LACHMANN, L. M. (1970), *The Legacy of Max Weber: Three Essays* (London: Heinemann).

LAKATOS, I. (1970), 'Falsification and the Methodology of Scientific Research Programmes' in Lakatos and Musgrave (eds.) (1970), 91–195.

LAKATOS, I., and MUSGRAVE, A. (eds.) (1970), *Criticism and the Growth of Knowledge: Proceedings of the International Colloquium in the Philosophy of Science, London, 1965, Volume 4* (London: Cambridge University Press).

LEA, J. (1979), 'Discipline and Capitalist Development' in Fine *et al.* (eds.) (1979), 76–89.

LENMAN, B., and PARKER, G. (1980), 'The State, the Community and the Criminal Law in Early Modern Europe' in V. A. C. Gatrell, B. Lenman, and G. Parker (eds.), *Crime and the Law: The Social History of Crime in Western Europe Since 1500* (London: Europa Publications), 11–48.

LESTER, A., and BINDMAN, G. (1972), *Race and Law* (Harmondsworth: Penguin).

LEWIS, N., and HARDEN, I. (1983), 'Privatisation, De-regulation and Constitutionality: Some Anglo-American Comparisons', 34 *Northern Ireland Legal Quarterly*, 207–29.

LEWIS, N., and WILES, P. (1984), 'The Post-Corporatist State?', 11 *Journal of Law and Society*, 65–90.

LIVOCK, R. (1979), 'Science, Law and Safety Standards: A Case Study of Industrial Desease', 6 *British Journal of Law and Society*, 172–99.

LLEWELLYN, K. N. (1930), 'A Realistic Jurisprudence—The Next Step', 30 *Columbia Law Review*, 431–65.

—— (1940), 'The Normative, the Legal and the Law-Jobs', 49 *Yale Law Journal*, 1355–400.

—— (1944), 'Group Prejudice and Social Education', reprinted in Llewellyn (1962), 451–67.

—— (1957), 'What Law Cannot Do for Inter-racial Peace', 3 *Villanova Law Review*, 30–6.

—— (1960), *The Common Law Tradition: Deciding Appeals* (Boston: Little, Brown).

—— (1962), *Jurisprudence: Realism in Theory and Practice* (Chicago: University of Chicago Press).

LLOYD OF HAMPSTEAD, LORD, and FREEMAN, M. D. A. (1985), *Lloyd's Introduction to Jurisprudence* (5th edn., London: Stevens).

LUHMANN, N. (1979), 'Trust: A Mechanism for the Reduction of Social Complexity' in *Trust and Power: Two Works by Niklas Luhmann*, transl. by H. Davis, J. Raffan, and K. Rooney (Chichester: John Wiley), 4–103.

—— (1985), *A Sociological Theory of Law*, transl. by E. King and M. Albrow (London: Routledge and Kegan Paul).

—— (1986), 'The Self-Reproduction of Law and Its Limits' in Teubner (ed.) (1986), 111–27.

—— (1988), 'The Unity of the Legal System' in Teubner (ed.) (1988), 12–35.

LUKES, S. (1973), *Émile Durkheim—His Life and Work: A Historical and Critical Study* (Harmondsworth: Penguin).

—— (1974), *Power: A Radical View* (London: Macmillan).

LUKES, S., and SCULL, A. (eds.) (1983), *Durkheim and the Law* (Oxford: Martin Robertson).

LUSTGARTEN, L. (1988), 'Socialism and the Rule of Law', 15 *Journal of Law and Society*, 25–41.

MCAUSLAN, P. and MCELDOWNEY, J. F. (1985), 'Legitimacy and the Constitution: The Dissonance Between Theory and Practice' in P. McAuslan and J. F. McEldowney (eds.), *Law, Legitimacy and the Constitution: Essays Marking the Centenary of Dicey's Law of the Constitution* (London: Sweet and Maxwell), 1–38.

MCBARNET, D. J. (1981), *Conviction: Law, the State and the Construction of Justice* (London: Macmillan).

MACCORMICK, D. N. (1978), *Legal Reasoning and Legal Theory* (Oxford: Oxford University Press).

MCCRUDDEN, C. (1988), 'Codes in a Cold Climate: Administrative Rule-Making By the Commission for Racial Equality', 51 *Modern Law Review*, 409–41.

MCDOUGAL, M. S., and LASSWELL, H. D. (1943), 'Legal Education and Public Policy: Professional Training in the Public Interest', 52 *Yale Law Journal*, 203–95.

MCGREGOR, O. R. (1981), *Social History and Law Reform* (London: Stevens).

MCGREGOR, O. R., BLOM-COOPER, L., and GIBSON, C. (1970), *Separated Spouses: A Study of the Matrimonial Jurisdiction of Magistrates' Courts* (London: Duckworth).

MACINTYRE, A. (1985), *After Virtue: A Study in Moral Theory* (2nd edn., London: Duckworth).

MCLENNAN, G. (1978), Correspondence, 7 *Economy and Society*, 193–205.

MAINE, H. S. (1861), *Ancient Law* (London: Dent, 1917).

MAITLAND, F. (1900), 'Introduction' in Gierke (1900), vii–xlv.

MALINOWSKI, B. (1926), *Crime and Custom in Savage Society* (London: Routledge and Kegan Paul).

MANN, M. (1970), 'The Social Cohesion of Liberal Democracy', 35 *American Sociological Review*, 423–39.

MANNING, P. K. (1982), 'Organizational Work: Structuration of Environments', 33 *British Journal of Sociology*, 118–34.

MARCUSE, H. (ed.) (1957), *The Democratic and the Authoritarian State: Essays in Political and Legal Theory by Franz Neumann* (Glencoe, Ill.: Free Press).

MARX, K. (1963), 'On the Jewish Question', transl. by T. B. Bottomore, in T. B. Bottomore (ed.), *Karl Marx: Early Writings* (London: Watts), 1–40.

—— (1970), 'Critique of the Gotha Programme 1875' in K. Marx and F. Engels, *Selected Works*, Vol. 3 (Moscow: Progress Publishers), 13–30.

—— (1976), *Capital: A Critique of Political Economy*, Vol. 1, transl. by B. Fowkes (Harmondsworth: Penguin).

MASSELL, G. J. (1968), 'Law as an Instrument of Revolutionary Change in a Traditional Milieu: The Case of Soviet Central Asia', 2 *Law and Society Review*, 179–228.

MATHIESEN, T. (1980), *Law, Society and Political Action: Towards a Strategy Under Late Capitalism* (London: Academic Press).

MATTHEWS, R. (1979), '"Decarceration" and the Fiscal Crisis' in Fine *et al.* (eds.) (1979), 100–17.

MAYER, J. P. (1956), *Max Weber and German Politics: A Study in Political Sociology* (2nd edn., New York: Arno reprint, 1979).

MEEHL, P. E. (1977), 'Law and the Fireside Inductions: Some Reflections of a Clinical Psychologist', 27 *Journal of Social Issues*, No. 4, 65–100.

MELOSSI, D. (1979), 'Institutions of Social Control and Capitalist Organization of Work' in Fine *et al.* (eds.) (1979), 90–9.

MERQUIOR, J. G. (1980), *Rousseau and Weber: Two Studies in the Theory of Legitimacy* (London: Routledge and Kegan Paul).

MERRY, S. E. (1988), 'Legal Pluralism', 22 *Law and Society Review*, 869–96.

—— (1990), *Getting Justice and Getting Even: Legal Consciousness Among Working-Class Americans* (Chicago: University of Chicago Press).

MILLER, A. S., and HOWELL, R. F. (1960), 'The Myth of Neutrality in Constitutional Adjudication', 27 *University of Chicago Law Review*, 661–95.

MILLS, C. W. (1959), *The Sociological Imagination* (Harmondsworth: Penguin, 1970).

MILWARD, A. S., LYNCH, F. M. B., ROMERO, F., RANIERI, R., and SORENSON, V. (1993), *The Frontier of National Sovereignty: History and Theory 1945–1992* (London: Routledge).

MITZMAN, A. B. (1970), *The Iron Cage: An Historical Interpretation of Max Weber* (New York: Knopf).

MOFFATT, G. (1992), 'Trusts Law: A Song Without End?', 55 *Modern Law Review*, 123–39.

MOMMSEN, W. J. (1974), *The Age of Bureaucracy: Perspectives on the Political Sociology of Max Weber* (Oxford: Basil Blackwell).

MONAHAN, J., and WALKER, L. (1986), 'Social Authority: Obtaining, Evaluating and Establishing Social Science in Law', 134 *University of Pennsylvania Law Review*, 477–517.

MOORE, S. F. (1978), *Law as Process: An Anthropological Approach* (London: Routledge and Kegan Paul).

MORRIS, P., WHITE, R., and LEWIS, P. (1973), *Social Needs and Legal Action* (London: Martin Robertson).

MUIR, W. K. (1967), *Prayers in the Public Schools: Law and Attitude Change* (Chicago: University of Chicago Press).

MÜLLER, H.-P. (1988), 'Social Structure and Civil Religion: Legitimation Crisis in a Late Durkheimian Perspective' in Alexander (ed.) (1988), 129–58.

NADER, L. (ed.) (1980), *No Access to Law: Alternatives to the American Judicial System* (New York: Academic Press).

NATIONAL DEVIANCY CONFERENCE (ed.) (1980), *Permissiveness and Control: The Fate of the Sixties Legislation* (London: Macmillan).

NELKEN, D. (1981a), 'Sociology of Law v. Socio-Legal Studies: The False Divide', Paper presented at University of Kent Conference on Critical Legal Scholarship, April 1981.

—— (1981b), 'The "Gap Problem" in the Sociology of Law: A Theoretical Review', 1 *Windsor Yearbook of Access to Justice*, 35–61.

—— (1982), 'Is There a Crisis in Law and Legal Ideology?', 9 *Journal of Law and Society*, 177–89.

—— (1990), *The Truth About Law's Truth*, EUI Working Paper No. 90/1 (Florence: European University Institute).

NELSON, W. E. (1976), *The Americanization of the Common Law: The Impact of Legal Change on Massachusetts Society, 1760–1830* (Cambridge, Mass.: Harvard University Press).

NEUMANN, F. L. (1944), *Behemoth: The Structure and Practice of National Socialism 1933–1944* (New York: Octagon reprint, 1983).

—— (1949), 'Editor's Introduction: Montesquieu' in C. de Montesquieu, *The Spirit of the Laws* (New York: Hafner Press), ix–lxiv.

—— (1953), 'The Concept of Political Freedom' reprinted in Marcuse (ed.) (1957), 160–200.

—— (1957), 'The Change in the Function of Law in Modern Society', transl. by K. Knorr and E. A. Shils, in Marcuse (ed.) (1957), 22–68.

—— (1986), *The Rule of Law: Political Theory and the Legal System in Modern Society* (Leamington Spa: Berg).

—— (1987), 'Rechtsstaat, The Division of Powers and Socialism' in Kirchheimer and Neumann (1987), 66–74.

NEWTON, K. (1982), 'Is Small Really So Beautiful? Is Large Really So Ugly? Size, Effectiveness, and Democracy in Local Government', 30 *Political Studies*, 190–206.

NEWTON, L. (1976), 'The Rule of Law and the Appeal to Community Standards', 21 *American Journal of Jurisprudence*, 95–106.

NISBET, R. A. (1962), *Community and Power* (New York: Oxford University Press).

—— (1967), *The Sociological Tradition* (New Brunswick: Transaction Books reprint, 1993).

NONET, P. (1976), 'For Jurisprudential Sociology', 10 *Law and Society Review*, 525–45.

NORRIE, A. (1982), 'Pashukanis and the "Commodity Form Theory": A Reply to Warrington', 10 *International Journal of the Sociology of Law*, 419–37.

NOVE, A. (1991), *The Economics of Feasible Socialism Revisited* (2nd edn., London: Harper Collins).

NOZICK, R. (1974), *Anarchy, State and Utopia* (Oxford: Basil Blackwell).

NUSSBAUM, A. (1940), 'Fact Research in Law', 40 *Columbia Law Review*, 189–219.

ODUM, H. W. (1951), *American Sociology: The Story of Sociology in the United States through 1950* (New York: Longmans, Green).

OFFE, C. (1984), *Contradictions of the Welfare State* (London: Hutchinson).

—— (1985), *Disorganised Capitalism: Contemporary Transformations of Work and Politics* (Cambridge: Polity Press).

O'HAGAN, T. (1984), *The End of Law?* (Oxford: Basil Blackwell).

OLIVECRONA, K. (1971), *Law as Fact* (2nd edn., London: Stevens).

PARSONS, T. (1937), *The Structure of Social Action, Vol. 2: Weber* (New York: Free Press paperback, 1968).

—— (1947), 'Introduction' in M. Weber, *The Theory of Social and Economic Organisation* (New York: Free Press reprint, 1964), 3–86.

—— (1962), 'The Law and Social Control' in W. M. Evan (ed.), *Law and Sociology: Exploratory Essays* (Glencoe, Ill.: Free Press), 56–72.

—— (1966), *Societies: Evolutionary and Comparative Perspectives* (Englewood Cliffs: Prentice-Hall).

—— (1967), 'Evaluation and Objectivity in Social Science: An Interpretation of Max Weber's Contributions' in T. Parsons, *Sociological Theory and Modern Society* (New York: Free Press), 79–101.

—— (1971), *The System of Modern Societies* (Englewood Cliffs: Prentice-Hall).

—— (1977), Book Review, 12 *Law and Society Review*, 145–9.

—— (1981), 'Revisiting the Classics Throughout a Long Career' in B. Rhea (ed.), *The Future of the Sociological Classics* (London: Allen and Unwin), 183–94.

PASHUKANIS, E. B. (1978), *Law and Marxism: A General Theory*, transl. by B. Einhorn (London: Ink Links).

—— (1980), 'Economics and Legal Regulation' in Beirne and Sharlet (eds.) (1980), 235–72.

PATERSON, A. (1982), *The Law Lords* (London: Macmillan).

PATON, G. W. (1972), *A Textbook of Jurisprudence* (4th edn., Oxford: Oxford University Press).

PATTENDEN, R. (1990), *The Judge, Discretion and Criminal Legislation* (2nd edn., Oxford: Oxford University Press).

PAULUS, I. (1974), *The Search for Pure Food: A Sociology of Legislation in Britain* (London: Martin Robertson).

PEARCE, F. (1989), *The Radical Durkheim* (London: Unwin Hyman).

PENNOCK, J. R., and CHAPMAN, J. W. (eds.) (1980), *Property* (New York: New York University Press).

PETRAZYCKI, L. (1955), *Law and Morality*, transl. by H. W. Babb (Cambridge, Mass.: Harvard University Press).

PHILLIPS, P. (1980), *Marx and Engels on Law and Laws* (Oxford: Martin Robertson).

PICCIOTTO, S. (1979), 'The Theory of the State, Class Struggle and the Rule of Law' in Fine *et al.* (eds.) (1979), 164–77.

PODGORECKI, A. (1974), *Law and Society* (London: Routledge and Kegan Paul).

PODGORECKI, A., and WHELAN, C. J. (eds.) (1981), *Sociological Approaches to Law* (London: Croom Helm).

PODMORE, D. (1980), *Solicitors and the Wider Community* (London: Heinemann).

POSNER, R. A. (1987), 'The Decline of Law as an Autonomous Discipline: 1962–1987', 100 *Harvard Law Review*, 761–80.

POSTEMA, G. J. (1986), *Bentham and the Common Law Tradition* (Oxford: Oxford University Press).

POULANTZAS, N. (1978), *State, Power, Socialism*, transl. by P. Camiller (London: New Left Books).

POUND, R. (1908), 'Mechanical Jurisprudence', 8 *Columbia Law Review*, 605–23.

—— (1917), 'The Limits of Effective Legal Action', 27 *International Journal of Ethics*, 150–67.

—— (1959), *Jurisprudence* (St. Paul, Minn.: West Publishing Company).

PROSSER, T. (1982), 'Towards a Critical Public Law', 9 *Journal of Law and Society*, 1–19.

PURCELL, JR., E. A. (1973), *The Crisis of Democratic Theory: Scientific Naturalism and the Problem of Value* (Lexington: University Press of Kentucky).

RABIN, R. L. (1979), 'Impact Analysis and Tort Law: A Comment', 13 *Law and Society Review*, 987–96.

RADCLIFFE-BROWN, A. R. (1933), 'Primitive Law', 9 *Encyclopedia of the Social Sciences*, 202–6.

—— (1934), 'Social Sanction', 13 *Encyclopedia of the Social Sciences*, 531–4.

RAJCHMAN, J., and WEST, C. (eds.) (1985), *Post-Analytic Philosophy* (New York: Columbia University Press).

RAWLS, J. (1972), *A Theory of Justice* (Oxford: Oxford University Press).

RAZ, J. (1979), *The Authority of Law: Essays on Law and Morality* (Oxford: Oxford University Press).

RENNER, K. (1949), *The Institutions of Private Law and their Social Functions*, transl. by A. Schwarzschild (London: Routledge and Kegan Paul).

RICHARDSON, G., with OGUS, A., and BURROWS, P. (1983), *Policing Pollution: A Study of Regulation and Enforcement* (Oxford: Oxford University Press).

RINGER, F. K. (1969), *The Decline of the German Mandarins: The German Academic Community, 1890–1933* (Cambridge, Mass.: Harvard University Press).

ROCHER, G. (1974), *Talcott Parsons and American Sociology*, transl. by B. Mennell and S. Mennell (London: Nelson).

ROCK, P. (1973), *Making People Pay* (London: Routledge and Kegan Paul).

ROMANO, S. (1975), *L'ordre juridique*, transl. from Italian by L. François and P. Gothot (Paris: Dalloz).

RORTY, R. (1980), *Philosophy and the Mirror of Nature* (Oxford: Basil Blackwell).

ROSHIER, R., and TEFF, H. (1980), *Law and Society in England* (London: Tavistock).

ROTH, G. (1965), 'Political Critiques of Max Weber: Some Implications for Political Sociology', 30 *American Sociological Review*, 213–23.

ROTH, G., and SCHLUCHTER, W. (1979), *Max Weber's Vision of History: Ethics and Methods* (Berkeley: University of California Press).

RUMBLE, JR., W. E. (1985), *The Thought of John Austin: Colonial Reform and the British Constitution* (London: Athlone Press).

SACHS, A., and WILSON, J. H. (1978), *Sexism and the Law: A Study of Male Beliefs and Legal Bias in Britain and the United States* (Oxford: Martin Robertson).

SANDERS, J. (1990), 'The Interplay of Micro and Macro Processes in the Longitudinal Study of Courts: Beyond the Durkheimian Tradition', 24 *Law and Society Review*, 241–56.

SANDERS, J., RANKIN-WIDGEON, B., KALMUSS, D., and CHESLER, M. (1982), 'The Relevance of "Irrelevant" Testimony: Why Lawyers Use Social Science Experts in School Desegregation Cases', 16 *Law and Society Review*, 403–28.

SANTOS, B. DE S. (1979), 'Popular Justice, Dual Power and Socialist Strategy' in Fine *et al.* (eds.) (1979), 151–63.

—— (1982), 'Law and Community: The Changing Nature of State Power in Late Capitalism' in R. L. Abel (ed.), *The Politics of Informal Justice. Vol. 1: The American Experience* (New York: Academic Press), 249–66.

SARAT, A. (1990), '". . . The Law is All Over": Power, Resistance and the Legal Consciousness of the Welfare Poor', 2 *Yale Journal of Law and the Humanities*, 343–79.

SARAT, A., and FELSTINER, W. L. F. (1988), 'Law and Social Relations: Vocabularies of Motive in Lawyer/Client Interaction', 22 *Law and Society Review*, 737–69.

SARAT, A., and SILBEY, S. S. (1988), 'The Pull of the Policy Audience', 10 *Law and Policy*, 97–166.

SCHACHT, J. (1964), *An Introduction to Islamic Law* (Oxford: Oxford University Press).

SCHMITT, C. (1976), *The Concept of the Political*, transl. by G. Schwab (New Brunswick, N.J.: Rutgers University Press).

SCHUCHMAN, P. (1988), 'The Writing and Reporting of Judicial Opinions' in S. Shetreet (ed.), *The Role of Courts in Society* (Dordrecht: Nijhoff), 319–31.

SCHWARTZ, R. D. (1954), 'Social Factors in the Development of Legal Control: A Case Study of Two Israeli Settlements', 65 *Yale Law Journal*, 471–91.

SCHWARTZ, R. D., and MILLER, J. C. (1964), 'Legal Evolution and Societal Complexity', 70 *American Journal of Sociology*, 159–69.

SCOTT, C. (1990), 'Continuity and Change in British Food Law', 53 *Modern Law Review*, 785–801.

SELZNICK, P. (1961), 'Sociology and Natural Law', 6 *Natural Law Forum*, 84–108.

—— (1969), *Law, Society, and Industrial Justice* (New Brunswick: Transaction Books reprint, 1980).

SHELEFF, L. S. (1975), 'From Restitutive Law to Repressive Law: Durkheim's *The Division of Labour in Society* Revisited', 16 *European Journal of Sociology*, 16–45.

SHILS, E. (1948), *The Present State of American Sociology* (Glencoe, Ill.: Free Press).

—— (1985), 'On the Eve: A Prospect in Retrospect' in Bulmer (ed.) (1985), 165–78.

SHKLAR, J. N. (1964), *Legalism* (Cambridge, Mass.: Harvard University Press).

SILBEY, S. S., and SARAT, A. (1987), 'Critical Traditions in Law and Society Research', 21 *Law and Society Review*, 165–74.

SIMPSON, A. W. B. (1986), 'The Common Law and Legal Theory' in Twining (ed.) (1986), 8–25.

SKOLNICK, J. (1975), *Justice Without Trial: Law Enforcement in Democratic Society* (2nd edn., New York: Wiley).

SMART, A. (1987), 'Criminal Responsibility For Failing To Do the Impossible', 103 *Law Quarterly Review*, 532–63.

SMITH, A. (1784), *An Inquiry Into the Nature and Causes of the Wealth of Nations* (3rd edn., Oxford: Oxford University Press annotated reprint, 1976).

SMITH, J. C., and HOGAN, B. (1992), *Criminal Law* (7th edn., London: Butterworth).

SOMMERVILLE, J. P. (1986), *Politics and Ideology in England 1603–1640* (London: Longman).

SPENCER, M. E. (1970), 'Weber on Legitimate Norms and Authority', 21 *British Journal of Sociology*, 123–34.

SPITZER, S. (1975), 'Punishment and Social Organization: A Study of Durkheim's Theory of Penal Evolution', 9 *Law and Society Review*, 613–37.

—— (1979), 'Notes Toward a Theory of Punishment and Social Change' in R. J. Simon and S. Spitzer (eds.), *Research in Law and Sociology: A Research Annual*, Vol. 2 (Greenwich, Conn.: JAI Press), 207–29.

SPOHN, C. (1990), 'The Sentencing Decisions of Black and White Judges: Expected and Unexpected Similarities', 24 *Law and Society Review*, 1197–216.

STEINER, H. (1980), 'Slavery, Socialism and Private Property' in Pennock and Chapman (eds.) (1980), 244–65.

STEVENS, R. (1979), *Law and Politics: The House of Lords as a Judicial Body, 1800–1976* (London: Weidenfeld and Nicolson).

—— (1983), *Law School: Legal Education in America from the 1850s to the 1980s* (Chapel Hill: University of North Carolina Press).

STINCHCOMBE, A. L. (1977), Book Review, 12 *Law and Society Review*, 129–31.

STONE, J. (1946), *The Province and Function of Law* (London: Stevens).

—— (1964), *Legal System and Lawyers' Reasonings* (London: Stevens).

SUGARMAN, D. (1986), 'Legal Theory, the Common Law Mind and the Making of the Textbook Tradition' in Twining (ed.) (1986), 26–61.

—— (ed.) (1983), *Legality, Ideology and the State* (London: Academic Press).

SUMMERS, R. S. (1971), 'Professor Fuller on Morality and Law' in R. Summers (ed.), *More Essays in Legal Philosophy: General Assessments of Legal Philosophies* (Oxford: Blackwell), 101–30.

—— (1977), 'Naïve Instrumentalism and the Law' in P. M. S. Hacker and

J. Raz (eds.), *Law, Morality and Society: Essays in Honour of H. L. A. Hart* (Oxford: Oxford University Press), 119–31.

—— (1978), 'Professor Fuller's Jurisprudence and America's Dominant Philosophy of Law', 92 *Harvard Law Review*, 433–49.

SUMNER, C. (1979), *Reading Ideologies: An Investigation into the Marxist Theory of Ideology and Law* (London: Academic Press).

SUMNER, W. G. (1906), *Folkways* (New York: New American Library, 1960).

TAYLOR, I., WALTON, P., and YOUNG, J. (1973), *The New Criminology: For a Social Theory of Deviance* (London: Routledge and Kegan Paul).

TAYLOR, M. (1982), *Community, Anarchy and Liberty* (Cambridge: Cambridge University Press).

TEUBNER, G. (1987), 'Juridification: Concepts, Aspects, Limits, Solutions' in G. Teubner (ed.), *Juridification of Social Spheres: A Comparative Analysis in the Areas of Labor, Corporate, Antitrust and Social Welfare Law* (Berlin: de Gruyter), 3–48.

—— (1988), 'Evolution of Autopoietic Law' in Teubner (ed.) (1988), 217–41.

—— (1989), 'How the Law Thinks: Toward a Constructivist Epistemology of Law', 23 *Law and Society Review*, 727–57.

—— (1991), 'La théorie des systèmes autopoiétiques: Interview de Gunther Teubner réalisé par V. Munoz-Darde et Y. Sintomer', *Journal M*, no. 44, February, 36–40.

—— (1992a), 'Social Order From Legislative Noise? Autopoietic Closure as a Problem for Legal Regulation' in G. Teubner and A. Febbrajo (eds.), *State, Law and Economy as Autopoietic Systems: Regulation and Autonomy in a New Perspective* (Milan: Giuffrè), 609–49.

—— (1992b), 'The Two Faces of Janus: Rethinking Legal Pluralism', 13 *Cardozo Law Review*, 1443–62.

—— (ed.) (1986), *Dilemmas of Law in the Welfare State* (Berlin: de Gruyter).

—— (ed.) (1988), *Autopoietic Law: A New Approach to Law and Society* (Berlin: de Gruyter).

THOMPSON, E. P. (1975), *Whigs and Hunters: The Origin of the Black Act* (London: Allen Lane).

THOMPSON, J. J. (1986), *Rights, Restitution, and Risk: Essays in Moral Theory* (Cambridge, Mass.: Harvard University Press).

TÖNNIES, F. (1955), *Community and Society*, transl. by C. P. Loomis (London: Routledge and Kegan Paul).

TREVES, R. (1974), 'Co-operation Between Lawyers and Sociologists: A Comparative Comment', 1 *British Journal of Law and Society*, 200–4.

TROELTSCH, E. (1934), 'The Ideas of Natural Law and Humanity in World Politics', transl. by E. Barker, in Gierke (1934), 201–22.

TRUBEK, D. M. (1984), 'Where the Action Is: Critical Legal Studies and Empiricism', 36 *Stanford Law Review*, 575–622.

TRUBEK, D. M., and ESSER, J. (1989), '"Critical Empiricism" in American Legal Studies: Paradox, Program, or Pandora's Box?', 14 *Law and Social Inquiry*, 3–52.

TUR, R., and TWINING, W. (eds.) (1986), *Essays on Kelsen* (Oxford: Oxford University Press).

TWINING, W. L. (1973), *Karl Llewellyn and the Realist Movement* (London: Weidenfeld and Nicolson).

—— (ed.) (1986), *Legal Theory and Common Law* (Oxford: Basil Blackwell).

TWINING, W., and MIERS, D. (1991), *How To Do Things With Rules* (3rd edn., London: Weidenfeld and Nicolson).

TYLER, T. R. (1990), *Why People Obey the Law* (New Haven: Yale University Press).

UNGER, R. M. (1976), *Law in Modern Society: Toward a Criticism of Social Theory* (New York: Free Press).

—— (1983), 'The Critical Legal Studies Movement', 96 *Harvard Law Review*, 563–675.

—— (1987), *False Necessity: Anti-Necessitarian Social Theory in the Service of Radical Democracy* (Cambridge: Cambridge University Press).

URRY, J. (1981), 'Sociology as a Parasite: Some Vices and Virtues' in Abrams *et al.* (eds.) (1981), 25–38.

VIDICH, A. J., and LYMAN, S. M. (1985), *American Sociology: Worldly Rejections of Religion and Their Directions* (New Haven: Yale University Press).

VILLANOVA LAW REVIEW (1965), Symposium on Lon Fuller's *The Morality of Law*, 10 *Villanova Law Review*, 631–78.

VOGT, W. P. (1983), 'Obligation and Right: The Durkheimians and the Sociology of Law' in P. Besnard (ed.), *The Sociological Domain: The Durkheimians and the Founding of French Sociology* (Cambridge: Cambridge University Press), 177–98.

VOLLRATH, E. (1976), 'That All Governments Rest on Opinion', transl. by H. Fantel, 43 *Social Research*, 46–61.

WALKER, D. M. (1980), *The Oxford Companion to Law* (Oxford: Oxford University Press).

WALZER, M. (1990), 'The Communitarian Critique of Liberalism', 18 *Political Theory*, 6–23.

WEBER, M. (1927), *General Economic History*, transl. by F. H. Knight (London: Allen and Unwin).

—— (1930), *The Protestant Ethic and the Spirit of Capitalism*, transl. by T. Parsons (London: Routledge reprint, 1992).

—— (1948), 'Religious Rejections of the World and Their Directions' in Gerth and Mills (eds.) (1948), 323–59.

—— (1977), *Critique of Stammler*, transl. by G. Oakes (New York: Free Press).

—— (1978), *Economy and Society: An Outline of Interpretive Sociology*, transl. by E. Fischoff *et al.* (Berkeley: University of California Press).

WECHSLER, H. (1959), 'Toward Neutral Principles in Constitutional Law', 73 *Harvard Law Review*, 1–35.

WEINBERGER, O. (1991), 'Institutionalist Theories of Law' in P. Amselek and N. MacCormick (eds.), *Controversies About Law's Ontology* (Edinburgh: Edinburgh University Press), 43–53.

WHITE, G. E. (1973), 'The Evolution of Reasoned Elaboration: Jurisprudential Criticism and Social Change', 59 *Virginia Law Review*, 279–302.

WIGDOR, D. (1974), *Roscoe Pound: Philosopher of Law* (Westport, Conn.: Greenwood Press).

WILKINSON, P. J. (1981), 'The Potential of Functionalism for the Sociological Analysis of Law' in Podgorecki and Whelan (eds.) (1981), 67–90.

WILLIAMS, P. J. (1991), *The Alchemy of Race and Rights: Diary of a Law Professor* (Cambridge, Mass.: Harvard University Press).

WILLOCK, I. D. (1974), 'Getting on with Sociologists', 1 *British Journal of Law and Society*, 3–12.

WIMBERLEY, H. (1973), 'Legal Evolution: One Further Step', 79 *American Journal of Sociology*, 78–83.

WINFIELD, P. H. (1928), 'Public Policy in the English Common Law', 42 *Harvard Law Review*, 76–83.

WINSTON, K. I. (ed.) (1981), *The Principles of Social Order: Selected Essays of Lon L. Fuller* (Durham, North Carolina: Duke University Press).

WOLFF, K. H. (ed.) (1950), *The Sociology of Georg Simmel* (Glencoe, Ill.: Free Press).

Author Index

Subject Index

Academic disciplines. *see* Disciplines, intellectual
Adjudication, institutional constraints on, 190
Altruism,
  individualism and, 246
  public. *see* Public altruism
Anthropology, 79–80
Autopoiesis theory, 105–8, 263, 302

Begriffsjurisprudenz, 159
Bills of Rights, 242
British Sociological Association Conference 1979, 86
Bureaucracy, 139, 148, 149

Collective participation,
  aspiration, as, 255–6
  community and, 20, 246
  concept of, 269, 332
  mutual interpersonal trust and, 332
  Rule of Law and, 271–2
  values of order and justice and, 333
Common law,
  democracy and, 224
  image of community in, 223–5
  nature of, 78–9, 169–71
Communitarianism, 309, 326
Community,
  authoritarianism and, 242
  collective participation and, 246
  concept of, 17–18, 20, 246, 300–1
  cultural diversity and, 246
  empirical conditions of, 244–5
  exclusion from, 246–7, 334
  'human scale' and, 331
  importance of concept, 325–6
  individualism and, 246
  institutions of, 248
  judge as representing, 247
  law and, 17–22, 193, 245, 300–1
  'loss of community' literature, 326–8
  moral distance and, 330–31, 332
  morality, 192
  mutual interpersonal trust and, 329–30, 332

  nation as, 334, 335
  orientations of social interaction, as, 329
  power in, 330
  plurality of communities, 20–21, 247, 248, 322
  privatized life-styles and, 19–20
  public altruism and, 246
  regulation of, 332–7
  self-interest and, 266–9
  shared values in, 19, 242, 245–6, 332
  sociological conceptions of, 223n, 326–9
  solidarity and, 268
  Taylor's conception of, 329, 330
  values, 235, 242, 245–6
  varieties of, 336
Community image of society. *see also* Legal images of society
  diversity of communities in, 322
  elements of, 222–7, 320, 321–5
  ideological character of, 321, 325
  individuality in, 233–4
  judge's role in, 231–2
  ratio and, 320
  scope of community in, 231
  unifying values in, 230
Consensus, value, 309
Contempt of court, 251
Contextualism, 76
Corporatism, 175
Courts, longitudinal studies of, 183
Criminology, British, 80, 82–3
Critical legal studies (CLS), 72, 88, 204–17. *see also* Critical theory
  choice of agenda of, 209
  contexts of, 204–5
  critique, concept of, 206
  critique, theory of, 207
  'fundamental contradiction' of liberal society, and, 165, 214
  general concepts, use of, 209
  law and society movement and, 297
  relation of law and society, on, 208